Into the Bermuda Triangle

Into the Bermuda Triangle

Pursuing the Truth Behind the World's Greatest Mystery

Gian J. Quasar

INTERNATIONAL MARINE / McGRAW-HILL

Camden, Maine • New York • Chicago • San Francisco • Lisbon • London • Madrid
Mexico City • Milan • New Delhi • San Juan • Seoul • Singapore • Sydney • Toronto

The **McGraw·Hill** Companies

7 8 9 1 0 DOC DOC 0 9 8

Library of Congress has cataloged the cloth edition as follows:

Quasar, Gian J.
    Into the Bermuda Triangle : pursuing the truth behind the world's greatest mystery / Gian J. Quasar. — 1st ed.
        p.   cm.
        Includes bibliographical references and index.
    ISBN 0-07-142640-X
    1. Bermuda Triangle. I. Title.
    G558.Q37 2003
    001.94—dc22   2003018090

Paperback ISBN 0-07-145217-6

To that vast horizon,
whose approaching will solve many riddles . . .

Contents

Photos follow pages 82, 143, and 208

1

The Bermuda Triangle:
A Riddle at a Nearby Shore

WITHIN THE WESTERN North Atlantic Ocean there exists what might be called a triangle of sea extending southwest from the island of Bermuda to Miami and through southern Florida to Key West; then, encompassing the Bahamas, it extends southeast through Puerto Rico to as far as 15° North latitude, and then from there northward back to Bermuda. This is the area commonly called the Bermuda Triangle. For all intents and purposes it appears like any other temperate sea. Yet in the annals of sea mysteries there is no other place that challenges mankind with so many extraordinary and incredible events, for this is where far more aircraft and ships have disappeared throughout recorded maritime history than in any other region of the world's oceans. With few exceptions the disappearances have been in fair weather, sending out no distress messages and leaving no wreckage or bodies. In the last twenty-five years alone, some seventy-five aircraft and hundreds of pleasure yachts have inexplicably vanished despite the fact that GPS is now extensively used, that communication systems are powerful and reliable, and that searches are immediately launched.

Disturbing as these numbers may seem, the circumstances surrounding many of the disappearances are what really give rise to the greatest alarm. From the files of several federal investigating bureaus, eye-opening details emerge that continue to present difficult questions that as yet have no answers within the scope of our present knowledge of the sea, aeronautics, and navigation. One such disappearance illustrates this point.

It was Halloween 1991. Radar controllers checked and rechecked what they had just seen. The scope was blank in one spot now. Everywhere else within the scope seemed normal, and routine traffic was proceeding undisturbed, in their vectors, tracked and uninterrupted. But moments earlier radar had been tracking a Grumman Cougar jet. The pilot was John Verdi. He and trained copilot, Paul Lukaris, were heading toward Tallahassee,

Florida. Just moments before, with a crackle of the mike, Verdi's voice had come over the receiver at the flight center.

He requested a higher altitude. Permission was quickly granted and the turbo jet was observed ascending from 25,000 feet to its new altitude of 29,000 feet. All seemed normal. Some thunderstorms had drifted into the path of the jet, and satellite imagery confirmed the area was overcast.

But that was no concern for Verdi. They were above the weather. At their present altitude they were just breaking out of the cloud cover, emerging into the brilliant sunlight.

The clouds must have been their typical breathtaking sight, billowing below in glowing white hills and arroyos.

They were still ascending. Verdi had not yet "rogered" that he had reached his prescribed flight level.

Radar continued to track the Cougar. Until, for some unknown reason, while ascending, it simply faded away. Verdi and Lukaris answered no more calls to respond. Furthermore, they had sent no SOS to indicate they had encountered any hint of a problem. Readouts of the radar observations confirmed the unusual. The Grumman had not been captured on the scope at all as descending or as falling to the sea; there had been no sudden loss of altitude. It just disappeared from the scope while climbing. One sweep they were there. The next—raised brows on traffic controllers: it was blank.

The ocean, sitting under convective thunderstorm activity, was naturally not conducive to a search. No trace, if there was any left to find, was ever sifted out of the Gulf. When it was all over, the whole incident was chalked under a familiar and terse assumption: "aircraft damage and injury index presumed."

So far, very few disappearances have ever been reported by the press and, if they are, they're reported with little attention to detail, or the reports studiously avoid any reference to the unusual. In 1978 and 1979 alone, eighteen aircraft mysteriously vanished, yet only two or three rated any space in newspapers. Among these missing planes was a DC-3 airliner; a large twin-engine charter on approach; and several private aircraft in the narrow corridor between Bimini Island and Miami, which are in view of each other from aircraft altitudes. Yet, nevertheless, all vanished as if surgically extracted by a hand being careful not to affect the surrounding heavy traffic on that route, which reported no signs of wreckage or unusual weather. Even apart from the strangeness of the events preceding and surrounding some disappearances, it appears fairly obvious by the number that something is very wrong.

Although it is often publicly recited that the Bermuda Triangle's reputation is based on twenty planes and fifty vessels posted missing over the last hundred years, official records vividly show that such a number can be and has been easily exceeded in any given two-year period. On an average, however, four aircraft and about twenty yachts vanish each year.

The frequency of those two years is alarming enough. But out of all the alarming elements in the statistics, it is not the isolated surges of losses that are the most intriguing. Dossiers on all aircraft accidents, which include missing planes, are still maintained, and behind-the-scenes they monotonously document the startling repetition. A "Brief Format," usually just called a Brief, is available for perusal from civil investigating authorities, particularly the National Transportation Safety Board in Washington, D.C. These handy and mostly terse one- or two-page chits preserve the known facts. Considering the brevity of the information, the nickname Brief is not a misnomer, especially prior to 1982 before the Board enlarged the scope of information contained on the sheets. Their pages, though, quietly testify to the actual number of missing planes in the Bermuda Triangle.

Computer searches of the database files of the NTSB for several time brackets reveal some sobering statistics. It is quite surprising to examine the Briefs and notice what is *not* in newspapers. For instance, between 1964 (the oldest dates for the "Brief" records) and 1974 thirty-seven planes vanished. The period from 1974 to 1984 show that forty-one aircraft have mysteriously disappeared in the Bermuda Triangle. The pattern was the same—mostly over the Bahamas; it continued: from 1984 to 1994 thirty-two vanished. And from 1994 to the present twenty aircraft have disappeared. Although it may appear that the number is on the decrease, this decrease mirrors the economic downturn of the late 1990s, and dropped sharply after September 11, 2001, when traffic was severely curtailed for a number of reasons.

There is no evidence, however, that the circumstances for disappearances are any less unusual than before. Mystery continues to strike. On Christmas Eve 1994, a Piper aircraft vanished over West Boca Raton, Florida—one of the few instances of a plane ostensibly disappearing over land. Although radar operators could never find a trace of it in their tracking readouts, a witness below clearly saw the navigation lights of the Piper. Investigation proved it must have belonged to Laurent Abecassis, who had taken the plane out earlier in the day for some practice flying. On May 12, 1999, an Aero Commander, while approaching Nassau, disappeared from radar for thirty minutes, then miraculously reappeared, though the pilot seemed unaware anything had happened, before the plane and the pilot vanished again, this time permanently. On February 1, 2001, Casey Purvis was in his Cherokee Six playing radar tag with a Coast Guard aircraft as a practice maneuver. Suddenly he reported himself in a fog, then vanished. Wreckage from the aircraft was later found near Marathon, Florida Keys, where he last reported himself. Weather from both the nearby Coast Guard aircraft and Marathon reporting station confirmed visibility was clear for 12 miles. On July 20, 2002, a Piper Lance mysteriously crashed after taking off from Freeport, Grand Bahama. After having been in flight long enough to have been halfway to Florida, its fuselage was found only 15 miles from its point of departure. Radar tracking cannot explain it. The phenomenon of the bizarre is not abating.

Factual aviation accident reports are available from General Microfilm, the National Transportation Safety Board's documents contractor, from 1978 onward. Those prior have been destroyed. Carefully sifting through these accident reports brings to light a pattern interwoven with tragedy and mystery. Together they create a sobering picture of sudden and many times bizarre disappearances at sea in a confined area. Quite often, when faced with the facts, the curious have come away badly jolted. The pages they read bare some recurrent themes in the losses and these, in turn, open the door to some potentially explosive issues.

Everybody involved in one particular case—tower and radar controllers and listening pilots alike—was dramatically affected by some frantic last words. Uttered in a desperate voice, they introduced other elements, stark and frightening, in the mystery of missing planes. While in flight near the coast of Puerto Rico, on June 28, 1980, about 35 miles out, José Torres, the pilot of an Ercoupe, signaled that a "weird object" in his flight path was forcing him to change course. Despite all his evasive maneuvers, the object continued to cut him off. That's not all—he reported his equipment was on the fritz, and he was now lost.

"Mayday, Mayday," he continued to call. Then, as astounded controllers watched, the plane vanished from the radarscope, with Torres and his passenger, José Pagan. Minutes later an object reappeared on the scope and then flitted away. In what manner it fled the scope the report would not comment.

A search that night cast beams of light on a dark ocean. It was the typical nothing: a bland ocean surface crisscrossed with streaming beams of Civil Air Patrol spotlights. The crests and swells were devoid of any trace of an accident.

Many of the other planes have simply vanished while in sight of land, while coming in for a landing, or after having just departed, occurring, it should be emphasized, between a single sweep of the radarscope (less than 40 seconds). Others have vanished over shallow waters, less than 10 feet deep, yet with equal lack of trace or silhouette to mark their position, as if magically they just faded away, while others have vanished during radio contact, as in the case above, blurting such words like: "Is there any way out of this?"; "Stand by, we have a problem right now"; "Oh, Jesus Christ . . . ! "; "What's happening to me?"; or reporting that their compass or directional gyro is going berserk.

The missing boats are not just specks lost on a big ocean. Many have vanished just at the edge of the harbor, others while cruising around a peninsula, and others have been found drifting shipshape, lifeless, the occupants gone without leaving any clue behind as to what happened.

In no search undertaken by the Seventh Coast Guard district (which has jurisdiction over the area of the Bermuda Triangle), for any airplane or vessel posted overdue and then eventually declared missing, has a body ever been recovered. Even when the vessel may later be found, it is always found deserted or, in the case of aircraft, it is found ditched in shallow water, the ignition key removed, the doors tightly closed, but no sign of the pilots or passengers.

The disappearances have not been limited to small craft. A whole squadron of five Navy torpedo bombers, the famous Flight 19, vanished on a routine training flight off Florida on December 5, 1945, after the flight leader radioed, among other things, that both his compasses were no longer working. Although the airplanes had the latest navigational devices and sea survival equipment, the patrol never found their way back, nor was any trace found. Passenger aircraft have included DC-3 and DC-4 airliners, plus several other four-engine models. Military aircraft have even included an eight-engine B-52 bomber. Large ships have included the 504-foot tanker *Marine Sulphur Queen*, the 520-foot *Poet*, and the 590-foot *Sylvia L. Ossa*. In the case of the *Ossa*, before she vanished she had just signaled she was near Bermuda—a dramatic reminder of the boundaries of the Triangle. Most of these vessels were carrying cargoes that are fairly safe to ship, such as coal and corn; some have even been in ballast—that is, empty and shipping no cargoes at all. None of these are as inexplicable as "reappearances," where a pilot's radio messages are captured receding hundreds of miles beyond where he vanished and hours after fuel exhaustion. In the case of the Grumman Cougar jet that vanished from radar while *ascending* to 29,000 feet, the summation of one observer that "there is just no logical explanation" seems to fit all these incidents.

There is a growing belief that there is something very different out in the Triangle as opposed to other seas. Since ships and planes disappear in like manner, there seems to be little possibility that ordinary mishaps such as pilot error, vertigo, fuel exhaustion, getting lost, disorientation, or natural disasters like tidal waves, cyclones, or whirlpools can be the sole culprit. While some of the above can be deadly to planes, they are not to ships and vice versa.

Furthermore, such destructive potential as some of these pose should also launch into motion devices called automatic alarms. An EPIRB (emergency position-indicating radio beacon) is designed to be activated when it floats free from a sinking ship, while an ELT (emergency locator transmitter) is jettisoned from or activated within an aircraft fuselage upon impact. Both continue to transmit their automatic electronic maydays for days, even weeks, not only alerting rescuers to an accident but also guiding them to the precise point where it occurred. While these signals are routinely picked up in other accidents around the globe, so far not one signal has ever been picked up from those planes and ships known to be carrying them which vanished in the Triangle, a total of well over 120 craft (!).

While it is true that this area is heavily traveled, there is an unshakable feeling shared by many of those who live in and about the Triangle that there is something far more compelling about these disappearances than just mere statistical losses. Continuing encounters by pilots and shipmasters, for one or more terrible moments, with unexplained forces involving electronic drains, radio dead spots, power blackouts, and spontaneous compass malfunction, with or without unusual fogs, hazes, or luminous phenomena, are contributing to the area's growing reputation as a unique place on this globe.

Attempts to correlate these phenomena to the disappearances have inspired some of the most innovative and equally unique theories. Some have seriously proposed that UFOs, utilizing nifty electromagnetic propulsion systems, enter Earth here and whisk away specimens of Earth life. The shallow Great Bahama Bank occupies much of the Triangle in its southern corner. Aerial surveys continue to reveal surprising geometric and apparently manmade ruins below the surface of the ocean. These have excited the followers of Edgar Cayce, a clairvoyant who believed that Atlantis was a super civilization of the past. According to his prophecies, given far in advance of the space age or the Bermuda Triangle concept, evidence for its advanced electromagnetic power sources, the abuse of which disturbed the magnetic and gravitational fields and sent it to the bottom thousands of years ago, would be found in the Bahamas. In this theory, the unexplained electromagnetic forces may be residual from sunken power complexes that continue to operate and cause disappearances through disintegration of a craft or misleading it until it is dangerously lost. Others have offered that Time itself may warp and send ships and planes to other dimensions, while still others have proposed a plethora of ideas like methane funnels from beneath the ocean, micro wormholes, static electricity, "gravity sink," and sudden rogue waves.

In the long run, however, the Bermuda Triangle's mystery is inseparable from its location, and its ultimate solution therefore must be found in solving the greater mystery of this Earth, this island at the confluence of the fabulous currents of mass and energy and time and space. For even now in the opening decade of the twenty-first century, we look beneath us to our past accomplishments rather than up to gaze at this vast and final horizon, where the secrets of the very force fields that hold this planet together remain more unknown to us than was the germ before Pasteur. The habits of these times are to sit in our parlors somewhat at peace in our assurance that we have now vanquished the unknown over the whole Earth, climbed her last high peak, sent bathyspheres to her deepest trenches below the sea, and swaddled her heavens in speeding satellites. We spin a globe of our Earth before us, bemusedly contemplating our dominion over it while blithely forgetting we neither understand nor can solve the forces involved in its rotation and revolution. As a matter of argument we are quick to add that we have long tested the strengths of the magnetic field. However, along with inconsistencies, this has given us a ponderous cache of unexplained vagaries.

Cold War atomic tests have revealed other mysteries of the magnetic field. All the Russian, U.S., and British atomic bomb drops in the Northern Hemisphere were followed by unusual auroras and lights in the ionosphere in the Southern Hemisphere at the exact magnetic opposite of the test site. After the atomic destruction of the city of Hiroshima in 1945, which lies near 36 degrees North latitude, these same lights and auroras were also noted at its magnetic opposite in the Southern Hemisphere near 36 degrees South latitude, south of Australia.

This phenomenon of Magnetic Opposition helps to illustrate the puzzling interplay between mass and its mysterious energy fields. Instead of

$$g = 983.22 \text{ cm per second}^2$$

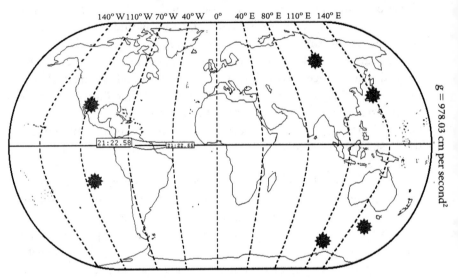

$g = 978.03 \text{ cm per second}^2$

Black stars represent points of magnetic opposition, as noted in atomic bomb drops. Also, an object actually falls faster at the poles than at the Equator, a phenomenon dependent on the rotation of the globe, causing bulging at the Equator and a flattening effect at the poles. The mathematical notations show in centimeters the acceleration of an unsupported body at each location per second². Very accurate atomic clocks have recorded time passing slightly faster at higher altitudes.

disrupting the entire field line, the energy travels to the exact opposite in the other hemisphere, where visible reactions occur.

Rotation of the Earth reveals mysteries of gravity. North of the Equator ocean currents turn clockwise, while south of the Equator they turn counterclockwise. It is intriguing to contemplate, when considering this, that the forces of magnetism and gravity may be subject to similar currents, eddies, and anomalies far independent of our knowledge of their fields, still waiting to be discovered, charted, and understood.

Acceleration of this sphere's rotation also varies the readings of gravity from pole to Equator, where, in the latter instance, an object will take longer to fall to the ground. But the most astounding mystery relating to mass has come via atomic clocks. Simultaneous readings at sea level and at orbital heights have revealed to us Time—itself the most mysterious force—is itself connected to mass and energy, and passes just ever so slightly faster farther from the center of gravity.

Subtle anomalies such as these, though interesting to contemplate for the time being, provide no apparent danger to travelers. But the Bermuda Triangle poses a different problem altogether inasmuch as its mystery is not one of permanent duration, and what is causing these unexplained disappearances remains annoyingly sporadic.

Thousands of planes and ships fly and sail through its boundaries on a weekly basis, but disappearances happen apparently randomly, without warning, sometimes within minutes and only miles from where another ship or plane is cruising without difficulty, and always without reason. There is no chartable location to record other than their recurrence in the general area of the Triangle.

Unexpected electromagnetic aberrations continue to be encountered by pilots and shipmasters at equally random locations in the Bermuda Triangle, and no plane or ship disappears without the suspicion amongst those who have experienced it that those who vanished experienced a more intense form of what they survived. Our growing awareness that the infinite horizon of electromagnetism extends through mass, across space, and beyond time is contributing to our knowledge of the alarming potential of anomalies. But if they are indeed the actual nemesis to ships and planes, what is causing them remains as mysterious as ever.

The sea itself over which these multiple mysteries occur would seem the logical first choice to blame. This hydrospace is vast and constantly in motion and far outside the scrutiny of our daily endeavor. We have, in due course, mapped the ocean bottoms with sonar and echo sounding. But that is hardly exhaustive. That is like saying that a NASA photograph of our land contours reveals the intricacy of our atmosphere. No mapping can unlock the potential of this hydrosphere nor expose its interplay with the thousands of electromagnetic wavelengths flitting about the Earth and those force fields inexorably tied to them like magnetism and gravity. Without this hydrosphere the sea bottoms are merely vast, dry deserts little different or less changeless than Sahara.

Even varying depths of the oceans and its temperatures have starkly different attributes and potential in terms of function and interaction with the atmosphere, surface and submarine currents, and even pressure and gravity. The *bathypelagic* zone includes most of the deepest waters, reaching more than 13,000 feet down, while the *mesopelagic* extends roughly from 3,000 feet upward to 700 or so feet below the surface. From there the *epipelagic* zone extends toward the surface, making this the zone that has the most potential interactions with atmospheric changes.

The mineral content of the ocean may provide us with some surprises as well. Just one of its many metals, mercury, when shaken has been proven to transmit radio signals.

Perhaps one indication of the mysterious energy interplay between the ocean and the atmosphere first revealed itself on very low frequency radio tests conducted by both the U.S. Coast Guard and the U.S. Navy back in the 1950s. Listening out over the ocean, both picked up sounds that can best be described as whispering and whistling. What exact force is creating these provocative sounds remains unknown. It continues to be picked up only over the oceans today, as verified by several independent VLF radio owners.

But although the sea and its currents have great untapped and even as yet mysterious potential, only the Bermuda Triangle stands out for its anomalies and mysteries to travel. Other areas of ocean continue to be equally traversed as the Triangle without incident or, at least, the intensity of mystery. The First Coast Guard district (off New England) handles about as many search and rescue cases each year (9,100) as the Seventh district (10,200), which encompasses the Triangle—a reflection of the similar amount of traffic and trouble encountered in both areas. But in the last decade the combined disappearances of planes off New England amounts to four or five in foul weather as opposed to the Triangle's twenty in fair weather. Also, accidents over surrounding land bordering the Triangle, though just as traveled, present no similar statistic for sudden loss of aircraft and subsequent impact into the ground. It is only after traveling into the Triangle that sudden disappearances occur.

More detailed mapping of the ocean bottom, in particular the Bermuda Triangle, has been prompted by several unexpected events and has contributed to the mystery of its missing ships and planes. After the tragic loss of the *Challenger* space shuttle in 1986, the Navy used sonar and underwater cameras to scour the Gulf of Mexico and the Atlantic up to North Carolina, which covers a large section of the Triangle. According to the orders, every square foot of ocean bottom down to 6,000 feet was to be examined and any piece of the shuttle larger than a dinner plate was to be retrieved. In addition, a $16 billion project called SOSUS (Sound Surveillance System) is maintained by the U.S. Navy to secure the ocean bottom from foreign submarines. Part of this is the careful painting of the bottom by hydrophone sensors to sketch an image from the ocean floor to the surface in order to detect any anomalous bottom changes that could indicate foreign subs poised for an attack. Nevertheless, there has

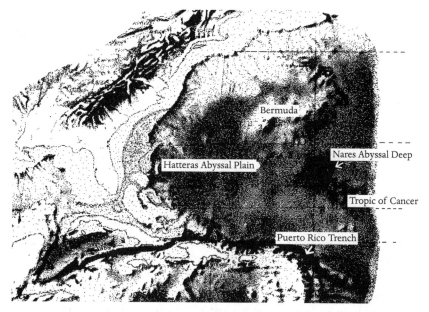

Despite underwater mapping, the Bermuda Triangle may hold considerable surprises for us. It has some of the deepest waters in the world, like the Puerto Rico Trench, a 220-mile-long fissure in the bottom about 5 miles deep, north of its namesake. Other areas of mystery include the deep and unapproachable undersea desert, the Nares Abyssal Deep, just north of the Tropic of Cancer, and the Hatteras Abyssal Plain.

never come any reports of finding the many large freighters, airliners, or other distinctive military vessels and planes that have vanished in the Bermuda Triangle, although it was over this area where they last reported themselves. It may be that no one was concerned with the shape of a vessel or plane on the scanner during operations if it didn't match the object of their search, nor thought to reexamine the readouts afterward in light of explaining old sea mysteries. But the release and reexamination of this data may help to solve some of the mysteries in this book, if the data is ever made completely public.

It may also mean that there is no mystery to catalog at all, a point of view the Coast Guard or any other authority is officially quick to embrace. Skeptics continue to point out that ships and planes vanish in greatest quantity where the traffic is the heaviest, implying the losses are not only expected but acceptable. In the case of the Triangle, however, a "statistically acceptable" number of accidents seem to be made up of a disturbing and unacceptably high proportion of disappearances.

There are those who would remind us that, given the powerful currents in the Triangle, like the tumultuous Gulf Stream that runs off Florida out into the Atlantic, any plane or boat can be broken up into bits and its pieces unidentifiable on the bottom or carried off far across the Atlantic until effectively it has "disappeared." For the Coast Guard's part, their feelings are summed up as follows: "The Coast Guard, in short, is not impressed with supernatural explanations of disasters at sea. It has been our experience that the combined forces of nature and the unpredictability of mankind outdo even the most far fetched science fiction many times each year."

Interpretation of this naturally depends on what one would consider supernatural. Is the currently unexplained, supernatural? Was wind shear or clear air turbulence supernatural before both were discovered? Would disintegration by electromagnetic aberrations be supernatural simply because there is as yet no cross-reference for them? Is travel through space or time supernatural? Often "natural" seems to get equated with "conventional."

There is no marine or aeronautic authority, including the Coast Guard, that would place such dogma in a report. Many of these reports, formerly restricted or secret, have included meticulously researched data, and have also included phrases or words like "north wall phenomenon" (referring to the Gulf Stream), "violent unknown force," and "beyond probability." As a part of the catalog of the meager debris retrieved, there is also included the notation that an unexplained "magnetic particle" was found imbedded in a recovered nose wheel of a missing aircraft.

While skeptics debate the very existence of the Triangle, even those who follow it find a bone of contention in its shape. The term "Triangle" dates only to 1952, when writer George X. Sand's "Sea Mystery at our Back Door" appeared in *Fate* magazine. In it he outlined its most enduring shape between Bermuda, southern Florida, and Puerto Rico, noting that "within this watery triangle . . . off the coast of Florida" ships and planes disappear "without leaving a single clue." The name "Bermuda Triangle" dates only to 1964, when Vincent Gaddis added it to the colloquial term "Deadly Triangle" in an article for *Argosy* magazine ("The Deadly Bermuda Triangle"). Out of those who have studied the phenomenon no two have agreed on a precise periphery, though most concur that the majority of disappearances occur within the triangle between southern Florida, Bermuda, and Puerto Rico. "Ellipse" or "lozenge" has been offered, as have a circle or ovoid body off the U.S. East Coast, alternate triangles connecting to Norfolk, Virginia, and a "limbo" encompassing the East Coast and even the Gulf of Mexico. To satellite engineers, the "Triangle" extends along the continental shelf farther down into the Caribbean, a periphery determined by places where satellites sometimes experience "glitches" and "fritz" but return to normal after passing over.

But long before the "triangle" and the publicity, unexplained disappearances had frequented the area and baffled contemporaries. The Spanish kept meticulous shipping records in Madrid (because gold was involved), and noted the high incidence of missing galleons. Derelict vessels found in the 19th century could not be explained by weather, piracy, or mutiny.

But when aircraft started disappearing, as ships had before, it added the greatest element of mystery to the Triangle, of suddenness and no impact because there were no Maydays and immediate searches found no debris. But none seem so inexplicable as the first publicly recorded incident in which planes vanished—an entire squadron of torpedo bombers during a routine exercise in 1945, and also of a rescue plane sent to search for them. In a sense we have come full circle, for it is this incident that started it all. The disappearance of Flight 19 is, without debate, the beginning of the Bermuda Triangle, the cause of its subsequent shape, name, and the most enduring part of its fame.

To appreciate the present we must go back—back to the past—to past events and man's confrontation with what he thought could never happen.

2

The Riddle of Missing Planes

THE CURRENT ENIGMA of the Bermuda Triangle grew out of an extraordinary event that took place December 5, 1945. This was the disappearance of not just one aircraft but *five* aircraft, flying together in formation, with a combined crew of fourteen, and then later that night the disappearance of one of the rescue planes, carrying thirteen crew. The disappearance of six aircraft and twenty-seven military personnel without trace in one night was so extraordinary that public interest in this mystery eventually led to journalistic review of earlier and later disappearances until the Bermuda Triangle's name and reputation were established.

The flight was designated Flight 19 as it was the nineteenth flight in the roster to take off that day from Naval Air Station Fort Lauderdale in Florida. At this base, about 20 miles north of Miami, prospective naval pilots underwent advanced navigational training before being assigned to sea duty on carriers.

Flight 19 was executing a basic training triangle. In their case this triangular flight plan started at 2:10 P.M. at Fort Lauderdale and was scheduled to last about 2 hours and 15 minutes. It would take them no farther from base than 123 miles east over the Bahamas, less than an hour's distance at their cruising speed of 140 mph, in case an emergency required them to fly straight back to the coast. Part of the exercise involved making dummy bomb runs at an old hulk near Bimini, about 56 miles east from base. Afterward, they would proceed farther easterly for 67 miles, following a heading of 091 degrees, then north-northwest on a heading of 346 degrees for 73 miles, then southwest back to base, finishing the triangle. Each of the three corners of the triangle was marked by a landfall or within sight of one. The weather was fair to average, with a gusting southwest trade wind pushing big, billowy clouds. Each plane was topped off with fuel and oil, giving the squadron a range of over 1,000 miles.

Navy Lieutenant Charles Taylor, the flight leader, was a veteran of combat in the South Pacific and had been flying since 1941. The other pilots were all seasoned servicemen who had switched to the Naval Air Force late in their military careers. All were graduate pilots with 350 or more flight hours under their belts. Marine Captain George Stivers Jr., pilot of FT-117, a 1942 graduate of the Naval Academy in Annapolis, was particularly honored, having been cited three times for gallantry in the South Pacific, twice at Guadalcanal and once at Tarawa. Marine Captain Edward J. Powers Jr., a graduate of Princeton and a marine since 1941, was an apt officer who had been assigned as a training instructor at Quantico, Virginia, throughout the war. Marine Second Lieutenant Jimmy Gerber had enlisted in the marines after Pearl Harbor and worked his way up to officer and pilot; and although Ensign Joseph Bossi had been in for only two years, he passed up his discharge so he could continue to fly planes like the Avenger. In addition to the pilot, each Avenger carried two crew, a gunner and a radioman, who were undergoing advanced training with their pilot; Taylor, however, as the flight leader, had veterans on his plane, FT-28. These crew, like their pilots, were mostly seasoned marines or naval ratings. When they took off that day they were one man short: the radioman in Gerber's plane, FT-81, failed to show up, leaving him with only his gunner, Billy Lightfoot.

Everything indicated the flight would be routine, if not dull. They carried out their scheduled bombing practice at Chicken and Hen Shoals, headed farther east, then headed northwest. Then something happened, suddenly and without warning. At 3:50 P.M. Taylor reported to Powers that his compasses were erratic. Then all the pilots compared their compass headings, but this merely led to another disagreement. Two out of the five were sure they should head west, but there was no consensus.

Meanwhile, another flight instructor, Lieutenant Robert Cox, flying in the vicinity of Fort Lauderdale, overheard the pilots discussing their headings and compasses. He contacted the flight moments later, and there ensued the following exchange:

Cox: Plane or boat calling "Powers," what is your trouble?

Taylor: Both my compasses are out and I am trying to find Fort Lauderdale, Florida. I am over land, but it's broken. I'm sure I'm in the Keys, but I don't know how far down and I don't know how to get to Fort Lauderdale.

Cox: Put the sun on your port wing if you are in the Keys and fly up the coast until you get to Miami, then Fort Lauderdale is 20 miles further, your first port after

Miami. The air station is directly on your left from the port. What is your present altitude? I will fly south and meet you?

Taylor: I know where I'm at now. I'm at 2,300 feet. Don't come after me.

Cox: Roger. I'm coming up to meet you anyhow.

Cox immediately left his squadron and proceeded to the Keys, where Taylor supposed himself to be. However, his reception got worse, not better as it should have, indicating that Taylor was nowhere in the vicinity.

The next messages overheard from Flight 19 were at 4:25 P.M. by the Port Everglades Rescue Facility. Taylor ordered Powers to lead the flight northeast (assuming he had a good compass). This was his attempt to bring them over Florida Bay to the southern Florida mainland. It was later asserted that the flight was over the Bahama Cays to the east of Florida and that therefore this direction took them dangerously far into the Atlantic, a point of view later shared by both the Board of Inquiry and Lieutenant Cox. While this is offered as an explanation for why the flight didn't get back to land, it overlooks the fact that Flight 19 did not take this northeast heading for more than 25 minutes before turning west—a heading that, presuming the above estimate was accurate, would have brought them to Florida's east coast and safety within an hour.

Military radio logs reveal that only 22 minutes after Flight 19 flew northeast, a certain amount of strain was already developing between the pilots when the coast of Florida did not come into view—proof they were not over the Florida Bay. Taylor said: "Let's turn and fly east 2 degrees. We are going too damn far north instead of east. If there is anything we wouldn't see it" —still assuming he was in the Gulf of Mexico. "Dammit, if we would just head west we would get home!" said another pilot (presumably Powers).

Only a minute or two later, at 5:11 P.M., a full-scale disagreement broke out between Taylor and Powers. Instead of flying east for 10 minutes according to Taylor's orders, Powers had apparently turned the flight on his own initiative. Taylor was heard to protest: "You didn't get far enough east. How long have we been going east?" Minutes later he or Powers was picked up saying "We are now heading 270 west," indicating Powers won the argument about direction. Then at 5:15 P.M. Taylor was heard to confirm fatefully, "We will head 270 until we hit the beach or run out of gas."

Now that they had begun their westward course back to Florida, tensions at Fort Lauderdale were considerably eased, as they had always assumed Flight 19 was in the Atlantic, and now they were sure this would lead them back to the coast. But although the flight was presumably heading closer to shore, the radio reception never improved enough for the tower to definitely determine what the problems were.

Lieutenant Taylor was heard to order the flight to close formation. "When first man gets down to 10 gallons of gas, we will all land in the water together. Does everyone understand that?" Although this came over clear, attempts to help direct the flight were thwarted by frustrating blackouts. Taylor's answers to repeated calls to change radio channels were: "Say again?"; "I can you hear very faintly"; "My transmission is getting weaker"; "Hello, Hello?"; "Repeat once again." After 30 minutes of this, at 5:54 P.M., finally refusing: "I cannot change frequency. I must keep my planes intact."

At 6:05 P.M., when radio operators were naturally expecting the flight to be confirming that the shoreline lights were in view, a surprising dialogue sequence was clearly picked up indicating no land was in sight and that Taylor, as a result, was becoming even more worried.

Taylor was overheard to again insist that they must be in the Gulf of Mexico and that flying west for the last 55 minutes had sent them dangerously into the heart of the Gulf far from any land. He was overhead to suggest that Powers turn the flight east yet again. There is no evidence, however, that Powers turned the flight and headed east, for they all knew that for the last hour anyway there had been no land behind them.

A high-frequency directional fix on their messages now added to the mystery. At the time of this dialogue it placed them roughly 225 miles northeast of Fort Lauderdale, about 150 to 200 miles off the east coast of Florida, between New Smyrna Beach and Jacksonville. Instead of dispelling the mystery, this fix confirms that the flight had flown much farther into the Atlantic than was possible and that all the while (almost an hour) they thought they had been heading west or northwest, they had instead been heading north. They should have covered 140 miles back to the coast in that time, but were still incredibly far out in the Atlantic.

By this time it was becoming increasingly obvious that this was not a typically lost flight. Several personnel at the bases became convinced that none of the equipment on Flight 19 was reliable anymore. This controversy, one of the most inexplicable surrounding Flight 19, has been sustained by an examination of several confusing statements that were overheard. One should remember that following a westward heading, even according to Powers's compasses, only took them north instead. Bits and pieces of other dialogue overheard throughout the unusual in-flight drama were noteworthy for the tone of mild panic even early on when, assuming normal circumstances, there seems to have been little reason for panic.

Indications of erratic equipment readings, including compasses, fuel gauges, airspeed indicators, and perhaps altimeters, might be suggested by the following recorded dialogue. Soon after announcing they were lost, Taylor expresses with a certain impatient frustration: "We don't seem to be getting far," referring to speed and covering ground. Again, when explaining to Cox how he thinks they got lost, he said, "We were out on a navigational hop and on the second leg I thought they were going wrong, so I took over and was flying them back to the right position, but I'm sure now that neither one of my compasses are working." Yet given these circumstances it seems remarkable and unexplainable that none of the other pilots bothered to point out to him they were on course to begin with. Instead they seem to be as surprised (and a couple of them as unsure) as Taylor when he asks for a comparison of compasses. Neither were IFF signals received from the planes, though the flight confirmed they were on, nor did their ZBX gear (homing device) detect Fort Lauderdale's beacon. At 5:55 P.M. one pilot suddenly interjects, "We may have to ditch any minute," though the gauges indicating the fuel crisis must soon have corrected themselves again.

During the last hour of contact with the flight the messages were the most broken and strained. "Powers, come in Powers," Lieutenant Taylor called. "Hello, Powers, I've been trying to reach you"; "What course are we on now?"—This Taylor was overheard to ask a number of times until 6:37 P.M., when this line was the last message overheard from him. The faint dialogue finally faded out altogether at 7:04 P.M. when Ensign Bossi's call sign, "Fox Tare Three . . . Fox Tare Three . . . Fox Tare Three," came in surprisingly clear and then abruptly ended.

Out of all the confusing elements of that night, the question of who was in command is yet another mystery. From earlier dialogue it had appeared obvious to many listening in that Captain Powers had taken complete command of the flight and was determined to go west no matter what. (Although a student, Powers was the senior officer, having five months' seniority on Taylor, and could have pulled rank.) In any case, by 6 o'clock Taylor was not giving orders but only "suggesting" course changes to Powers—something that piqued the interest of the Board of Inquiry. It is nonetheless irrelevant who was in command. Flight 19, with their fuel and a westward direction, should have made land.

The mystery of where their compasses were directing them is compounded by the mystery of radio reception. The signals were strangely erratic: clear one moment, they faded to barely audible the next moment, died out altogether, or were obscured by heavy static. Pensacola had a far greater range (a high-frequency directional finding station) than Fort Lauderdale, but though they were about the same distance from Flight 19 at this time, their reception was little better, with the same frustrating blackouts. Every time a direct message to help the flight was attempted, there was interference, but interplane chatter was sometimes surprisingly clear. This mystery had begun early in the flight; clear or prolonged radio reception had never been possible even when, as in the beginning, they had been closer to shore.

This, the mystery of the radio reception, has a counterpart in the mystery of their ETA. The Navy was certain it was 5:23 P.M. This was, however, an hour past the correct landing time of 4:23 P.M. As a result, the Navy did not undertake aggressive rescue operations until over an hour after the flight had been due and, furthermore, about two hours after it had become lost.

1. The Triangle represents Prob. Nav. 1. **2.** Taylor last reported: "We just passed over a small island. We have no other land in sight" just before they headed 030 degrees northeast. Most assume it was Walker Cay, Bahamas. Following his course orders, by 6 P.M. the flight should have been approaching Banana River. **3.** Instead, a directional fix found them within a hundred-mile radius of this area.

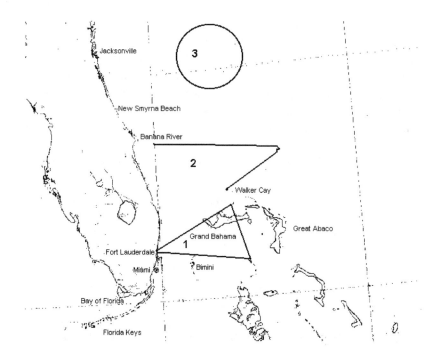

Then there is the mystery of their fuel endurance. Their fuel was originally estimated to be exhausted by 6:30 P.M., then 7 P.M., then lastly by 8 P.M. that night. But these estimates did not take into account the possibility that the pilots would adjust their control settings and throttle back. This way they would stagger their fuel and prolong their already impressive fuel range—though they would be cruising at a reduced speed. This may account for the appearance that they had been making little progress back to the coast but not explain, of course, how they got so far north in the first place. They could possibly, as some TBM Avenger pilots emphasize, have extended their total flight time to 7 or 8 hours. This would have given them a flight time of possibly 2 hours after the flight's last brief message was received at 7:04 P.M.

Then there is the mystery of the delayed call sign "FT . . . FT" heard by search pilots hours after the flight was estimated to have exhausted their fuel. They were dismissed as wishful thinking, though in retrospect, assuming they throttled back, they very likely *were* from the flight. But this adds yet another element of mystery: where were they during these hours?

Then there is the mystery of the search by a big PBM Mariner, with thirteen crewmen. It was airborne only 20 minutes, heading directly out to Flight 19's last known position, when it too was swallowed up into the void. Off the east coast of Florida, at 7:50 P.M., the sky tore across a color amber and red, as a fireball 100 feet high pulsed with explosion. The freighter *Gaines Mill* reported it was directly overhead. Meanwhile, the USS *Solomon's* radarscope lost the PBM blip in the precise area. Regardless of being in the immediate vicinity, the *Gaines Mill* could locate nothing but an oil slick. Nor did any of the other search aircraft, being redirected to this area, locate anything.

Besides the mystery of the PBM, the actual search for Flight 19 presents many peculiar mysteries of its own, including unexplained lights described variously as streaking or dancing or as flares. They were seen as far as from the Keys to the Atlantic off Jacksonville, labeled inconsistently as red, green, or white, but their sources remained unidentified—a phenomenon seen to this day after other disappearances.

Daylight search operations started at 6 A.M. the next morning. This included all aircraft from the entire east coast of Florida and numerous warships and civilian merchant ships that had been rerouted during the night and were still continuing to search. This search, maintaining an average of 200 planes each day and dozens of search vessels, was finally discontinued on December 10, with appended advice to "keep a sharp lookout and report anything pertinent," a command which three decades later one author, Richard Winer (*The Devil's Triangle*), emphasized was never rescinded.

To this day no trace of the five Avengers has yet been found despite undersea cameras, sonar, and extensive bottom mapping of the area of the Gulf and the Atlantic as far as North Carolina, every place Flight 19 could have reached. Weeks after the incident members of the Naval Board of Inquiry that had been convened to unravel the case were not able, in the words of the information officer, Captain W. C. Wingard, "to make even a good guess as to what happened." Captain William O. Burch, the Fort Lauderdale NAS commanding officer, gave the following formal statement: "What happened is unbelievable. Only fifteen minutes before the squadron of Avengers left our base at 2:10 P.M. that Wednesday, another flight of five similar planes took off, flew exactly the same course and returned safely without incident. It encountered no unusual weather conditions, except the wind picked up ten or fifteen knots." After the adjournment, the subheads in the *Kansas City Star* were typical of many: "Navy Still Makes No Explanation of Mysterious Disappearance of Five Planes on a Routine Flight Over Florida, Nor Why the Sixth, a Rescue Plane, Also Never Returned."

Some of the search pilots, still considering this incident today, are of the opinion that they had not been searching far enough north. They are quick to mention that the orders were to search as far north as Jacksonville, Florida. However, if the flight ditched north of here, the Gulf Stream's northward current would sweep debris beyond the search parameters.

Joe O'Brien, a member of Flight 22 that day, has considered the incident over the last fifty-eight years. Along with Bob Cox, he was one of the few pilots who had any even fleeting radio contact with Taylor after he initially announced he was lost. He is of the opinion, as are others, that the flight may have flown over the peninsula of Florida by that evening and ironically ended up in the Gulf, where Taylor first thought he was. While the last stations that overheard Flight 19 clearly both bordered the Gulf of Mexico, namely Pensacola, Florida, and Houma, Louisiana (high-frequency direction-finding stations), neither recorded anything after about 6:45 P.M. It is unlikely then that Flight 19 headed toward the Gulf since a continuation of this course would naturally have brought them closer to Pensacola and Houma and their radio signals would have become clearer, not fade away as they did.

Captain Don Poole, then a lieutenant commander and the flight officer at NAS Fort Lauderdale, who took over the operations from the tower and tried to guide the flight back, perhaps still has the only fair summation of the many inconsistencies and mysteries of that night: "I'll be the first one to admit that we don't know where in the hell those planes finally ended up."

David White, then a lieutenant and one of the search pilots, recalls having their evening poker game disturbed by the duty officer when he burst in and told them to muster at 5 A.M. "We take off at 6 A.M. We have an entire squadron missing." He recalled his reaction. "I thought, how could we have lost five planes!" A similar reaction came from Joe O'Brien, who recalled that at one point in a conversation with a buddy that night, he said: "What are people going to say twenty years from now if we lose an entire flight?"

In the decades since 1945, these sentiments, along with their ninefold of consternation, have been embraced by a greater and greater number of people. There seems to be no logical explanation for the disappearance of five aircraft or for the many confusing reports that night. Attempts to blame Taylor overlook the fact that Powers could not bring the flight back, even with enough fuel and following a "westward" heading. Blaming any pilot cannot explain the lack of debris or bodies at sea. When pondering all of these, it is not surprising that the enigma of the Bermuda Triangle developed and in turn maintained a tight grip over the incident. An entire flight of five planes plus one rescue plane—carrying a combined total of twenty-seven men—completely vanished.

If this had been an isolated incident, it would remain a great mystery of aviation. However, continuing disappearances of aircraft afterward, many in the same area and some with drawn-out and confusing radio messages like Flight 19's, indicate that perhaps it is only one of many, all sharing a similar cause or at least some crucial factor before meeting the same fate.

On July 3, 1947, a big four-engine C-54, the military equivalent of a DC-4 airliner, vanished. The military cargo flight left Bermuda early that morning for Morrison AFB in southern Florida. A search eventually found a large oxygen bottle and cabin paneling, indicating the aircraft must have been obliterated. A later study of the radio communications and reported headings curiously revealed that never once had it been on its correct course. Nor, apparently, were its many navigational errors apparent to the pilot, Major Ralph Ward, a veteran of considerable reputation.

The disappearance of the Tudor IV airliner *Star Tiger* just seven months later, in the predawn of January 31, 1948, is one of the most startling events in the Triangle. The airliner, with twenty-nine passengers and crew, had left hours earlier from Santa Maria, Azores, one of its many fuel stopovers from London to Havana, Cuba. While approaching Bermuda the pilot, Captain B. W. McMillan, made the expected contact with Kindley Field, his next stopover, requesting a radio bearing to calibrate his navigation and make sure he was still on course. The response indicated the plane was slightly off course. Its position was corrected after Bermuda relayed a first-class bearing of 72 degrees from the island. At this point, *Star Tiger* was less than 2 hours away from Bermuda, and it confirmed its ETA at 5 A.M., an hour late due to headwinds. This was the last transmission ever heard from the aircraft.

Rescue operations were aided by the fact that the plane's last known position report was precise, placing its disappearance within a confined track line northeast of Bermuda. In spite of this, no trace was ever found, and the search operation was discontinued, with negative results.

The report issued by the Civil Air Ministry contains an impressive official recital of what could *not* have happened to the plane: "There would accordingly appear to be no grounds for supposing that *Star Tiger* fell into the sea in consequence of having been deprived of her radio, having failed to find her destination, and having exhausted her fuel." Whatever occurred, it was concluded that it did so extremely rapidly: "There is good reason to suppose that no distress message was transmitted from the aircraft, for there were many radio receiving stations listening on the aircraft's frequencies, and none reported such a message." Weather information proved "the weather was stable, there were no atmospheric disturbances of a serious kind which might cause structural damage to the aircraft, and there were no electrical storms." The aircraft could not have gone off course. After the broadcast bearing from Bermuda, with the winds prevailing, *Star Tiger* would have been brought to within 30 miles of Bermuda: "The aircraft could hardly have failed to find the island in a short time, in the conditions of visibility which prevailed." Engine trouble as a possible cause was ruled out since at this late stage in her flight, without the added weight of her fuel, she could have flown safely on three or even two engines instead of the four she had. The possibility she could lose three engines was considered absurd.

Faced with all the evidence, the board of investigation soberly addressed the loss of *Star Tiger* in some of the most eloquent language ever entered into any accident report:

In closing this report it may truly be said that no more baffling problem has ever been presented for investigation. In the complete absence of any reliable evidence as to either the nature or the cause of the accident to *Star Tiger* the Court has not been able to do more than suggest possibilities, none of which reaches the level even of probability. Into all activities which involve the co-operation of man and machine two elements enter of a very diverse character. There is the incalculable element of the human equation dependent upon imperfectly known factors; and there is the mechanical element subject to quite different laws. A breakdown may occur in either separately or in both in conjunction. Or some external cause may overwhelm both man and machine. What happened in this case will never be known and the fate of *Star Tiger* must remain an unsolved mystery.

The mystery of the *Star Tiger* was compounded in a stunning way just one year later. On January 17, 1949, her sister airliner *Star Ariel* inexplicably vanished south of Bermuda. She had just taken off from Bermuda on a fine early morning, carrying nineteen crew and passengers, bound for Kingston, Jamaica. About an hour later her captain, John C. McPhee, sent this radiogram to Bermuda, Kingston, and New York's Oceanic Air Control: "I departed from Kindley Field at 8:41 A.M. hours. My ETA at Kingston 1:10 P.M. hours. I am flying in good visibility at 18,000 ft. I flew over 150 miles south of Kindley Field at 9:32 hrs. My ETA at 30° N is 9:37 hrs. Will you accept control?"

Shortly afterward at 9:42 A.M. he sent a last brief message: "I was over 30 degrees North at 9:37. I am changing frequency to MRX"—both Nassau and Kingston's radio frequencies. However, although he indicated he was just switching frequencies, neither aerodrome ever received any word from him. After 1:10 P.M., the scheduled ETA, *Star Ariel* was listed as overdue and a search began within two hours. This search was aided by military vessels in the area, Coast Guard cutters and life stations, and other aircraft flying that same route. It was finally discontinued, with the same results as in *Star Tiger*'s case—negative.

The investigation of this disappearance was perhaps even more intense than that to which *Star Tiger* had been subjected, yet with equal lack of logical explanation. "There were no weather complications at all. A study of the weather reports gives no indication of any abnormal conditions. . . . There were no clouds above 10,000 feet over the whole route. . . . The freezing level was 14,000 feet, so there was no question of icing."

Unexplained radio interference was reported during the plane's flight time, beginning close to its time of departure and ending eerily around its

ETA. This ranged from "blackouts" to hazy reception that came and went without reason, affecting certain stations while not affecting others, and then vice versa. An examination of this interference, however, yielded no clue to why a distress signal was not picked up, since a Mayday is an all-points bulletin and some station would have heard one. The report, under John Moore, Lord Brabazon of Tara and head of the investigation committee, concluded it was lost suddenly: "The Captain's procedure was correct. That he did not re-establish communication with Bermuda after failure to contact Kingston or any other Caribbean Station must be assumed to have been because of inability to do so."

One must inject "lightning-like" since this "inability" struck between switching frequencies.

While sabotage was suspected (but without evidence) because both aircraft belonged to the same corporation, an equally astounding disappearance had happened only a few weeks earlier of an aircraft of an entirely different carrier, on a completely different route (though still within the Triangle), that is even more impossible to explain.

This was a big DC-3 airliner, a twin-engine aircraft considered to be the most reliable type of airplane ever built. It took off from San Juan, Puerto Rico, at 10:03 P.M. on December 27, 1948, with a full complement of passengers and crew totaling thirty-one people. NC16002 (its official registration number) circled the field until its transmitter was completely charged. (The battery was discovered to be low on water when it had landed.) After successful contact with San Juan, it headed northwest to its destination of Miami.

At about 3:40 A.M., shortly before its ETA of 4:03 A.M. at Miami, Robert Linquist, the DC-3's pilot, was overheard reporting himself just 50 miles south of Miami—in terms of time just beginning his approach. The flight was on schedule. The weather was perfect, without any complications whatsoever.

Nevertheless, the large airliner, with all its passengers and crew, was never seen again. No explosions were reported—the usual cause of sudden loss. A thorough search even included the Everglades, because the flight's approach to Miami was over shallow, transparent water. The inexplicable lack of trace of the aircraft in these conditions suggests it might have suffered an unknown navigational breakdown and may have been far off course. Although this might sound logical, it also presupposes that the radio ceased to function in the interim as well and that Linquist did not recheck his position by astral navigation. A combination of the above, it should be remembered, was declared "beyond probability" in the case of *Star Tiger.* Again, the lack of debris cannot be blamed on any mechanical or human failure.

A number of unexplained radio quirks during NC16002's flight time cannot be blamed on its radio. When the plane was only an hour from San Juan, Linquist reported his altitude at 8,300 feet. Yet he was not heard by San Juan but was overheard by Miami, 700 miles away. When 50 miles south of Miami, it was actually New Orleans, 600 miles northwest, that picked up the message and relayed it to Miami. This disturbing coincidence of unusual "voids" in the atmosphere, interfering with the lost plane's radio communication, will be noteworthy in other disappearances.

On December 21, 1952, a Curtis C-46 cargo flight disappeared at night in the same area, with apparently equal suddenness, with its crew of three, after the pilot signaled he was descending from 8,000 to 6,000 feet, en route to land at Miami. The weather had been perfect, and the pilot was within sight of the coastline lights.

Possibly one of the most tragic disappearances in the Triangle happened to Flight 441 on October 30, 1954. This was a huge Lockheed four-engine Super Constellation airliner in military transport service, designated an R7V-1. It was carrying forty-two passengers, all of them family of U.S. Navy servicemen overseas. Everything indicates that the flight encountered nothing unusual; its messages were routine from its base of Patuxent River NAS, Maryland, as far as Bermuda, where it would pass northward on its course to Lajes, Azores, where it was subsequently determined to have inexplicably disappeared, by lack of radio messages thereafter. Its cargo adds another peculiar aspect to the mystery. It was carrying five life rafts, 111 life jackets (!), forty-six exposure suits, pillows, and 660 paper cups. An intensive search found no bodies, no parts of the plane or cabin paneling, nor any sign of its very floatable cargo.

The final conclusion of the Naval Board of Inquiry perhaps best summarizes what can be said of any missing airplane in the Bermuda Triangle: "It is the opinion of the Board that R7V-1 BuNo 128441 did meet with a sudden and violent force, that rendered the aircraft no longer airworthy, and was thereby beyond the scope of human endeavor to control. The force that rendered the aircraft uncontrollable is unknown."

Among the most astounding disappearances of military aircraft is that of *Pogo 22,* an eight-engine Boeing B-52, on October 14, 1961. This was the first time a jet aircraft disappeared in the Triangle. Operating out of Seymour Johnson AFB in North Carolina along with five other B-52s,

Pogo 22 (its squadron name) was participating in Sky Shield II, a secret Cold War maneuver for strike deterrent preparedness. Its return trip to base was a large arc extending from Nova Scotia to Bermuda, where the six B-52s split up to a 10-mile lateral separation and headed west for base. *Pogo 22* was last seen by its "white cell" partner *Pogo 13* when 3 miles distant during the separation. The other five B-52s cruised into base on schedule, with the exception of *Pogo 22*.

An immediate search by Coast Guard cutters, Navy destroyers and cruisers, and C-130 Hercules planes, not to mention all the civilian vessels in the vicinity, covered 280,000 square miles of sea, roughly twice the area of California.

Wreckage from a B-52 normally should not be hard to locate, since this type of aircraft is 160 feet long, has a 186-foot wingspan, and is 40 feet high. It also vanished within a very specified route heading toward the coast, at all times only 10 miles away from *Pogo 13*. Any explosion would have been seen, and any ditching would have been preceded by a Mayday, no matter how terse. Perhaps a simple explanation for this aircraft's disappearance can be found; however, its last location in the Triangle is in itself a disquieting coincidence with the others.

A KB-50 aerial tanker with the squadron handle of "Tyler 41" disappeared next in this same area on January 8, 1962. This large four-engine aircraft, a design based on the B-29 bomber, carried large quantities of fuel for mid-air refueling. About an hour after it took off from Langley AFB, Virginia, carrying eight crew, the following message was picked up: "This is Tyler 41. I am at 37°15' North latitude, 70° West longitude at 12:17 P.M. My flight level is 23,000 feet. I am flying on instruments, heading 085 degrees. My ground speed is 385 mph. Endurance is 11+ hours. My destination is Lajes. Am estimating 37°30' North latitude 65° West longitude at 1 P.M. and 37°35' North latitude 60° West longitude next. I request that you relay this to New York Oceanic Air Control."

A peculiar radio communication void preceded the KB-50 disappearance, as well. The 1 P.M. ETA mentioned would place it in the Triangle almost due north of Bermuda. When they reached this area, Tyler 41 made several unsuccessful attempts to contact "Harmon Control" on the east coast of the United States to inform them they were on course and schedule. Then for the next 15 minutes they tried to contact other stations along the U.S. East Coast, with equal lack of success. Knowledge of this comes from a Navy transport plane approximately one hour behind, also en route to the Azores. They attempted to relay Tyler 41's messages, but encountered the same lack of response. At 1:20 P.M. both gave up and continued on their course.

However, when the Navy transport landed without incident at Lajes, Azores, they were informed that Tyler 41 was overdue. Though traveling behind her on the identical course, they had not seen anything indicating a horrific explosion, nor did they receive a Mayday indicating trouble.

According to COMEASTAREA and COMUSFORAZ, the Air Force's various command areas, 162 search and rescue sorties were flown in a combined 1,369 flight hours by the U.S. Air Force alone, with an additional seven sorties and forty-nine search hours by the U.S. Navy and twenty-three sorties in 236 hours by the U.S. Coast Guard. So frustrating was the lack of trace that five Coast Guard cutters, one abreast the other, sailed the entire flight track of the KB-50 from Langley to the Azores, a 412-hour search covering 440,820 square miles of the Atlantic, to date the most extensive search for any lost plane or ship. "No trace of any survivors or wreckage was ever found," the investigation concluded, "thus preventing the accident Board from obtaining any physical evidence upon which to base their investigation."

Only five months later, on May 27, 1962, a huge C-133 Cargomaster left Dover, Delaware, for Lajes, Azores. In this case, the bizarre nature of its disappearance was verified by radar. The pilot, James Allen Higgins, had just rogered reaching 17,000 feet altitude. Minutes afterward, at precisely 9:25:50 A.M., the C-133 vanished from the scope. The search, concentrating in this area, at first found nothing, but eventually a nose wheel was found and retrieved. Examination of the tire by the FBI lab revealed minute particles of aluminum, steel, plywood, and paint chips embedded in the rubber—a pathetic cross section, molecularly speaking, of all that the Cargomaster had been, along with its 50,000 pounds of cargo consisting of crates, boxes, bags, machinery, etc., though now unusually disintegrated. The lab also found a "magnetic particle," but added that "no significance is attached to the presence of the very small magnetic particle," although they admitted they did not know what it was. Tests also concluded that no explosive material was found on the wheel. This is just one case of a huge aircraft suddenly disintegrating for no apparent reason. As a final mystery, this C-133 was carrying 85,000 pounds of fuel, most of which had not been expended yet, but no oil slicks were located.

By a disturbing coincidence, another C-133 disappeared from radar in the same location more than a year later, September 22, 1963, after leaving Dover. Before it vanished there was unusual electronic interference, as noted by the radar return. The operator had trouble picking it up on his scope, so he requested that the pilot "indent," that is, turn on a signal that makes an SIF (selective identification feature) appear on a controller's scope to magnify an aircraft's image.

Radio reception was also unusually poor for this time of early morning and for the flight being so close to such major hubs of air traffic as New Jersey and New York. Pilot Dudley Connolly's reply was faint: "Roger, roger." Nonetheless, no such SIF amplification of the return ever showed on the controller's scope. At 2:55 A.M., Connolly was heard to say, "For your information—ah, we're 30 miles out of the Sea Isle on the one thirty eight radial," to which New York responded, "Report reaching one-four-thousand." Connolly's last words were "Roger, roger." Only five minutes later the C-133 blip vanished from the scope.

For the record, this C-133 was carrying 48,593 pounds of cargo and 88,000 pounds of fuel. This time the search found absolutely nothing.

If the disappearance of this last C-133 received little publicity, it was because in the month before, on August 28, 1963, an incredible disappearance involving two KC-135 jet Stratotankers engrossed the press. Flying in formation on a return trip to Miami from a point about 300 miles southwest of Bermuda, they disappeared, apparently simultaneously, while maintaining about a mile separation in flight, with the lead aircraft at 36,000 feet and the other 500 feet lower.

A massive search was launched after they failed to arrive at Homestead Air Force Base. The search finally located debris identified as coming from *one* of them, then days later debris from the other nearby. But it remained mysterious how they could have collided in midair. We will see later, however, other incidents where planes suddenly slowed or changed altitude for no reason, possibly explaining some of the mysteries still surrounding these two Stratotankers.

The June 5, 1965, disappearance of a C-119 "Flying Boxcar" contains more unexplained radio quirks that serve only to deepen the mystery surrounding it. This Air Force utility flight took off from Homestead Air Force Base, south of Miami, with ten crew, and headed toward its destination of Grand Turk Island, where it was to drop off engine parts for another C-119 that had lost an engine and made an emergency landing the day before. Shortly after takeoff at 7:47 P.M., Major Louis Giuntoli informed Miami he was picking up the "Yankee Route" at 9,000 feet altitude and would follow this air highway all the way to Grand Turk. Giuntoli's last transmission at 10:03 P.M. was from the last check-in point on this route, designated Yankee 2, roughly 200 miles from Grand Turk. What is strange is that he was not picked up by any local control, several of which ring the area, nor by any of the other aircraft flying in the vicinity, nor by Miami, which was expecting the call. He was picked up by New York, some *1,300* miles away, as if nearer there than to the Bahamas. They in turn informed Miami.

When the Boxcar failed to arrive in the next hour, a full though fruitless search was launched. An examination of the weather provided no clue. "After a thorough investigation of the synoptic situation and evaluation of numerous pilot debriefings it has been determined that the weather between Yankee 2 and Grand Turk at the time and altitude that C-119 was in the area was VFR [visual flight rules] with no apparent hazards."

Although the disappearance of Flight 19 is the first recorded disappearance attributed to the Bermuda Triangle, a number of aircraft, mostly military, had vanished during the war years. These remained unknown because documentation for those lost during the war was not available until more recently. The most surprising of these involve several PBY Catalinas, amphibians that can land on water should trouble arise. One with nine Free French crew left Norfolk, Virginia, July 27, 1944, and disappeared; another went missing off St. Augustine, Florida, February 21, 1944; two others were lost in the Gulf June 5, 1942, and October 2, 1943, with combined crews of eighteen. Sometimes dates are not even given but location is, like another Catalina with eleven crew that left San Juan and disappeared, with only a few "minor parts found." Numerous Avengers and Douglas Dauntlesses have vanished, like one that went missing off NAS Norfolk March 7, 1943, with three aboard; a Dauntless went missing east of NAS Miami at night on September 11, 1944; another one vanished about 40 miles east of Fort Lauderdale March 6, 1945. A Lockheed Ventura disappeared July 10, 1943, while itself on a search mission, with five crew, out of Guantánamo, Cuba; another Ventura, on convoy cover duty out of Trinidad, vanished with six crew November 13, 1943; yet another Ventura was on a search mission September 7, 1943, and went missing with six crew; and another Lockheed Ventura, with five crew, disappeared August 7, 1943, believed shot down by an enemy sub. PBM Mariners lost on routine and training patrols have included one on July 10, 1945, while over the Bahamas on night patrol, with twelve crew; only a few days later on July 18 a Navy Privateer also vanished over the Bahamas while on routine patrol; and a B-24 Liberator on a ferry flight near Bermuda was lost February 7, 1945.

Postwar losses include a Grumman Hellcat, off Key West, Florida, on November 27, 1950; a Grumman F9F-2 Panther jet after leaving New Jersey September 11, 1950; and a Lockheed Texan after leaving Cherry Point, North Carolina, December 5, 1953.

While smaller civilian aircraft have disappeared since the 1940s as well, these events have been obscured by ruined records before 1964 or, in the case of the military records above, remain unindexed and will one day be relocated or extracted with more pertinacious research. Records for aircraft accidents show that roughly four aircraft vanish on an average each year. Sometimes there have been single years when no plane vanished, but then followed by a glut when as many as nine or ten have vanished in a given year. There is no overall model or make affected. The only similarities are the location, lack of radio reports (or confused reports), and lack of wreckage. This last point strikes a disquieting chord because many of the planes vanished over shallow water.

On February 8, 1964, a twin engine Piper Apache, in charter service with pilot and three passengers, disappeared between West Palm Beach, Florida, and Grand Bahama. December 5, a Cessna 140 with two persons vanished off New Smyrna Beach, Florida. A Cessna 182, a high-wing, reliable aircraft often used for aerial scouting and pleasure flying, disappeared over the crowded Florida Keys while en route from Marathon to Key West, with pilot and passenger aboard, October 31, 1965. December 29, 1965, a Piper Cherokee took off from Caicos Island, heading for San Juan, Puerto Rico, with pilot and two passengers; it went missing.

A rather unusual disappearance of a cargo plane took place April 5, 1966. Carrying a decidedly nonhazardous load of frozen chickens, the aircraft, a converted B-25 Mitchell bomber with the civilian tailmark of N92877, was headed from Fort Lauderdale to Aruba and then to South America. The last radio report indicated it was somewhere over the Tongue of the Ocean, the deepest water in the central Bahamas. Thereafter, however, the expected routine radio contact never came from the pilot, Gene Nattress. An exhaustive search found no trace.

Disappearances are sometimes disturbingly frequent. In the first week of January 1967, three aircraft vanished. The first one, a Chase YC-122, was lost January 11 between Fort Lauderdale and Bimini, with four persons aboard, while carrying supplies for an Ivan Tors movie shoot. The second was on January 14, when Dr. R. van Westerborg and his friends took off in his Beechcraft Bonanza from Key Largo, south of Miami, and disappeared over shallow water. The last, on January 17, was a Piper Apache en route from San Juan, Puerto Rico, to St. Thomas, piloted by an extremely qualified pilot, John Walston, who was carrying three passengers.

Though these received a lot of attention in the press and later contributed to this period being dubbed Black Week, they were only three out of a total of eight disappearances in 1967 alone. The others received little if any attention, among them a Cherokee that vanished July 2 near Mayagüez, Puerto Rico, with four occupants; another Piper Cherokee in the short span between Miami and Bimini (about 50 miles) on August 6, carrying three people; and yet another Piper Cherokee between Great Inagua Island and San Juan, Puerto Rico, on October 3. Great Inagua is the most common halfway rest and refueling point for flights heading from Florida toward Puerto Rico, and vice versa, thus ruling out fuel exhaustion as a possible cause in the last case. When getting lost on this route, one can easily find land at Hispaniola to the south. Yet no trace of the aircraft was found and no Mayday was received. Although it is still easier to get lost on long overseas routes, as in the above cases, it is not likely on short routes, as in the case of a Cessna 182 that disappeared November 8 over shallow water between George Town, Great Exuma, Bahamas, and Nassau, Bahamas, carrying the pilot and three passengers. Lastly, a Cherokee with four persons aboard went missing November 22 in the vicinity of Cat Island, Bahamas.

On May 29, 1968, a Cessna 172 vanished around Grand Turk Island, with two persons aboard, after the pilot shouted over the mike: "Engine quit!" This incident was sensationally revisited a year later when another Cessna 172, this one with the tailmark N8040L, vanished June 6, 1969, after a chain of confusing radio messages. The pilot, Carolyn Coscio, accompanied by her boyfriend, Richard Rosen, was trying to find Grand Turk to refuel and then head to Kingston, Jamaica. When she should have been at the island and requesting approach instructions, she radioed instead that she was lost and was circling two deserted islands and that her navigational equipment could not detect the Grand Turk homing beacon. In desperate tones, she finally transmitted "Is there any way out of this?" before she disappeared. A full search found no trace despite calm seas.

Six other aircraft disappeared in 1969, most of them twin-engine aircraft with skilled pilots. In none of these incidents did the pilots send any Mayday, though even if they had lost an engine there should still have been ample time to do so before ditching. Two of them were along an identical course—Great Inagua to San Juan—while the others were along busy routes well within range of several flight unit facilities.

A Piper Comanche disappeared while overflying the Bahamas November 23, 1970, en route from West Palm Beach to Kingston, Jamaica.

On December 20, 1973, a particularly surprising disappearance involved a Lake Amphibian—an aircraft designed to land on water—between Nassau and Bimini, a route mostly over shallow water. Nevertheless, the plane vanished with its three occupants.

While many planes have vanished on long routes, the disappearances have nevertheless primarily been confined to the Bahamas, an area that consists of *hundreds* of islands and some of the shallowest ocean depths in the world, thousands and thousands of square miles being the Great Bahama Bank, with an average depth of only 50 feet and often as shallow as 5 or 7 feet. This latter depth covers many square miles, even far from any visible land.

Of all the disappearances, the most unusual have been those lost on short routes between the Bahamas and Florida, unusual because the element of suddenness is inescapable in any conclusion. Often the routes are so short that a plane is at its cruising altitude for only minutes before descending. These short routes are usually crowded with other air and sea traffic—a battery of potential witnesses and rescuers—and the hundreds of islands and their beaches make potential repositories for debris. Although many times these disappearances happen over the Gulf Stream, the Coast Guard takes into account an object's drift when searching for any lost plane.

Nevertheless, no trace has been found of any of the following aircraft that vanished over these waters: a Forney Ercoupe on December 6, 1965, between Fort Lauderdale and West End, Grand Bahama; again on July 8, 1968, a Cessna 180 between Grand Bahama and West Palm Beach, a flight distance of 65 or so miles; a Piper Comanche between Nassau and Opa Locka, Florida, near Miami, January 17, 1970; a Cessna 177 between Andros Island and Miami on March 20, 1971, timed at 3:18 P.M. by an unqualified call for help; March 28, 1973, a Cessna 172 after leaving West Palm Beach, Florida; a Navion A16 on May 25, 1973, between Freeport, Grand Bahama, and West Palm Beach. In this last disappearance the pilot, Bob Corner, had been informed of thunderstorms on his route and was rerouted along with all the other traffic, including a plane close behind. Amidst this traffic, he vanished without trace. On August 10, 1973, a Beech Bonanza disappeared between Fort Lauderdale and Marsh Harbor, Great Abaco, with six aboard. A Cessna 172 vanished on a coastal flight in the vicinity of Fort Lauderdale July 28, 1975, one of two that had vanished

The busiest part of the Triangle: its southwest corner containing southern Florida, the Keys, and the exotic islands of the Bahamas and West Indies spanning the distance between San Juan and Miami, the two radial hubs of traffic.

in less than three months. Previously, on May 2, a twin-engine Cessna Skymaster had vanished in the same area.

Though weather records are scanty for some of these, and thus bad weather cannot be ruled out, an alarming possible cause might be gleaned from a disappearance in 1971 in nearby waters.

Considerable official silence still surrounds the disappearance of *Sting 27*, a Phantom II jet fighter, September 10, 1971. It was on a short, routine maneuver out of Homestead Air Force Base, south of Miami, where it took off at 8:05 A.M. Its last radar return was at 8:22 A.M., 82 miles southeast. The jet was in a right turn after having come out of Mach 1 speed. At this time "Blissful Control" noticed *Sting 27*'s SIF (selective identification feature) get weaker. "*Sting 27*, your SIF feature is fading. We're having trouble identifying you. Is that you at the boundary of Alpha six?" Lieutenant Norm Northrup, in training under Captain John Romero in the back seat, responded, "Roger, I am in a port turn at this time." Radar confirmed Northrup's message. *Sting 27* turned left to a northerly heading, then right again: "During the right turn, radar contact was lost at 8:22 A.M." states the report.

Despite other Phantoms in the area, and the Coast Guard cutter *Steadfast* (which had earlier taken note of *Sting 27* in the sky by two sonic booms as it exceeded Mach speed), no trace was found of the aircraft and no automatic alarm was detected.

The report on this disappearance is highly redacted. Even the standard summary sheet, with its many questions and accompanying boxes, has been subjected to a skilled razor. This extends even to the answer box for the question "What type of accident?" Usually the answer is "missing/unknown" and does not require editing. However, at the back of the report there is a map showing *Sting 27* at various points of its flight path. Among a number of boxes with arrows highlighting key parts of this path, there is a box reading "suspected point of impact," miles (according to the scale of the map) before a pinpointing arrow that leads to another box reading "radar contact lost." This vague and overlooked point in the report, intimating some form of collision or encounter in midair, adds alarming ramifications to an "object" seen by *Sting 29* and *Sting 30* when they were immediately vectored to the last radar spot.

According to the report, only minutes after *Sting 27* vanished, *Sting 29* dropped down to 1,500 feet to get a closer look at an "area of disturbance" in the ocean and then described it—in the words of the report—as "an area of water discoloration, oblong in shape, approximately 100 by 200 feet, with its axis running north/south; its southern tip appeared to be

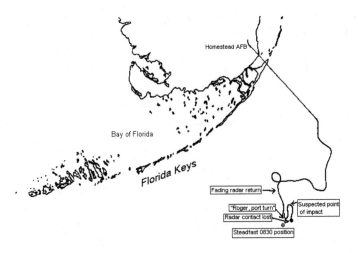

This map is based on the official U.S. Air Force Mishap Report map showing *Sting 27* at crucial points of its last moments. "Suspected point of impact" comes miles ahead of where *Sting 27* finally vanished. What was it?

below the surface and the northern end appeared to be above." The report does not offer it as a "UFO" or its submarine equivalent "USO," for a gap takes the place of any Air Force opinion or clarification—the explanatory paragraph is neatly hacked out.

Since an oil slick cannot be both above and below the water, nor disperse cross-current, these facts strongly suggest that this was not an oil slick, as the current, in this case, would have dispersed it northeastward. Adding to this deduction is that the Coast Guard cutter *Steadfast* was only 5 nautical miles away when *Sting 30* signaled it to investigate. When it arrived shortly afterward, it found no trace of the "discoloration." Moreover, this area was searched by sonar in order to find any trace of *Sting 27* on the bottom to confirm it impacted with the sea, but no trace was found in a 5-square-mile grid search.

Equally alarming circumstances surrounded the disappearance of *Fighting Tiger 524* on February 22, 1978. While en route from NAS Oceana to the carrier USS *Kennedy,* only 100 miles off shore, the pilot, Lieutenant Paul Smyth, blurted "Stand by," followed moments later by the copilot, Lieutenant Richard Leonard, saying "Stand by, we have a problem right now."

Moments later the KA-6 attack bomber vanished from the *Kennedy*'s radarscope, judged at only 30 miles distant. As soon as the "downed aircraft" symbol went up, the strike controller in CIC (Combat Information Center) noted a "raw radar return." Unlike the one received from the KA-6 attack bomber, this was devoid of any IFF but was definitely a verified aircraft trail or, one might say in this case, an object trail, since it could not be definitely confirmed as the KA-6. This heading was completely different from the one the attack bomber had been on. (They were last heading 270 degrees, being vectored for landing.) This "raw radar return" appeared 12 miles southwest of *Fighting Tiger*'s last position, heading 220 degrees. It lasted for a couple of minutes. But during this time neither Leonard nor Smyth, if this was them, sent any clarifying message or answered repeated hails. This radar return then vanished from the scope.

An extensive but fruitless search and thorough investigation could only produce the following opinion:

It is evident that two minutes prior to AB524's disappearance, the crew was having some difficulty or experiencing a minor emergency as revealed by the voice tape transcripts. Due to the lack of further radio transmissions, no hypothesis can be made as to the type or severity of the initial difficulty. It is suspected, however, that a catastrophic situation developed after the final radio transmission and Lieutenant Smyth and Lieutenant Leonard were incapable of coping with the situation. It is further believed that the crew did not attempt to eject as the concurrent failure of both URT-33 beacon radios [automatic alarms triggered by ejection] was unlikely. Thus, this investigation concludes that a catastrophic emergency situation developed, incapacitated the crew to the point that they were unable to eject and were subsequently lost at sea.

This incident was merely an unsettling foreshadowing of what was to come. In 1978 more aircraft disappeared in the Triangle than in any other year. Their courses varied; so did the types of aircraft that vanished. There seems to be no pattern, except for the disturbing and already apparent one.

On March 25, 1978, a twin-engine Aero Commander 680 disappeared between Opa Locka, Florida, and Freeport, Grand Bahama. The aircraft was reported overdue by a client of the pilot, who had been waiting to inspect his boat on Grand Bahama with the intent of purchasing. The weather had been beautiful that day, with no hazards of any kind over the Bahamas.

On April 27, 1978, a Piper Aerostar left Pompano Beach, Florida, with its pilot, Dr. Anthony Purcell, en route to Panama City, Florida. Again, the weather provided no explanation for the disappearance. After it vanished from radar, a 5-second-long auto alarm signal was picked up but was abruptly silenced. Hours later two more 2-second signals were heard, then silenced. These were not identified as coming from the Aerostar, or from any plane for that matter, and their origin remains unexplained.

While the search for the Aerostar was underway, a Cessna 172 disappeared in unusual circumstances on April 30, 1978, en route to Daytona Beach. The crew of a fishing smack noticed an airplane overhead fighting power loss, its engine sputtering and skipping. Despite this, the plane continued on without making any attempt to contact the vessel, even by visual means. This, and its steady course, plus absence of a radio Mayday, suggested to the crew that the pilot may no longer have been aboard. This unusual scenario, implying a derelict aircraft, has been noted in other sightings of aircraft that were later reported missing. This plane had left Dillon, South Carolina, with George Hotelling, a pilot of considerable experience. The plane continued on until out of sight and sound. No trace was ever found of it.

It was May 19, 1978, when a Piper Cherokee Arrow III, with four persons aboard, disappeared between Fort Pierce, Florida, and Nassau, Bahamas. As part of the investigation, the local flight service unit went over a recording of Lon Amason, the pilot, in conversation with the radio operator about weather fronts and scattered thunderstorms in which the operator informed him of a large break in the weather near his position. Amason's last words were: "Affirmative, I see a spot here just about due east of my position. It's clear through there."

On May 26, 1978, at 4 P.M., a Beech Queen Air departed Port-au-Prince, Haiti, on a short, 45-minute trip to nearby Providenciales Island in the Bahamas. The weather was perfect. Thirteen minutes after takeoff, the pilot made his last radio contact, saying all was well.

On July 18, 1978, a large twin-engine charter Piper Navajo left Santa Marta, Colombia, for Port-au-Prince with two pilots and disappeared over the Caribbean.

Among the disappearances in 1978, one of the most remarkable happened to Argosy Flight 902, a DC-3 charter airliner, south of the Florida Keys. On September 21 the pilot, George Hamilton, obtained U.S. permission for a flight to Havana in order to pick up twenty-one U.S. citrus growers on tour there. He and his copilot, Pete Rustinburghe, were accompanied by his wife, Barbara Hamilton, and a friend, Pauline Lowe, who acted as stewardesses. Shortly after takeoff from Fort Lauderdale, Rustinburghe contacted Miami with his typical levity. "This is Pete Rustinberghe of Argosy Flight 902. We'll be going to Havana, Cuba, and I'd like to get the weather along the route and all the goodies if I could, please." The reply was for fair weather along their course.

When the DC-3 departed the area of the Keys and headed south to Havana, it began to experience hazy radio communications—a presentiment of disaster, as we have seen in other losses. After about 15 minutes of this, Havana picked them up loud and clear and tracked them on radar. The last sweep of their scope, at 12:43 P.M., showed Argosy 902 making a slight turn to the right of course. The next sweep, the scope was blank.

Miami and Havana coordinated an immediate search. U.S. Air Force and U.S. Coast Guard units raced to the scene, while the Cuban air patrol made overflights within the first hour. By afternoon the Coast Guard cutter *Steadfast* was coordinating the surface effort. The search was expanded to all traffic, plus four more cutters, a helicopter, and a C-131 with the following cable: "All shipping Straits of Florida-Nicholas Channel Argosy Airlines Flt. 902 (N407D) is overdue on a flight from Fort Lauderdale to Havana, Cuba. Desc: white with blue trim. 4 persons on board. All ships are requested to keep a sharp lookout for debris, yellow life jackets, people in the water. Signed U.S. Coast Guard Miami, FL."

There were thirty-two yellow life jackets on board Flight 902. The blue-gray seat cushions were the floatable kind. On September 24 the search was discontinued, with negative results. The DC-3 also carried an ELT (emergency locator transmitter), but, as in the many other disappearances in the Bermuda Triangle, no transmission was ever received.

Comment on radio and television was lively and up to the minute. At one point it excited one erratic mind to call the UPI (United Press International) in Miami, invent a terrorist organization of which no one had heard, then claim responsibility for blowing up Argosy Flight 902, before abruptly hanging up. Although little credence is usually given such calls, the authorities followed this one up and found it to lack credibility. Anyway, if the DC-3 had blown up it would have scattered debris over a fairly wide territory, something that would not have gone unnoticed during the search. In addition, Argosy 902 would not have turned to the right of its course before a surprise explosion.

Every available fact about Argosy 902 only leads to improbable suppositions: if the airplane had exploded, this would explain why it vanished from the radarscope; on the other hand, debris would also have been found scattered over a wide territory; if it plummeted to the sea, for whatever reason, the blinding impact and implosion would have scattered debris everywhere as well.

If this incident is hard to believe, less than two months later a twin engine, ten-seat Piper Chieftain charter aircraft vanished in even more alarming circumstances. Caribbean Flight 912 disappeared at 7:19 P.M. while coming in for a landing at Harry S. Truman Airport, St. Thomas. Its last position off the runway was clearly marked by radar and by visual confirmation by the air traffic controller, William A. Kittinger, who estimated it to be within 2 miles of the runway. The landing light was clearly visible as a bright and steady beam. At this moment, Kittinger remembers he looked down at the radarscope to make sure a Heron DH-114 was taking off all right. To his surprise, he noticed the radarscope was blank except for the Heron climbing to altitude. He immediately did a double take back out the tower window and saw no more landing light. Urgent radio calls went unanswered, and he declared an emergency.

The search began within minutes when Kittinger redirected a Cessna 172 on approach to search the area. This was followed up by a thorough four-day-long Coast Guard search. Despite the Chieftain's last position being less than 2 miles from the runway, the search found no trace of it.

The mystery of Flight 912 grows more complicated. The Chieftain had ample radio equipment, which was working only minutes before. The

The radarscope readings as taken from the NTSB report. The X shows the last position of Caribbean Flight 912 in relation to the runway.

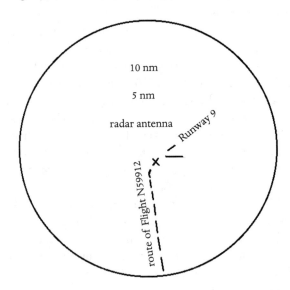

pilot, Irving C. Rivers, the sole occupant, was a charter pilot with more than 5,000 flight hours; he had just taken off from nearby St. Croix to come pick up passengers; there is no hint of pilot fatigue or pilot error. The aircraft also carried an ELT, yet no signal was received.

This exact scenario had played itself out before at St. Thomas. On February 10, 1974, a Pilattus-Brittan-Norman Islander "signaled approach; failed to arrive St. Thomas" at 7:31 P.M., as the official brief so briefly summarizes. (Earlier that same day another odd disappearance happened in the Triangle, near the Bahamian island of Great Abaco, after a Cessna 414 with only the pilot on board left the port of Treasure Cay.) A fruitless search lasting several days in both locations failed to find a clue. In 1982 a charter Navajo vanished near St. Thomas in familiar circumstances. It left nearby Anguilla October 20 and headed for St. Thomas. A complete search failed to locate a trace of the Navajo (N777AA) or its complement of eight persons and luggage.

In a disturbing encore, eight aircraft utterly vanished in 1979. Most of these were over the Bahamas and in and about the nearby islands. Only one pilot sent a message to indicate they had encountered trouble. The pilots' amount of experience was very good to excellent. No trace was found of any of them despite well-coordinated searches.

These aircraft included a Beechcraft Musketeer with pilot Roy Ziegler, a professional airplane mechanic, and his friend, Brian Fines; it was last heard from over the Exumas on January 11. In this same general location Jim Catron was last heard from in his twin-engine Beech E18s while en route from Fort Lauderdale to Cat Island on April 2. On April 24 a Piper Cherokee signaled it was turning around while only about 5 miles off at Fort Lauderdale; the radio transmission was suddenly poor. The pilot stated no reason (though a rain shower was beginning); it then vanished from the scope. Along the short route between St. Croix and St. Thomas, a Cessna 150 went missing on June 30. On October 4, 1979, an Aero Commander 500 left Andros Town, Andros Island, for West Palm Beach and was last seen passing Bimini. A twin Piper Aztec left Montego Bay, Jamaica, bound for Nassau, Bahamas, on October 27. It never arrived. A comparatively crowded route lay below the flight track of a Beech twin Bonanza that disappeared November 19, 1979, while en route from Delray Beach to Key West, Florida. The pilot, Jack Houston, was planning to scuba dive in the Keys. Another Aztec disappeared December 21, 1979, bound for Caicos from Anguilla, with four persons aboard.

Not only have aircraft disappeared within sight of land, abruptly halting any radio dialogue, but, even more strange, on a couple of occasions radio messages from vanished planes have continued to be picked up by far-flung receiving stations hours afterward. This element to the mystery, as if to imply the messages were being received as they receded farther away in *time* or *space,* is echoed in the following cases.

The most extraordinary example is that of a Beech Baron 58 that left St. Thomas and headed for Miami February 11, 1980. The pilot was a young Civil Air Patrol student (last seen boarding his plane in his uniform) named Peter Jensen. Jensen last reported himself near Miami at 8:38 A.M., 4 hours and 23 minutes after takeoff. He said he was only 6½ miles east of Miami; both engines had quit and he was about to ditch. What is extraordinary, however, is that this was overheard by Fleming Flight 667 while in the vicinity of Bermuda, roughly 1,000 miles away, but it was not heard by Miami.

Jensen's last words would seem to preclude further contact. Yet at 8:53 A.M. two more flights picked up his Maydays. They were American Flight 667 and Eastern Flight 924, both, like the Fleming flight, around Bermuda. Jensen now reported himself at *150 feet* altitude, descending to ditch, but he was now completely disoriented in strange *clouds.* (The weather off Miami at the time was ideal, confirmed by an immediate Coast Guard helicopter search.) Not once did Miami pick him up. Their search was completely fruitless, including the inability to pick up an ELT signal.

Was it a disoriented novice pilot who was lost and far off course? Is that all there is to it? If that is the case, then how can one explain an odd incident that night? The tower on Caicos Island (about midway between San Juan and Miami, 600 miles away) picked up a radio message at 8:05 P.M. They distinctly heard the call letters N9027Q, the tailmark registration number of Jensen's plane. They described it as "a young man's voice." He reported that he was 10 minutes away and wanted permission to land. Although the tower waited, no aircraft ever arrived. An intense search also failed to locate a trace here as well.

Subsequent investigation established beyond a shadow of a doubt that the plane only had 5 hours of fuel on board. Yet 16 hours after takeoff, Jensen was picked up as still flying. This placed him 600 miles away from where he last reported himself and over 1,000 miles from where he was last heard by the airliners . . . and 11 hours after it was even possible!

In developing the ramifications of all this, it is pertinent to note that there is no place where an aircraft could land and refuel without being logged in and out; Jensen was not initiating his own disappearance; and it was not being reported on the news so that some crank would try and imitate Jensen and then think to do so 600 miles out to sea by an isolated island.

In later incidents we will see how "electronic fogs" have precipitated unusual events, as described by those who survived them, some of them seemingly implying aberrations of time and space. Some might also propose that Jensen was suspended in a "holding area" or "limbo" where the fuel was not used before he was released—or escaped. This last suggestion, intimating direct intervention of the flight by alien or other intelligences, has also been suggested to explain other cases. Although this may sound somewhat like an erudite view, only a few months later a plane disappeared in circumstances that add an alarming dimension to this supposition.

It was a clear summer evening on June 28, 1980. José Maldonado Torres was flying with his friend, José Pagan, to Puerto Rico in an Ercoupe 4-15D N3808H. At 8:03 P.M. the Remote Communications Air to Ground (RCAG) log records the following transcript: "Mayday, Mayday, Ercoupe ocho cero, eight zero zero hotel [sic], we can see a strange object in our course, we are lost, Mayday, Mayday [25 seconds later] . . . Mayday, Mayday, We are lost. We found a strange object in our course."

Iberia Flight 976, flying north of San Juan, intercepted the message and replied:

Station calling one two one five Mayday, Mayday, Iberia nine seven six, go ahead.

Ercoupe 4-15D N3808H: Ah, we are going from Santo Domingo to, ah, San Juan International but we found, ah, a weird object in our course that made us change course about three different times. We got it right now in front of us at 1 o'clock. Our heading is zero seven zero degrees . . . our altitude is one thousand six hundred at zero seven zero degrees. . . . Our VORs got lost off frequency.

Iberia Flight 976: Station calling one two one five Mayday, Mayday, Iberia nine seven six, go ahead.

Ercoupe 4-15D N3808H: Mayday, Mayday, this is Ercoupe three eight zero eight hotel in flight from Santo Domingo to San Juan, Puerto Rico. We have a very weird, ah, object, in front of us that made us lose our course . . . our present heading is 130 degrees at one thousand five hundred feet, sir. . . . We lost signal off of Aguadilla VOR.

Torres's last message came at 8:05:45: "Right now we supposed to be about 35 miles from the coast of Puerto Rico but we have something weird in front of us that make us lose our course all the time. I changed our course a second [unintelligible] our present heading roughly now is 300. We are right again in the same stuff, sir."

At 8:07 P.M. N3808H vanished from Atlantic Fleet Weapons Range radarscope while 35 miles out to sea. At 8:15 P.M., in startling similarity to other aircraft disappearances, an object appeared on the scope, this time tracking 266 degrees. It was never identified and answered no calls. And, if it was the Ercoupe mysteriously reappearing, Torres sent no more Maydays. It then permanently vanished. The Ercoupe also carried an ELT, yet no signal was received.

The search for this aircraft was quick and thorough, rippling outward from the precise location where it vanished from the radarscope. One search pilot who was obsessively diligent was José Pagan Jiménez, Pagan's father and the owner of the airplane. He was also a lieutenant in Puerto Rico's Aero Police. He flew many missions looking for his son, including the last one in his own helicopter, before search operations were suspended with negative results.

On July 18, 1980, Lieutenant Commander M. R. Adams issued what might be considered the official opinion of the Coast Guard in a "to whom it may concern" letter addressed to investigating bureaus in Washington. He observed: "As of this date nothing has ever been found to indicate positively the ultimate fate of N3808H. The Coast Guard has suspended active search and barring the development of some new, positive information indicating the whereabouts of the airplane and/or its crew, no new search efforts will be undertaken."

Inexplicably, aircraft have been found ditched and abandoned. Salvor Graham Hawkes found one such plane by accident between Miami and Bimini at the bottom of the deep Florida Straights. By pure chance his underwater cameras came across a Piper sitting peacefully in the bottom mud. The remote camera zoomed in on its interior to reveal a surprising sight. The ignition key had been removed—yet the doors were tightly closed. There were no signs of personal effects inside. Hawkes, also on camera in the control room on the research vessel, commented with understandable surprise: "Come on, you don't ditch a plane and then remove the ignition key." A Piper Apache is reported to have been found in the same circumstances. On May 4, 1997, it was reported overdue. Despite the search, the plane was not found. Then on June 7, 1997, it was discovered just 5 miles south of Bimini in only 7 to 8 feet of water, as though it had been dropped there only recently. There is no explanation for why the aircraft was never seen for a whole month in such shallow water. Its pilot is declared dead, but no final report has ever been issued, and few details exist.

Time and radio discrepancies are unavoidable when examining the case of the disappearance of a Beechcraft Bonanza, N5805C, on January 6, 1981. The plane, with four persons, was headed from Opa Locka, near Miami, to Nassau, with an ETA of 11:21 A.M. At 11:41 A.M. the Bonanza was just technically overdue. However, 100 miles southeast of Nassau near George Town, Great Exuma, where the plane could not possibly have been yet, a pilot picked up a Mayday indicating the Bonanza was having some kind of problem and had to ditch. All stations were alerted but none, including Nassau, had heard the SOS. The pilot climbed higher and tried to regain contact with the Bonanza, without success.

Several hours later, 30 minutes after fuel exhaustion, around 3:00 P.M., the messages once again revived. The tower on Normans Cay, one of the Exuma chain of islands but much farther north and closer to Nassau, reported a garbled SOS from the Bonanza. In another eerie postscript, the pilot of N2712L reported that, at 5 P.M., he too heard a Mayday from the Bonanza, receiving clearly the call letters and the description. This was *over* an hour and a half after fuel exhaustion. Yet again the problem could not be discerned.

A bizarre chain of events not only preceded but also followed the disappearance of Flight 201, a twin-engine Cessna 402B charter aircraft flying between Miami and Bimini on March 31, 1984. For this trip it carried six people, all employees of the charter company. The pilot was Chuck Sorren, copilot, Al Warton, and extra pilot, Gerald Lancaster. The others aboard were Anne LaTarte, Tammy Christie, and Glynis Bernhard.

The aircraft was tracked on radar, with nothing unusual observed. Then, not even midway to its destination, the target slowed to a dangerously low airspeed of a mere 90 knots. They continued like this for an estimated 4 minutes, without any indication from the pilots that something was wrong. The plane then "plummeted in a 5,400 foot per minute dive until it vanished from radar."

A clue to the fate of Flight 201 only deepened the mystery. An eyewitness at Bimini reported seeing a plane plunge into the sea about 1 mile off the northeast corner of the island. Further corroboration came from a man who said he too saw a huge splash in the ocean, though he saw no plane. They both pegged it between 8:30 and 9 A.M. Although this is during the flight time of the aircraft, all the information points to the airplane disappearing at least 30 miles *away* from Bimini. If one supposes that the "ghost aircraft" that crashed was Flight 201, then it never reappeared on radar and there had been no SOS in the interim. The incident was completed with another mystery: the water in this area is only about 18 feet deep, yet a search uncovered no wreckage and no trace of the plane on the bottom.

Aircraft disappearances over the succeeding years have been on both long and short routes and have included a twin Cessna Skymaster carrying four persons which vanished off the Florida east coast after a routine radio position report on January 14, 1985. A Cessna T210K disappeared on a long flight from Miami to Port-au-Prince, Haiti, the following May 8; a Piper disappeared between Nassau and Opa Locka on July 12, 1985, with four people aboard; on August 3, 1985, a pilot in his Cessna 172 disappeared, apparently near Fort Myers, Florida; and on September 8, 1985, a Cherokee disappeared about 20 miles northeast of Key West after a routine radio communication at 10:08 P.M. that night.

But of all these, the disappearance of another charter Piper Chieftain testifies in a vivid way to the unexplained. Its flight route was short, very short, only 100 miles between Miami and its destination of West End, Grand Bahama Island. It was carrying six people including its pilot, José Villa, in absolutely perfect weather on March 26, 1986. Villa's last message stated he was 10 miles from West End—in terms of their ETA, about 5 to 7 minutes. Nothing was ever heard from him again. There was no SOS, no ELT, no wreckage, and no witnesses. This last fact is especially surprising since West End is a customs port of entry into the Bahamas and the waterway below is often speckled with approaching boats. None reported any whine or sputtering overhead or any crash into the sea.

This is just another example of a lightning-like disappearance where a plane seems to "dematerialize" while coming in for a landing—a fact underscored by the impressive list of what could not have happened in that short time, such as getting lost, missing the island (which was in sight), losing its radio, or being affected by any navigational aberrations.

Some more unusual circumstances surrounded the disappearance of a Cessna 402C on May 27, 1987. In this case the plane was clearly seen to pass over its destination of Marsh Harbour, Great Abaco Island, and to continue eastward as if the pilot had never seen his destination below. This course would take it out into the middle of the Atlantic, as there is nothing beyond Great Abaco. There appeared to be no trouble with the plane, and the large island was clearly visible in the better than average weather. No trace of the aircraft or its pilot was ever found. He sent no distress call of any kind or, that is, none was received.

On June 3, 1987, a large Cessna 401 disappeared between Freeport, Grand Bahama, and Crooked Island, Bahamas, with four persons on board.

No trace was found despite broadcasts to be on the lookout for a number of bright orange life jackets carried on board and to listen for an ELT signal.

On December 2, 1987, Victor Arruberena disappeared along with his Cessna 152 on a short route between La Romana, Dominican Republic, and San Juan, Puerto Rico, a course that reminds one of Torres and Pagan's tragic flight in 1980.

Among those that have vanished on short routes, there is the interesting case of a Cessna 152 during an instructional flight, in perfect weather, off the east coast of Florida on January 24, 1990. Although they were always in view of the coastal lights of West Palm Beach, the flight simply vanished without a trace . . . or a peep over the radio or from its ELT.

Another aircraft lost on a short route was a Cherokee N7202F on June 5, 1990, between the islands of St. Martin and St. Croix. The last words of the pilot, Mary Pomeroy, were unusually faint, consisting of "Zero two foxtrot four five at the boundary, over," indicating she was entering U.S. airspace. Then she faded away for good.

Another unusual disappearance on radar happened on October 31, 1991, when a Grumman Cougar jet was being tracked on radar over the Gulf of Mexico. The pilot, John Verdi, had just requested ascent from 23,000 feet to 29,000 feet. Radar tracked the aircraft during its climb until, for some unknown reason, it simply faded away. Radar readouts confirmed the unusual—the jet had not been captured as descending or falling to the sea. While there was convective thunderstorm activity noted in the area, the cloud tops were at 27,000 feet and the jet was last observed above the weather while on its ascent.

In the last decade, disappearances of aircraft have been along familiar routes as those before, around Florida or over the Bahamas. On September 30, 1993, a Cessna 172 disappeared between Miami and Marco Island, near Florida Bay. The pilot was last heard in routine chatter by other planes; the weather was clear, without complications. A Cherokee 6 went missing between Treasure Cay, Bahamas, and Fort Pierce, Florida, on August 28, 1994. On September 19, the following month, a Piper twin-engine Aztec disappeared over the Caribbean with five persons. And on the following Christmas another Cherokee disappeared near Florida, over land, possibly last being seen fighting power loss while flying over a house. In this last sighting, the pilot never reported a problem.

An Aero Commander 500 performed some unexplained maneuvers before it vanished from radar near Nassau on May 12, 1999. The Aero 500 was clocked by Nassau radar as steadily descending, but at no time did the pilot, Enrique Esme, report anything unusual. The radar then registered 000 altitude (this was not an amphibian). But 30 minutes later he reappeared, requested to land at Nassau, did unusual maneuvers which angered the controller (though Esme seemed unaware of them), then climbed to 1,300 feet, where the plane completely and finally vanished. A part of an aircraft wing was found in the search, not definitely determined as coming from the plane, though it did have gold and blue paint, the same color scheme as the charter plane.

On October 27, 2000, Hubert Helligar disappeared after leaving Winter Haven, Florida, to cruise locally near the Everglades in a Cessna 150, N11214. It was the only time he left without his GPS or cell phone.

Most recently, a Piper has vanished. On September 6, 2002, while in contact with Nassau Control, the pilot of Pawnee N59684 was reporting himself en route from Fort Lauderdale to St. Croix. Suddenly, his voice stopped. The radarscope revealed that his "blip," which had shown he was just 20 miles southeast, was now gone.

Throughout the reports a number of pertinent factors quickly become evident. Each disappearance was very sudden and unexpected. The average qualifications of the pilots ranged from good to excellent, with several hundred to thousands of flight hours' experience under their belts. Some figures jump out immediately, like 5,000, 11,000, 15,000 and, in one instance, 18,000 flight hours' experience.

Engine loss, oil leaks, smoke in the cabin, and fuel exhaustion are all more "routine" events that have been experienced by any number of pilots and have precipitated terrible accidents. Nevertheless, in such cases pilots are able to transmit their problems and often ditch the aircraft and survive. One pilot, for instance, set out on a long flight without a functioning radio. Near Caicos Island he ran out of fuel, but he was still able to use a handheld radio and reached Caicos Tower, informing them he was ditching. He survived.

By contrast with these more "routine" and familiar hazards that befall aircraft, the disappearing aircraft at best are capable of sending only confusing and sketchy Maydays, if any, and still never seem to ditch properly, leave debris, or impact with the ocean and leave an ELT signal; and no occupants ever survive.

To belabor the point, there is a disquieting contrast between disasters of known origin and disappearances. For example, in one disaster in 1980 a DC-3, fully loaded with thirty-four people and flying from Fort Lauderdale to Freeport, Grand Bahama, while coming in for a landing was struck by lightning and crashed into the sea. Rescuers came upon a veritable debris field of cushions, plywood, life jackets, and numerous bodies. But in the case of DC-3 NC16002's disappearance in 1948 in excellent weather while on approach to Miami, there was no trace whatsoever. It was the same for the DC-3 N407D in 1978; also for the charter Chieftain at St. Thomas in 1978 while only 2 miles or less from the runway. There are dozens of other such disappearances in fair weather that have a comparable opposite number of disasters in bad weather where debris is commonplace.

While it is often argued by those who seek to explain away the Bermuda Triangle mysteries that they are nothing more than statistically acceptable accidents, others note that the unusual element seen in many of them is far more important and crucial to any discussion than the number. They point out that an accident is different from a disappearance. The waterways off California and New England, for example, bustle with activity, and the catastrophe, with all its gambols, is frequent. On the other hand, these areas are comparatively low in disappearances.

The dividing factor is, of course, the presence of wreckage. The absence of an SOS may indicate the lightning-like speed with which the aircraft was destroyed. The absence of an ELT signal might also suggest that the force was so destructive that it obliterated the device before it could transmit. But what is so fast and so destructive as to preclude any debris whatsoever?

It may be perfectly natural to assume that the sea is the primary culprit. After all, unlike land, the sea can hide the remains of a simple crash or disperse it before rescuers come upon the scene. But this can by no means explain what caused the aircraft to crash in the first place. Nor can the sea always remove the trace of an aircraft in shallow water a few feet deep or prevent wreckage from washing up on a beach only 1 mile from the area of suspected impact.

It is true that in past centuries to be 50—or even a few—miles from the shore was to be a long distance out at sea. The disappearance of a ship, and later of a plane, did not indicate anything unusual in itself. Often a disappearance went unnoticed until the ship or plane was declared overdue, which could be hours or days later; and long journeys would confront rescuers before arriving at the suspected scene of the accident.

But radio and radar coverage and the fast speeds that aircraft travel—50 miles being only minutes timewise—have shrunk the ocean considerably and thus the amount of time and space it takes for anything unusual to happen. Continuing disappearances without trace, without Mayday, without ELT, even in such narrow corridors as 1 to 5 miles from land, beggar the imagination. The temptation to reject their occurrence would seem easy, were it not for the fact they have been so well documented and investigated.

These aircraft have disappeared in spite of every precaution of flight service, which includes flight plans (a handy file for tower operators to refer to a plane's departure time, course, planned altitude, and ETA), which allows a tower operator to declare a flight overdue within minutes of its failure to report itself in the traffic pattern; several navigational devices that safeguard the pilot from human error, like VOR (very high frequency omnidirectional range or just variable omnirange), radio guidance signals sent out from a base station that guide the aircraft to that destination; DME (distance measuring equipment) that lets the pilot know where he is in relation to various airfields; transponders that identify an aircraft on the scope so a controller can sort out which blip is the plane that signaled itself in trouble, allowing him to quickly judge its altitude and location and render immediate assistance; weather radar, carried in the larger commercial aircraft, that detects the immediate weather instead of leaving a pilot dependent on reports from distant stations on what the weather *may* be like along his course.

Rescue operations are aided now by helicopters and hydrofoil cutters that travel at fantastic speed, set into motion by the Flight Service Stations which monitor the frequencies in use. The moment a Mayday is received, the Coast Guard is notified. Immediate broadcasts are made to all local traffic to be "on the lookout." The speeds of the local currents and probable drift are standard computations in any search and rescue operation. But none of these have done away with disappearances in the Bermuda Triangle at all, nor explained why in other oceans the opposite stands true of overwater accidents where debris is still more consistently located, retrieved, and examined.

Aircraft accidents happen anywhere in the world, with sudden and frightening speed. Airways and seaways over the Mediterranean, around Hawaii, or off Australia are busy with traffic. Yet none have a reputation as a "devil's sea" nor, interestingly, have they ever had. But long before the 20th century the same general area of ocean known today as the Bermuda Triangle was known by other names by virtue of the many sea mysteries that frequented it. Our records of modern missing aircraft are only our generation's contribution to the history of this area, one that unites it with the many missing freighters and drifting, empty sailboats of the past, a contribution that equally unites us in bewilderment with earlier generations in contemplating an area of ocean that has been an observed mystery for hundreds of years.

3

The Riddle of Vanished Ships

SHIPS HAVE BEEN disappearing in the Bermuda Triangle for a considerable period of time. Because many of these disappeared in the days before radios and scheduled position reports, the exact location where they vanished was never known with precision. However, after the Avengers disappeared in 1945 a review of earlier disappearances of ships revealed that they were concentrated along routes that took them through the area now called the Bermuda Triangle. Contemporaneous reservations were no doubt held that storms and mutiny could account for some of them. But whatever the cause, we today are left with the dramatic picture of great sailing ships turning toward this area of sea, their masts hidden in shrouds of billowing canvas, before slipping over the horizon, never to be seen again.

"Sea of Doom," "Graveyard of the Atlantic," and "Sargasso Graveyard" were names given in the 18th and 19th centuries to specific areas in the Atlantic, all of which traverse the modern Bermuda Triangle or are areas sometimes included in the Triangle's boundaries. "Sea of Doom" was a general area of the sea lanes around Bermuda, while "Graveyard of the Atlantic" specifically meant the Virginia and Hatteras capes, and "Sargasso Graveyard" was applied to the Sargasso Sea, the westernmost part of which overlaps the entire center of the modern Bermuda Triangle.

The Sargasso Sea has been a mystery since it was discovered. Essentially ovoid or elliptical, it covers the central Atlantic Ocean from 20 to 35 degrees North latitude and 30 to 72 degrees West longitude—starting about 300 miles off the U.S. East Coast and extending into the eastern Atlantic. The Sargasso Sea is often considered one of nature's greatest oddities, for while the North Atlantic is cold and tempestuous, this area is largely an immobile body of warm water with weak currents. Its relative calmness may largely be the result of strong surrounding currents completely interlocking and isolating it, making the currents within it largely entropious (that is, rotating inward and remaining weak).

But the sky above the Sargasso Sea is also plagued by deadly calms. Its warmer temperatures make the area high in evaporation, more stable, and less prone to wind. The Spanish became victims of this first when many of their galleons en route to the New World would lie becalmed, deprived of wind and with no strong currents to carry them out. The Doldrums traverse here, calling attention to the depressed and melancholy nature of the area, and so do the Horse Latitudes, a name that comes from the gruesome sight of bloated dead horses floating about, for during the stagnant weeks of waiting for wind the Spanish were often forced to kill and throw overboard their war horses to conserve water.

But the Sargasso Sea receives its name from its greatest oddity— a unique form of seaweed that floats lazily over its entire expanse called sargassum, a Latinized word from the Portuguese meaning grape or grapelike. Tiny, hollow grapelike bladders grow from the stems of the sargassum and keep it floating. This unique characteristic has fascinated

The area covered by the Sargasso Sea in the central Atlantic. The entire body of water slowly rotates and changes location, though only slightly, within the Atlantic.

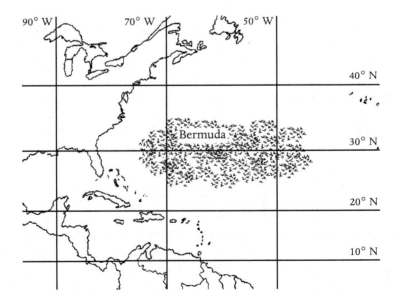

and confused sailors since it was first observed by Christopher Columbus, who recorded in his log the following over a period of two weeks, as later compiled by Brother Bartolomé de Las Casas in his *Diario* (September 16–October 3, 1492):

Here they began to see many bunches of very green vegetation. . . . When dawn came they saw much more vegetation and what seemed to be river weed . . . and they saw much weed, although the day before they had seen none. . . . At dawn [Friday, September 21] they found so much weed that the sea appeared to be solid with it and it came from the west. . . . For part of the day there was no weed; later it was very thick [Saturday, September 22]. . . . The weed was plentiful and they found crabs in it . . . the sea had been calm and smooth. . . . The sea became very calm, because of which many sailors went swimming. . . . They saw much weed. . . . The sea was always smooth and good, many thanks be given to God always, says the Admiral [Columbus]. Weed was coming from the east to west, contrary to its usual direction. . . . There was much weed, some very old and some very fresh, and it bore something like fruit [Wednesday, October 3].

This last observation no doubt refers to the little bladders or pods that grow from the stems.

Prior to this, seaweed was seen only along the coasts, where it grew from rocks in the shallows. Columbus, it is said, even sounded the area, thinking land must be nearby. In his case, the nearest land was miles below on the Nares Abyssal Plain. No bottom reading was particularly alarming to his crew and one might imagine even to Columbus himself, especially after weeks of seeing so much seaweed with no land in sight. Moreover, since the weed was greeted as a portent of land nearby, Columbus had to be ready each time to dissuade his nervous crew from possible mutiny by claiming the weed they saw came from nearby, though unseen, islands just over the horizon—although its presence must have equally baffled the Admiral.

Now that the oceans of the world are completely charted, the Sargasso Sea is confirmed as genuinely unique. Seaweed, and the Sargasso Sea's other anomalies of wind and sea, provide us with a keen insight into the greater mystery that the shape, mass, and rotation of our planet play in this one area, for there is no other area in the world's oceans where this occurs. Almost all currents of the world are circuitous and interlock large ovoid seas in the middle of our great oceans. For example, there are the South Pacific and Mentor currents, which form the circumference of the South Pacific, and the Benguela and Brazil currents in the South Atlantic.

Charted though they may be, and frequently traveled besides, none has a peculiar history, nor have they indigenous growth so thick and inexplicable. But why is the Sargasso Sea different?

The Sargasso Sea has received popular and often tabloid press for generations before the Bermuda Triangle mythos developed, a mythos that may be partly a 20th century incarnation of the earlier legends. Lithographs showed sailing vessels becalmed and being devoured by the sargassum, and even at the turn of the 19th century, seamen continued to tell tall tales about schooners and barkentines still being found sitting weed-shrouded in this stagnant void, along with ancient Roman and Phoenician triremes.

If anything were needed to dispel these old myths, it is provided by modern steam engines and the development of aircraft. For neither calms nor sargassum can affect aircraft, nor can they waylay large freighters that plow through the seaweed easily and steam through calms with little effort.

Of course the mysteries of the Sargasso Sea remain unsolved, a fact made clear by continuing disappearances and unusual power losses in and about it and the Triangle. Even within the last twenty years derelict boats have been retrieved, like the yacht *Penetration* found on July 26, 1982, and a nameless British yacht found derelict a hundred miles away one month later, or the sailboat *Sophie,* missing for a year, then found dismasted and a shambles in March 2001. Unusual power loss now extends mysteriously to electrical generation as well. A dramatic total power loss befell the 13,000-ton refrigerator ship *Andra,* which suddenly went dead in the water some two hundred miles from Bermuda in August 1999. Fortunately, its weak SOS was picked up by two vessels within a day's steaming, a sister ship *Frio Vladivostok* and the tug *Powhatan.* The tug towed *Andra* to Bermuda while *Frio Vladivostok* stayed alongside, supplying her with power to save her 17,000 tons of frozen chicken.

Since so much of the Triangle overlaps the Sargasso Sea, the Triangle's connection with loss of power, whether wind or electrical, may be said to be a recorded mystery for hundreds of years. It seems more than coincidental that the one place on Earth where nature remains a mystery should also be a place where travel remains an equal mystery. The conundrum of missing planes and ships may be no greater than the conundrum of the very place where they so utterly vanish.

The most reliable records of ship disappearances in the Bermuda Triangle date back to the 18th century. The earliest registers list the following U.S. warship. In 1780 the *General Gates* mysteriously vanished. An engagement with a British warship is a possible explanation, but no warship claimed to have engaged her.

Long after the American War of Independence, terse entries in marine journals continued to list disappearances. Curiously, many of them are warships—more mysterious than merchant vessels, one might imagine, since they are sturdily built, heavily gunned, and manned by large numbers of well-trained crews. In September 1799 the USS *Insurgent*, a thirty-six-gun French-built warship with 340 crew, vanished. The USS *Pickering* disappeared on a voyage to the West Indies in 1800, around August 20. The USS *Wasp*, which mercilessly pummeled British shipping in the War of 1812, mysteriously disappeared in the Caribbean in October 1814. This fate was anticlimactic to her last sighting, an engagement with the British brig *Atalanta*, which she won by capturing the vessel and sending her back with a prize crew. She then sailed off on her next cruise and was never seen again.

The voyage of the USS *Epervier* in 1815 had an auspicious occasion. She carried the peace proposals for ending the War of 1812. She left Algiers for Norfolk, Virginia, and vanished, delaying the ending of hostilities.

The USS *Wildcat*, with thirty-one crew; the schooner Lynx, with forty men; and the schooner *Hornet* (which had won a notable victory over HMS *Peacock* in 1812) all vanished in 1824.

The first recorded merchant ship lost to mystery was actually not the ship at all but her crew. In August of 1840 the *Rosalie* sailed through the Sargasso Sea bound for New Orleans and was found abandoned in the Bahamas in perfect condition and then brought into Havana. An astute *London Times* reporter recorded:

A singular fact has taken place within the last few days. A large French vessel, bound from Hamburgh to Havannah, was met by one of our small coasters, and was discovered to be completely abandoned. The greater part of her sails were set, and she did not appear to have sustained any damage. The cargo, composed of wines, fruits, silks, etc., was of a very considerable value, and was in a most perfect condition. The captain's papers were all secure in their proper place. . . . The only living beings found on board were a cat, some fowls, and several canaries half dead with hunger. The cabins of the officers and passengers were very elegantly furnished, and everything indicated that they had only recently been deserted. In one of them were found several articles belonging to a lady's toilette, together with a quantity of ladies' wearing apparel thrown hastily aside, but not a human being was to be found on board. The vessel, which must have been left within a very few hours, contained several bales of goods addressed to different merchants in Havannah. She is very large, recently built, and called the *Rosalie*. Of her crew no intelligence has been received.

The writer's mistake in naming her destination as Havana may be attributed to the fact that another derelict, the *Rossini*, which was bound for Havana, had run aground and been abandoned by her crew. She was picked up around the same time as the *Rosalie* and taken to Nassau. Her crew got to shore. However, the fate of the crew of the *Rosalie* was never known. Records today merely list her launch date as October 1838 and note that she was built of 222 tons of wood.

Subsequent disappearances include another U.S. schooner-warship *Grampus* in March 1843 after sailing south of the Carolinas. The passenger ship *City of Glasgow* vanished with 450 passengers after she left New York in 1854 en route to Liverpool (taking the southern route). A particularly tragic disappearance is that of the British training brig HMS *Atalanta* in 1880. She had departed Bermuda for home with 290 cadets and was never seen again.

The upsurge of interest in nautical history has extended to the information age. Hugh Brown, a former London police officer, now a shipwreck researcher in Canada, maintains the International Registry of Sunken Ships, containing a database of several thousand entries on shipwrecks, salvage operations, and treasure discoveries extending back several centuries. Some of these include piquing and precise data on Spanish armadas down to individual ships, like the caravel *El Dorado,* which left Santo Domingo, Hispaniola, with thirty-one other vessels in July 1502. Heavily laden with gold and treasure, she was subsequently lost in a hurricane that sank all but five ships of the armada in the Mona Passage, near Puerto Rico. Records even exist as to the rumor she was carrying a gold table weighing one and a half tons! Ten of the vessels have so far been located, but *El Dorado,* along with seventeen other vessels, remains undisturbed somewhere below the Triangle.

Brown's continuing searches and updates of his records have brought to light a number of missing ships as well, aside from his general interest in underwater archaeology and his goal of wreck discovery. These records include the 385-ton Canadian brigantine *Arbutus,* which disappeared January 1, 1899, on a voyage between Jamaica and New York; the schooner *Chicopee,* 55 tons, last reported in the Gulf of Mexico on September 29, 1915, heading toward the Triangle; the 382-ton schooner *Doris,* last seen in the Gulf of Mexico on August 8, 1915; the steamer *Mountain Girl,* last reported in the Gulf on May 5, 1896; the 5,273-ton *Santa Rita,* which set sail from New Orleans to New York on October 20, 1921; *Theodor,* a Norwegian steamer-barkentine of 2,638 tons, which sailed from Tampa, Florida, to Yokohama, Japan, on March 2, 1906; the *Thomas B. Schall,* a 62-ton sailing yacht last reported in the Caribbean on December 14, 1942; the 1,555-ton *Benjamin F. Poole,* which went missing after leaving North Carolina and heading south in January 1914; the 605-ton schooner *Sedgwick,* which was last seen off South Carolina on February 11, 1922; the cargo schooner *Annie Hendry,* which left Turks Island in cargo of salt on December 16, 1911; the eighteen-gun Spaniard *Ardilla,* which was probably carrying silver when she vanished en route from Louisiana to Spain in 1808; the steamer *Arkadia,* of over 2,200 tons, which left Louisiana in October 1910; the 790-ton schooner *Baghdad,* which sailed from Key West on October 27, 1921; the steamer *City of Everett,* which departed Santiago, Cuba, on October 1, 1923; the 139-foot Canadian cargo schooner *E. E. Armstrong,* which left Kingston, Jamaica, British West Indies, on August 17, 1918, in cargo of flour and mangrove bark destined for the French colony of Martinique; the 243-foot Austrian clipper *Miroslav* bound for Fiume, Italy, from Delaware via the Bahamas, which disappeared in February 1886; the 150-foot Canadian *Nova Queen,* of 432 tons, which was bound from Turks Island to Nova Scotia in cargo of salt and disappeared on December 4, 1934; the submarine *Dorado,* which disappeared between New London, Connecticut, and her destination, Panama, but was suspected sunk between Cuba and Florida by friendly fire around October 1943.

A converted bark/steamer.

It is impossible in any discussion of sea mysteries not to mention the strange case of the *Ellen Austin,* later relayed to British naval officer, Rupert T. Gould. She was a 210-foot schooner, one of Grinnell, Minturn & Co.'s Blue Swallowtail Line of London–New York packets. North of the Sargasso Sea in August 1881, she encountered an unusual sight, a derelict schooner. Her captain, A. J. Griffin, placed a prize crew aboard to sail her in tandem back to New York. After the vessels had been separated for a couple of days by a squall, the *Ellen Austin* again came upon the schooner, sailing erratically. The vessel was once again completely and mysteriously deserted.

In 1909 the famous solo world circumnavigator Joshua Slocum sailed out of Miami on his treasured yawl *Spray.* He was never seen again and no trace was found. Theories included the possibility that he was run down by a freighter.

But freighters also disappear without any reason. By the 20th century the steamer had command of the sea lanes. Welded steel double hulls and dual engines, plus flares and several lifeboats, were together thought to amount to a guaranty for secure passage on the ocean. Plus, a new invention was about to change the picture. As Warren Tute, in his *Atlantic Conquest,* writes, "By the time the twentieth century dawned, although Marconi had proved his invention, the crew of a ship in any kind of trouble still fought a battle for life in utter loneliness when in fact help might be there to hand a few miles beyond the horizon. Wireless telegraphy was to deprive the sea of its ancient terror of silence." Of course, like steel hulls, steam engines, flares, and lifeboats, wireless telegraphy and then radiotelephony have failed to provide a fail-safe for disappearances. The modern terror of the sea is now a silence qualified.

No SOS messages were picked up from the following ships.

Between March 6 and 27, 1917, the 1,579-gross-ton freighter *Timandra,* bound for Buenos Aires from Norfolk, Virginia, in cargo of coal, disappeared; she carried twenty-one crew, under Captain Lee.

The fact that the U.S. Navy collier *Cyclops* never sent any kind of distress signal before disappearing was considered one of the greatest mysteries surrounding her. She left Rio de Janeiro in cargo of manganese ore for Baltimore, Maryland, in February 1918; 309 Navy crew and passengers were on board, including the U.S. consul in Rio, Alfred L. M. Gottschalk. She made an unscheduled stopover on March 3 at the British colony of Barbados, where her master, George Worley, raised some eyebrows by requesting extra money from the U.S. consul, Brockholst Livingston, to pay for more coal and more food supplies, alleging that his coal was inferior and wouldn't burn properly. Although Livingston was unusually reluctant to pay the sum ($775), he nevertheless did. He found Worley personally unlikable and also noticed that the *Cyclops*'s crew stayed away from local British crews.

The *Cyclops* left the next day and was last

USS *Cyclops,* lost 1918, sister ship of *Proteus* and *Nereus,* lost 1941.

heard to report "All's well." Over the next two days she was twice seen by a British patrol boat, which each time found her off course and guided her back to her correct heading. After this, the *Cyclops* fades away into the annals of sea mysteries. She sent no distress call, and no trace was ever found in an incredibly large and prolonged U.S. Navy search.

The mystery hardly stops there. The loss of the *Cyclops* is literally chock-full of coincidences that can suggest almost any unusual theory. First, both Gottschalk and Worley were discovered to be very pro-German. (The *Cyclops* was operating in American waters because during her last voyage, off France, certain acts of sabotage had been committed aboard, including lifeboat falls tampered with, gun lenses put in backward, and an unauthorized signal lamp attached to the top of the mainmast.) This led to the belief that pro-German elements aboard the *Cyclops* betrayed her to the Germans, and she was interned into a German port. Sabotage was considered also because a Rio newspaper published a notice that a requiem mass was to be held "for the repose of the soul of consul Gottschalk who was lost when the *Cyclops* went down at sea," but it was published before the *Cyclops* was posted overdue; at this time only the upper echelons in the Navy knew she was overdue. It was wondered if this article was not some form of tip-off by German spies signaling that a sabotage attempt on the *Cyclops* had been successful . . . but how would they have been informed unless someone survived?

Mutiny was also suggested. Consul Livingston sent a telegram to Washington detailing his personal investigation on Barbados. It contained, in part, the following: "Master alluded to by others as damned Dutchman, apparently disliked by other officers. Rumored disturbances en route hither, men confined and one *executed*. . . . Number telegraphic or wireless messages addressed to Master or in care of ship were delivered at this port. . . . I have to suggest scrutiny here. While not having any definite grounds, I fear fate worse than sinking though possibly based on instinctive dislike felt towards Master."

The *Cyclops* carried three prisoners being returned to the United States, one for a twenty-year sentence, another for life, and the third to be hanged. It was not certain if there was trouble over these prisoners or if Livingston merely misunderstood someone saying there were prisoners aboard and that one was destined for execution. (Worley would never have held a banana court and an illegal execution at sea unless he had been sure he was not going home to Baltimore.) Livingston also discovered that Worley's excuse about his need for coal and food was a lie. "From different sources gathered the following: He had plenty of coal, alleged inferior, took coal to mix, probably had more than fifteen hundred tons. . . . I have ascertained he took here ton fresh meat, ton flour, thousand pounds vegetables"—all of which suggests a prolonged sea voyage.

The mystery of the *Cyclops* deepened after the war. Immediate searches of German ports proved the *Cyclops* had not been captured or betrayed to them by Worley and taken to Germany, as many rumors had insisted during the war. German records revealed no sabotage attempt planned against her.

Any number of theories prevailed afterward, including splitting in two, capsizing, cargo shifting, and combustion caused by coal dust (from her earlier cargo) in contact with manganese ore (her present cargo).

Splitting in half was proposed as much as forty years later by Conrad A. Nervig, who wrote a delightful (and possibly fanciful) story in the Naval Institute *Proceedings* about his voyage south to Rio on the *Cyclops* as an officer on board. He not only painted Worley as mentally unstable (given to striding around the *Cyclops* in his long johns, walking cane, and derby hat), but said that the *Cyclops*'s deck creased up and down with the waves. Nervig's story and insights have been widely circulated despite Bureau of Navigation records proving that no officer named Conrad Nervig was on board the *Cyclops* on her voyage south.

In any case, what the *Cyclops* amounts to in the end is a veritable riddle of the sea. As much as ten years after the fact, newspapers still referred to it as "The Greatest Mystery of the Sea" whenever rehashing the incident. The Navy opinion, maintained by its historical society, concludes: "The disappearance of this ship has been one of the most baffling mysteries in the annals of the Navy, all attempts to locate her having been proved unsuccessful. Many theories have been advanced, but none that satisfactorily accounts for her disappearance."

Subsequent disappearances of freighters have included the tramp steamer *Cotopaxi,* which last signaled herself in difficulty off the Florida east coast on December 1, 1925. She reported she was listing from damage in the Number 1 hold, then went silent.

(The 770-foot *Leader L.* experienced a similar problem in March 2000 while northeast of Bermuda. But in this case twelve crew were able to get off and be rescued. Contradictory reports from them still cloud exactly what happened to the huge vessel. The first report was that a metallic object struck the vessel and sank it in 45 seconds; a second report states that a 45-foot hull plate fell off. The last would explain the flooding of one hold, but not the flooding of other holds enough to sink the vessel or sink it so rapidly. A third scenario considered that both the previous reports were accurate: that an object hit the *Leader L.* in one hold with such force that it penetrated the hull and shuddered the vessel so violently that a loose hull plate fell off, causing two holds to flood and drag the vessel under in less than a minute.)

Disappearances have included the *Suduffco,* with twenty-nine crew, which sailed in March 1926 from New York to Los Angeles with 4,000 tons of assorted cargo. Although the waterways to and from the Panama Canal and U.S. East Coast are heavily traveled, no ship reported hearing any distress call or seeing any wreckage.

In 1938 the 420-foot *Anglo Australian,* bound from Cardiff, Wales, to British Columbia, with a crew of thirty-eight under Captain Parslow, last signaled herself off the Azores—"Passing Fayal this afternoon. All well."—and was not heard from again. Her course to Panama would next take her through the Triangle.

Various theories such as mines (the Spanish Civil War was in progress), sudden tidal waves, and piracy were entertained to explain this incident as well as other disappearances. However, in the case of the *Samkey,* the Board of Investigation went way beyond speculation and insisted that the vessel keeled over. The *Samkey,* with a crew of forty-three, was last reported in the same vicinity of the Azores in February 1948. Her last transmission was the same: "All well." Although some stray mine from World War II might have crossed her path, the Board was adamant and insisted that she had capsized, although the vessel had only been in ballast (no cargo) and there wasn't a scrap of evidence found to suggest anything. Her course would have taken her through the Triangle, with her next position report due just as she would have been entering the area.

During World War II a torpedo often spelled sudden death for freighters. However, in many cases survivors were able to scramble to a life raft or onto floating wreckage of some kind to be rescued later by passing vessels. Although both the *Anglo Australian* and the *Samkey* were sailing in peacetime, they were heading deep into the Atlantic, far from any rescue station and passing vessels.

But freighters sailing along the busy U.S. East Coast have also disappeared. The 185-foot coaster *Sandra,* with a cargo of DDT, left Savannah, Georgia, for Puerto Cabello,

A small coaster, like the *Sandra.*

Venezuela, on April 5, 1950. She last reported herself off Florida.

The coastal freighter, *Imbross,* with seven crew, vanished on December 18, 1975, after a brief and garbled SOS. The vessel had been en route to

Québec from Mobile, Alabama, with assorted cargo. A court case involving her was not settled until 1998. The court, not being able to establish any bad weather, blamed the owners.

Disappearances of smaller vessels (yachts, sailboats, schooners, and fishing vessels) are more numerous. The Bahamas attract many yachters from Florida and the U.S. East Coast. Moreover, the Bahamas are themselves, in a way, like a huge Venice, where a boat is indispensable for traveling between settlements on nearby islands. A boat is valuable property in the Bahamas, which remain one of the few places in the world where piracy is still punished by hanging.

It can be variously estimated that anywhere from a couple of hundred to 10 times that amount have vanished in the last twenty-five years, depending on how the Coast Guard wishes to incorporate boats into "statistics," while at the same time constantly reminding any inquirer that they maintain no statistics on missing boats. But district offices can maintain a database list of vessel names, for whatever reason, and within these can be found the designation "overdue," which for the pedantic is considered a very different thing. Asking for information on "overdue vessels" can produce about 120 such cases a year in the Seventh District alone. Although they may be searched for or alerts raised to be on the lookout for them, since the Coast Guard cannot investigate them (nor does the NTSB), the ultimate outcome remains forever in limbo if a boat is not quickly found.

A rough idea of the nature of some of the vessels lost over the last fifty years can be gleaned from inexplicable circumstances documented in other, more detailed, cases. While he was head of the U.S. Coast Guard Search and Rescue, Captain John Waters observed: "When a vessel equipped with reliable long-range radio disappears, we must presume that whatever occurred was the result of such sudden and overwhelming disaster that the stricken ship was unable to transmit even a brief call for help."

A perfect example of this may be found in a case Captain Waters personally remembered. The *Home Sweet Home* left Bermuda for St. Thomas January 13, 1955. A weather front was scheduled to move into the area from Louisiana in a day or two. But Waters remembers a radio call coming into RCC (Rescue Coordination Control) Bermuda only hours after it left. "RCC Bermuda, this is the HSH."—"It was a calm, steady voice," Waters recalled. Nevertheless, *Home Sweet Home* never replied to Bermuda's hail to go ahead. No trace was found of the sailing yacht and its four persons in a subsequent search.

Other yachts have disappeared without trace, though not always so dramatically between routine calls. In January 1958 the schooner *Bounty* disappeared when sailing between Miami and Bimini, a distance of only fifty miles; on April 16, 1960, the *Ethel C.* went missing off the Virginia capes en route to fishing grounds; around April 5, 1961, the *Callista III* was sailing from Norfolk to the Bahamas; in 1962 the schooner *Evangeline;* in November 1962 the 56-foot schooner *Windfall* disappeared en route to Bermuda with five crew; the 36-foot ketch *Dancing Feathers,* in 1964 en route from the Bahamas to North Carolina; the *Enchantress,* a 58-foot schooner, on January 13, 1965, 150 miles southeast of Charleston, after it signaled a strong wind had suddenly heeled it over; *L'Avenir* in November 1977, en route to Bermuda from Maryland with four persons. The only vessel to leave a trace was *Revonoc,* an all-weather racing yawl that set sail from Key West to Miami January 1, 1958. This was its dinghy *Revonoc Jr.,* which turned up 80 miles north of Miami at Jupiter Inlet.

The dinghy of the yacht *Evelyn K.* was also found in bizarre circumstances in March 1948. Al Snyder (a famous racing jockey) and two friends went fishing on the *Evelyn K.,* but it was then later found moored in the lee of one of the Florida Keys without a soul on board. There was no immediate worry since the dinghy was gone and the three were thought to have taken it to do some fishing closer to shore. A search, however, found the dinghy weeks later across the Florida Bay in an area called the Ten Thousand Islands. The dinghy was damaged, its motor ripped off, and it seemed that one of the men had tried to tie himself down in it to prevent being taken.

Among the cases of missing boats, the case of the *Sno' Boy* has a stunning element to it as well. A PT boat converted into a fishing vessel, it left Kingston, Jamaica, for Northeast Cay on July 2, 1963, with forty paying passengers aboard. When it failed to return from a two-day fishing excursion, a search was mounted that found among its floating fishing poles its two dinghies, one right side up but completely empty. Not one of the forty made it into a lifeboat or, if any did, they did not remain for very long.

In the catalog of inexplicable disappearances, the case of the *Witchcraft* is the most striking. On December 22, 1967, it left Miami with its owner, hotelier Dan Burack, and his friend, Father Patrick Horgan. Horgan had at long last accepted Burack's invitation to go out in his 25-foot cabin cruiser to see Miami's Christmas lights from the sea. They were going no farther than 1 mile from shore, remaining in the vicinity of buoy number 7 at Miami harbor's entrance.

At 9 P.M. RCC received a call from Burack for assistance. He told them he would need a tow back into Miami, for he thought he had struck something underwater and damaged his prop. A Coast Guard cutter was dispatched immediately, and at 9:19 P.M. it was in the general vicinity awaiting a flare Burack had promised to fire to pinpoint his position. But no flare was ever forthcoming and an expanded search out into the Gulf Stream as far as 1,200 square miles never located a trace of the *Witchcraft*.

Burack was keen on boating safety and had a number of life jackets aboard; also, all his seat cushions were floatable. He had also taken the precaution (and extra expense) of adding built-in flotation to the boat. Although this does not imply buoyancy, it does mean that some part of the vessel, even when waterlogged, should remain visible above the water.

A cryptic conclusion by the Coast Guard, "We presume they are missing but not lost at sea," may have been influenced by the fact that everything points to the impossibility that the cabin cruiser could so utterly vanish. Although a squall hit later that night, it could not have drawn the disabled *Witchcraft* beyond the reach of the Coast Guard in 19 minutes.

In March 1974 the 54-foot luxury yacht *Saba Bank* disappeared while on her maiden voyage, with four crew, in the Bahamas. *Dutch Treat* was sailing between Cat Cay (near Bimini) and Miami on July 24, 1974, and never arrived. A year later, *Meridian,* bound to Bermuda from Norfolk, never made port. The motorsailer *High Flight* disappeared between Bimini and Miami in April 1976. On December 16, 1976, a 40-foot sloop with seventeen passengers disappeared between St. Kitts and Dominica.

In April 1980, the 43-foot *Polymer III* disappeared between the Bahamas and Florida. The yacht belonged to Lester Conrad, the former CEO of a chemical company (hence its name). Along with his friend, William Faulkner, the two were returning to the United States from a vacation. The failure to find any trace prompted Conrad's wife to post a $25,000 reward for any information about her husband.

A long-distance yacht, like *Polymer III.*

During the night of November 5–6, 1984, the 32-foot sports fisherman *Real Fine* also vanished between Freeport, Grand Bahama, and Fort Lauderdale, with three crew aboard. Two Canadians vanished with their 25-foot cabin cruiser between Freeport and West Palm Beach on February 22, 1985.

Although fishing vessels and oceangoing tugs are usually better equipped for sea, a number have strangely disappeared in the Triangle without any clue as to what befell them. On April 22, 1975, the 73-foot shrimper *Dawn* was last seen at sunset off Smith Shoals Light, near Key West. The next day she was gone, along with her four crew. The ocean-going tug *Boundless* vanished in December 1975. The *Mae Doris,* with four crew, left Cape May on October 27, 1992, and was never seen again. On April 15, 1999, the *Miss Fernandina,* of Fernandina Beach, Florida, an 85-foot shrimper, last reported herself experiencing an electrical drain and that her net was caught in her propeller. Other nearby boats responded, and subsequent Coast Guard overflights spotted what appeared to be one of her life jackets floating on the water.

When a boat disappears in any of the Triangle's southern waters (Bahamas and the Straits of Florida, near Cuba), the possibility of piracy or hijacking must always be kept in mind. This suspicion has proven valid on a number of occasions. In one instance, a pertinacious investigator was able to prove, some eight years after the fact, that the yacht *Flying Dutchman,* which had vanished in 1976, was still around and trafficking drugs.

Piracy even surfaced in 1963 in the case of the *Marine Sulphur Queen,* a 504-foot T-2 tanker with thirty-nine crew. Her last report placed her approaching the Keys from the direction of the Gulf of Mexico (she had departed Beaumont, Texas, for Baltimore with a cargo of molten sulfur). The message consisted of a personal call from one of the crewmen to his stockbroker about a purchase. When marine radio tried to send the reply several hours later it could not raise the ship; no contact could be made. The Coast Guard later used this time period to establish her disappearance around February 4 between 1:30 A.M. and 11 A.M., roughly placing her approaching the Dry Tortugas.

An intensive search operation was ordered February 7 when she failed to arrive in port. This search involved numerous cutters and aircraft, eventually covering 348,400 square miles of ocean in 499.6 search hours. Not one shred was found of her. (As an aside, the Coast Guard located forty-two other vessels that might have seen her, but all signaled negative—an indication of how busy the traffic is along the Gulf Stream.) On February 13 the search was discontinued.

Yet one week later, near Key West, debris was spotted. This jump-started a new search, which eventually turned up a couple of life rings, life jackets, a fog horn, and even a broken wooden signboard bearing part of the vessel's name: "arine Sulph." Where the debris had come from remains a mystery, for a sonar search conducted between March 20 and April 13 in the area indicated to be the most likely, according to drift tabulation, revealed no hulk of a sunken vessel near the Dry Tortugas that could not be explained as another sunken vessel.

One piece of debris was particularly suggestive of manipulation. This was a life jacket around which was tied a seaman's shirt. The shirt was examined by the Bureau of Fisheries, which concluded it had been worn by a sailor. They also noted several thrash marks on it consistent with those caused by blows from predatory fish. Before this discovery several stories had been circulating about the *MSQ* having been hijacked to Cuba, which was at its most volatile since Castro had taken over. The discovery of the debris seemed to conveniently belie these arguments, although it remains hard to explain why a crewman would tie his shirt around a life jacket, or why a shark would attack a shirt without a man in it. But no trace of the *Marine Sulphur Queen* in Cuba has ever come to light and nothing could ever be proved, however obvious a clue the shark-thrashed shirt on the life jacket appears to be.

Other large vessels have since vanished, all of them on routes within the Bermuda Triangle but far from Cuba. Among these, the disappearance of the 590-foot *Sylvia L. Ossa* is noteworthy. Relaying from on the scene, one Coast Guardsman observed: "It's not easy to miss a 590-foot long ship on a day with visibility of more than 40 miles and calm seas. So it doesn't seem too hopeful that the ship is still afloat."

Her last message, on October 17, 1976, was a routine position report indicating her ETA at Philadelphia, where she was bound from South America with a cargo of ore. Her last position was given as 140 miles southwest of Bermuda, from where it was later determined she must have suddenly disappeared. This was shown by the discovery (as in the case of the *MSQ*) of a piece of her shattered wood signboard reading "L. Ossa" floating in the near vicinity. Then a lifeboat was found, intact. But the lifeboat had not been launched; it had been ripped from the ship by a terrific force.

The *Poet*, a 520-foot cargo ship carrying grain (number 2 yellow corn to be precise), was last known to be within only a few hundred miles of this same area in 1980 before she and her thirty-four hands disappeared without trace. In her case, there is the added element of no EPIRB signal being picked up. She had been in transit between Cape Henlopen,

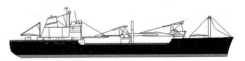

SS *Poet*, in final configuration, 1980.

Delaware (which she had left October 24, 1980), on a rhumb-line course to Port Said, Egypt. Her next position report was due October 26, when she should have been northeast of Bermuda. Since the report was never forthcoming, it was deduced that she vanished before this while passing north of Bermuda.

Theories about the *Poet's* disappearance included a "freak storm" with 70-mile-per-hour winds that came from nowhere; a "rogue wave" (which had sunk the ketch *Wandering Angus* in the same vicinity on October 26, as well as the yacht *Polar Bear;* both crews survived, making the disappearance of the 11,000-ton *Poet* intriguing by comparison); the idle accusation that she was a "rust bucket" was disproved (a common accusation after any ship disappears); also disproved was an imaginative theory that her cargo of corn may have gotten wet from a leaky hatch and expanded until it burst the hull and sent her down like a rock. A combination of the above, like a rogue wave and a leaking forward hatch, was also considered. The Marine Board of Investigation favored the hypothesis that she capsized in quartering or following seas, but the commandant overruled this in favor of a "loss of hull integrity." An "ingress of water could have gone undetected by the crew" until the ship sank by "plunging, capsizing or foundering." There was also acrimony involving her owners, Hawaii Eugenia Co., for not reporting her overdue after she failed to send her October 26 position report. But ultimately there was no trace upon which to base any theory.

The *Poet* was not the first vessel to vanish without even its automatic alarm signal being detected. The 337-foot freighter *El Caribe* vanished as utterly, in calm seas, in October 1971, after signaling itself only two days from its destination of Santo Domingo.

Among the many mysteries that have come to pass in the Bermuda Triangle, the occurrence of deserted ships are the most striking. There is nothing more provocative than boarding a lifeless ship and gazing at the reminders of interrupted life. The sensation has caused even the most level-headed to elaborate upon their discovery with innumerable adjectives to the point of sensationalizing it. Not a few have been Navy and Coast Guard officers who were first to board such vessels. Such is the case with the *Ruth* in 1997 and the *Rubicon* in 1944, both of which turned out to be easily explained by having broken their moorings and drifted out to sea while their crews were ashore.

Unexplained derelicts, however, usually recur within similar locations within the Triangle. A disturbing number happen where ships often tend to disappear more frequently as well. The luxury yacht *Connemara IV* was found abandoned 140 miles southeast of Bermuda in September 1955. The vessel was sturdy enough to have survived three successive hurricanes without a crew before it was discovered. It then conveniently sank while under tow by the freighter *Olympic Cloud*. What had happened to the crew was never answered, since the clues, if there were any, went to the bottom of the sea with her.

Several yachts continue to be found derelict east of the Triangle and southwest of the Azores. This can be explained by the east-northeast current of the Gulf Stream conveying a pilotless ship. In 1969 alone five yachts were found derelict northeast of the Sargasso Sea. Two of them were found keeled over, and one of these was noted to have barnacles on it—a good indication it had been floating aimlessly for awhile before being spotted by a passing freighter. One vessel found upright was identified as the *Vagabond,* belonging to Peter Wallin of Stockholm, who had been sailing around the world. Where exactly the crews had disappeared, jumped ship, or were removed, is not known, but the currents in the area suggest they may have been in the vicinity of the Sargasso Sea or on its perimeter in the stronger Gulf Stream currents, north of Bermuda.

This appears to be the scenario in the case of other deserted vessels: after the crews had left (or been removed) the unguided boat succumbs to subsequent rough seas. In the case of Michael Plant, his sailing yacht *Coyote* may have drifted hundreds of miles on the North Atlantic Drift until it was found, capsized and deserted, near the Azores in 1991. Plant was last heard from north of Bermuda in a radio message that was both weak and unintelligible. Earlier he had reported to a freighter that he had lost electrical power and the use of his long-range radio.

Most of these yachts had only one person on board. The most prosaic explanation is that they all fell overboard. Although tethering is common and recommended practice, each skipper may have fallen off when not tethered, when an unexpected wave hit the boat or a sudden gust surged the vessel and heeled it over before it righted itself again.

But deserted vessels have been found that had had more than one man aboard—in some cases from three to eleven crew. The late biologist Ivan Sanderson, an accomplished sailor and British secret agent during World War II, made an independent study of the Bermuda Triangle, which he published in many articles and books. On the inexplicable nature of derelict vessels, he observed in *Invisible Residents:* "Certain facts should be noted. First, even an inexperienced or leaderless crew seldom if ever abandon ship because of [a] storm. To do so is obviously asinine, because if the ship won't hold up, no yawl, gig, or other small lifeboat can do so."

In each of the following cases there is no reason why the crews abandoned ship, like the eleven crew of the *Carroll A. Deering* off North Carolina in January 1921, although murder and mutiny were possible. The *Lucky Edur*, having left port with three fisherman aboard in 1971, was found abandoned, throttle engaged, and out of fuel off Cape May.

The British cargo schooner *Gloria Colita* was found derelict in unusual circumstances in February 1940. The schooner was waterlogged but not sunk; her cargo of lumber had prevented her from sinking. The crew was, however, gone. There were indications they had been stopped in the middle of rigging sail since one of the lines was found fouled and dangling. Bad weather no doubt came along afterward and swamped the unattended vessel. The boarding party of the patrol boat *Cartigan* noted that her lifeboat was gone, but it was not certain if it had been launched or washed off by the subsequent bad weather.

Among the more modern is the unusual case of the *Hawarden Bridge*, a coastal freighter credited with having been the first Allied vessel to enter Dunkirk Harbor after its liberation in 1944. Sold off to a Barbados company, she plied her trade along the West Indies until she became a modern *Mary Celeste*. When she was found drifting on March 14, 1978, on her course to Miami, the Coast Guard boarded her to discover and record: "Cargo holds dry/empty. Two life rafts missing, no gyro, magnetic compass removed, no communications equipment, engine room flooded. No persons on board." Neither Lloyd's nor the Coast Guard could find a trace of what happened to the entire crew, nor was evidence left behind to suggest why they fled, other than the unexplained flooded engine room.

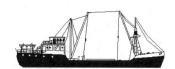

The *Hawarden Bridge;* she had from five to seven crew.

Derelict vessels have continued to turn up in unusual circumstances at every corner of the Triangle. Off the Carolinas, in May 1985, three marines and three children disappeared off an outboard boat, though it was later found at the end of a trail of their floating life jackets. On January 2, 1998, the recreational boat *Formosa* was discovered deserted. And on August 5, 1999, an 18-foot day cruiser was found abandoned except for a barking dog, the pet of the owner, who had taken the boat out to do some day fishing. Most recently, a 28-foot cabin cruiser was found derelict off South Carolina on May 19, 2001. The condition of the vessel, with empty fuel tanks and the throttles wide open, suggests that the skipper, Derrick Smith, forced the boat to the highest speed possible before disappearing. While the Coast Guard noted that Smith's wallet was found on board, they did not note if it was found with his clothes.

In another incident, off Miami on May 11, 1975, a 20-foot day cruiser was found derelict and splattered with blood, and its skipper, a Miami doctor, was missing. On April 30, just two weeks earlier, a 27-foot cabin cruiser was found cruising in circles 14 miles off West End, Grand Bahama; blood splattered the boat; the clothes of both occupants were found, as well as the owner's wallet with more than $100 in it, meaning that whoever perpetrated these incidents was not interested in clothes, money, or the value of the boat, merely the people.

This same scenario applies to another derelict discovered in July 1980. The 38-foot sailboat *Kallia III,* belonging to Bill and Patty Kamerer of Fort Myers, Florida, was found near Pipe Cay in the Exumas of the Bahamas. Harry Yourell, an Illinois state legislator, was the first to come upon it. As he circled it in his fishing vessel, *Shark II,* the dinghy came into view. In it was the dead body of a man, his head and upper body hanging over the side into the water and his lower half covered with "something blue."

By the time authorities were able to overfly the area a few days later, they noted that the body was still in the dinghy. Upon closer investigation the next day by boat, the body, after all those days, had conveniently disappeared. A description of what they found:

There were apparent blood stains in the pilot area of the stern of the boat and what appeared to be gunshot marks on the left side of the stern of the boat. There were also what appeared to be bullet holes in a red two-gallon tin which was tied to a rail on the right side of the boat's stern.

Two spent flare cartridges and four live flares were found at the stern of the boat. The flare gun was not found. A pair of glasses with brown frames was found on the deck of the stern. In the galley there were apparent blood stains. . . . There was a small amount of water in the bottom of the dinghy and on its right side were apparent blood stains. There was a large amount of maggots on the right side.

There is something of excessive ambiguity in the report on points that should have been more than clear by the date it was issued (October 1980 and then only because of international pressure). Allegations of a cover-up continued, especially since by this time blood and bullet holes could be easily proven.

Then there is the peculiar mystery of Great Isaac's Light near Bimini. This government lighthouse station was found abandoned in August 1969 when a launch came from Bimini to check on it. The two lighthouse keepers, Ivan Major and B. Mollings, were gone, leaving the islet deserted and silent except for the chatter of nearby passing boats over the lighthouse CB radio.

Other derelicts in this area include the schooner *City Belle,* with ten persons aboard, found on December 5, 1946. Later reports by Lloyd's indicate survivors were found in a boat and taken to Exuma, Bahamas. However, the case was then dropped and nothing else was heard, nor was the story ever confirmed.

On March 23, 1973, the 88-foot yacht *Defiance* was seen from Cap du Môle, Haiti, heading out to sea with sails set but her four crew missing. She had left Puerto Plata, the Dominican Republic, the previous day bound for Port-au-Prince, Haiti.

Without any definite explanation one way or the other, several other yachts have turned up derelict and are still under investigation, such as the 45-foot *Scarlet* found near St. Martin in 1994, and the fishing vessel *Hemingway* off Cuba in 2001, abandoned by captain and crew.

If those who feel Norfolk and the Chesapeake Bay area constitute a fourth nodal point in the Triangle are correct, then the continuing disappearances there may be considered, like the *Erica Lynn* on August 10, 1998, which was not known to have disappeared until a life ring was found with its name stenciled on it. The *Carolina* vanished in November of that same year. On November 15, 1999, a 22-foot day cruiser with two persons on board went missing in the short distance between Frying Pan Shoals and Frying Pan Light.

In the Triangle's more southern waters, the 65-foot *Intrepid* disappeared 30 miles off Fort Pierce, after a garbled SOS on October 14, 1996, with sixteen persons reported on board. The 74-foot *Interlude* was posted overdue on a cruise around the Caymans sometime in November 1998. The last course of the vessel was uncertain, though its owners had listed Cayman Island as their destination.

More recent disappearances of merchant vessels include the *Kurika,* which left Bermuda for the Azores in April 1991 and was posted as an overdue vessel by Lloyd's of London; the same for the 357-ton *Jamanic K.,* en route to Miami from Cape Haitien in March 1995. The motor vessel *Genesis* last spoke with another vessel off the Leewards on April 20, 1999, at 5:30 P.M. She was in cargo of 465 tons of brick, water tanks, and concrete slabs. When it was determined she was overdue, a 33,100-square-mile search failed to locate the vessel.

It is perhaps easier to minimize the significance of the disappearance of ships and boats, as opposed to aircraft.

A small, interisland general-purpose cargo freighter.

After all, the sea is very large and a ship moves relatively slowly over its expanse as compared to an aircraft. As a result ships are out of sight of land, both visually and from radar, for long periods, allowing more opportunity for something to happen and, frankly, more time for it to happen. During transit, contact is often only every two days, and this is limited to terse position updates. Weather can turn foul suddenly, and at a ship's slow speed it is hard to avoid it, whereas an aircraft can divert around it in a matter of minutes. For smaller pleasure boats, there is absolutely no schedule. Neither do they have to report their departures or ETAs. They leave the U.S. East Coast and Caribbean islands en masse. Often their destination or course is unknown except to a friend or business associate, who may not become alarmed for their safety until days later, when the boater does not show up at home or for work.

Storms and hurricanes continue to take their toll on shipping, causing disappearances anywhere in the world. But to be lost in the Bermuda Triangle implies an element of the unexplained, raising questions about whether they were lost naturally or from some as yet unexplained phenomenon. Technically, any incident that occurs within the Bermuda Triangle is a candidate for mystery, but the term would be a misnomer if applied too broadly. Once the occurrence of a storm is established, the incident is removed from the litany, since it is in this sense not a unique event, as a storm can strike anywhere in the world and provide ample force to send a ship down.

Because a ship's track is often thousands of miles between ports, some have been posted missing in the Triangle by virtue of the fact it lay on their course. However, when their last position reports become available, these place them thousands of miles beyond it, as in the case of the freighter *Ithaca Island,* which disappeared en route to Manchester, England, from Norfolk, Virginia, in November 1968, but last reported herself between the Azores and England, heading north. The Greek tanker *Milton Iatrides* left New Orleans for South America and disappeared, but last reported herself south of the Equator, off the hub of Brazil.

It stands to reason the opposite is true as well. It is impossible for the

U.S., British, Canadian, and Bahamian Coast Guards, those authorities most often concerned with the Triangle seas, to keep track of traffic in it. Hundreds of vessels sail through it uncounted each month. In essence, the words of Captain John Waters still ring true: "Small boats, yachts, and fishing vessels in uncounted numbers disappear. Long searches produced no sightings and no clues, only speculation."

Even when a list of vessel names is extracted (with persistent prodding, one might add) from the Coast Guard, the information can be ambiguous. The Seventh Coast Guard District does not, in the words of Lieutenant Commander Ruvolo, "track the number of persons missing or presumed dead at sea; it does track lives lost in our area of responsibility." A cautionary note added: "Please be aware that at times it is very difficult to accurately account for the exact number of people on board a vessel because of poor reporting." This note may serve to elucidate the following chit for part of fiscal year 2000 where an overdue vessel's name is followed by essentially nothing but zeros until it reads "case closed" (see table beginning on next page).

Of the 130 or so cases for 2000 alone where the vessel is posted as "overdue," "odu," "ovd," or "unreported" (depending on who is keying in the results), some of the boats may have made port later, but the Coast Guard is unaware of it. It may also mean a missing vessel was reported but with such little information presented there is absolutely no way for the Coast Guard to even commence a detailed search and evaluation. Or, it may mean that the Coast Guard never found the boat and therefore does not know how many persons were on board. Even the clarification appended to the list does not help—it represents a "statistical listing of all cases we have kept on file," although it is not clarified why these were kept on file. Dozens of missing boats may not have been retained while potentially insignificant incidents are listed.

U.S. Coast Guard headquarters in Washington, D.C., likewise maintains that no such statistics for missing boats are kept. It does, however, provide outcrops that may reflect a culled-down version of those maintained by district offices. "Missing Recreational Vessels" (which can mean sunk or not recovered as well) for fiscal years 1990–2000 (for the Fifth and Seventh Districts) are divided according to cause—weather, hull fractures, fire, etc. It is not these which are of interest here, since if the cause is known it means it was a sunken boat from which the crew were rescued. But on an average sixty boats per year are placed in the category "caused by other factor," which is statistical parlance for "nobody really knows." (cont. p. 77)

Overdue Vessels: Incidents as Reported by U.S. Coast Guard Seventh District, part of fiscal 2000

Case Title	Geographic Location	Case Number	Date Opened	Date Closed	Vessel Name	DOC/REG#	Vessel Description	Flag	Lives Saved	Lives Lost	Property Saved	Property Lost	Case Description
16FT P/C overdue	IVO Creek Stake, Hudson, FL	166	10/18/99	10/18/99	Stump Knocker		P/C	US	0	0	0	0	
S/V Xanadu	IVO Cuba	207	10/15/99	10/15/99	Xanadu		S/V	MX	0	0	0	0	closed
F/V La Pescadora overdue	Guayama, PR	226	10/16/99	10/16/99	La Pescadora		F/V		0	0	0	0	closed
Overdue Kayak-1 POB	Miami Beach	228	10/16/99	10/16/99			P/C		0	0	0	0	closed
P/C Bella-overdue	Biscayne Bay	286	10/18/99	10/18/99	Bella			US	0	0	0	0	
16FT P/C overdue	IVO Stake Creek Point	314	10/18/99	10/18/99	Stump Knocker		P/C	US	0	0	0	0	
M/V Viking Sky	Caribbean Sea	329	10/22/99	10/23/99	Viking Sky		M/V	PN	0	0	0	0	closed
Overdue PWC	North of Aguadilla, PR	358	10/24/99	10/25/99			PWC		0	0	0	0	suspend

continued

Case Title	Geographic Location	Case Number	Date Opened	Date Closed	Vessel Name	DOC/REG#	Vessel Description	Flag	Lives Saved	Lives Lost	Property Saved	Property Lost	Case Description
ODU 25FT Mako	IVO Creek Naples, FL	368	10/26/99	10/26/99	No Plan		P/C Mako	US	1	0	0	0	closed
P/C Vector	Apolla Beach, FL	382	10/27/99	10/28/99	Vector		P/C		0	0	0	0	closed
S/V Manyana	Key West, FL	391	10/28/99	10/29/99	Manyana		S/V	US	0	0	0	0	closed
P/C First Strike	FT Myers, FL	556	11/5/99	11/6/99	First Strike		P/C	US	0	0	0	0	closed
S/V Miss Rosey	Tampa Bay, FL	567	11/6/99	11/7/99	Miss Rosey		S/V	US	0	0	0	0	closed
16FT Hobie Cat	Key Biscayne, FL	573	11/7/99	11/7/99			S/V		2	0	0	0	closed
M/V Kemo Sabi overdue	Carrabella to Marco Island	654	11/12/99	11/12/99	Kemo Sabi		M/V	US	0	0	0	0	closed
N20442C A/C OVD	Key West	660	11/12/99	11/12/99		N20442C	A/C		0	0	0	0	closed
S/V Camelot overdue	State Road 84 New River	673	11/14/99	11/14/99	Camelot		S/V	US	1	0	0	0	closed
22 P/C overdue	Clearwater Pass	676	11/13/99	11/14/99			P/C	US	4	0	0	0	closed

continued

Case Title	Geographic Location	Case Number	Date Opened	Date Closed	Vessel Name	DOC/REG#	Vessel Description	Flag	Lives Saved	Lives Lost	Property Saved	Property Lost	Case Description
S/V Abobday	St. Johns River	687	11/14/99	11/15/99	Abobday		S/V	US	0	0	0	0	closed
17FT P/C	IVO Hudson	688	11/14/99	11/15/99			P/C		1	0	0	0	closed
14FT P/C		690	11/14/99	11/15/99		SC4814AJ	P/C		0	0	0	0	
16FT P/C		747	11/15/99	11/15/99			P/C		0	0	0	0	closed
S/V Islandia (UK) Overdue	Dominican Republic enroute Cuba	756	11/17/99	11/17/99	Islandia		S/V	UK	0	0	0	0	closed
P/C Damsel Fish-Odu	Florida Straits	881	11/26/99	11/27/99	Damsel Fish		P/C	US	0	0	0	0	closed
S/V Knot Limited-Overdue	West End, BF	905	11/28/99	11/22/99	Knot Limited		S/V		0	0	0	0	closed
S/V Estrolita Overdue	Key West to Cape Coral, FL	997	11/28/99	11/29/99	Estrolita	FL9364 HD	S/V		0	0	0	0	closed
S/V Begin Again-Overdue	Bimini enroute Nassau	1139	12/19/99	12/10/99	Begin Again		S/V	US	0	0	0	0	closed

Abbreviations: A/C = aircraft; F/V = fishing vessel; M/V = motor vessel; MX = Mexico; P/C = pleasurecraft; PN = Panama; PWC = personal water craft; S/V = sailing vessel.

Allowing a certain amount for hijacking, the number for truly unknown disappearances could tally around twenty to thirty per year.

These are just a couple of examples of how difficult it is to actually establish a boat "disappearance." Of the 130 cases for 2000, long searches were undertaken for *Vidar,* Aruba to Roatán, November to December 1999; *Adanac,* North Carolina to British Virgin Islands, November 1999; *Lucky Dog,* destination Florida, December 1999; *Intrigue,* Bahamas to San Juan, February 8, 2000—the names go on and on, finally ending with an appropriate *Insanity,* overdue from Key West to Costa Rica, September 2000.

Beyond this chit there is little information. Requests for Search and Rescue Reports are the only way to determine what might be the fate, what the weather was like, and if there was any unusual radio contact or SOS. "Report" is, however, a broad term, since there is no investigation. They are mere records or dispatches sent between vessels and RCC (Rescue Coordination Center) headquarters relaying vague details and hours spent searching this or that location. And if you are determined to be a nosy inquirer, even these become unattainable, as the Coast Guard can discriminate among who gets them free and who must pay high research and photocopy prices.

Some, however, may reveal surprising elucidation. Clues found aboard derelicts like the *Alyson Selene,* December 27, 1999, indicate its master, Coast Guard Petty Officer Bobby Powell, was peacefully fishing in shallow water 7 miles northeast of Andros Island, with the ignition off, before he vanished from the boat without trace; and that something disturbed retired Navy Captain Tom Olchefske on his 38-foot sailboat *Tropic Bird,* causing him to stop his noonday log entry on June 8, 2000, and come topside. The *Tropic Bird* was next found deserted hundreds of miles away, gently beached on an Antiguan reef on June 22, out of fuel, frozen food rotten, freshwater barely touched, with an interrupted entry in the log: "12:56 P.M. Off Grenada, making good time" without finished longitude and latitude notation.

For fiscal year 2001 a comparable number is found. Names run the gamut: *Hardtimes, Fat Cat, Far Side, Shady Lady, O'Daly, La Sabia, Veronica Jovi, Calypso, Folie Adeaux, Slo-M-Ocean, Imari Trader, Hanna B., Halfway to Heaven, Sea Hunder, Folle-E-Duex, Cosmic Hippo, Pluto, Antares, Free Spirit*— and so forth. Some are found quickly, others are not.

While it is as true today as it was forty years ago—that the sea is large and a boat relatively small by comparison—it is not as easy to dismiss these disappearances as "routine" anymore, at least beyond general satisfaction. The disappearances within the last twenty years must be viewed within the context of the vast network of modern electronics, satellite tracking, GPS, and automatic distress signaling. On the face of it, the sailing challenges appear the same today, but in reality the sea is only as broad as the length of time it takes a radio beam to speed across its surface.

RCC Bermuda's Marine Harbor Radio is at the center of an Atlantic swept by signals. Its log details a host of scenarios. Within the last two fiscal years, Bermuda picked up the 406 MHz EPIRB signal from the tanker *Chevron South America* (November 2000), accidentally activated during routine tests off Brazil. In December another 406 MHz alarm was traced to the yacht *Sokar*, which was immediately contacted and apologetic for inadvertently tripping the signal. A few days later a 121.5 MHz EPIRB set the direction-finder working at Harbor Radio, which traced it to the Bermuda South Shore area, to *Ginger Pepper*, at anchor; the EPIRB had fallen because of a broken bracket and started transmitting. While 200 miles east of Madeira the *Chiquita Joy* also accidentally tripped her 406, and Bermuda immediately traced it. March 2001: Falmouth, England, picks up another signal registered to a Bermuda ship, which was discovered all right off the Azores; another accidental transmission. Another Bermuda-registered EPIRB, to the vessel *Loretta Anne*, traced her to the Caribbean—another inadvertent triggering. *High Noon* started taking on water 850 miles southwest of the Azores, and the two crew abandoned the boat and activated the EPIRB. The Coast Guard immediately diverted the bulk carrier *Putney Bridge* to the scene to rescue them. April 2001: RCC Cyprus couldn't raise one of its vessels; RCC Bermuda started transmitting, also without success; RCC Norfolk finally located her south of Bermuda, having radio trouble. *Pasha 1* washed ashore on Bermuda after having been abandoned in November 2000 by her ill crew 380 miles northwest of Bermuda. May 2001: another 406 was activated by accident, this at the airport in Luton, England, and traced by Bermuda. Another 406 at 470 miles west-northwest of Bermuda; a C-130 overflew and discovered it to be *Vesper*; water ingress activated the EPIRB and the signal was secured. *Solitude* lost her mast 160 miles north-northwest of Bermuda in a gale; the crew opted to abandon to container ship *Sealand Performance*, and the derelict drifted on as a navigational hazard. August 2001: RCC Halifax picked up another 406 from a Bermudian passenger vessel, *European Envoy*. Harbor Radio traced the vessel to the Irish Sea and confirmed it was an accidental transmission. Near Bermuda the *Gringo* picked up wreckage from the freighter *Sea Breeze*, lost December 2000 off Virginia.

November 2001: *Bon Secour* was disabled in rough seas and the crew abandoned to Naval Auxiliary *Gold River,* the derelict was posted as a navigational hazard. Bermuda aircraft 406 was picked up; it was discovered safe in Grenada, 1,500 miles south of Bermuda. December 2001: another 406 was picked up, unidentified by registration; RCC Madrid located the vessel and rendered assistance off the Spanish coast. On January 27, 2002, urgent calls began for the 34-foot sailboat *Manx,* overdue from the Canaries to Miami, without success. May 2002: lightning struck the mast of the 60-foot sailboat *Amule* 40 miles north of Bermuda, damage extended from mast to deckhouse; received help from passing freighter *Bermuda Islander.* Another 121.5 EPIRB signal was received; the transmitter fell overboard from the vessel in St. George's Harbour. Another 406 was received from *Leopard Bay,* south of the equator—battery faulty and disconnected. June 2002: *Caliente* was found derelict 220 miles northwest of Bermuda by *Boomerang;* it was confirmed that the Coast Guard had airlifted the ill crew while it was 50 miles off Hatteras, North Carolina. *Joss* hit an underwater object and transmitted a distress signal, quickly monitored by Bermuda and located 1,300 miles south, off Aruba. An accidental 406 came from *Bombarino,* 160 miles northwest of Bermuda. *Bienstar* via satellite phone informed Bermuda their boom and rigging was lost 200 miles northwest of Bermuda.

Even twenty boats disappearing without sound or trace within such a web of communication would seem to suggest the unusual, even if the number itself did not. Even more weird, as in a 121.5 EPIRB beacon picked up on May 4, 2002, only 50 miles south of Bermuda, quick overflights can find no trace but the signal continues, as if from another point in *space* or *time.*

Sometimes this is the only clue to a vessel's presumed position in the Triangle—a garbled and ambiguous SOS. Reports from AMVER (American Merchant Vessel Emergency Report) vessels record a variety of such encounters: "M/V *Raleigh Bay* reports VHF-FM Channel 16 Mayday call. . . . *Hermina* and *Sea Monarch* diverted thru area. No distress sightings. Search suspended pending further developments" or "M/V *Alabama* . . . possible explosion . . . confirmed sighting flash, diverted to investigate. . . . No significant findings."

This also underscores the amount of unknown activity in the waters of the Triangle. The sources for the numerous sightings of unexplained lights and brilliant flashes on the surface, as above, when investigated by passing freighters have never been determined, adding yet another element of mystery to the goings-on in the Triangle. In many of the search operations for missing vessels and planes these same lights, often described as white luminescence, have been reported but never tracked down and confirmed as flares. It is more likely that these lights are always present but are unnoticed or unreported unless there is a reason, as when a ship is alerted to a possible missing vessel or downed plane. Notwithstanding, it is a curious fact that their source always remains elusive. In one recent search, Admiral Richard Rybacki admitted: "We'll never know if we were seeing signals for help, the lights were so far away and lasted just a few seconds. . . . Each time we had a sighting, it gave us new hope as we sent ships and aircraft to investigate. Despite a thorough search, we were disappointed each time to find no one in the area."

One Coast Guardsman expressed himself more frankly: "It might be a mile away, or it might be 30 miles away. There are no geographical references at all on the ocean. On land there are mountains and hills, but on the ocean all you've got is the horizon."

Although the list of vessels lost in the Bermuda Triangle is always changing, as some are added and some are removed, those removed have never been caused by the finding of any vessel firmly established as missing. The removals have always come after the presence of a storm or by verifying a vessel had long passed the Triangle while sailing its course. The same applies to smaller aircraft and boats. Never has any hulk been found, even in the shallow waters over which many were known to have been sailing.

With relatively few exceptions, most disappearances take place in the southern waters of the Triangle, in and about the Bahamas archipelago and southern Florida, where the underlying continental shelves are, in some cases, so shallow the water is transparent.

Scuba diving is a major attraction in the Bahamas and Florida Keys, with treasure or salvage being the ultimate goal. The shallows of the banks of the Bahamas and Keys are a breeding ground for relics, both old and new. They are also a mine of historical artifacts dating back to the Spanish treasure fleets that used the Gulf Stream to hasten their return to Spain, artifacts from the many luckless galleons that went aground during storms and hurricanes.

The grass-studded bottom sands of the Keys constantly yield cannons, anchors, wood spars, ships' bells, and occasionally, medallions and more valuable items. It is hard to tell how valuable the material being brought up is, as the more valuable finds are seldom reported. It is no exaggera-

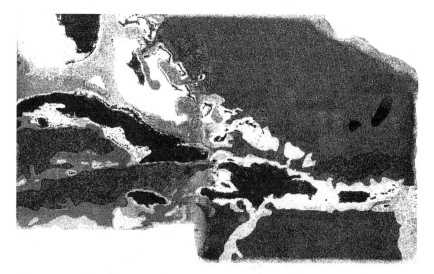

Clear areas within the map outline contours of the shallow banks of the Bahamas and the Caribbean. The changing depths of the ocean around them are indicated by the varying shades of dark. The landmasses are shown in black. The largest underwater bank is the Great Bahama Bank into which extends the odd Tongue of the Ocean, a deep canyon of unusual geologic shape. Many of these banks are only a few fathoms deep.

tion to say that the ocean floor is a veritable museum of artifacts—one that is all too easily accessible to some of the rankest and most thoughtless amateurs.

Potholes and trenches are found blown and cut into the sandy bottoms where some enthusiastic salvors used pumps to blast the sand away from promising (or random) spots to find artifacts. These depredations are a constant worry to marine biologists who are interested in preserving the indigenous sea life and a nuisance to archeologists who would like to preserve the historical value of the ancient shipwrecks for future study.

Several of these finds turn up later. Cannons, anchors, and other Renaissance metallurgy gild the fronts of shops or stand vigilant outside restaurants. They may not last for as long above water as below, as the elements are corroding them at a faster rate.

Florida Keys residents have made a museum and placed it in an authentic atmosphere, on the sea bottom off Key Largo. Divers can view pieces of wrecks, such as cannons lying in the bottom grass, a prostrate spar, an anchor, and other vintage nautical items, all of which have been dredged from the Keys's sandy bottom and spared the dubious antiquities dealers' divers.

But 20th and 21st century contributions to the seafloor aren't like the old galleons, brigs, and Cape Horn schooners. Our ships and planes are steel and fiberglass, sturdy and sometimes incredibly big. They don't rot away quickly. They lie broken and snapped on the bottom, a putrid color green, crusted with coral and crawling with sea life. The wrecks usually look fantastic, sometimes cloaked in secrecy, and occasionally mystery, but they are always there. It is true that smaller boats and planes can be broken up in the tides around coral heads and in the rocky shallows. But the banks vary in depth from tumultuous shallows to peaceful, though easily accessible, depths of 40 or 50 feet, where a mantle of Technicolor blue is seldom disturbed.

Of course there is the possibility that many of the missing in the Bermuda Triangle have been seen but do not attract special attention. They may sit peacefully covered by a thin layer of sea dust, stripped of their valuables a long time ago by salvors who were little interested in cross-referencing the wreck.

All of the ships and yachts are not just gone in the sense of physical wreckage—they sailed away silently without one word or clear SOS, even without their automatic alarms to indicate they sank. Their apparent lack of existence on the bottom seems to confirm this. An aircraft may spiral into the ocean, thereupon breaking up into bits that could never be identified by any diver. On the other hand, vessels sink and remain intact, easy to be identified, cataloged, and investigated.

Observers of these mysteries, both scientist and lay alike, have not been reticent to consider a wide variety of theories to account for them. Some have reached out to laws of physics while others have proposed exceptions to our own physical laws. Still others suggest that the disappearances cannot be natural and therefore entities from outer or inner space are intercepting them, and yet others feel the answer may lie not in the Triangle itself but in the greater confabs of matter, time, and space.

Although we must consider all these in working toward a conclusion, we must, in a way, follow the knee-jerk reaction of many and reach out to where many prefer to remain. We must first take into consideration some of the most common problems in over-water navigation that might affect both pilots of planes and helmsmen of ships, and silently and unexpectedly lead them into oblivion.

The TBM was the largest single-engine aircraft used in World War II. It was designed to carry three crew: pilot, gunner, radioman. (National Archives)

An example of an actual Fort Lauderdale–based FT (Fox Tare). The "F" stood for Fort Lauderdale, "T" for Torpedo. (National Archives)

Some of the drama of Flight 19 played itself out here, in Operations Radio below the tower. (Author's collection)

Two PBM Mariners in flight off Banana River, Florida, in 1945. Just as shown, Training 49 and Training 32 took off to scour the Atlantic for Flight 19 on December 5, 1945. Training 49 would disintegrate, while Training 32 (at right) would return safely. (National Archives)

Attempts to solve the mystery of Flight 19 have even included concocting false information about its leader, Lieutenant Charles Taylor, labeling him a drunk, sloppy, and a careless navigator. He was in reality an excellent pilot, a light drinker, and a conscientious leader. (Author's collection)

A big C-54. This was the military transport version of the DC-4, the largest airliner of the time. (Author's collection)

A BSAA Tudor IV, an hermetically sealed aircraft. BSAA and BOAC operated Tudors around the Western Hemisphere, but only two disappeared, both in the Triangle, causing the plane to be withdrawn from service. Freddie Laker later led a move to reinstate the Tudor IV as a cargo plane. As the Super Trader it clocked more than 3 million miles around the world without incident. (Courtesy Joan Beckett, from the collection of J. C. McPhee)

John Clutha McPhee, pilot of *Star Ariel*, was a highly qualified RAF pilot, a quiet, popular, "intellectual type." (Courtesy his sister, Joan Beckett)

The DC-3 was the standard airliner of its time. (The disappearance of NC16002 in 1948 would be equivalent to the disappearance of an MD-80 today.) Thousands of DC-3s were used as military cargo and paratroop planes in World War II. (Author's collection)

A C-46 Commando. Many such surplus U.S. Air Force aircraft were converted to cargo service after the war. The disappearance of one of these while approaching Miami on December 21, 1952, is yet another example of inexplicable losses in the Triangle. (Author's collection)

A Lockheed Super Constellation. When a Navy version of this aircraft disappeared in 1954 the Naval Board of Inquiry was only able to deduce that it "did meet with a violent and unknown force." A twelve-day search found no trace. (National Archives)

What can explain the disappearance of *Pogo 22* during a routine maneuver in 1961? (Author's collection)

The KB-50 was an aerial tanker based on the design of the B-29 bomber. The search for one of these in 1962 is probably the largest search ever conducted for a missing plane. (Author's collection)

A C-133 Cargomaster, the largest USAF plane in service. Two of these vanished from radar, near land, full of cargo and fuel, one without trace, the other leaving only a life raft and a nose wheel with an unidentified "magnetic particle." (National Archives)

A KC-135 Stratotanker. Can the unexplained turbulence and "funnels" of the Triangle explain the loss of two jets like this in 1963? (Author's collection)

A C-119 "Flying Boxcar." The last message from this aircraft was picked up 1,300 miles away from its course. It vanished without trace or reason. (National Archives)

An ever-reliable, rather bulbous, Piper Apache. (Author's collection)

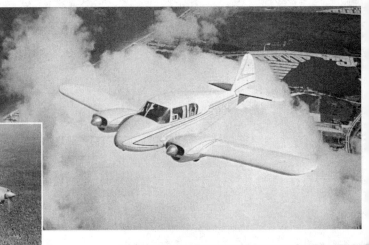

A Comanche. (Author's collection)

A standard Piper Cherokee Warrior. (National Archives)

A Beechcraft Musketeer, competitor to the Piper Cherokee. (Author's collection)

A Beechcraft executive Queen Air 65. (Author's collection)

Rockwell's Aero Commander, 500 series, a popular heavy twin-engine plane. (Author's collection)

Rockwell's prototype Aero Commander. (Author's collection)

The ever-popular Beechcraft V-tail Bonanza. (Author's collection)

A Cessna Skylane, another popular airplane. (Author's collection)

A Cessna 310, a rugged light twin. (Author's collection)

A Cessna 210. (Author's collection)

A Beechcraft Baron. (Author's collection)

A Beechcraft Travel Air. (Author's collection)

An F-4 Phantom II in a right turn. In such a maneuver *Sting 27* vanished from radar, one of the most puzzling cases in the Triangle. It left no trace and no automatic alarm; an unidentified "oblong" shape was seen in the water moments after, which itself then quickly disappeared. (National Archives)

Captain John Romero, pilot of the *Sting 27*, holder of two Distinguished Flying Crosses. (Courtesy John Romero III)

The DC-3 is considered one of the most reliable aircraft ever built. Out of the nearly 11,000 DC-3s built in the 1930s and 1940s, hundreds are still in service, many in southern Florida and the Caribbean islands, where the short distances and small airfields make their size ideal. The disappearance of this plane, N407D, in 1978 defies explanation. (By and courtesy of Alexandre Avrane)

Even more inexplicable was the disappearance of a Navajo Chieftain on November 3, 1978, less than 2 miles from the airport and while under visual supervision for landing. (National Archives)

One of the few disappearances with any clue to what was happening. José Pagan, shown here, and his friend vanished in this plane, N3808H, on June 28, 1980, after a desperate Mayday describing a "weird object." (Courtesy Evelyn Rivera)

What can explain the bizarre disappearance of a charter Cessna 402 over the Gulf Stream in March 1984 and the ghost image of another aircraft crashing off Bimini at the same time? Did a mirage cast an image of its final moments to the shallows off Bimini? (National Archives)

What overwhelmed an A-6 attack bomber while approaching the carrier? It happened so fast there was no time for the pilots to eject. (Author's collection)

On July 10, 1945, a PBM on patrol over the Bahamas disappeared. Tom Garner, shown here, was one of the gunners. The many aircraft disappearances before Flight 19 are emerging from the records today. Left, standard Navy telegram informing Garner's family. (Courtesy Don Garner)

WESTERN UNION

REGRET TO INFORM YOU THAT YOUR SON THOMAS ARTHUR GARNER AMM3C MISSING SINCE ABOUT 0215 JULY 10 1945 WHILE ON A ROUTINE TRAINING FLIGHT SEARCH BEING CONDUCTED WILL KEEP YOU PROMPTLY ADVISED=

COMMANDING OFFICER NAS BANANARIVER FLO 111944.

A number of Venturas went missing during World War II while on routine antisub patrols or search missions. (Author's collection)

A big Privateer vanished on July 18, 1945. (Author's collection)

USS *Cyclops*. In one of the greatest mysteries of the sea she vanished in the Triangle in fair weather with 309 crew, leaving in her wake rumors of treason, sabotage, mutiny, madness, and, most of all, mystery. (U.S. Navy History Center)

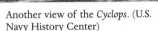

Another view of the *Cyclops*. (U.S. Navy History Center)

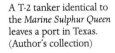

Coming upon the derelict *Gloria Colita*, February 4, 1940. Coast Guard photo taken from the *Cartigan*. (National Archives)

A T-2 tanker identical to the *Marine Sulphur Queen* leaves a port in Texas. (Author's collection)

The *Poet* in wartime configuration as the *General Omar S. Bundy*. Part of the weather data obtained from the *Star Ariel*'s flight came from the *Bundy*. Her turn to disappear would be in 1980, north of Bermuda, with all hands. (Author's collection)

4

Can It Be That Simple?

THOSE WHO BELIEVE there isn't any such phenomenon as the Bermuda Triangle tend to blame the disappearances on very conventional causes like mechanical malfunction, basic bad weather patterns, and human error. They also tend to regard the subject only in passing and ascribe popular interest in it to gullibility, sensationalism, and ignorance. They might also tend to generalize a solution to the subject by noting that on occasion a writer or columnist reported a ship's position in error and that it was really thousands of miles away from the Triangle when it vanished. They imply or state outright that all research therefore falls under suspicion, and they assert that if reporting were better done, a simple solution would be found for all disappearances in the Bermuda Triangle for which there is at present no explanation.

In general, they tend to believe that any point of view beyond this can only be expressing a desire in the supernatural or the occult. Because they do not display a broad or protracted interest in the subject, they do not pursue any solution to it beyond that of citing known cases of poor seamanship, bad navigating, careless flying, and so on, and then they apply these to the broad list of missing vessels and planes. The fact is, however, that those many cases were known because the participants survived to recount what happened and to be embarrassed by their mistakes.

The assumption is made that the survivors of mishaps at sea were simply the lucky ones. The others who disappeared simply were not so lucky, and that no trace of them was found was simply coincidental. They offer the reassurance that these are just statistical losses that can be placed under conventional categories because they have never heard of, or prefer to dismiss out of hand, any stories from survivors—the "lucky ones"— of anything odd or unusual about their accidents.

They are also more likely to insist on a strict adherence to the triangular shape for the area, and then they exclude any incident from consideration that happened outside it, even if by only a few miles. This naive approach to argument and debate is tantamount to saying there is no mystery because there is no triangle.

In a way, however, they are quite correct—there is no triangular shape. After all, there is no other reference point in the entire western Atlantic Ocean except Bermuda, without referring to the cumbersome and nondescript coordinates of latitude and longitude. Miami and San Juan are well-known cities and ports, and besides being radial points their names instantly bring geographic recognition to most people's minds. When Vincent Gaddis coined the term Bermuda Triangle he did so with this journalistic codicil: "in and about this area."

Others have sought to delineate the area more laboriously and have subsequently come up with varied shapes and sizes. Ivan T. Sanderson, who dealt extensively with it in *Invisible Residents,* stated categorically: "It is not a triangle, and its periphery is much greater. . . . In fact the area . . . forms a large, sort of lozenge-shaped area . . . which extends from about 30° to 40° North latitude, and from about 55° to 85° West." Investigator Richard Winer in *The Devil's Triangle* proposed: "The 'Devil's Triangle' is not a triangle at all. It is a trapezium, a four-sided area in which no two sides or angles are the same." He adds: "The area commonly called the 'Devil's' or Bermuda Triangle is actually only one quarter the size of the actual triangle or trapezium." According to John Wallace Spencer in his *Limbo of the Lost,* the first book entirely devoted to the subject, it extends from "Cape May, New Jersey, to the edge of the continental shelf. Following the shelf around Florida into the Gulf of Mexico, it continues through Cuba, Jamaica, Haiti, the Dominican Republic, Puerto Rico, and other islands of the West Indies, and then comes up again through the Bahamas . . . then up once more to Bermuda." Ironically, this amorphous body harkens back in some ways to the very beginning of interest, as seen in E. V. W. Jones's Associated Press article in 1950 that first broached the subject of an area of mysterious disappearances off the U.S. East Coast.

Alternative triangles have also been proposed by others connecting Bermuda, Key West, Chesapeake Bay, San Juan, or Miami—take your pick. The most seriously considered alternative is the port of Norfolk, Virginia, about 600 miles northwest of Bermuda. Drawing a line on a map between all these points would essentially bring to light a sea graphed by four

Three varied shapes as opposed to the "typical triangle": the triangle linking Bermuda, Chesapeake Bay / Norfolk, Virginia, and the Florida Keys; the dotted line is an estimate of John Spencer's "Limbo of the Lost"; and the broken line represents Richard Winer's trapezium or "Devil's Triangle."

triangles. Envisioning a somewhat similar territory, John Godwin, in his book, *This Baffling World,* amusingly labeled his area the "Hoodoo Sea."

In any case, for those who believe there is no mystery, there is no shape. Any disappearance is first blamed on the pilot of a plane or skipper of a boat. Usually this is the first choice because weather information proves there were no hazards. No matter how often this excuse raises its head, it does so as an accusation, not as an explanation. Since nothing is left from a disappearance, human error simply becomes a category of suspicion.

So far, the most outspoken proponent of the theory that human error is a major culprit is the U.S. Coast Guard. They made their position clear in a two-page form letter prepared about thirty years ago by their headquarters in Washington. The continuing disappearances have warranted them, plus many other U.S. Government bureaus, to keep it on hand for the inquirer, would-be traveler, and curious correspondent.

Triangles represent an approximation of where major aircraft and ship disappearances have occurred based on known course and position last reported by radio or radar. Because of long courses, scant radio messages, or vague boat plans, many locations cannot be estimated for those traveling in the Bahamas or to Bermuda, though within the last forty years a large number must have vanished.

The "Bermuda or Devil's Triangle" is an imaginary area located off the southeastern Atlantic coast of the United States, which is noted for a high incidence of unexplained losses of ships, small boats, and aircraft. The apexes of the triangle are generally accepted to be Bermuda, Miami, Fl., and San Juan, Puerto Rico.

In the past, extensive, but futile Coast Guard searches prompted by search and rescue cases such as the disappearances of an entire squadron of TBM Avengers shortly after take off from Fort Lauderdale, Fl., or the traceless sinking of USS *Cyclops* and *Marine Sulphur Queen* have lent credence to the popular belief in the mystery and the supernatural qualities of the "Bermuda Triangle."

Countless theories attempting to explain the many disappearances have been offered throughout the history of the area. The most practical seem to be environmental and those citing human error. The majority of disappearances can be attributed to the area's unique environmental features. First, the "Devil's Triangle" is one of the two places on Earth that a magnetic compass does point towards true north. Normally it points toward magnetic north. The difference between the two is known as compass variation. The amount of variation changes by as much as 20 degrees as one circumnavigates the Earth. If this compass variation or error is not compensated for, a navigator could find himself far off course and in deep trouble.

An area called the "Devil's Sea" by Japanese and Filipino seamen, located off the east coast of Japan, also exhibits the same magnetic characteristics. It is also known for its mysterious disappearances.

Another environmental factor is the character of the Gulf Stream. It is extremely swift and turbulent and can quickly erase any evidence of a disaster. The unpredictable Caribbean-Atlantic weather pattern also plays its role. Sudden local thunderstorms and water spouts often spell disaster for pilots and mariners. Finally, the topography of the ocean floor varies from extensive shoals around the islands to some of the deepest marine trenches in the world. With the interaction of the strong currents over the many reefs the topography is in a state of constant flux and development of new navigational hazards is swift.

Not to be under estimated is the human error factor. A large number of pleasure boats travel the waters between Florida's Gold Coast and the Bahamas. All too often, crossings are attempted with too small a boat, insufficient knowledge of the area's hazards, and a lack of good seamanship.

The Coast Guard, in short, is not impressed with supernatural explanations of disasters at sea. It has been our experience that the combined forces of nature and unpredictability of mankind outdo even the most far-fetched science fiction many times each year.

Enlarging somewhat on their hypothesis, the reason there is "compass variation" on Earth is that there is a difference between true north and magnetic north. The magnetic field of this planet can be likened to a bar magnet, with the two ends representing the north and south magnetic poles. The bar or central line between these two points is its axis or, as it is called in geophysics, the Agonic Line.

Although we associate the North Pole with the absolute geographic north on this planet, the compass actually associates magnetic north with true north. This would present no problem except that the northern magnetic pole (magnetic north) is located at Prince of Wales Island in the frozen Northwest Territories of Canada, about 1,500 miles *south* of the North Pole. This causes a great discrepancy for a navigator in the cardinal points of north, south, east, and west because the compass has a tilted perspective of the Earth.

At the Azores, for instance, magnetic north and true north are about 24 degrees off. A navigator would have to add 24 degrees to his course to maintain a true heading north. If heading north, he must steer 024 degrees. Even at the Agonic Line the compass still points to magnetic north, but here one is, longitudinally, directly south of Prince of Wales Island, which in turn is directly south of the North Pole. Therefore the compass needle points to true north incidentally because they are briefly in line.

For practical purposes, the Coast Guard solution could never really apply, since the Agonic Line is a very narrow corridor of longitude in the overall Triangle. When the Coast Guard wrote its little chit, the Agonic Line was off the east coast of Florida. Already at Bimini Island (only 50 miles from Miami) there was a 2-degree charted westerly variation. Failing to compensate for this slight variation would not have resulted in a plane lost before Bimini. (Incidentally, if flying over Bimini at 10,000 feet, one can see Miami.) Moreover, a navigator can get lost from inaccurately adjusting his heading anywhere in the world, whether there be a 12-degree difference, 2 degrees, or none. Yet other parts of the world do not have so many disappearances.

Today their statement is completely outdated (though still in wide circulation) because magnetic north subtly shifts over time in response to rotational changes in the molten core of the planet. The Agonic Line is now off the *west* coast of Florida, beyond Key West—to those detractors of the Bermuda Triangle enigma completely outside it. Yet disappearances still continue, many of them along the same routes as before. Most of them are clearly not in the Gulf of Mexico, where the lack of compass variation now exists.

Although the Coast Guard blames this simple element of navigation for most of the losses, it overlooks the fact that if a navigator becomes lost he can still transmit an SOS. A pilot who is lost and slowly running out of fuel realizes he's in trouble and starts calling for help. Nor can it explain the lack of any debris after, presumably, a plane must have crashed.

The records show that pilots reported themselves lost on only a couple of occasions. How they got lost we do not know, since they then vanished. Others vanished after blurting a few sudden words, apparently not having had prior warning, and some vanished while on radar, in sight of landing. Lost planes that seem to justify the Coast Guard's scenario are few and far between.

What is applicable to aircraft is not necessarily so for boats and ships. There are, in fact, so many islands along the Bahamas that a boat captain can easily steer by point-of-sight navigating without using his compass. Should the boat become lost, there is still time to call for help. When it

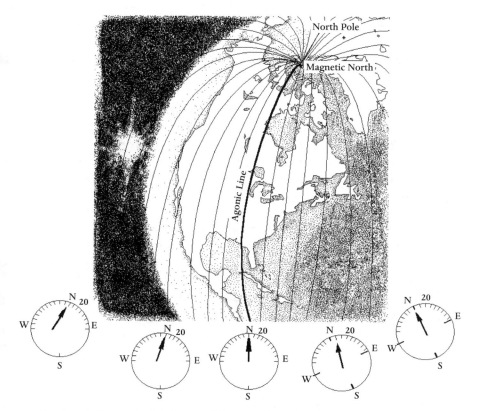

The Agonic Line today. It is far out of the strict Triangle and continuing to move westward. The compasses show how "compass variation" happens. Each compass always points to "N," meaning magnetic north. But as one circumnavigates the Earth the disparity between true and magnetic north widens because the compass remains fixed on magnetic north, not on the actual true North Pole. Thus "N" can be up to 20 or more degrees either west or east of actual geographic north.

runs out of gas, it does not fall thousands of feet to the surface—it remains static on the ocean. Yet far more boats have vanished in this area than aircraft.

Considering the simple and brief lack of compass variation as a viable cause, the Coast Guard synopsis presupposes that the majority of pilots and navigators who vanished failed *not to compensate,* were not able to call when they realized they were lost, and had subsequently traveled so far off their course that no debris was recoverable. A combination of the above was deemed "beyond probability" in the assessment of *Star Tiger's* loss.

It also ignores the fact that many of the pilots were local and well-experienced charter pilots with thousands of hours flight time. They were, obviously, familiar with the area's charted magnetic variations.

Nevertheless, human error doesn't have to hinge on the compass variation issue. It can stem from many other factors. Retired pilot George Smith, who was trained at Banana River, Florida, in Martin Mariners and later flew extensively in the Bermuda Triangle, is wary of people who come to hasty conclusions about the supernatural and calls these explanations "just bull." From his experience he prefers to concentrate on some of the basic mistakes in flying, plus some of the area's unique hazards, as recorded in a conversation at his home:

You can get confused very easily. Rapid movements of the head, movements of the aircraft and whatnot. . . . I know specifically of one guy who told me one night that he was having a hard time making upside down right. He couldn't tell whether the stars were the land where he had seen some lights or whether it was the other way around. He kept rolling that F-3H Demon around trying to discover which was up and which was down!

Question: The sea off Florida's east coast is often noted for a white, humid haze. Have you ever experienced a "white out" in which there is no horizon, where the ocean and sky blend together?

That's not as uncommon as you think. You can get it in snow, too. You lose your equilibrium—you get vertigo is what you can do. It's not that uncommon at all in the Florida area if you're out over water. . . . There are different types of cloud layers and situations that you fly through at some point in time that you better put your ultimate faith in your instruments inside the airplane. . . . Lock your eyeballs inside that airplane and keep your instruments where they belong and believe them that you're right side up or in a left turn or right turn or whatever. Because if you start trying to follow your eyes on the outside of the airplane, the next thing you'll be doing is what they used to call a 'deadman's spiral'; you just go down and down and go into the water, and you don't even know it. Your mind is telling you that you're flying straight and you aren't; that's typical vertigo.

Sometimes we think of clouds as being up and down or they're nice horizontal layers . . . and they're not always that way. You have some that drift in sideways or something like that, and maybe you don't see the ocean and sometimes you think you are. You just don't know! So I don't have a problem with a pilot being confused. But he better be looking to his instruments and believe them.

But he concludes grimly: "If they're wrong, you're in real trouble."

The National Transportation Safety Board has expressed that overwater navigation may have been the culprit in some disappearances. To avoid the strictures of investigative red tape, they list their conjecture as a "remark," such as the "pilot exceeded his experience / ability level" or just "pilot's first overwater flight." This was expressed in the disappearance of the Musketeer N922RZ (Ziegler and Fines) on January 11, 1979, although in itself this isn't proof that human error played a part in the loss. In the dossier on the flight of Anthony Purcell, the pilot of the Ted Smith 601 (Aerostar), the NTSB recorded that the altimeter on the aircraft was known not to have been working properly. It is noteworthy that Purcell vanished while descending. Without a working altimeter, he may have misjudged his rate of descent and banked the plane into a deadly spin, plunging it into the sea.

There were a few more aircraft disappearances where the pilot had a low number of flight hours experience. But it is interesting to note that most of the astonishing disappearances were charter aircraft, with the pilots possessing thousands of hours experience.

The cases where human error could even be inferred, or at least should be listed tentatively, are still relatively few. So far that leaves us with an unacceptable amount of losses where there was no official conjecture offered beyond the Spartan and somewhat annoying "Aircraft Damage and Injury Index Presumed."

Ship and boat losses from human error seem harder to accept, at least with the same degree of danger faced by a pilot, for vertigo cannot result in a boat plunging miles to the sea and being obliterated by impact. At the comparatively slow speeds boats travel, getting lost is not going to take them out of radio range quickly.

Nevertheless, some boat disappearances may be preceded by some calamities genuinely unique to yachting, like torching the boat from knocking over the barbecue. In one case, a fisherman spilled gasoline over his boat which seeped quickly down into the bilge. Desiring to get rid of the potentially flammable liquid, he opened the bilge plug to let it drain out, forgetting that the ocean would instead flood into his boat! In another, a cigar-chewing skipper dribbled gas all along his deck while refueling his motor from a portable tank. Desiring a smoke he lit his cigar, took a satisfying drag, then, though there was an ocean around him, threw the match down on the deck. VARHOOM! . . . He still survived though somewhat more charred.

Mechanical failure in an airplane is often harder to imply because, again, at sea it can only be an assumption. But it happens often enough in accidents over land where the debris can be sifted and the mechanical problem exposed. Since disappearances only occur over the ocean, it is often said that there is really no mystery in these losses whatsoever. The ocean, with its many currents and its deep trenches, merely covers up the remains of what otherwise would have been exposed as a "normal" accident had it happened over land and been accessible for investigation.

It is a fact that some of the most treacherous currents in the world do exist in the Triangle, such as the Florida Current and the Gulf Stream. The former, off Florida, moves at the incredible speed of 4 knots—close to 5 MPH. Merely drifting in this current, a boat can be exceeding harbor speed limits. Moreover, the Gulf Stream is full of tangential currents below, eddies and undertows. A plane or ship that crashes or sinks here would effectively be spread out quickly and even be further broken up as it sank through tumultuous colliding currents beneath.

Coast Guard searches, however, do take into account the drift and speeds of this current and compensate for it in defining their search areas. This is dependent, of course, on knowing that an aircraft or boat is in trouble over this area. But with the lack of SOS in most cases, searches can be hours or days late. In such a scenario it is not surprising that no debris is found. Nevertheless, there are dozens of accidents over this area each year in which wreckage is recovered quickly and examined thoroughly.

Power loss in the Gulf Stream's turbulent waves, especially when its northbound course is buffeted by southbound winds, can swamp and founder a boat with low freeboard. It can be such a turbulent ride that many seasoned yachters prefer to head down to the Keys and use the Gulf Stream as a conveyor belt rather then cut directly across it, and then glide off at the Bahamas.

Boats hitting "unknown objects" in the Gulf Stream is not uncommon, and it accounts for many known sinkings. Much of this is debris pulled from the Gulf by the strong current. It can range from tree trunks to the hulls of boats that do not sink all the way because of corking or built-in floatation. Whatever they all are, the Coast Guard is routinely called upon to destroy "underwater navigational hazards."

An example of to what extent people have sought to embrace a prosaic and quick solution to the mystery of the Bermuda Triangle can be found in the continued promotion of a near thirty-year-old book by Larry Kusche, *The Bermuda Triangle Mystery Solved* and his claim to have exposed the "true" and banal facts of each case . . . chiefly via the method of browsing old newspaper articles.

His title and conclusion, however, become a ghastly canard when the results of his newspaper browsing is compared to the contents of lengthy and detailed official accident reports, the repositories of some of which he knew. Nevertheless, he repeatedly defers to inaccurate or incomplete sources. For instance, in the case of Tyler 41 he relies on an obscure newspaper report erroneously claiming Tawney's last message was sent from a location where the search later found an oil slick, implying the plane merely plummeted to the sea. The official U.S. Air Force Mishap Report made it clear that the KB-50 was heard hours later and hundreds of miles past the spot. In another case, he "solved" a nonexistent accident with hearsay information, believing a C-54 in 1947 was a B-29 bomber hundreds of miles away.

Out of the other sixty or so cases Kusche bothered to present, ambiguity is the common conclusion. Most cases remain unsolved, and he avoids or is ignorant of such hot cases as the two C-133 Cargomasters, *Sting 27*, dozens of military flights, plus thirty-seven civil aircraft losses between 1960 and 1972 and Coast Guard statistics on forty-seven missing vessels between 1970 and his writing (1974). But he nevertheless claims he found twice as many that disappeared outside of the Triangle (though he mentions no names), and deduces that "mystery writers" must have ignored them in order to make the Triangle stand out.

An example of his investigative process can be gleaned from the following. For one of the most tragic disappearances in the Triangle, Flight 441 in October 1954, he merely reproduces verbatim a *New York Times* article then adds this strategic addendum: "the search was abandoned on November 4 [actually November 11] because of 'extreme weather conditions' "—thereby misrepresenting the entire incident, for the accident report clarified the weather was "typical" for this time of year (isolated thunder showers), and that Flight 441 carried weather radar and was flying over it. "The weather that Lt. Leonard [pilot] was thought to have been subjected to was not beyond the capabilities of R7V-1, nor was it thought to be beyond his own capabilities," the Board of Inquiry assessed.

His "meticulous research" led to his overlooking the 1,500 papers amassed on the USS *Cyclops* and the ten-year search and investigation, contained in such unimaginable repositories as the National Archives (boxes 1068–1070, Modern Military Branch). His desire to solve it based on his own hunches led to a statement that could make even Ripley sit up and blink: "I confidently decided that the newspapers, the Navy, and all the ships at sea had been wrong, and that there had been a storm near Norfolk that day strong enough to sink the ship." The documents at the National Archives and Records Administration make it clear there was no storm. Yet Kusche wrote: "Contrary to popular opinion, there never was an official inquiry into the disappearance. . . . Had there been any investigation, the weather information would surely have been discovered." He claimed there was a storm on March 10 off the Virginia capes. But throughout his entire recital he never mentioned the *Cyclops*'s ETA at Baltimore on March 13. If he had, his wishful storm of March 10 would have been exposed as long before the *Cyclops* was even due off the Capes.

In the final analysis the acrimony he directed at others can be returned to him. His solutions were based merely on faulty newspaper articles, elastic conclusions there from, and on the whole trying to explain away why there was no debris or SOS. Combined with his inability (or reluctance) to even travel near the Triangle, his research was no more informed than anybody who browses their *Daily Blatt* during their morning coffee. The result was a debunk on popular discourse on the Triangle, rather than actually documenting it.

In an interview by Wanda Sue Parrott (*Riddle of the Bermuda Triangle*), Kusche rendered what is his own impression of his work. "I don't like the word debunk because it carries with it the connotation that someone set out to prove someone else wrong, which was not what I did. My purpose throughout was not even to find a solution but merely to write a book that reported each incident as objectively and honestly as possible. The solution was completely unintentional and an added bonus."

Whether Kusche added the idea of the solution or whether a publicity department did, it is in Kusche's statement of his work that *The Bermuda Triangle Mystery Solved* might best still be viewed, for it fits the contents of his book—it is as a look at the incidents. Many of the cases he lists neither solve nor, in some cases, even debunk the Triangle. There is truth and there is error. But it is in comparing the content of the book with its title that the greatest disillusionment is found with the work.

Although the Coast Guard has also been eager to affix blame for disappearances to many simple causes, it itself has been blamed for not actively pursing vigorous searches, not just in the Triangle but in less hazardous areas like a lake. In one case, a spokeswoman replied to the press proposal of using sonar to find the fishing boat *Linda E.*, missing in Lake Michigan, with: "We have done the investigation to the extent that is appropriate for this agency. We are not in the salvage business." When Congress became interested in the case, the young lady found out that the Coast Guard does as ordered to do—and the *Linda E.* was found two days later by sonar.

The point is expanded by some who see a correlation with the Bermuda Triangle: because of financing, the depths of the ocean, and the speed of currents, sonar is seldom used, and searches on the surface are often ritualistically carried out and discontinued in a few days or even hours. (However, sonar has been employed twice to find missing craft and still uncovered nothing.)

And, quite frankly, the more bold will take up this lead and follow it to the investigation process. Investigators are not allowed to go beyond listing factually the known circumstances of any accident of undetermined origin. In fact, on the NTSB instructions sheet for the investigator, always included with every report so the reader knows under what conditions and to what purpose the report is being made, it reads under item 21: "This report, when submitted as the NTSB factual aircraft accident report, must not contain any opinions or conclusions. All attachments should be legible, reproducible original documents . . ." The rest of the instructions concern bureaucratic and interagency handling.

In essence, the case is investigated accurately with only the purpose of putting together a chain of events, sterile of any insight, devoid of any desire to draw comparisons or plot cause and effect. The facts are then filed away. The only items entertained are those that would be considered to have an immediate impact on the case—those, one must suppose, that fit the criterion of item 21. Presumably, the facts should be forthright enough to suggest the obvious answer.

In practice, the Air Force operates under less strict guidelines laid down by their AFRs—Air Force Regulations. However, according to AFR 4-33, paragraph 15e, often recited to an inquirer, they cannot and will not release the opinions or conclusions their investigators come to. These pages are left out altogether, or such an opinion is expurgated by a razor, leaving nothing but a large open square in the text of the page—a daunting sight.

It is understandable on the part of investigating bureaus, even advisable, that they make no conclusions or opinions, since there is nothing left from a disappearance upon which to base any conclusion. Most evidence is only circumstantial, however impressive the repetition may become.

But the investigation of the mystery of this sea does not end here. There is a growing body of evidence from the experiences of those who actually sail and fly the Bermuda Triangle to suggest that very unexpected elements may have played a role in some of the disappearances. For decades sailors have spoken about weird mirages, time lapses, strange fogs and vapors, and ubiquitous electromagnetic anomalies and aberrations, as though the very fundamental laws of nature ceased to operate in a manner with which we have taken for granted. While it may be easy for some to dismiss these as modern sea superstitions, the persistence of the stories, the similar lines along which they continue to play, and the fact that official reports now contain allusions to such hot topics as time gaps in radio calls and weird objects in the sky, the stories are not being laughed off by an increasing number of conscientious observers.

5

Those Who Lived to Tell

WHILE IN FLIGHT at 29,000 feet on July 8, 1999, a Continental Airlines airliner with 155 passengers was struck by two unexplained "jolts" that caused the aircraft to drop precipitously by 600 feet before the flight crew could recover. The airliner, a Boeing 737, was about 160 miles south-southwest of Bermuda at the time, en route to San Juan, Puerto Rico, from Philadelphia.

A vivid account of what happened comes from one cabin attendant, Leslie Thomas: "The crew had just completed the meal service and I was in the back in the aft of the main cabin, approximately row 29, picking up trays from the meal service. The seat belt sign was off and we were flying in smooth air with no sign of turbulence. Then all of a sudden, the aircraft dropped abruptly which caused my body to fly upward hitting my head on the ceiling. I fell back to the floor on my knees. Approximately 10 seconds later, the aircraft dropped again, causing my head to hit the ceiling once again. At that point I lost consciousness. When I awoke, I was very dazed noticing my head bleeding, arms cut and bruised, and back and shoulders sore."

The airliner went into a dangerous nose-down descent. The plane's captain, Joe Moore, noticed the speed was already approaching MMO (maximum mach operating speed). Had he not quickly corrected the air-liner's sudden descent, it would have increased speed until it would have been impossible to recover. In commenting on the incident, he confirmed "no reports of turbulence were reported by ATC [Air Traffic Control] along our route of flight or in our dispatched paperwork," while the First Officer added "it had been smooth . . . there were no visual clues to an adverse ride. Both radars were on when the aircraft was hit."

Whatever force this was, seventy-one passengers were injured, causing Moore to immediately call Bermuda for permission to divert his course and land.

In another incident of this type, American Airlines Flight 935, a Boeing 757, was cruising at 31,000 feet approximately 300 miles west-southwest of Bermuda on April 7, 1996. Unexplained turbulence suddenly shook the aircraft up and down so violently that an aisle cart became airborne, striking a flight attendant on the leg and resulting in a serious injury. Flight 935 immediately diverted course and landed at Bermuda as well.

Questions naturally arise whether these are normal CATS (clear air turbulence) or some other unknown phenomenon. While meteorology has come far in being able to predict where CATS are likely to strike, in these cases there was no warning whatsoever. Had there been any fore-warning of these SIGMETS (significant meteorological information) would have been in effect and would have been a part of the preflight weather briefing package, or notice would have been immediately flashed to the crews when information became available.

It could be, of course, that these were not CATS in the strictest sense, but something else significantly affecting the atmosphere that might contribute to sudden disappearances of aircraft less resilient than big jumbo jets.

A particularly pertinent fact about this observation involves their locations. They occurred approximately—and in one instance almost exactly—in the same position where the two KC-135 Stratotankers were mysteriously destroyed in 1963 and where the Tudor IV *Star Ariel* vanished in 1949. Investigation into the weather along its course indicated that the chance for clear air turbulence was "practically nil."

Unexplained turbulence or "pulses" and "chops" continue to be reported by airliners. Their onset is always sudden and their duration is very short. These incidents have caused a number of injuries, since the pilots, flight crews, and passengers have absolutely no warning. In each case, the weather radar in the aircraft showed no weather conditions that could instigate turbulence.

In the case of United Airlines Flight 990 on October 22, 1993, while at 35,000 feet over the Bahamas en route to Miami from Rio de Janeiro, the encounter began with a "light" to "moderate" chop that lasted almost a minute, resulting in three injuries.

A particularly interesting encounter happened on January 7, 1997, when American Flight 2009, while en route to San Juan, Puerto Rico, from Philadelphia was hit at 33,000 feet by "two pulses" separated by only

8 seconds. Each pulse had a maximum of 1.6 g (force of gravity). This brief but violent encounter caused one serious injury and five minor ones. This incident is particularly interesting because it happened at "Champs Intersection," where the two C-133 Cargomasters had suddenly vanished decades before in 1962 and 1963.

An indication these may represent as yet unknown forces in the Triangle comes from a surprising incident involving a light plane. A Cessna 172 was just about to touch down at the airport at Culebra, Puerto Rico, on February 15, 1994. The winds were light, only 6 to 8 knots easterly. As the plane began the landing flare, two severe "blasts" from the right jolted it. John Macone, an aerobatic pilot of considerable caliber, immediately regained control and brought his plane back in line with the runway. Seconds later, however, a third "blast" picked the plane up and threw it 60 to 80 feet to the left over buildings, over tension wires, across a road, and then slammed it down into an alleyway, despite any evasive action Macone tried. Both he and his student, Herman Vander Heide, survived with minor to serious injuries. In summing it up, Macone recalled: "In thousands of hours of mountain and aerobatic flying, I have never encountered a condition approaching the severity of this whirlwind nor the sense of helplessness it created."

Highly unusual and extremely sudden winds at sea level are a recurring theme in the Bermuda Triangle. The tall ship *Pride of Baltimore,* which was on a goodwill cruise that encompassed part of the Bermuda Triangle, was suddenly lost 250 miles north of Puerto Rico on May 14, 1986. Bob Foster, deckhand and one of the survivors, told how: "At that time, the winds were just from 30 knots that we had been sailing under to God knows what, 70 knots and above I've been told, but I couldn't judge. Looking back aft, I could see horizontally blown spray coming up off of the top of the waves, and I could see the wind—actually the wind—hit the sail, and at that time the boat just started to slowly roll . . . roll over on her side. It wasn't a fast motion, it wasn't . . . a rapid motion, it was just a slow heeling over."

Captain Chuck Willis experienced a more sudden way to disappear in the Bermuda Triangle while off the Gulf Stream. While asleep in the early morning hours of May 1, 1998, something happened to his fishing boat *Miss Charlotte II.* "The dishes, glasses, everything came crashing onto the cabin floor. . . . A huge wind had suddenly hit us. It threw us out of our bunks and cleared everything off our deck." Since the weather had been dead calm and the seas perfectly flat, Willis at first thought a waterspout had hit them and radioed that the deck had been cleared of all gear and that they were checking for damage. Then, however: "Twenty-foot waves hit our boat and sank us in under 2 minutes. We were told later that Cape Lookout registered 74 mph winds at this same time." Willis was able to save himself and his crew by staying together in the ocean. After 6 hours, they were picked up by a Good Samaritan vessel and brought to shore.

Captain Don Henry is perhaps one of the most impressive observers of anything unusual at sea. He is frank, direct, and strikes one as being a true "sea dog." It is immediately apparent that he is accustomed to being in charge. When he politely invites you to sit down, it sounds like a command. He has a regulation Navy crew cut, and even in his early seventies, he is a large, powerful man. When he speaks, his keen eyes return to the sea. His career at sea extends from World War II until his retirement in the 1980s, covering every aspect of salvage. He has been a free diver, hard hat, and tug captain. In his various capacities he has salvaged Japanese warships in Tokyo Bay and captained underwater salvage operations along the entire U.S. East Coast and in the Caribbean.

But out of all the seas he has sailed there is only one event in his long career he could not explain. It was back in 1966, in the Bermuda Triangle. Don Henry offers it in a plain and no-nonsense way, without digressing into any theoretical guesswork. It is best to let him tell it in his own words.

Well, we were heading to the Miami area where I had a salvage company at the time. We were on a return trip from Puerto Rico, with a barge in tow. My tug was the *Good News*. She was a 160-foot tug with a lot of power, 2,000 horsepower. The barge itself was about 2,500 tons. We had it on a 600-foot towline. It had carried petroleum nitrate, but was empty now. We were over the Tongue of the Ocean, about three days out of Rico.

It was daytime, in the afternoon. I had been on the bridge for some time since the morning, so I had gone to my cabin for a little rest, which is just aft the bridge. While I was in my cabin, I heard a great deal of commotion coming from the bridge. The crew was hollering and screaming. I came running out onto the bridge and yelled: "What the hell is going on here?!"

The chief officer was there, and he told me to look at the compass. I walked over and looked. The gyro was tumbling, and the magnetic compass was going completely bananas. It was simply going around and around. I had never seen anything like that before.

We had no communications of any kind over the radios. There were no lights. We lost the generators—they were running but produced no energy. There was just some kind of electronic drain at this time. There was just nothing. A case of fifty batteries I had picked up in San Juan had to be thrown away. They were completely shot. This we found out later. We didn't know this at the time.

I went out on the bridge. . . . I was going to check on the tug but the sky caught my attention first. There was no horizon now; you couldn't see where the sky ended and the water began. I looked down on the ocean. All I saw was foam; it was like milk. The sky was the same color. There was just no definition between the two as there always is, so that's why I say there was no horizon.

I automatically looked aft to the barge; it was a reflex action. But there was no barge! I knew it had to be there but I couldn't see it. The towline was leading back, the way it was supposed to be, but there was simply no barge.

I ran to the afterdeck, then down to the towing deck, and started to pull the towing hawser—You can't pull a 2,500-ton barge, of course, but you can tell if something is attached. It was. The line was tight. It was very taut. There was something on the other end all right.

I still couldn't see it, though. There was a fog or something around it, like clouds, and the towline was running aft into that. It's hard to explain. I've likened it to the old Indian rope trick. The towline was just sticking out of a fog . . . but the fog was nowhere else. It was just around where the barge should be. The water was also more choppy immediately around where the barge should be.

I had heard about the Bermuda Triangle at this time; most every seaman about those waters had. I thought: "I don't want to be another statistic!" I ran back up to the bridge and kicked those throttles full ahead. It wasn't like "full ahead and clear for action"—it was full ahead and let's get the hell out of here!

We plowed ahead . . . or tried to. It seemed that something was pulling us back. It was like being in the middle of a tug-o-war. We were trying to go forward under our power but we were being restrained. When you've been at sea for any amount of time, especially on the same tug, you get a feel for it; you can tell when it is moving and when it's being restrained; there is a vibration in a ship that is there all the time; you can tell when it's going and when it isn't.

Now coming out of this thing was just like coming out of a fog bank. We could see the horizon again. We got everything back: the radios, the lights, the gyros, the generators. We got the damn barge back! The line was leading back to it. That fog was gone.

We plowed ahead for some time. As soon as we got out of that spot, I wanted to make sure everything was all right, that the line hadn't weakened at the coupling during our struggle. I put a boat over the side and went back. The barge was warm, much warmer than it should have been. It wasn't hot. You could touch it. But it was much warmer than would have been normal.

Like I've said, this encounter never scared me out of sailing the Bermuda Triangle afterward. I mean, it scared the hell out of me, but I was never leery about going back down in there. You can't avoid the area, anyway. It's just something that happened and, as I've said a number of times, it sure made me into a "believer."

Question: How long did this last?

The whole incident took only about, oh, I don't know, 7 to 10 minutes, from the time I came onto the bridge until the barge came out of that fog.

Question: What had the weather been like before this?

. . . The sea had been flat calm. Visibility had also been good, more than 10 miles.

Question: Had you ever experienced any changes like this in your compass before?

Not like this. I knew a compass could tumble but never saw that on a tug. You just don't get that much acceleration. When this happened all I could think of is My God, I'm next!

Retired Coast Guardsman Frank Flynn gives a remarkable account of another unexplained phenomenon at sea level. In his case, he experienced this while an ensign aboard the Coast Guard cutter *Yamacraw* on an August night in 1956. His account has pertinent and surprising relevance to other cases of unexplained fogs and vapors and electronic drains. He recalled that at the time of the incident the weather was absolutely perfect; the sea flat calm, and visibility and ceiling just about unlimited. They were heading out to sea from the Florida coast, into the Triangle.

At about 1:30 in the morning, we observed on the radarscope a solid line approximately 28 miles away. We were a little concerned about it at first; it had a strong resemblance to a landmass. However, a quick check of our navigation equipment indicated that we were right on course approximately 165 miles offshore.

We tracked it and found it was dead in the water. So we carefully approached it and approximately one and a half hours later we got down to about a half of a mile from the radar target, and we carefully moved closer to it.

About 100 yards from the strange object, the cutter turned on her searchlight. The mass was so dense that the light beam reflected off it, and the carbon arc couldn't penetrate it. They moved closer, with the searchlight beamed on it. At this point they started a gentle left turn to avoid approaching the unknown vapor mass head-on. After moving in still closer, they nudged it with the starboard wing. They veered off several times and returned to nudge it again. Since it proved not to be solid, they returned to normal cruising speed and entered the unknown mass.

Flynn recalled that visibility was about zero within the vapor mass. On penetration of the mass a surprising phenomenon also happened: the engine room called up, saying they were losing steam pressure; the situation was becoming serious. When their speed was down to 4 knots, they decided to reverse course. Moments later they broke out of the mass. At the same time all engine and electronic gear returned to normal. Flynn summed up: "Now, as to what we might have encountered that night, I really have no way of speculating. Over the years after this happened I talked to many oceanographers, and none of these people could shed any light whatsoever on what it might have been."

Don Welch and Ron Reyes's encounter with an unusual fog at sea level is another incident that might be considered a close call with forces in the Triangle. It was in 1996, off Port Canaveral, Florida.

It was early morning and we were heading out with a moderate wind and seas at about 2–3 feet. At approximately 5–6 miles offshore we entered a small fog bank. After just a few minutes, we entered an area with clear skies, extremely calm wind, fog all around us, and an eerie feeling. It was sort of like entering the eye of a hurricane. We went from a moderate wind into a fog bank and then into an opening in the fog bank which was a dead calm with sunshine and no sounds. We stopped to talk about it and have a cigarette and watched our smoke stay in front of us for a couple of minutes. We then proceeded back into the fog and then back into moderate winds with light seas. All I know is that it was a very eerie event. We have told this to many friends and they think we are making up a story.

—A reaction that has often proven to be a barrier to those who innocently seek logical explanations.

William "Al" Kittinger is yet another man who is intimately familiar with the ocean and sky of the Bermuda Triangle. He has flown them many times as an experienced pilot based in St. Thomas, Virgin Islands. Al is also, perhaps, the closest person to being an actual eyewitness to a disappearance in the Triangle. He was the controller on duty at Harry S. Truman Airport, St. Thomas, on the night of November 3, 1978, when the charter Piper Chieftain disappeared while coming in for a landing, a disappearance that happened between Al's glance out the window at its landing light and his double check of it on the radarscope. After 1981, when the nation's air traffic controllers were fired by then-President Ronald Reagan, Al became a fisherman in the Bahamas, a job that made him intimately familiar with its many islands and weather conditions over the next ten years of his career. Along with being an astute and particularly qualified observer, he is a gregarious and level-headed man who now channels his energy to teaching Tae Kwon Do in southern Florida.

As a pilot and former air traffic controller, Kittinger is also a certified weather observer and an excellent source of information on visual phenomena in the Bahamas. On a number of occasions he would see fogs hovering over the ocean in the distance. They attracted his attention because the weather conditions were not right for creating fog. Taking them only as weather oddities, he never bothered to investigate them more closely. He is not without his firsthand encounters, however. On one occasion, while flying his Cessna, Al experienced a spinning of his compass. He had just taken off from Great Inagua when "I noticed the compass spin around one full time. I thought it was merely deflected to something nearby. Then it did it again. That's unusual. It finally came back onto course. If you know what's beyond Great Inagua—*nothing*—you'll know how spooky it is to think you are about to lose your navigational equipment."

A more prolonged encounter with unusual vapors and fogs, with accompanying electromagnetic phenomena, did not result in fatal consequences due in part to the exceptionally experienced pilots. This was the flight of a restored Catalina PBY-6A flying boat, en route between Bermuda and Jacksonville, Florida, on June 11, 1986. One of the passengers, author Martin Caidin, an expert pilot and engineer, has a complete knowledge of every aspect of aviation and its history. He has been a test pilot, instructor, and investigator. Besides this, he has flown almost every type of aircraft in most every place on this globe and is intimately familiar with numerous and varied weather conditions. It is best to let him recount what happened, with all his candor and directness, as he described in his book *Ghosts of the Air*, a compendium of unexplained aviation stories.

Now the weather was perfect. We had range up the gazoo. We had a couple of million bucks worth of special avionics gear. . . . We wanted to know what the weather was like, we didn't even have to look outside, we were getting direct printout photos on maps from satellites more than 20,000 miles above. . . . One of those days when you could see forever.

The perfect weather disappeared . . . [we] could only see the nose right in front . . . the wingtips disappeared into what looked like the inside of a milk bottle. . . . Maybe it looked more like inside a batch of eggnog. You looked up, you saw a tiny patch of sky; everything else was yellow mud (or eggnog). You looked down, and you saw a tiny patch of ocean, and the rest, you guessed it, was eggnog.

. . . the magnetic compass began to rotate. It picked up speed and went whirling around as if it were a whirligig. We checked the photo printout from the weather satellite. . . . The metsat picture showed us in absolutely clear air. The nearest clouds were two hundred miles south of us.

But we couldn't see out the airplane. . . . just about that time the metsat print machine died. . . . The electronic innards of the Catalina, all two million clams worth, shriveled up inside. The LORAN went out. The electronic fuel gauges sogged to fuzzy markings. The long-numbered navigation gear [digital] read 888888888. The radios died. Everything still had power, but nothing worked. . . Why didn't we simply hold heading with the directional gyro? Because it was trying to imitate the magnetic compass. We went down low. You could see tiny details of spray, but not fifty feet ahead of us. We climbed up to 8,000 feet. Lots of eggnog up there too.

. . . About an hour out of Jacksonville we seemed to penetrate a curtain. Of an instant, no more eggnog. We could see forever and ever. The mag compass settled down. The directional gyro quit its foolishness and steadied. The electronics emerged from their funk, and everything worked perfectly.

The great aviator Charles Lindbergh was himself a victim of an unexplained haze and magnetic anomalies in the Triangle in 1928 while flying his famous *Spirit of St. Louis.* After a night departure from Havana, he headed northward into the Triangle. Shortly afterward, he noticed his compass begin to rock left to right and eventually it began to spin. His earth induction indicator (an early navigational instrument) began to wander and give unreliable readings. Shortly thereafter a haze enveloped his plane, preventing him from using any form of astral navigation. It was impossible to make out the sea below (and thereby tell by the whitecaps the direction and speed of the wind). When dawn finally broke, he noted the sky was a peculiar "dark milk." This continued for hours, and then the haze parted and disappeared and land came into view beneath him. At this same time, his navigational equipment returned to normal. Using his charts he was able to discern his position by the matching outline of the coastline. This, however, contributed to the mystery, since it proved he had gone farther than his fuel could have carried him. In his book, *Autobiography of Values,* in 1976 he first mentioned this incident. One might imagine because the Bermuda Triangle popularity at the time took some of the stigma off a pilot reporting the completely unexplained.

Weird navigational discrepancies that neither register to navigation equipment nor to pilots, but go hand-in-hand with time and distance discrepancies, have also been reported in the Triangle. Remember the case of the C-54 in 1947 that was never once on course, nor from the transmitted position reports did it seem apparent to its pilots. Alan Oneida, a retired Air Force electronics engineer and radar operator, experienced this same, though not fatal in his case, way of disappearing. It was back in 1980 when Oneida was radarman aboard an S3A on ferry flight from Bermuda to Jacksonville, Florida, along almost an identical course as the C-54. He recalls the Sun set when they were about 150 miles off the mainland. It was now dark, but the weather was perfect. Soon after, when they picked up the lights of the coast, the pilot initiated calls to Jacksonville Approach, all to no avail. "Finally one of the pilots excitedly exclaimed, 'We're over Miami, we are nowhere near our ADIZ (Air Defense Identification Zone) penetration area, the fighters could scramble on us.' "

Far outside of their radio sectors, they were incapable of contacting any base and informing them who they were. The pilot immediately commenced evasive maneuvers and dropped down to an altitude of 200 or 300 feet and then followed the coast up to Jacksonville until, at St. Augustine, they climbed once again and made contact. Oneida, however, recalls how close they were to being shot down (the Cold War was still "hot" in 1980) or, just as bad but a more mysterious fate, how close they were to missing the Florida mainland as a landmark altogether. "It is my contention that another 30–40 miles south of Miami and our crew would not have made it to Jacksonville. We had no idea we were off course. . . . We were 300 miles off course; that is a large deviation in my book, especially since Bermuda isn't all that far (about 700 miles)." Miami is, however, 1,000 miles from Bermuda. There is no explanation how the flight arrived on time at Miami yet was 300 miles beyond its course. One is tempted to feel, however, that the flight may have just skirted the phenomenon that had cost so many others their lives.

Everywhere along the Triangle evidence for electromagnetic phenomena is accumulating. Reports of ships disappearing from land-based or ship-based radar momentarily or for several hours before reappearing unharmed have persisted over the last twenty-five years. It is later discovered that the ship that had so mysteriously vanished was experiencing unexplained power drains at the precise time it was invisible to radar or to the searchers looking for it. As recently as May 23, 2002, the cruise ship *Destiny* lost almost all power while off the Leeward Islands en route from a Caribbean cruise to San Juan, Puerto Rico. According to one passenger,

Marsha Pilgeram, during this time it was impossible to contact any outside line or relay, cell phones were inoperable, and no electrical system would function, including elevators, air-conditioning, and navigational equipment, resulting in a completely stranded ship. When the Coast Guard was finally raised, the large cruise ship could not be found either by radar or by search craft, but drifted for eight hours completely disabled until power returned and it cruised to St. Lucia harbor. "After being in St. Lucia for 4½ hours longer than they said we would be there," she recalled, "a man boarded carrying a briefcase and a bag. As soon as he was on board we left. Someone said the Coast Guard was on board with us."

Further evidence of electromagnetic phenomena interfering with equipment is the continued and unreliable depth readings recorded by a number of ships. One such incident involved the Navy spy ship USS *Harkins* on a cruise through the Triangle north of Puerto Rico in 1972. When going east the vessel's depth recordings were 450 feet, but when returning along the same course only a day later, instruments indicated a depth of 1,700 feet. During this time one incident occurred that was particularly interesting. One of the new Bell helicopters carried on the vessel had just landed. After the helicopter crew disembarked, the chopper shuddered and split in half by about one inch apart along a jagged line from nose to tail. Navy engineers and the manufacturer's representatives waited for the ship to return to port, where the helicopter was unloaded—and no more was heard about that.

Unexplained magnetic anomalies seem strangely concentrated around Bimini Island in the Bahamas. One witness to these is author Dr. David Zink, who, during his protracted research and dives around Bimini studying its famous rock formations, began to note some recurrent and unexpected compass readings. "In 1975 at the same time of year [August], we had apparently experienced a 6-degree magnetic anomaly. What our findings meant so far was that, in addition to local charted 2 degree westerly variation, we had observed an additional 6-degree variation in August of 1975, and an additional 3 degree variation in August 1976." He added: "These observations added to my growing awareness of unexplained magnetic problems in the Bahamas."

There may be a simple reason why this sporadic phenomenon has not gained greater public recognition. Bill Keefe is a no-nonsense diver, with over eighteen years' experience in the Bimini area. He is also owner and operator of Bimini's only dive shop, Bimini UnderSea. He knows the seas around Bimini, literally from top to bottom. He notes that much of the navigating done by the local fishermen is point-of-sight, in which there is little need to refer to one's compass. Locals instantly know where they are by noting a familiar landmark on the horizon. He adds, however, that during his eighteen years on Bimini "There have been a number of times when we have looked at our compasses and noticed that they were pointing in the wrong direction. We jokingly say, 'Look, it's the Bermuda Triangle.' "

It is also possible, as Dr. Zink's observations imply, that such anomalies are prevalent only at certain times of the year. Perhaps somewhat tentatively linked to this phenomenon are the rashes of unexplained grounding of ships in the Bahamas and Florida Keys. In one week alone, three vessels went mysteriously off course and grounded on the same reef.

A possibility that these could be sideline events of acute electromagnetic aberrations occurring elsewhere is suggested by the intensity of the unexplained electromagnetic disruption experienced around Bimini by Bruce Davies, captain of the 26-foot *Grandpa's Toy*. While participating in the Bimini Extravaganza, a promotional boat race to Bimini sponsored by *Salt Water Sportsman* magazine, he was approaching Bimini on June 5, 1997, when all of his electronic and navigational equipment suddenly "fritzed" and he was unable to home in on the island. When he was finally able to get his VHF radio to work, he was eventually located and discovered to have overshot the island by 8 miles. He was escorted to Bimini by another boat where, upon arrival at the dock, all his equipment started working normally again. His pithy reaction is somewhat typical of those who sail the area, "The Bermuda Triangle did a number on us!"

For aircraft there appear to be levels of intensity to these moments, often when near unusual or isolated clouds or fogs. The compass seems the most easily affected. But if the encounter is more severe, the GPS will go out, as well as the radio. In grading these events one must consider the encounters where only the compass was affected to be a mild one, although those who have experienced it confide that this hardly diminishes the initial scare or the potential dangers of getting hopelessly lost.

Pilot David Angstrom's summation is perhaps the most concise of what every pilot has expressed. He was flying two friends (one of them new to flying) from Andros, Bahamas, to Miami in January 1996. When approaching Bimini a cloud "came out of nowhere." His compass started to spin and his RPMs dropped way off. "I basically almost shit my pants at this point, but there is no point being afraid. Besides, the new guy was in a right state by then." He was able to turn around and luckily found his way back to Andros.

Bruce Gernon's experience, involving the formation of a strange meteorological phenomenon, while passing Andros Island and approaching Bimini on December 4, 1970, is a graphic illustration of what might be termed a severe encounter with an unknown "electronic fog."

It was about 3 o'clock that afternoon and just after takeoff from Andros Island when Gernon, in company of his father Bruce Gernon Sr. and business associate Gus Lafayette, saw a lenticular (lens-shaped) cloud sitting very low over the ocean. They noticed it because it was lower than anything they had seen before, about 500 feet above the surface, Gernon estimated. Continuing his angle of ascent (about 1,000 feet a minute), they noticed that the lenticular cloud was undergoing a metamorphosis into a huge towering cumulus cloud, which seemed to be rising about as fast as they were. For a few minutes it engulfed the Bonanza until Gernon climbed atop it and entered clear skies at 11,500 feet altitude. Gernon, looking behind him, noticed that the cloud had built into an enormous squall, extending in the shape of a semicircle behind them. Shortly after this, they noticed another cloud building before them. When coming closer, they noticed that the cloud originated from the surface of the ocean, like the cloud they had left behind, but in this case it extended about 60,000 feet high. Gernon decided to fly around it. But after several miles they realized that it curved around them to the east. It was then they realized that this was the same cloud. Beyond their vision it had formed into a giant doughnut, extending around them. Gernon felt it must have had a 30-mile diameter, since visibility was about 10 miles that day and the clouds extended far beyond his view.

Gernon admits he felt as if he were hemmed in—the cloud was too high for his Bonanza to fly over, and it was impossible to descend to get under it. The doughnut-shaped cloud was continually constricting around them until it was now only about 4 to 5 miles interior diameter. Extraordinary bright white flashes burst about the inside of the cloud, and it grew increasingly darker.

Gernon takes up the narrative:

I noticed a large U-shaped opening on the west side of the doughnut cloud. I had no choice but to turn and try to exit through the opening. As we approached, we watched the top ends of the U-gap join, forming a hole. The break in the cloud now formed a perfect horizontal tunnel, one mile wide and more than 10 miles long. We could see the clear blue sky on the other side.

We also saw that the tunnel was rapidly shrinking. I increased the engine RPM, bringing our speed to the caution area of 230 miles per hour. When we entered the tunnel, its diameter had narrowed to only 200 feet.

I was amazed at what the shaft now looked like. It appeared to be only a mile long instead of 10-plus as I had originally estimated. Light from the afternoon sun shone through the exit hole and made the silky white walls glow. The walls were perfectly round and slowly constricting. All around the edges were small puffs of clouds of a contrasting gray, swirling counterclockwise around the airplane.

We were in the tunnel for only 20 seconds before we emerged from the other end. For about 5 seconds I had the strange feeling of weightlessness and an increased forward momentum. When I looked back, I gasped to see the tunnel walls collapse and form a slit that slowly rotated clockwise.

All of our electronic and magnetic navigational instruments were malfunctioning. The compass was slowly spinning even as the airplane flew straight. . . . Instead of the blue sky we expected, everything was a dull grayish white haze. Visibility seemed like more than 2 miles, yet we could not see the ocean, the horizon, or the sky. The air was very stable and there was no lightning or rain. I like to refer to this as an "electronic fog," because it seemed to be what was interfering with our instruments. . . . We were in the electronic fog for 3 minutes when the controller radioed that he had identified an airplane directly over Miami Beach, flying due west. I looked at my watch and saw that we had been flying for less than 34 minutes. We could not have reached Miami Beach—we should have been approaching the Bimini Islands. I told the controller that he must have identified another airplane and that we were approximately 90 miles southwest of Miami and still looking for Bimini.

Suddenly the fog started breaking apart, in a weird sort of electronic fashion. Long horizontal lines appeared in the fog on either side of us. The lines widened into slits about 4 or 5 miles long. We saw blue sky through them. The slits continued expanding and joined together. Within 8 seconds, all the slits had joined, and the gray fog had disappeared. All I could see was brilliant blue sky as my pupils adjusted to the abrupt increase in brightness. Then, I saw the barrier island of Miami Beach directly below.

Both fascinated and bewildered by his experience, he began to do some math. He checked his watch. He had been in flight only 47 minutes. Yet the course must have been at least 250 miles. There was no way he could have traveled it so fast. "I could not logically understand what had happened during the flight, although I felt it was significant and reviewed it in my mind several times a day."

He heard about the Bermuda Triangle in 1972 and about the theories of time warps causing some to disappear. "It was then that I realized time was the key. It should have taken about 4 minutes to travel through the tunnel, since it appeared to be between 10 and 15 miles long. Instead, this is precisely how long it took for us to leave the storm and reach clear skies. The remarkable thing is that we did not come out of the storm 90 miles away from Miami as we should have. . . . We had traveled through 100 miles of space and 30 minutes of time in a little more than 3 minutes."

Question: Did you notice any blue-green glowing phosphorescence before, during, or after your experience?

I didn't notice any colors other than shades of gray. It was the color of fog; that is one of the reasons I call it Electronic Fog.

Question: Was any turbulence associated with your experience?

I did notice some turbulence related to the fog. When my airplane reached the end of the tunnel and made its exit from the storm, I felt the sensation of zero gravity. I also felt as if we were being given a boost in forward momentum. At the same time and length of this feeling, contrails formed on the edges of the wingtips for about 10 seconds.

It was at this point the electronic fog attached itself to the airplane. I believe the airplane was flying in clear weather but it appeared to be IMC [Instrumental Meteorological Conditions] because the fog was attached to the airplane. In other words, I wasn't flying through the fog, I was flying with the fog. It takes a different perspective of the mind for a pilot to realize this, and this could be the reason for a pilot to become immediately spatially disoriented.

While most pilots and ship captains are resigned to accepting their encounters as unexplained and sudden events, over the last thirty years Gernon has continued to puzzle over what happened to him. His studies have led him to the conclusion that after the storm has dissipated, the electronic fog is capable of drifting around for many hours.

In developing this possibility, many, but perhaps not all, of the encounters in the Bermuda Triangle with unexplained fogs and electromagnetic anomalies might have occurred in the aftermath of this type of meteorological formation. But considering the excitement many have expressed over the sudden appearance of these "electronic fogs" out of nowhere, they seem to form randomly and dissipate just as quickly without building any storms.

Gernon, having considered what happened to him, has been very alert when traveling the areas of the Bermuda Triangle thereafter. He has built up thousands of flying hours' experience in the area. He is an excellent *in situ* observer, with a keen eye for detail and an excellent memory for recall.

On a number of occasions he has noted other phenomena. About three months later, he observed a "UFO" speeding at him. He recalls a peculiar coincidence between it and his previous unexplained experience.

We were flying at night about 9:30 P.M. in February and the weather was CAVU [ceiling and visibility unlimited]. We were over Miami at 10,000 and headed due east toward Bimini. When we got a few miles offshore we noticed an amber light far to the east of us. Suddenly it came toward us at an incredible speed. It was on a collision course with us and within seconds it was right in front of us. It was bright amber and shaped like a saucer with a diameter of about 300 feet. It was massive and I felt that its mass was of a solid nature and not just a form of light. I banked to the left to avoid a certain collision. When I looked back to see where it was, it had vanished. It may have been an illusion—although we both saw the exact same thing. It is interesting to note that the UFO was on the same flight path that I had traveled when I went through the time tunnel and encountered the electronic fog.

UFOs and USOs are frequently seen in the Bimini area and in other areas of the Bermuda Triangle. Dr. J. Manson Valentine, retired professor of oceanography at the University of Miami, cataloged many of these during his near fifty years of zoological and oceanographic work in the waters of the Triangle. He observed: "There are more sightings in this area than at any other place. There have been many sightings of aircraft that we know are not planes and undersea craft that we know are not regular submarines."

In collating dozens of UFO/USO reports in the Triangle, Dr. Valentine has noted how localized fogs and electromagnetic anomalies seem to go hand in hand with their arrivals and departures. At normal cruising or hovering, however, they appear merely as unidentified objects or glowing lights. The shape of a USO is usually described as more oblong than a saucer, many times 100 or 200 feet long (this last feature was also noted in the area of "water discoloration" after the Phantom II disappeared in 1971), but they display abilities none of our submarines are capable of.

Examples of Valentine's data include the following account related to him by Robert Kunhe, a part-time fisherman in Miami. While a few miles off Fowey Rock, Key Biscayne, in May 1975, he noticed a massive gray-white object beneath his boat that looked like an underwater cloud. Its presence "fritzed" his depth-finder and sonar, and he decided to get out of the area quickly. Another encounter with a similar USO was experienced by fisherman Don Delmonico in April 1973 near Great Isaac Rock, near Bimini. The object was light gray, about 100 to 200 feet long, and seemed to be smooth, without fins, portholes, elevators, superstructure, or any type of propulsion. It raced underneath his 35-foot boat, traveling about 75 miles per hour. In assessing such cases, Dr. Valentine has offered that these may not be objects at all but magnetic fields forming underwater, intense enough to create cloudlike formations caused by the actual object materializing or disturbing the magnetic field before it does materialize.

UFOs and USOs are often seen around the Tongue of the Ocean or areas of "drop-off," the colloquialism for the places where the shallow banks suddenly drop off to the deep blue abyssal depths. They seem oddly concentrated around Bimini, reported mostly around Great Isaac Shoals north of Bimini or south at Moselle Reef, although Bimini's ever redoubtable fishermen are more than ready to ad-lib some good stories.

An encounter at Bimini by two members of the oceanographic crew of the *New Freedom* is, however, an unimpeachable account of a UFO at hovering or normal cruising. This was seen during a stroll along the beach after dinner on a very starlit night, August 2, 1975. Dr. Jim Thorne, its expedition leader and chief eyewitness, made the following report to Dr. Valentine:

> A single star seemed to detach itself from the others and come towards us. It hovered directly above us and then moved to the right. It maneuvered first to the right, then to the left, and back again. It appeared to stop dead in the sky and hover over different parts of the island and sea around it. I would calculate its speed at several thousand miles per hour. It seemed to be a bluish-white and also to vibrate. At times we thought we heard a buzzing sound or, rather, a steady oscillation of sound. We observed it for a full 3 1/2 minutes. It was close enough for us to see its shape. When it got close I saw it was lighted with blue-white lights. It started away very fast.

Unusual lights in the sky dematerializing or materializing in association with strange atmospheric clouds and vapors continue to be reported in the area of the Bermuda Triangle. The experience of two boaters, Paul Vance and Doug Gerdon, on June 25, 2001, happened while cruising to the Bahamas from West Palm Beach, Florida, on Vance's 26-foot sailboat *Rare Form*. Vance, a commercial pilot, is particularly qualified to identify size, distance, and speed of anything in the atmosphere. He reported what he saw in a pilot's cool and spontaneous reportorial style.

Eleven miles offshore I looked up in the sky to the northeast and witnessed something strange. There was a single light—I'm guessing about 3 to 5 thousand feet in altitude—which I assumed to be an aircraft with its landing light on although not very brilliant. The light then appeared to turn downward which then made me think it may be a helicopter with a searchlight, although again it wasn't a brilliant light. A swirling mist then engulfed the light as the light slowly drifted down into the mist. The whole mass of mist then glowed a short time and then dissipated along with the light. Stars could then be seen and the sky was clear. This happened at 9:30 P.M. EST, and my friend witnessed it too and tried to videotape it but the boat was pitching too much to get anything.

Questions: What color was the light? Did it disappear as though it landed? Did you hear any noise in the sky? Was the Moon about to rise?

The light was white. It didn't disappear as though it landed because the swirling mist didn't extend to the ocean surface. Our engine was running so if it made any noise we probably couldn't hear it. The moon was already up at about 70° toward the south. The feeling I got was that the light appeared, waited a moment until the swirling mist began beneath it, and then it descended through the mist tunnel and disappeared. It's like the mist was a door.

It is best to let Vance elaborate on the sighting, as noted in subsequent conversations.

The light turned downward and descended into the swirling cloud, making the whole cloud glow. When the cloud dissipated the glow dissipated with it. It was a single white light. I'm a licensed commercial pilot with an instrument rating so I know what planes look like at night. My common sense tells me it was atmospheric, but it sure looked like it was passing through a passage. The weather was CAVU with a puff of cloud here and there. Wind was light from the east. We don't know what we saw but both agreed it lasted 2 to 3 minutes.

Question: Did you notice any changes or deviations with your compass, navigational equipment or motor?

The motor lost power at the same time we saw the light. It didn't quit; the rpms dropped way off and it ran rough. We were so amazed at what we were seeing, though, we hardly took note of the engine. The wind was out of the east so we had to sail back to West Palm and never made it to the Bahamas. The next morning we were swimming off the boat and noticed a lot of black soot around the exhaust and I immediately suspected the fuel pump diaphragm as the problem. After getting back to Indiana, I began checking out the engine and found the FPD to be OK. Upon checking the ignition system, I discovered a cracked coil. The coil would barely jump the spark plug in open air so I doubt that it would fire much under cylinder pressure. I didn't mention the engine before because it never got better after the sighting so I didn't possibly see how the crack could be related. I'll have to admit though, when the engine faltered and I saw that swirling mist, I thought to myself, "My God, there's something to this Bermuda Triangle stuff!"

A recent UFO encounter involved the cruise ship *Celebrity* when four passengers stargazing for constellations were surprised when one of the "stars" started to move, much as in Dr. Thorne's encounter. The incident took place on October 11, 2001, between 12 and 1 A.M. The ship was a day out of Nassau, near Bimini, en route to Miami. The sky was clear and the stars were shining brightly. The object began to circle, moving alternately in clockwise and counterclockwise motions. After 15 minutes of this, it started to home in on the ship, in a maneuver that might be regarded as reconnoitering. "All movements were very deliberate and were not haphazard." Three rows of lights in the form of a triangle became visible on its underside, and they strobed, blue, white, red, green. The exact shape of the object could not be distinguished beyond these under-carriage lights. It then recessed to the point of looking like a star again. Although preferring to remain anonymous in any forum related to the Bermuda Triangle, two of the witnesses (a corporate attorney and his wife, a doctoral student in health) did report it to the ship's personnel at the reception desk and were assured by a purser that a crew member would be sent out to verify it. "Her reaction led us to believe that they get such reports often."

At the opposite end of the spectrum is Columbus in the early hours of another October 11 long ago. He is, without doubt, the first person to record unusual phenomena and a strange light associated with those seas we today call the Bermuda Triangle. His logbook speaks in an impressive way over the vault of time, along similar lines with affidavits of more recent explorers and sailors. During his first voyage to the New World, no less than five times he recorded unexplained phenomena, thrice involving the compass, once involving the sea, and once involving an unexplained faint light rising up and hovering in the distance. Although his log was eventually lost to posterity, much of its annotations and entries were preserved by Fray Bartolomé de Las Casas in his *Diario:*

Thursday 13 September 1492

On this day at the beginning of night the compasses northwested and in the morning they northeasted somewhat.

Monday September 17

The pilots took the north [North Star]; marking it, they found that the compasses northwested a full point [11¼ degrees]; and the sailors were fearful and melancholy and did not say why. The Admiral [Columbus] was aware of this and he ordered that the north be marked again when dawn came, and they found that the compasses were correct. The cause was because the North Star appears to move and not the compasses.

Sunday 23 September

Because the sea had been calm and smooth the men complained, saying that since in that region there were no rough seas [Sargasso Sea], it would never blow for a return to Spain. But later the sea rose high and without wind, which astonished them. . . .

Sunday, 30 September

The Admiral says here when night comes the compasses northwest one quarter, and when dawn comes they align with the [North] Star exactly.

The unexplained light, rising and then hovering in the west, is perhaps the most propitious phenomenon recorded in the Triangle. It happened on the eve of discovering the New World, and it inspired Columbus and his crew to sail on and discover the Bahamas. Columbus saw it first, then Pero Gutiérrez, then "After the Admiral said it, it was seen once or twice; and it was as a small wax candle that arose and lifted up." What both *arose* (alçava) and *lifted up* (Levatava) imply is hard to say—whether it means it rose up, hovered, and then disappeared upward or merely vanished while levitating is unclear. Today, it is hard for landfall specialists to explain it, since Columbus was too far at sea to have seen any bonfire or torch on land, and local island fishermen would not have been so far at sea at night with torches to attract catch.

Scholarly debate has subsequently offered to explain the erratic compass readings by the apparent revolution of Polaris around the celestial pole, an optical effect for an observer, although this is only visual and not something mechanical that comes and goes. Aside from this, it has also been suggested that the dusk and dawn readings varied because during the evening readings a crewman unwittingly placed the compass too near a bucket of nails, a sword, or some other metal object, which then deflected it.

Whatever the cause, Columbus may be pardoned for his necessarily expeditious explanations for these encounters, knowing how a crew can panic when faced with the unexplained. Whether Columbus believed his story or not or whether he was simply trying to keep his crew calm and protect his venture (and life) is another conjecture altogether. It was easier to say Polaris moved than to admit their equipment was ceasing to work; that, in essence, the rules that had always governed navigation and seamanship had ceased to operate in a normal, predictable way.

A similar motive may be responsible, though innocently, for our own tidy explanations for the unexplained events so often reported in the Bermuda Triangle. It is perhaps easier to blame our equipment or ourselves when we find ourselves on unfamiliar ground than it is to admit there may be something beyond our own present knowledge or control.

It is for those who believe these accounts are not so easily dismissed to draw parallels between them and the many cases of planes and ships that simply vanished in fair weather, some in very unusual circumstances, some, indeed, in unbelievable circumstances. Even the Coast Guard allows an "open forum" by noting in their chit's bibliography the work of other writers, including Vincent Gaddis. The simplest solutions, however, continue to be promoted by both the Coast Guard and Lloyd's of London, agencies that are naturally not eager to promote mysteries and that endorse enthusiastically any theory that seems the most conventional and readily understandable.

But an open forum sweeps into the door some refreshing debate, none of which is allowed in official investigation. The evidence that "believers" in the Triangle present for their theories is often very impressive, many times more impressive, and sometimes embarrassingly more impressive than dry facts accumulated by the limitations of official inquiry. The disappearance of planes while coming in for a landing; radio calls from planes long vanished and long out of fuel; reports of "weird objects" harassing planes; plus the pattern of electromagnetic disturbances reported by many who survived unusual events, form a springboard into a pool of fascinating and disturbing conjectures. Scientists and researchers into geophysical data and those involved in the search for new forms of energy, plus many pertinacious observers *in situ* in the Bermuda Triangle, have compiled data individually that, when placed together in a broader perspective, may provide a startling solution to some of the mystery.

To understand how an object can disappear we must look at the very foundation of operating systems, at forces that are themselves invisible.

6

Space-Time Vortices, Zero-Point, and Sunken Worlds

THOSE WHO SAY that the Bermuda Triangle is not unique are, in one sense, correct in that disappearances do happen in other parts of the world. This, however, does not imply an even spread to these disappearances over the Earth's oceans. Ships and planes travel all over the seas, with accidents happening anywhere. Disappearances, on the other hand, seem to happen more frequently in groupings, such as the Great Lakes of the United States and Canada and the seas off Japan, between the Mariana Islands and the East China Sea.

This last area is the only other place to achieve special recognition like the Bermuda Triangle, inasmuch as Japanese seamen have long dubbed it the Devil's Sea because of its history of unexplained disappearances and unusual events. Also, in the 1950s the Japanese government declared the area dangerous because of its unpredictable volcanic activity. This activity may explain some of the electromagnetic disturbances of compasses, loran, and other electronic equipment also reported here, as well as some disappearances from huge and sudden displaced seas swamping a vessel before it can get off an SOS.

But the so-called Devil's Sea also shares another interesting coincidence with the Bermuda Triangle: it is located on the exact opposite side of the Earth and between the same latitudes of 20 to 30 degrees North. But while this similarity is of apparent interest, it is not half as piquing as its *dissimilarities*. These include the lack of treacherous currents over the shallow banks of the Bahamas and the lack of strong Gulf Stream currents—factors for which disappearances are so mundanely blamed in the Triangle are *completely absent* off Japan.

Nevertheless, disappearances are not only frequent in the Devil's Sea, but some have been singularly spectacular. The most recent cases have included the Japanese fishing vessel *Dairyu Maru No. 3,* which disappeared with fifteen crew February 14, 1992. The large freighter *Vast Ocean* last reported itself off the Japanese island of Kyushu almost exactly one year later, on February 15, 1993, and was never heard from thereafter. On November 21, 1995, the *Alkashem* last reported herself approaching this area en route for Onahama, Japan, and disappeared without trace. The *Yuko Maru No. 8,* carrying twenty-five tons of fish, was found derelict off Japan on January 7, 1992, smoldering between her deckhouse and stern. No trace of any of her crew was found, nor exactly how they left the ship. Most recently, the 23,000-ton *Honghae Sanyo,* with twenty-eight crew, on April 11, 2001, sent off a Mayday similar in some respects to those in the Bermuda Triangle, saying that a strong wind had suddenly hit it. It was southeast of Japan at the time. No further messages were received. When a search was mounted, only her empty lifeboats were found. Later one body was located and patches of oil were sighted rising up from beneath the sea. There is nothing readily available to blame, since tumultuous seas are absent. Piracy is often rampant in the Orient, though usually closer to China, in the South China Sea, in the Straits of Malacca, and off the Malay Peninsula.

In general, no particular kind of vessel seems prone to disappear. The dominant type of traffic through an area seems to be the victim, no matter what it is, whether huge merchant ships or daily charters, a fact underlined by the other area of mystery, the Great Lakes, where there are certainly no strong currents or pirates or volcanoes.

From 1964 to the present, about thirty private and charter aircraft have disappeared while navigating over the Great Lakes. Accident records for the bordering states of Michigan, Wisconsin, Illinois, and Ohio do not reveal statistical similarities for sudden loss, that is, involving planes that plummeted to the ground before a Mayday could be sent—the scenario one must assume happened over the Great Lakes, the only difference being that the waters cover any remains. Most of the accidents in these states happened during landing or takeoff, often in the winter when drifting snowbanks and flurries can confuse a pilot. Since landing and takeoff maneuvers are not done over the lakes, the disappearances in flight over the water stand out as even more disproportionate.

Considering the many dissimilarities between these areas, several independent researchers have used a process of elimination to uncover any underlying thread, a process that has led them all to one common denominator—strong geomagnetic lines. This coincidence raises the question about the potential of this force field.

Magnetic field readouts are the oldest scrutinized geophysical data available. Their strength, vagaries, and anomalies have been studied for the past century and a half. Nevertheless, repeat readings and tests continue to offer puzzling and conflicting results, leaving us with an unstable foundation for even interpreting its potential. Our inability even to crack the shell of its origin still elicits qualified opinions similar to those expressed by Dr. J. Manson Valentine: "To begin with, it happens to be the only inanimate phenomenon for which we have been unable to conceive a mechanistic analogue. We can visualize electrons traveling along a conductor and thus 'explain' electric current, or we can envisage energy waves of different frequencies in the ether and thus 'explain' the heat-light-ratio spectrum. But a magnetic field defies a mechanical interpretation. There is something almost mystical about it."

The association of this still mysterious force field with an even more mysterious force—Time itself—opens the door on some intriguing theories on time warps. The possibility of space-time warps is gaining greater recognition in scientific nomenclature, not only as a model but as theoretical science. Time's association with magnetism and gravity is vital to Einstein's Theory of Relativity, which regards gravity not as a force but as a curvature of space near a massive object. Einstein predicted that even light, itself an electromagnetic wavelength, which traditionally follows straight lines, would bend while traveling through curved space (this was empirically observed when Sir Arthur Eddington detected a change in a star's position during a total eclipse in 1919). General Relativity went on to predict that gravity also distorts time. This was later confirmed by extremely accurate atomic clocks ticking a few microseconds per year faster at high altitudes where the Earth's gravity is weaker.

However, in our experience thus far, these vagaries seem only minute, as minute as the temperature changes on a spring day or in the slightly shifting breeze in the dead of summer: an atomic clock records Time passing faster in less gravity; an object falls faster at the Poles than at the Equator. But nature is subject to violent shifts: a summer breeze to a strong foehn, a bright spring day to a sudden thunderstorm, a calm morning obliterated by a tornado into which everything in the surrounding atmosphere is drawn into its vortex. Are magnetism and gravity subject to the same tumults, the changing of the subtle variations into sudden and terrifying aberrations?

Places characterized both by concentrations of disappearances and by the persistence of unexplained electromagnetic (EM) field anomalies raise the possibility that these areas may contain transient magnetic vortices capable of warping gravity locally and in turn even space or time itself. Ships and planes traveling through or near one of these vortices at the right moment (or wrong moment, according to your point of view) might simply disappear by being held in time.

An appreciation of this possibility can be had from the generally accepted geophysical theory that magnetic vortices do swirl into and out of existence within the body of the Earth, caused by factors of rotation and possible shifts of the mantle disturbing the generation of the field. Considering that this same incline is key to the wide array of weather fluctuations on the surface may help us to envision how certain areas of the Earth, like the Triangle, may likewise be prone to magnetic vortices extending to its surface while others are not, just as these same factors contribute to tornadoes and cyclones—very visible atmospheric vortices— to swirling into existence only along the same latitudes, with great ferocity, but in others are nonexistent or freak events.

The greatest mysteries like Time, however, are not found in the minutiae of scientific hairsplitting, but are often found in those things we take for granted, things so omnipresent they are rendered invisible. For instance, we often erroneously think that we live in three dimensions of space and therefore we are confused about where to place the domain of time. In fact, we *occupy* three dimensions of space, but we *live* in the fourth dimension of time. We do not often consider that we *are* traveling in time and that there may be varying rates of progression of time depending on the strength of the curvature of space. By its mass and velocity through space, the Earth *is* curving space around it and thereby slowing time fractionally within its gravitational field, as opposed to its orbital heights. It stands to reason that the same effect can be created or intensified by the action of a vortex, itself a smaller version of the great rotating orb of the Earth and therefore capable of infinitely faster speeds and with this a greater potential to bend space and then slow time within its clutches.

This is predicated on the belief that the spinning nature of a vortex is the most essential for creating a "torsion field" around it. If strong enough, the "torsion field" becomes, in a highly anodyne sense, a vacuum that could be capable of bending space and thereby redirecting all the frequencies in a local place, drawing them into a different curvature of space than they would normally take. Since we see along electromagnetic wavelengths, the vortex would be invisible, and any aircraft or ship coming within its field would presumably suddenly vanish, just as in the case of a mirage, itself the result of fractionally bending space.

We must remember that everything is in vortex kinesis. The effect of energy is to cause rotation: from the largest galaxies to the tiniest building blocks of matter—the nuclei of atoms rotate on their axis and the electrons revolve at tremendous speeds around them. To create a dangerous vortex is merely to intensify the natural action of energy. It is now understood that the atom, of which *all matter* is composed, is essentially electric in nature.

However esoteric this may sound, the atomic age has given us a very real understanding of the possibilities of a magnetic vortex. There are a little over a hundred atoms in the universe that we know of, which make up the structure of all matter. The building blocks of the atom are the charged particles protons and electrons. Any atom consists of a nucleus that holds an equal number of protons as there are electrons in orbit around it. The simplest, hydrogen, is a nucleus with one proton inside and one electron in orbit. The next is helium with two protons in the nucleus and two electrons in orbit. An atom with three protons in the nucleus and three electrons in orbit is not a gas anymore; it is the silver-white metal lithium. An atom that has eight, although a heavier atom, is once again a gas—oxygen. Lead, a heavy metal, has eighty-two; but radon, which is heavier, is nevertheless a gas again; it has eighty-six. The point is clear: they are all protons; they are all electrons; one atom is no different than the other except in number. Therefore the structure of all matter must be the energy the varying numbers generate and the fields the different numbers create, and by their positions interlock, bend, divert, or whatever, not in the basic makeup of the particles.

When director of the Moody Institute of Science, Dr. Irwin A. Moon once observed that the appearance of the atom is that of a mini-solar system, most of it space. All this space is the electromagnetic energy between these charged particles that bind substance together. He added: "Take away the space from matter and all you have left are particles so tiny as to be invisible even under the most high-powered microscope."

Phenomenal examples exist within our own scientific reference of deadly and destructive energy being made to pass through mass (a denser form of energy) without affecting it adversely by simply changing its frequency—in other words pass an electric current (electron particles) through a body (made up of molecules, a combination of atoms). For instance, it is a fact that 1 million volts of high-frequency electricity at 60 cycles alternating current will be instantly fatal to a human being, but 1 million volts at 65,000 cycles can be channeled through the body

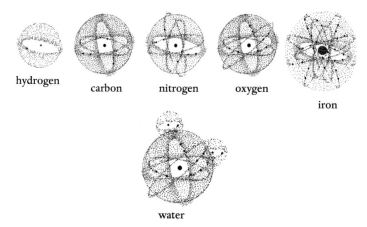

hydrogen carbon nitrogen oxygen

iron

water

Reality. The atomic structures of five common elements: hydrogen; carbon; nitrogen; oxygen; iron. All atoms are made of protons, electrons, and neutrons (except hydrogen, which has no neutron). Protons and neutrons (nucleons) rotate within the nucleus, while electrons orbit the nucleus at tremendous speeds. No matter what anything looks like, everything in the universe is made up of a combination of these three charged particles. In relation to the galaxy and the universe our solar system can be viewed as one atom within the greater "molecule" of all creation. What greater electromagnetic energy exists throughout all space and "matter" for an infinite potential of effects, for communication, travel, time, and being? Manipulation of electromagnetic energy is limitless power.

and discharged out the fingertips like lightning if metal thimbles are provided as a point of discharge. In essence, an individual may, at the right frequency, channel through the body trillions of the same particles that together compose the most impregnable bulwarks.

Noting this, Dr. Moon directs our attention to the fact that it is not the particles in atoms that prevent us from walking through a wall, but the mutually interactive frequencies of forces between the wall's particles and ours. If an entirely undetectable spectrum of electromagnetic frequencies exists, then: "It is within the realm of scientific possibility that there could be two worlds, coexistent, occupying the same part of space at the same moment of time, each world just as real as the other, with its mountains, valleys, rivers, trees and people, and that each world could pass freely through the other world without being conscious of the existence of the other world if you grant just one thing: atomic forces within the material substances of these two worlds which are not mutually interactive."

The idea of a space warp and coexistent worlds, as envisioned above, might be easier to imagine if using a spectrum or hologram card as an analogy. Retuning the electromagnetic frequencies may be like turning the spectrum or adjusting the card and seeing a different image—no mass or space has changed, but light now brings to our eyes a whole different realm.

Providing what is perhaps a logical extreme, Dr. Valentine further offers: "It is therefore reasonable to suppose that a genesis of unusual magnetic conditions could effect a change of phase in matter, both physical and vital. If so it would also distort the time element which is by no means an independent entity. . . . Like a tornado, the magnetic vortex would be self-augmenting and could well bring about an interdimensional transition for anyone caught up in it."

Recent breakthroughs testify to the remarkable power even a weak magnetic vortex has on the mystery of gravity and therefore possibly on different curvatures of space and electromagnetism. A 12-inch-diameter device invented by Russian scientist Dr. Evgeny Podkletnov in 1996 at Tampere University laboratories in Finland appears to have unexpectedly nullified gravity. The circular device was a doughnut-shaped ceramic superconductor ring placed over solenoids to levitate it magnetically and start it spinning. The ring was encased in an outer steel casing which contained liquid nitrogen to cool the ring as it spun.

Although the purpose of the test was not "antigravity," this effect, or more correctly "gravity shielding" as Dr. Podkletnov prefers to put it, was noticed when an assistant's pipe smoke drifted over the operating device and straightaway rose to the ceiling, where it hovered. When the ring was made to spin at 5,000 rpm, objects suspended over the device lost a percentage of their weight. When Dr. Podkletnov tested the area directly above the device, even to the top floor of the building, he discovered a circular funnel 12 inches in diameter of less gravity that went through all floors and perhaps then extended upward into space.

Wilbert B. Smith, a Canadian physicist, discovered something that could be considered a natural counterpart to Dr. Podkletnov's gravity-shielding funnel. His global surveys with Project Magnet in the 1950s discovered similar funnels measuring about 1,000 feet in diameter, extending from the ocean surface to very high altitudes, wherein the magnetic and gravitational readings gave indication of less attraction to the Earth. He referred to these mysterious funnels as areas of "reduced binding," and noted that they were far more common and pronounced in southerly latitudes like the Triangle.

Like an invisible tornado, these areas moved or disappeared. "When we looked for some of them a few months later, we could find no trace." Commenting on the degrees of intensity of these "holes in the sky,"

Smith reported: "Some planes, of course, would not be affected by the conditions, others might fly to pieces in a storm of turbulence."

The varying intensity of these areas might suggest they are indeed magnetic vortices. The intensifying factor could be from subsolar storms, in which the Earth and the Triangle in particular are being bombarded by charged particles. These particles would be attracted to the magnetism of the vortex and then turn it into a vortex of charged particles, perhaps even until it becomes a visible atmospheric phenomenon like an "electronic" spiraling cloud.

Detection of spiraling clouds on September 26, 2001, after a subsolar storm, was enough to cause NASA to postpone a launch. Photographs taken of the clouds captured a telltale clue. They had long whorls—corkscrew tails—created by the charged particles spiraling around the lines of force of the magnetic field.

This bears a remarkable resemblance to Bruce Gernon's description of the sudden formation of a lenticular cloud and then the formation of a vortex within this cloud through which he exited. It is possible that this cloud contained charged particles. As a matter of interest, he was flying in the direction of the magnetic field's lines of force, and this tunnel opened up along this same path.

This "tunnel" sounds more or less like a natural horizontal counterpart to Dr. Podkletnov's magnetic vortex. Gernon even reported a sensation of zero gravity. Perhaps this could have prevented him from detecting any g-forces caused by a hyperacceleration this "magnetic tunnel" would have given a speeding airplane, much like the smoke that zoomed to the ceiling in Podkletnov's lab. If so, this also would explain how he could have covered so much distance in less time and without expending the required fuel. However, this meteorological formation did not extend near where Gernon emerged from his "electronic fog." This once again raises the confusing conjectures about magnetic vortices and curvature of space and time.

Perhaps more than anyone else, Ivan Sanderson associated swirling ocean currents and their patterns with a catalyst for possible "vile vortices" in the world. Studying disappearances around the world revealed they recurred in roughly lozenge-shaped areas, tilted to the right, the most volatile to the east of continents. Plotting these areas on a globe revealed a curious discovery: the areas were at precisely 72-degree intervals, latitudinally. The total number of areas also was interesting. There were no fewer than twelve areas or vortices—five in the Northern Hemisphere and five in the Southern—with the Bermuda Triangle and the Devil's Sea coincid-

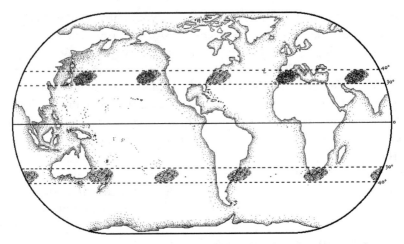

Sanderson's concept of areas prone to natural vortices based on the strong swirling currents and the sharp contrasting temperatures. He attributes the prevalence of anomalies in the Triangle to the fact that it is more heavily traveled.

ing mathematically as two of the vortices, and with one each at the Poles.

Each area shared strong, swirling currents colliding tangentially, which, according to Sanderson, were "all precisely in curious areas where hot surface currents stream out of the tropical latitudes toward the colder waters of the temperate. These are the areas of extreme temperature variabilities which alone would predicate a very high incidence of violent marine and aerial disturbances. What more likely areas for storms and wrecks and founderings, and even magnetic anomalies?"

He offers an intriguing supposition that the plane or vessel might be the catalyst for these anomalies if they "just happened to lock into a phase with some natural frequency over the area in which they were flying—say a vortex caused by a cold whirlpool of lower air over a hot sea surface—to produce something quite else which happened to be the trigger which set off other natural procedures in that area." Since "every tiny bit of our universe," this planet, "we and all other life forms are essentially electrical devices," he rhetorically asks: "What could not happen?"

An answer may come from a surprising source. Unusual and hitherto "impossible" phenomena have been generated by lay scientist John Hutchison in his Hutchison Effect, with startling ramifications. A consideration of his discoveries, authenticated by videotape, film, and personally observed by several accredited scientists, aspects of which were then independently duplicated, is in order.

Hutchison might be described as the proverbial boy tinkerer. Since his childhood he has experimented with electromagnetism and electrical induction. He stumbled onto his "effect" in 1979 when he was attempting to study the longitudinal wavelengths of Nikola Tesla (an electrical and radio waves pioneer). Limited by space in his Vancouver home, he crammed into one room a variety of devices that emit electromagnetic fields, such as Tesla coils, Van de Graaff generators, radio frequency (RF) transmitters, signal generators, and others. When he turned them on, over a period of time things began to happen. While he was working on his equipment something hit him in the shoulder—an object he wasn't expecting because it was actually levitating! With further experimentation he has produced a number of astonishing effects.

Videotape captured a nineteen-pound bronze cylinder rising grandly into the air. This fact was not only surprising, to say the least, but the distance it rose was extraordinary: some 80 feet from the center of the "device"—that is, all the various equipment he had assembled. More inexplicable still, this marvel was achieved, as its creator admits, with only "110 volts AC."

Wood, plastic, copper, zinc, Styrofoam, rubber, and even a sixty-pound cannon ball have all levitated. Objects have suddenly appeared and disappeared, and water (or any liquid) in buckets, containers, or even drinking glasses has spontaneously swirled (mild vortex kinesis), and corona manifestations (exotic lights) have filled the lab.

The antigravity effects are not limited to mere hovering, as noted by electromagnetic researcher Albert Budden:

The Hutchison device produces effects which can basically be divided into two categories, propulsive and energetic. It can induce lift in objects made of any material and also propel them laterally. It has been noted that there are four types of trajectory that affect objects weighing a few pounds, and all of these upward movements begin with a twisting spiral movement. Also, there has to be a particular geometry in relation to the direction of gravity, i.e., downwards of these objects, for them to be affected in this way. Some objects will not take off if you turn them on their sides, but will if you stand them on their ends. It is evident, therefore, that the relationship of their physical forms to the fields which swirl invisibly around them is important.

Hutchison's work has been subject to broad though varying degrees of interest and approval over the last twenty-two years. Three nations have aired his work; he was courted by scientists in Japan; he was accused of treason in Canada when he went to Germany for funds to continue; his laboratory was ransacked by Canadian officials who seized his equipment under the pretense of confiscating his antique gun collection, which was, however, later returned with no explanations or charges. Los Alamos National Laboratory has done research on the Hutchison Effect; in 1990 once again the Canadian government seized his crated lab equipment while in transit to Germany (and never returned it despite a court order) when he was seeking financial aid to continue his studies; the military of Canada and the United States have expressed a covert interest; he regularly receives Christmas cards from the White House; he has been arrested by the Canadian government and handcuffed on his doorstep while his lab was ransacked and investigated again (under the excuse of checking his antique gun collection again). This last incident was March 17, 2000, and may have been instigated by a neighbor who complained to the police after he thought he might have experienced an unexpected levitation.

Because of all this, which has been ongoing for more than twenty-three years, Hutchison's lab has undergone numerous changes, from completely disappearing into government hands to vital pieces having been sold off later because of financial problems.

Nevertheless, Hutchison has continued his work. He has tinkered with and adjusted his equipment and continues to get varying and remarkable results, many of which have been documented and photographed by McDonnell Douglas Aerospace and the Max Planck Institute in Germany.

Some of these results give us an alarming view of the potentiality of electromagnetic effects on matter, its destruction, and transmutation. Metal turns white hot (but does not burn surrounding flammable material), 1-inch metal bars split, shred at the fracture point, wriggle like a worm, and flutter like a rag in the wind; fires start around the building out of nonflammable materials like cement and rock; metal warps and bends and even breaks (separating by sliding in a sideways fashion), and in some instances it crumbles like cookies.

Perhaps no other scientist has gone as far in reproducing the Hutchison Effect as noted electrical engineer Dr. George Hathaway. His observations of his and Hutchison's joint duplications are worthy of note. Hathaway reported, among other startling effects, that a aluminum rod was distorted out of shape and another "was blown into little fibres." Molybdenum's melting point is $5,000°F$, but after subjecting molybdenum rods to Hutchison's electromagnetic fields, "we watched these things wiggle back and forth." He concludes: "In general . . . the collection of pieces of metal shows that they have been blasted apart or twisted."

Another effect is equally astounding. In describing this, one observer, Mark A. Solis, notes that "dissimilar substances can simply 'come together,' yet the individual substances do not disassociate. A block of wood can simply 'sink' into a metal bar, yet neither the block of wood nor metal bar come apart." He adds: "There is no evidence of displacement, such as would occur if, for example, one were to sink a stone in a bowl of water."

But perhaps one of the most remarkable aspects of the Hutchison Effect is spontaneous invisibility of metallic materials in the "active zone" of his Pharos-type Hutchison Apparatus. Hutchison speculates that if his equipment were properly adjusted, the "cronons" and "gravitons" generated by his technology could cause entire buildings to disappear.

Observers of Hutchison's experiments and demonstrations (he has given over 750) have uniformly expressed astonishment at the weak electrical power that seems to be sufficient to produce very stupefying results. Since basic outlets in any house supply enough power to operate his many machines, the power that unleashes all these astonishing effects is believed to lie elsewhere, such as where the various electromagnetic fields invisibly interplay. But how these independent fields interact is still largely a mystery. Even where they interact can be perplexing. Sometimes one must wait for days for something to happen, and 99 percent of the time nothing happens at all. To draw an analogy, it is like trying to boil water without being able to determine the strength of the heat—in such a scenario it is not surprising that it might take different amounts of time to produce the boiling effect.

Since the effects and the materials vary greatly, it seems logical to assume there is some form of disruption of the basic atomic structure, considering that fusion of nonidentical materials, fires, levitating objects, invisibility, etc., have nothing in common but the energy from these building blocks of matter.

Hutchison has long considered this plethora of effects. He suggests that somehow the surface skins of the masses undergoing this effect may become excited "and their atoms . . . create an unstable space-time situation." He further theorizes: "This might allow the fields from the Tesla coils and RF-generation equipment to lock up in a local space-time situation. My thought is that now a small amount of energy is released from the vast reservoir in space-time at the subatomic level to create a disruptive or movement effect."

A possible source for all this power is suggested by Mark Solis. "It is surmised by some researchers that what Hutchison has done is tap into the

Zero Point Energy. This energy gets its name from the fact that it is evidenced by oscillations at zero degrees Kelvin, where supposedly all activity in an atom ceases. The energy is associated with the spontaneous emission and annihilation of electrons and positrons coming from what is called the 'quantum vacuum.' The density contained in the quantum vacuum is estimated by some at 10^{13} joules per cubic centimeter, which is reportedly sufficient to boil off the Earth's oceans in a matter of moments."

One can only pause at this moment to consider what unlimited power the Earth may have to randomly unleash micro-moments of such energy if its electromagnetic wavelengths and frequencies are sufficiently disrupted—and equally to be alarmed at what the results might be to a ship or plane in the vicinity.

Hutchison is keenly aware of similarities in the Hutchison Effect to many of the reports in the Bermuda Triangle. In commenting on the applied ramifications, he has speculated: "It is highly probable that nature can form these fields on her own and create the right situation for the ship or aircraft to either totally disintegrate or disappear into another dimension or domain."

But his observation of another effect produced in his lab provides perhaps the most concrete link between electromagnetism and the Triangle. "I have personally experienced the grayish-type mist when I was doing my high voltage research; and this mist would appear and disappear. To look at it, it looks like metallic. I couldn't see through it. So it exists." Somehow it is easy to recall what Frank Flynn described from the Coast Guard cutter *Yamacraw* and also the many fogs and vapors reported by pilots that seem to possess "electronic" properties. One might also recall Gernon's impression that the "electronic fog" seemed to travel with his plane and that the plane was not traveling through it—a prescient correlation to a "cling of a gray fog" that Hutchison has observed and even filmed (on 8mm) materializing around objects during some tests.

Recalling the unusual spiraling clouds and vapors in the Triangle, and the effects such spinning matrixes could have on gravity, leads one to further speculation on the ships and planes missing in the Bermuda Triangle. Caught in such invisible magnetic vortices, could an object disappear "up" instead of down, with bits and pieces ultimately raining down far away? For, despite official denials throughout history, the fall of man-made objects and biological aquatic life—and even flesh and blood—from the sky on clear days have been recorded; these remain unexplained.

Aside from his electromagnetic pursuits, Hutchison has continued to experiment with a wide range of alternative energy sources. Experimentation with crystals has produced surprising energy results. Using crystals of barium titanate, a material capable of capturing the pulses of certain radio frequencies, Hutchison was able to create his Hutchison Converter. A demonstration model of this device ran a small motor without batteries or fuel and without any connection to an electrical outlet. In 1996 Hutchison took a smaller version to Japan, where he demonstrated it before an audience of five hundred in Hiroshima—where it is still working nonstop.

He believes that this form of energy could be produced by inexpensive refrigerator-size cylindrical batteries that theoretically could be linked in a series and network in harmony. He further believes this power system could generate up to 110 to 130 volts and apparently work forever.

Hutchison has noted that all this energy is free; one must simply tap into it—possibly why several elements look unfavorably on his pursuits. There are other concerns. Tapping into too much zero-point energy can be dangerous. He warns: "If you draw too much from the electromagnetic jitter of zero-point energy, you'll get a minor meltdown. I've had to clean this area up once because of this."

One is tempted to believe that the Hutchison Effect is not an effect at all but the "device" that creates the observed effects of levitating, burning, disappearance, and so forth. To be more explicit, one is tempted to think of this invisible interaction between these fields as an invisible device itself—a vortex or warp, whatever you may call it—created not by Hutchison's machines and their weak electrical power but by some field or fields they create in tandem. Hutchison may indeed be the only inventor in history to have invented an "invisible device"—with astonishing results.

Hutchison's creation of this portal into the subatomic structure of the Universe is only a discovery; it has yet to be harnessed or directed or even consistently reproduced. In a way, he has like a fisherman dipped his net into the vast ocean of universal forces and pulled out what he chanced at first to find.

We can now only somewhat wistfully wonder what the harnessing of such a device might bring. At the very least we should not doubt its inevitability. We have long been used to satellite communications and television in which voices and pictures travel on frequencies through the atmosphere. In a sense we have projected sounds and one-dimensional images, almost immediately, through space to another point thousands of miles away and reassembled them for a television audience. These same frequencies—the billions of fluctuations of zero-point—that Hutchison uses or warps may indeed one day be able to send a three-dimensional object just as speedily to another point in space *or time.*

It might well be wise for us to consider what abusing these invisible wavelengths can do. Machine or machines capable of creating or harnessing this invisible energy are capable of altering the very structure of matter and redirecting the energy inherent in it. The effects seem limitless, as limitless as the building blocks of matter. It is estimated that the Universe consists of 10^{80} atoms, as far as our minds can comprehend today—infinite. Since all structures are composed of atoms, a harnessing of such power as exists in the Hutchison Effect could be employed for everything: for medical purposes (to eradicate cancer and tumors, to rejuvenate dead tissue into living), for communication, for transportation and exploration . . . and even for destruction.

In many ways such machines and a civilization capable of harnessing and directing electromagnetism through them are starkly reminiscent of the readings of clairvoyant Edgar Cayce (1877–1945). Cayce gained worldwide recognition during his lifetime because of the advice he gave while in trances, usually involving cures for various maladies undiagnosed by then conventional medicine. His readings, however, covered a variety of topics because he was called on to answer many people's questions while in his trances. Although he was often called the "sleeping prophet," many of his readings dealt not with the future but with the past.

Between 1924 and 1944 Cayce made startling statements about areas which today are key parts of the Bermuda Triangle. According to his readings, areas in the Bahamas still hold the remains of a vast prehistoric civilization that sank beneath the sea in tragic increments. He associated this civilization with our tales of Atlantis, which, according to Plato, our only Western source, sank some 11,400 years ago in a sudden catastrophic event after the civilization had thrived for thousands of years in peace and glory but then spiraled into cruelty, abuse, immorality, and war.

As far as our knowledge extends today, we are little better off than was Plato in our understanding of this dark epoch in our own history. Everything before 3100 B.C. is obscured in the vast vault of "prehistory," since we have no written records antedating that time. The only records describing that era are vague, the product of possibly hundreds of years of oral tradition, until they were written down in the 3rd to 2nd millennia B.C. It is more than interesting that some of our earliest recorded folktales speak of a past and glorious civilization, a time of the "gods," of floods and catastrophes and the scattering of mankind. This is not surprising considering that writing materials, whether clay tablets or papyri, were not in great abundance and therefore reserved for the most important information.

What is interesting about Cayce's readings is that he often called this prehistoric civilization Atlantean or Atlantic based and also credited it with the use of what seems to be the technology mentioned above. He spoke in terms that suggested devices using wavelengths and frequencies, machines that could overcome even gravity, and machines using forces that could send information through the air and direct and power any type of aircraft or vessel. He said, furthermore, that the Atlanteans built and designed these devices to draw upon "universal forces"—and he outright blamed Atlantis's destruction and its eventual breakup and submersion on the misuse of these power sources. Although these power sources are often called "forces in the light" or "lights," he referred frequently to crystals or "stones," which were part of the apparatus used to harness and direct these energies and give them practical use.

Cayce, it must be remembered, was not a scientist. He was a lay healer. He often described what he saw as best he could. Considering that light—itself an electromagnetic wavelength—is merely the expression of energy, his repeated references to light as a power source draw an apt parallel with zero-point energy only now being considered by our own civilization as the ultimate and limitless power source.

In developing the prescience of what Cayce was trying to convey, one must remember that these readings were given long before any concept of these energies. He repeatedly said the machines used forces "not of the present," meaning not known or understood circa the 1930s. In referring back to Atlantis, he added: "And as we find, it was a period when there was much that has not even been thought of yet, in the present experience." These machines came about after the understanding of the "law of universal forces" from which the machines derived their energies. Also from "elements that are found and not found in the Earth's atmosphere."

A patchwork quotation from a 1933 reading illustrates Cayce's attempt to describe the apparatus and its housing:

About the firestone. . . . In the center of a building which would today be said to be lined with nonconductive stone something akin to asbestos with . . . other nonconductors. . . . The building above the stone was oval; or a dome wherein there could be . . . a portion for rolling back, so the activity of the stars, the concentration of energies that emanate from bodies that are on fire themselves. . . . The concentration through the prisms or glass (as would be called in the present) was in such a manner that it acted upon the instruments. . . . The preparation of this stone was solely in the hands of the initiates at the time . . . among those who directed the influences of the radiation which arose, in the form of rays that were invisible to the eye but acted upon the stones themselves as set in the motivating forces.

An oddly prescient statement surrounds the electromagnetic vehicles used by this ancient prehistoric civilization. In a reading in January 1943, far antedating any concept of the Bermuda Triangle, UFOs, or USOs, Cayce described them as "things of transportation, the aeroplane as called today, but then as ships of the air, for they sailed not only in the air but in other elements also."

Even more surprising, Cayce directly linked a harnessing of electromagnetism to effects only recently discovered: "In Atlantean land at time of development of electrical forces that dealt with transportation of craft from place to place, photographing at a distance, reading inscriptions through walls even at a distance . . . overcoming gravity itself, preparation of the crystal, the terrible mighty crystal; much of this brought destruction." This destruction, as suggested by a careful reading of Cayce's statements, continued over a long period of time because the Atlanteans were completely unable to grasp what was causing the upheavals. As in the case of the phenomena associated with Hutchison's electromagnetic tests, the side effects built up unpredictably.

The catalyst of a period of upheaval and submergence shows a striking resemblance to John Hutchison's warnings about the misuses of zero-point energy: "[They] brought destructive forces by setting up in various portions of the land the kind that was to act in producing powers for the various forms of the people's activities in the cities, the towns and the countries surrounding same. These, not intentionally, were tuned too high; and brought the second period of destructive forces to the people in the land."

It was the last portion of Atlantis to sink that Cayce directly associated with the Bahamas or, actually, the Great Bahama Bank upon which the Bahamian islands today are but mere tips of its former low-lying hills. Cayce called it Poseidia and said it was only a fraction of the landmass of the original Atlantean continent.

Cayce often comes back to trying to describe these machines more than the forces they manipulated—understandably, because he could "see" the machines and not the forces. Enduring substances such as crystals and glass

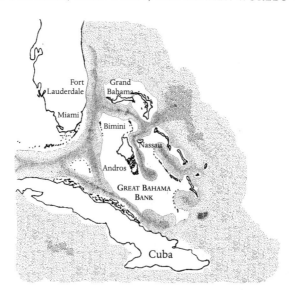

The Great Bahama Bank is the only underwater bank in the world that would form a huge island if the level of the oceans were only 50 feet below their present levels.

and the firestone cut with crystalline facets were repeated themes. Several of his followers maintain that these ruined machines or parts of them could still be below the ocean in the Bahamas. According to their view, thermal energies in the Earth and their wavelengths or frequencies might still exert an influence on these crystal devices, which in turn capture and convert them and then, using this pulse of energy, randomly affect a vessel or plane in the nearby vicinity. They contend that this explains the electromagnetic anomalies and, in some cases, even contributes to the disintegration of a ship or plane.

From our perspective today, the idea of machines without the limiting need for continuing electrical power, which is dependent on some sort of fuel or generator, is absurd. The machinery would also be subject to the need for maintenance, to deterioration over time, and to the physical and eroding effects of entropy. But however absurd it seems, our own civilization is being made acutely aware of small versions of these machines, such as the Hutchison Converter, which even Hutchison believes could run forever and to which crystalline power sources are vital.

Other devices have existed that are remarkably similar to those in Cayce's readings of Atlantis. Knowledge of these has recently been unearthed by

Nick Cook in *The Hunt for Zero Point*—an unexpected coincidence between the "universal forces" Cayce mentioned and zero-point energy, a coincidence made more intriguing by the fact that neither inventors nor Cook were even aware of Caycean Atlantis.

One seems to be revealed from secret tests conducted by the Germans in the closing days of World War II by which they were attempting to create energy by a torsion-field effect. The tests were codenamed *Lanternentrager* (lantern holder) and *Chronos* (time). They suspended a bell-shaped metal object down a mine shaft into a specially prepared chamber lined with nonconductive tiles or rubber and spun it at speeds sufficient to bend space around the orb or channel elements in the atmosphere into vortex kinesis, reminiscent in some ways of Cayce's great power sources contained in chambers with nonconductive material and long columns for centralizing energy.

Cook notes that the change in code names for the same project may indicate that they discovered that time was also being affected and then pursued that angle, only then to be stopped by the end of the war and subsequent capture. Cook also notes that when questioned by the Polish courts in secret and the Russian NKVD after his capture, one general, Jakob Sporrenberg, overseer of security for the tests, used such words as "vortex compression" and "magnetic fields separation," conveying pieces of phraseology he had picked up from the scientists he had been guarding.

These tests may originally have been trying to duplicate, only on a grander scale, a device developed by a German scientist, Viktor Schauberger. In 1939 this device first worked successfully. An understanding of its mechanism will lend startling body to the expression "vortex compression." The device, called the Repulsine, operated literally on "air" by swirling into a dense emulsion charged particles such as protons and electrons in the atmosphere. The Repulsine, shaped like a large bonbon, with a cone-shaped turbine and air intake on top, had a small motor that drew in air via the intake. This air was channeled through a whorl-shaped interior (the spiraling shape of a corkscrew or certain sea shells) between the turbine and its bonbon baseplate. The vortex movement of the air within the machine rapidly cooled and "condensed" it, reducing its volume and creating a massive vacuum and suction which continued to suck in more air on its own. The motor could then be turned off and the device operated purely on (what is the first reference to) "free energy"—the vortex collision and annihilation of charged particles. This provides yet another corollary to Cayce's machines that operated on elements "in the atmosphere."

Schauberger was visionary enough to see that a machine capable of channeling the subatomic world of charged particles, in essence, of matter in its dematerialized state, was capable of producing limitless power. He believed that machines capable of vortex compression could power almost anything, provided that a short burst of energy began the self-augmenting vacuum. Believing the power of these machines could be engineered to reduce energy to its matter form, he considered the potential of a man-made vortex: "I stand face to face with the apparent 'void,' the compression of dematerialization that we are wont to call a 'vacuum.' I can now see that we are able to create anything we wish for ourselves out of this 'nothing.'"

Before Cayce, interest in the ancient legend of Atlantis was restricted to Plato's dialogues *Timaeus* and *Critias* (4th century B.C.) which first told the story of a prehistoric civilization "beyond the Pillars of Hercules" (Straits of Gibraltar). Plato, however, did not claim it as a Greek original, but rather openly explained how it came from an even earlier period of knowledge of which the Egyptians were still the custodians. "In the Egyptian Delta, at the head of which the river Nile divides, there is a certain district which is called the district of Sais, and the great city of the district is also called Sais. . . . To this city came Solon [the Athenian lawgiver], and was received there with great honour; he asked the priests who were most skillful in such matters, about antiquity."

Many great and wonderful deeds are recorded of your state [Athens] in our histories. But one of them exceeds all the others in greatness and valour. For these histories tell of a mighty power which unprovoked made an expedition against the whole of Asia and Europe, and to which your city put an end. This power came from the Atlantic Ocean, for in those days the Atlantic was navigable; and there was an island situated in front of the straits you call the Pillars of Hercules [Straits of Gibraltar]; the island was larger than Libya and Asia put together, and was the way to other islands, and from these you might pass to the whole of the opposite continent which surrounded the true ocean; for this sea which is within the straits of Hercules is only a harbour, having a narrow entrance, but the other is a real sea, and the surrounding land may be most truly called a boundless continent.

Plato can be pardoned for skewing the tale of Atlantis into glorifying the Athenian state, which did not even exist 11,400 years ago. But if his tale is entirely fable, it is hard to explain his knowledge of the Atlantic, of its size disparity as compared to the Mediterranean, of the islands beyond (presumably the Caribbean), and then of America, "the boundless continent" beyond them. This is something even Columbus did not suspect; he thought he would reach India and China on his voyage—the reason why Native American peoples were first called Indians, and why the islands of the Caribbean and the Bahamas are called West Indies.

There is no reason to suppose that anything more than just the barest snippets of information trickled down to Plato's time, leaving him to fill in the rest. It can be said that the Great Bahama Bank was once "an island beyond the Pillars of Hercules," and in many ways the present Bahamas also fit his broad description of the aftermath of the Atlantean subsidence: "The consequence is that, in comparison of what then was, there are remaining in small islets only the bones of that wasted body, as they may be called, all the richer and softer parts of the soil having fallen away, and the mere skeleton of the country being left."

Anyway, Plato's tale seems a great composite, a mixture of flood stories (popular throughout the ancient world) and the attack on the entire eastern Mediterranean by the "sea peoples," of whom the Philistines were a branch, and which Egypt, not Greece, was able to rebuff. Plato referred to a stunning alloy called orichalcum (Latin aurichalcum) that made up the fabulous wall of the citadel of Atlantis. It is hardly unknown; it is a mixture of gold, brass, and copper. Josephus even said that the altar washbasin outside the Temple at Jerusalem was made of orichalcum. If the tale is an admixture, with Plato's skewing of it to fit Athens into the picture added, then the tale as we know it today (or even for the last 2,400 years) is so convoluted that if such a prehistoric civilization existed, our exact knowledge of it is denuded of facts beyond the repeating ones of submergence and great destruction and that the Atlantic was the epicenter of this.

Because of Plato's obvious borrowings, the actual location of ancient Atlantis and its time period have been questioned for centuries. Generations of scholars have suggested it was the Azores or an island in the Aegean or Israel, Sicily, India, or, inevitably, after Columbus's time, America. Edgar Cayce was the first one ever to associate any part of the Bahamas with the fabled "continent."

Needless to say, this bold assertion only underscores the already obvious differences between Cayce's Atlantis and Plato's and these other conjectures. But it is nevertheless in this assertion that it becomes the *only one* that has ever been corroborated by evidence, which exists in a most remarkable prophecy and an even more remarkable discovery.

For his one and only time, in what as a result becomes his most surprising reading, Cayce actually mentioned a specific island in the Bahamas and then directly associated it with the novel electromagnetic power sources of that prehistoric age:

As for a description of the manner of construction of the stone: we find it was a large cylindrical glass (as would be termed today); cut with facets in such manner that the capstone on top of it made for centralizing the power or force that concentrated between the end of the cylinder and the capstone itself. As indicated, the records as to ways of constructing same are in three places in the Earth, as it stands today: in the sunken portion of Atlantis, or Poseidia, where a portion of the temple may yet be discovered under the slime of ages of sea water near what is known as Bimini, off the coast of Florida.

Earlier, he foretold this temple's destruction and reemergence: "As given, the temple was destroyed at the time there was the last destruction in Atlantis. . . . Yet, as the time draws nigh when the changes are to come about, there may be the opening of those three places where the records are one. . . . The temple by Iltar will then rise again."

In another reading, given in 1940, Cayce added an unexpected and terse codicil to his Poseidia predictions: "Poseidia will be amongst the first portions of Atlantis to rise again—expect it in '68 and '69—not so far away."

Whether Cayce meant this record exists in some written form or in an excavation of an actual machine is not specified. Yet to mention the obscure island of Bimini in 1933 draws us strangely to the only location out of all those offered above where ruins have been found underwater that cannot be associated with or credited to any known civilization on Earth.

These surprising discoveries were indeed made in 1968, more than twenty years after Cayce died, at the unlikely location where he said remains would be found—the Great Bahama Bank—and in some equally remarkable circumstances. The unusual chain of events began in routine overflights. The tides seemed to have been sweeping in different fashion than usual and had uncovered several odd shapes below. Dimitri Rebikoff, an underwater photographic inventor and amateur archeologist, first sighted a rectangle measuring about a quarter of a mile long that seemed too perfectly formed to be natural. In July, pilots Bob Brush and Trig Adams photographed a partitioned rectangle near Andros Island that was suggestive of the floor plan of a ruined building.

But the most extraordinary finds were on Labor Day at Bimini. Dr. J. Manson Valentine, professor of oceanography at the University of Miami, diving into the shallow waters off Paradise Point on the island's northwest shore, discovered several huge polygonal stones. By their op-

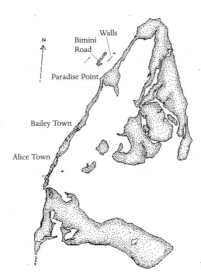

Bimini in the Bahamas. It is a small island about 50 miles from the Florida coast, with only a couple of settlements, Alice and Bailey Town. The deepest water in the immediate vicinity is only 18 feet. Off Paradise Point on the northwest shore lie the Bimini Road and Bimini Walls: the inverted "J" is the Road; the parallel sections of polygonal stones are the Wall. Most of the eastern part of the island is marsh.

posing edges it seemed they had once been cut to fit each other with precision, much like the mysterious pre-Inca stone walls in Peru. Although they had pillowed by this time—that is, their edges had been worn and eroded by the action of the surf or currents—it could still be clearly seen how their angles had at one time fit into the opposing stones. With three other divers (Jacques Mayol, Chip Climo, and Bob Angove), Valentine glided over a larger edifice to estimate its size. It extended for about 1,900 feet and was shaped like an inverted J. This structure, later named the Bimini "Wall" or "Road" because it resembles either a fallen wall or a broad paved stone road, was constructed, as its discoverer observed, "of stones which were absolutely rectangular, sometimes approaching perfect squares. The larger pieces, at least 10 to 15 feet in length, often ran the width of parallel-sided avenues, while the small ones formed mosaic-like pavements covering broader sections."

In commenting on his first reaction to this unexpected sight, Valentine said: "When I saw the regular pattern of these enormous stones I was so surprised I lost my weight belt. . . . I could hardly believe it; it was like a dream. I followed it for hundreds of yards to the big stones that go under the sand."

Expanding his searches from the air, Valentine, accompanied by Dimitri Rebikoff, discovered an array of geometric forms on the shallow Great Bahama Bank, either by outlines from bottom growth tracing their pattern or by the lack thereof. In all he has counted thirty sites where, in his own words, "there are probably man-made remains either on the sea bottom or below it. For example, between Diamond Point and Tongue of the Ocean there is a network of modular straight lines intersecting at right, obtuse, and acute angles. It resembles an architect's plan for a complex urban development with still more lines in the distance which I call 'ghost patterns' since they are vague outlines of other structures too deeply buried to be traced in detail. . . . All this suggests to me the one-time presence of ancient peoples."

Valentine and his discoveries have been subjected to varying degrees of criticism to this day, with some underwater archaeologists flatly denying that the Bimini Road (the only one they have heard of) is man-made or after a brief visit making the unsubstantiated claim that they are granite or beach rock. Others have first agreed that they were man-made but then have recanted, possibly because of peer pressure from many archaeologists, most of whom have never visited any of the sites but are hostile to the theory of an unknown civilization.

The Bimini Road. It is made of huge stones, and forks past the main lead. The shape suggests a giant bar magnet in its complete form. The most mysterious cultures of ancient Peru also built temples in a giant U-shape, the remaining half of which the "Road" seems to suggest.

Parallel sections of the Bimini Wall. They run at an angle to the Road and look very much like huge fallen Peruvian walls.

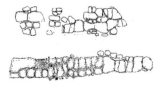

Valentine has subjected the area a much more prolonged and objective investigation. In commenting on the composition and alignment of the Bimini stones, he has observed: "These are not squares of beach rock arranged by nature in neat rows to fool gullible underwater archaeologists. Many of the stones are of flint-hard micrite, unlike soft beach rock. The lines are closely fitted, straight, mutually parallel, and terminate in corner stones. The stone avenue does not follow the curving beach rock-line, which follows the shape of the island, but is straight." He adds: "Perfect rectangles, right angles, and rectilinear configurations are unaccountable in a natural formation."

Perhaps no other person has examined the site as carefully after Valentine than author David Zink. On two expeditions in 1975 and 1976, in successive dives he mapped and photographed many of the stones of the "Bimini Road." In his book, *The Stones of Atlantis,* Zink notes the discovery of several critically placed stones shaped like a wedge, an arrow, or a "chockstone" that match "sacred geometry" used by Earth's earliest and still mysterious megalithic cultures.

Although these discoveries have excited the followers of Edgar Cayce, they have not proven any claims of a past supercivilization contained in his readings. The discoveries have been controversial enough even with just the bare inference that they represent an unknown culture highly skilled in building, much less one with the capabilities Cayce's adherents believe once existed in the Bahamas. It is equally true that their belief that the Bermuda Triangle's anomalies can be explained by this vanished civilization's power complexes hinges only on these readings and on what are only vague outlines underwater—no matter how striking or intriguing they may be.

Nevertheless, considerable enigma has been added to Cayce's readings by evidence supporting the idea that the Bimini stones are in fact man-made by some unidentified prehistoric culture. A case in point is the fact that a representation of them has recently been found on the Piri Reis Map, the earliest surviving map of the Americas, dated to 1513 and rediscovered only in 1929, when the dethroned Sultan's Topkapi Palace in Istanbul was being cleaned out. On the map the stones are shown as a row of polygonal, prostrate stones marking the center of an island in the Bahamas group—a gesture on the part of old cartographers to indicate a unique or salient feature of a specific location—also a clear indication the Spanish were amazed by them. The native Taino tribe of the Bahamas also seems to have been aware of their presence on land, referring to Bimini as the "island of the fallen wall."

Every time an uncanny parallel develops in our technological progress with that of Cayce's past Atlantis, interest in his readings reaches a new peak. Today, companies such as TeraBeam and AirFiber are developing the means to direct Internet and visual information via beams of invisible light from base stations to various relay towers that would in turn direct them to a dish at one's house or office—a completely cordless transmission of ideas, sound, pictures, and energy, surprisingly similar to Cayce's Atlantis and its hubs of buildings and temples with relay crystals atop them (although neither company was aware of or is remotely interested in Cayce's readings of the past).

It is natural, of course, to seek an explanation for the ruins in the Bermuda Triangle, as well as for the persisting yet unpredictable electromagnetic anomalies in the area. This is especially important since these anomalies may represent an actual or perceived danger to any traveler in the area and contribute directly or indirectly to a disappearance.

But if one cannot believe the stones are generating them, then where else can one look for their origin? Somewhere in the past of this planet is a good guess, with its many geologic scars testifying to horrendous upheavals. We may find an answer that can explain how a prehistoric civilization could be cataclysmically destroyed, how parts of it could sink, and how latent tensions and forces could develop as a result. These electromagnetic anomalies may be not the cause of a continent's submergence but stresses left over from a catastrophe that may very well connect them to "Atlantis" in a most unexpected way.

For this answer to the Triangle we must go deeper down, not into any fathoms of water . . . but into the murky mists of the past.

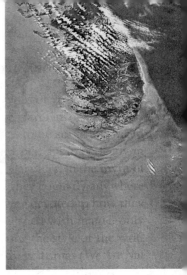

The "drop-off" into the Tongue of the Ocean. (NASA)

Infrared satellite photo showing Miami and southern Florida on the left and Bimini Island toward the center. Within this short distance of 50 miles countless ships and planes have vanished. (NASA)

A closer view of Bimini. The drop-off of the Great Bahama Bank shows clearly. The "white waters" south of Bimini are the currents breaking in the lee of Moselle Reef. Bimini remains a hotbed of mysterious disappearances, strange lights, and unexplained electromagnetic anomalies. (NASA)

An upstanding wheel from the undercarriage of an aircraft at Bimini, showing how shallow the waters are off Bimini and on the Great Bahama Bank in general. (Courtesy Bruce Burgess)

Far from land, the mysterious bulb of the Tongue of the Ocean. The surrounding rippled bottom sands are only a few fathoms deep, while the dark blue (seen as black here) of the Tongue is 6,000 feet. The dark color, upper left, is the Exuma Sound, another area of deep water. Along here at the edge of its drop-off runs the Exuma chain of islands. (NASA)

The *Sapona* looks today as she did when Flight 19 used her for bombing practice in 1945. Wrecked near Chicken and Hen Shoals in a 1929 storm, she is in 12 feet of water and rises 25 feet above. (Courtesy Bruce Burgess)

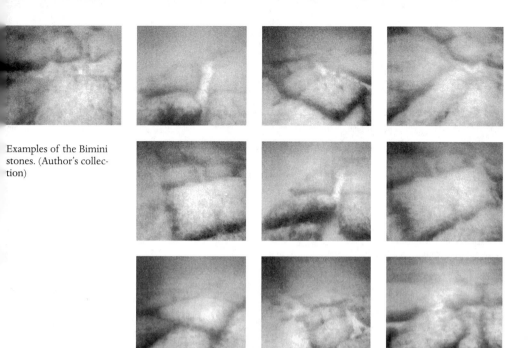

Examples of the Bimini stones. (Author's collection)

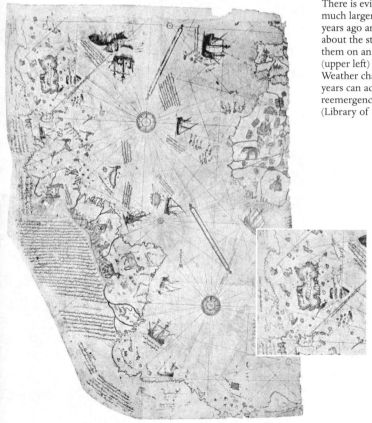

There is evidence that Bimini was a much larger island only five hundred years ago and that the Spanish knew about the stones. A cartographer drew them on an island in the Bahamas group (upper left) in this Piri Reis Map of 1513. Weather changes in the last thousand years can account for the stones' reemergence and then resubmergence. (Library of Congress)

In this enlargement of the photo at left, the center of the island is marked by a row of fallen polygonal stones and a stone construction, indicating they were on land in 1513. (Library of Congress)

Effects somewhat reminiscent of Edgar Cayce's prophecies are now being produced from free-energy sources in electromagnetism. One of the pioneers is Canadian scientist John Hutchison. Shown here are shattered ingots. (Courtesy John Hutchison)

Levitating a 60-pound cannon ball. (Courtesy John Hutchison)

Hutchison at the controls. (Courtesy John Hutchison)

Fusion of dissimilar materials (a block of wood and a metal bar). (Courtesy John Hutchison)

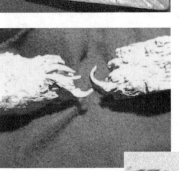

Two views of the cold melting of metal. These are just some of the astounding effects produced by Hutchison. (Courtesy John Hutchison)

Working on batteries that may run forever. (Courtesy John Hutchison)

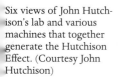

Six views of John Hutchison's lab and various machines that together generate the Hutchison Effect. (Courtesy John Hutchison)

An astounding photo of the "white waters" taken by Bruce and Lynn Gernon on April 26, 1999, off Andros Island. The area is almost exactly where the lenticular cloud developed and turned into a ringed doughnut cloud. This picture shows a remarkable vortex of clear water in the middle of the glowing waters. Another is in the upper left, without any vortex action. Taken from 6,500 feet. Cloud tops at 3,500 feet. Gernon estimates each blotch covered 10 acres. (Courtesy Bruce and Lynn Gernon)

Spiraling clouds form corkscrew tails. (Courtesy Walter Nemanishen)

Ball lightning in formation over Bimini. (Courtesy Bruce Gernon)

These may be the oldest worked stones in the world. The great foundation stones of the Temple of Baal at Baalbek, Lebanon, are 65 feet long by 14 feet high and wide, and each weighs 1,200 tons. A classical Roman temple was built over them, but no one knows who originally cut and moved them or for what purpose. (Author's collection)

The largest worked stone in the world, at Baalbek, 68 feet long by 15 feet high and wide. What stopped the building? What toppled these prehistoric buildings? (Author's collection)

At Baalbek, at one side, the Roman temple falls short of the stones. (Author's collection)

Baalbek stones from another angle. Some of the stones on top match the style of those at Bimini. (Author's collection)

Sacsahuaman, Peru. Terracing up the hill. (Courtesy Judith Marx)

Sacsahuaman. Parts of the ancient ramparts are much decayed. (Courtesy Judith Marx)

Sacsahuaman. Three photos showing the beveling and the detail of the intricate joins of the stones. (Courtesy Judith Marx)

Sacsahuaman. These stones show more than just a little resemblance to those of Bimini and to the mysterious culture of the Bahama Bank. (Courtesy Judith Marx)

Sacsahuaman. There are miles of such polygonal stones. (Courtesy Judith Marx)

Sacsahuaman. Note the modern work with small rocks compared with the perfectly faceted boulders. (Courtesy Judith Marx)

Sacsahuaman. Note the detail in just one short section of the wall. (Courtesy Judith Marx)

An interesting compromise. A free-standing church steeple? Actually, it's a relay tower for wireless communications, its design dictated by the fact that the property of a church was the best area to receive and transmit signals. The tower was modeled on a church steeple to conform it with the theme of the property. A similar concept is found in Cayce's readings for past Atlantis. Are we going too far? (Author's collection)

7

Clues from a Shifting Paradigm

EVER SINCE THE 1960s it has been established that gravity anomalies can pinpoint areas of tectonic stresses that are otherwise invisible. This was determined first by gravimetry and then by artificial-satellite orbit perturbations. Tracking satellites are so precisely calibrated that even minor variations in the measurement of gravity by as little as plus or minus 0.04 centimeter per second^2 will affect the system, and their locations must be previously computed before launching.

An overall survey of the gravitational field of the Earth reveals "zones of compression," areas where continental masses abut and compress against each other, where the continuing force possibly directs crustal mass back into the mantle, creating pressure and density that register in readings of gravity. Zones of tension also exist, great upward thrusts from deep within the Earth into the crust. The pressure outward supposedly affects gravity in the reverse of zones of compression. This is no doubt a partially cyclical process, where the crustal displacement downward at the zones of compression displaces the viscous mantle, which then pushes up into the crust toward the surface at the zones of tension.

The layout of these zones draws our attention quite squarely to the Atlantic. The zones of compression are on the side of the continents that face away from the Atlantic, that is, in the areas of the Pacific Ocean where the ocean floor has been buckled by the massive force of the Euro-Asian continent pushing headward against the seafloor; along the Alpide Region where the Asian subcontinent and Euro-Asia compress; and on the western sides of Mexico and South America where the American continental mass has swept so much seafloor before it, it too shows signs of being compressed like a massive carpet.

In contrast, the Atlantic seabed has virtually no zones of compression. Zones of tension exist there, following precisely the great undersea

Midatlantic Ridge, where the crust has split open and billions of tons of magma have uplifted the sea bottom by thousands of feet.

In some places the Midatlantic Ridge has risen to break the surface and these peaks and seamounts form such distantly placed islands as the Azores in the North Atlantic, off Portugal, to Ascension Island in the South Atlantic, and even down to Tristan Da Cunha much farther south, roughly parallel with the bottom of the African continent.

Underwater mapping of the Atlantic has confirmed that the shape, convolutions, and contours of the Midatlantic Ridge correspond to the continental shelves on both sides of the Atlantic. Echo sounding has also confirmed that its vast inclined slopes directly correspond to the width between the continents—where the Ridge is wide, the distance between the continents is widest, and where the Ridge is narrow, at the Romanche Gap, near the Equator, the distance between the continents is the narrowest.

All this collectively calls our attention to the theory that there was once one great "megacontinent" on Earth, which, for some still unknown reason, fractured, spread apart, and created the present appearance of the Earth, the seafloors, and the ocean currents, and, possibly, because of weight redistribution, even tilted the Earth on its axis, initiating our seasonal weather patterns.

Dark lines trace "zones of compression," while the dual lines trace "zones of tension" in the gravitational field of the Earth. They follow geological stresses.

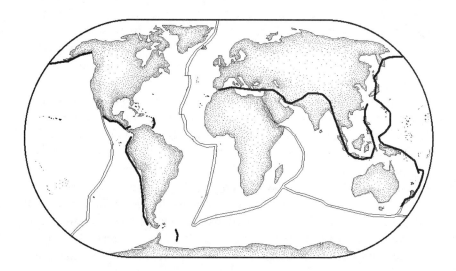

Examples of what kind of truly earthshaking force must have been mounted to uplift the Ridge can be found in more modern (though minuscule by comparison) cataclysms. When only one volcano blew up in 1883, on the island of Krakatoa in the Java Sea, for instance, the shock waves were registered in England 11,000 miles away, and minor tidal waves were also noted in the English Channel. But the Midatlantic Ridge is itself around 10,000 miles long—a network of immense parallel ridges on opposite sides of a central rift valley. In some areas this central rift is 6 miles wide and as much as 2 miles deep. When considering that this is the feature of much of its length, it gives the impression of being a huge scar that split open and uplifted along *almost one entire side* of the Earth.

A project carried out over the last decade under the guidance of Drs. Deborah K. Smith and Joe Caan has mapped and confirmed as many as 481 active volcanoes along only a 500-mile segment of the Ridge, some ranging as tall as 1,800 feet from the bottom. Extrapolating this, it is estimated that there are 85 million volcanic seamounts on the ocean floor, with 2.5 million ranging over 600 feet high.

Of all the places in the world, the Atlantic seafloor remains the most unstable part of this planet. Thousands of earthquakes strike along the Ridge as bottom plates move and as more magma boils and oozes out along its course. Extending outward from the Ridge, toward the continental shelves, the bottom is literally peppered with volcanoes in the form of coalesced seamounts. Trembling bottoms cause frictions and rogue waves, and massive lava flows the size of some countries span huge sections of its floor. These seem to be explained by the past movement of the continents over the sea bottom, the changing weight passing overhead having upset the mantle below. All of these have the potential to shift the bottom and abut and compress huge sections of seafloor, potentially affecting both the magnetic and gravitational fields.

Even a minuscule shift can change pressure over thousands of square miles of sea bottom. Gravity anomalies *are* known to exist over land around areas of postglacial uplift, where huge glaciers melted and the land became free of its former weight. Transient gravity anomalies in the Bermuda Triangle might play along the same theme, only in reverse. Past ocean level increases have added additional weight to the continental shelves, and this can affect former coastal faults and strata. Portions of the continental shelf north of the Bahamas seem to have incrementally plunged, from Blake Terrace east of Florida down to Puerto Rico, leaving the vast Great Bahama Bank as a massive plateau awaiting inundation.

Upward pressure from the mantle counterbalancing the plunging weight of the shelf might keep sections of the bottom in a touchy teeter-totter harmony. Tracking satellite glitches, sometimes reported over this area, might be the only evidence for these brief tugs-of-war.

Phases of the moon may even temporarily affect the magnetic field lines if they have been made touchy by a past cataclysm. According to Russian engineer Dr. A. J. Yelkin, some unexplained magnetic deviations recur in the Triangle frequently enough to be plotted. These have been at the new moon, full moon, and when the moon is closest to the Earth.

Satellite imaging shows the continental shelves of the Triangle. East of Florida, Georgia, and South Carolina they plunge gradually, possibly all the way down to Puerto Rico, leaving several freestanding banks, like the Great and Little Bahama Banks, on the greater continental shelf.

Yelkin deduces that the magnetic deflections at these times are caused by lunar solar tides. This would also explain Dr. David Zink's reports of unexplained magnetic deviations at Bimini each year in early August, a time coinciding with a full moon.

Areas of the Bahamas, near the deep drop-off, are also the only place in the world subject to the phenomenon of the "glowing" or "white waters," plumes of smoky white water venting up from somewhere in the bottom. They float and disperse with the currents, giving the appearance of wisps of clouds being rippled by the wind. While their source remains mysterious, tests of the water indicate a high sulfur and possibly lithium content—perhaps released by the subsurface instability near these deep underwater cliffs.

While it would seem that the unstable nature of the Atlantic would give rise to numerous reports of odd electromagnetic anomalies everywhere, the reason for the Bermuda Triangle's fame may be that it is simply more traveled, and hence mathematical probability dictates a better chance that these anomalies will be encountered there and give rise to comment. It may also mean that the continental shelves and the deep bottoms of the Triangle provide more potential for shifts and force-field anomalies, whereas the bottoms far from the continental shelves are more static.

Vestiges of the Atlantic-centric catastrophe are not only omnipresent on the Atlantic seafloor; they literally girdle the globe. There is ample proof that most of the major mountain ranges and geologic formations in the world were created in response to a cataclysm in the Atlantic. The great mountain ranges of the Earth are all located away from their Atlantic side, that is, for North America the Sierra Madre, Cascades, and Rockies, which extend through western areas of the United States, Canada, and Mexico; for South America, the Andes along its western half; and for Euro-Asia and Africa toward their center or eastern halves—essentially those parts of the continents where buckling would be expected if they were moving *away* from a central point in the Atlantic.

The great earthquake belts also lie on those sides of the continents that would have borne the brunt of the friction as they were pushed away from the Atlantic, like the west coasts of the United States, Mexico, and South America; and the east coasts of Asia and Japan; and the Great Rift Valley on Africa's eastern coast.

Features exist in every continent to suggest cataclysmic quaking. An inland sea seems suddenly to have emptied into the Gulf of California, creating the Grand Canyon; the Sahara Desert appears to have been very recently an inland sea that drained into the Atlantic. Vast lava beds are pierced through the continents. In the northwest United States, the Columbian Plateau covers 200,000 squares miles and is several thousand feet thick; in India, the Deccan Traps is a lava flow the size of France (since magma does not retain its liquidity very long after reaching the cooler crust, these can only be explained by massive eruptions). Ayres Rock in Australia, one of the largest boulders in the world, is 1,100 feet high, with a 5-mile circumference, and seems to have been literally kicked and rolled to its present place in a desert from a mountain 20 miles away—and all this leads us back to the theory that one great megacontinent was split violently apart at the Midatlantic Ridge.

Just such an event is indelibly etched into the earliest history of mankind. Almost every ancient people preserves vivid accounts of one great earthquake coming just before our first civilization, and that there was the "shaking, shifting, and splitting" of the whole Earth. Sumerian tablets record that the entire Earth was divided and mountains were born. The Inca Indians have distinct cultural memories of the Andes mountain range violently uplifting from what had previously been a plain. The Hopi Indians preserve the legend that during this cataclysm the Earth spun off its axis—a remarkable statement showing advanced knowledge by ancient peoples of the shape of the Earth and its rotation and that this "splitting" so redistributed the weight as to change the incline of the planet. (This ancient view is surprisingly prescient, since many geologists today feel that continental movement can explain the current incline of the Earth on its axis by 23 degrees, aside from the evidence for sudden climatic changes, glacial melting, and ocean-level changes.)

Among the Teutonic tribes of Norway there is a remarkably similar recollection: "The whole Earth trembled. The Yggdrasil tree was shaken from its root to its topmost branches. Mountains crumbled and split from top to bottom. All were driven from their hearth and the human race was swept from the surface of the Earth. The Earth itself was losing shape. The stars were coming adrift from the sky and falling into the gaping void. . . . Flames spurted from fissures in the rocks . . . everywhere there was the hissing of steam. And now all the rivers, all the seas arose and overflowed. From every side waves lashed against waves . . . the Earth sank beneath the sea . . . mountains arose anew." A rather accurate account of what *would have* happened while the continents divided, with mountains building where the land buckled, lands sinking, tidal waves crashing over land and backing up rivers while the land catastrophically moved to its new position and the Earth tilted, as shown by stars apparently moving in the sky and sinking over the horizon.

Religious texts as far apart as the *Popul Vuh* of the Mayans and the *Vedas* of India preserve accounts of the destruction of a great civilization by division, scattering, and confusion, while Genesis records a similar event (Babel) happening just before our own histories begin. Even the isolated Cyapo Indians of the Amazon recall that the great corn tree was cut down and mankind was scattered—a recollection, though in impoverished terms, of Genesis and the Tower of Babel.

An explanation for the mysterious ruins in the Bermuda Triangle, along with a search for the unknown civilization that built them, might best begin by probing into the philosophical controversy that buried them more deeply than the sea did. Understanding the shifting interpretation in geology may resurrect them more visibly than the shifting sands of the Bahama Banks.

The past problem with correlating the Midatlantic Ridge with this cataclysm and a destruction of civilization was one of timing. Its discovery in 1876 through mapping carried out by HMS *Challenger* occurred during a revolution in geology brought about by a then new philosophy called *uniformitarianism*. This ideology was based purely on the belief in the uniformity of nature throughout time, and therefore it could not accept that any global cataclysm could have struck the Earth, since, by Victorian standards, none had been observed to do so. Embracing the maxim "the present is the key to the past," uniformitarianism could only come up with ridiculously long ages to accomplish any geological event because every minute change noted today was extrapolated backward to provide a dating method—thus all geological formations on Earth, whether canyons, mountains, valleys, or just the general topography, had to be accounted for by contemporary weather patterns . . . if only given enough time.

Uniformitarianism's philosophical father was Charles Lyell, an English barrister turned amateur geologist, who, after traveling around the globe, began to publish in journals his observations of geologic change. These later culminated in his voluminous book, *The Principles of Geology.* In 1858 he first introduced the concept to the world with his study of Niagara Falls's 3,500-foot-long gorge. Claiming that the falls receded by a foot per year, he extrapolated this backward and applied it to the length of the gorge. His conclusion was that it therefore took 35,000 years for the pounding action of the falls to have created this long canyon. He used this logic on every other feature of geologic activity and came up with phenomenally long ages to accomplish every formation.

For example, the deep layers of sediments (that is, rock created by the swift movement of wind or water) covering the continents were explained using the present slow buildup of sandstone at river mouths. Since, in some cases, continental sediments are miles deep, it was adduced that roughly 600 million years were required to lay down much of these sediments, since it takes an average of several thousand years for rivers to lay down 10 feet of sandstone. It was also proposed that the fossils of dead animals (dinosaurs, mastodons, primates), and foliage found in them were preserved in the same slow way in the course of everyday nature.

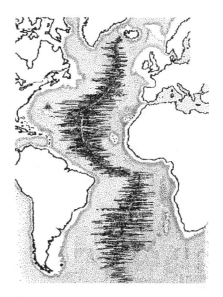

The Midatlantic Ridge in relation to the continental shelves. Viewing the angles of the continental shelves it is easier to see how they fit into place with each other: North Africa into the eastern shelf of the United States; South America into the western shelf of southern Africa. This also shows how much water now covers areas of former land, and the potential for sunken civilizations.

Lyell and uniformitarianism organized these strata into neat "time periods" to classify the developing "ages" of the Earth. This Geologic Column became the cyclical dating method for anything found buried in the sediments. Each time period's duration was determined by its thickness, its thickness being determined by the repeating type of fossils found vertically throughout it. Each layer represented millions of years, since they were hundreds of feet thick. This column should reflect, in neat ascending order, the progressive evolution of species to the present Holocene epoch (beginning 10,000 years ago), from the most primitive sea invertebrates of the Cambrian Period (beginning 600 million years ago, according to uniformitarianism), and contain the sum total of the Earth's geological history.

When "continental drift" became established in the 1960s by apparent measurements of the continents "drifting" *away* from the Atlantic by a minuscule 2 centimeters per year, this same theory was used to determine a date for the division. The 2 centimeters was extrapolated backward linearly, much as in Lyell's Niagara Falls computations, and it was determined it would have taken the continents 200 million years to move to their present positions from the Midatlantic Ridge. The Ridge itself had to come about by equally slow means, according to the current process of slowly oozing magma—always assuming the maxim "the present is the key to the past."

Before the unusual conceptions of the uniformitarian paradigm rose to dominate geology in the late 19th century, the Catastrophist mentality pervaded, accepting the ancient and biblical records of a huge global flood having wiped out a prehistoric civilization, and then thousands of years later another civilization destroyed by scattering and division. Evidence for the first was accepted by the fact that great sheets of sediment—waterlaid rock—covered the continents. But for the second, the scope of destruction had been so large it was not even guessed these ancient accounts, like Babel, were referring to a global event.

In the 16th century when mapping of the Americas became more extensive, Sir Francis Bacon was the first to note the curious fact that the Americas seemed to fit roughly into the west coast of Africa. However, it was not until 1858 that a French scientist, Antonio Snider-Pelligrini, proposed that the Atlantic was created by powerful forces that tore apart one great continent. In the last twenty-five years this approach has been solidly embraced by a greater and greater number of geologists, now called Neo-Catastrophists, who note that direct field examinations have always refuted uniformitarianism.

Lyell's own calculations for the Niagara Falls gorge were blatantly false. (An eminent geologist of the time, named Blackwell, told Lyell in person that the locals had observed the falls recede by over 3 feet per year, making the falls, by Lyell's own uniformitarian criterion, only around 12,000 years old.) Modern studies indicate that the falls actually recede between 4 and 5 feet a year, reducing its age to around 5,000 years.

Since about three-quarters of the continents are caked with sediment, it is hard to conceive that ancient rivers or basic wind patterns created them. Even where they are miles deep, they show only depositional action—laid down successively and not disturbed by other events like vast ecosystems, thriving forests, and the like; it's only miles of water-laid rock.

These sediments also do not reflect the Lyellian and uniformitarian geologic column. "Time periods" are often discovered out of the chronological order proposed on paper by uniformitarianism, that is, "earlier" time periods sitting on top of "later" time periods. This is evident because the fossils entombed in them actually show "later" developed animals coming long before "earlier" animals. Such a common paradox is called a deceptive conformity—deceptive because, in essence, it does not justify uniformitarian ideology and conformity because the sediments conform to each other perfectly, meaning they were laid down successively without any time elapsing between. In the Grand Canyon, where the geologic column concept is most visible, the entire Permian Period is missing, but the sediments sit comfortably on each other. The simple fact is that there are no index fossils here attributed to the Permian Period to identify anything as Permian.

The fact that fossils universally exist in the Earth's crust underscores the theory of a huge flood. Fossilization would not result if the animal had merely dropped dead, was subsequently eaten, or rotted and was dispersed—the fate of all animals if they are not buried quickly by a load of sediment—that is, water-laid rock—which is required for fossilization to commence. If entire species are missing, it simply indicates that those animals were not indigenous to that area and therefore it is not surprising that they leave no fossilized trace. Catastrophists note that since animals would be deposited according to variations in weight, time of death, and strength of the currents, there is little reason to expect "chronological order" in the deposits.

Other discoveries support the theory that the strata of the Earth are neither slowly laid down nor particularly ancient, but rather the result of catastrophic floods or, to use the biblical terminology—the Flood. For instance, many fossils actually exist in "graveyards" around the world and, in particular, the Cumberland Bone Cave of Maryland contains fossils from a wide variety of species, from bats to mastodons, and from several inimical species—all of which indicates huge volumes of water sweeping over the land. Robert Broom estimates that the Karoo Supergroup of Africa contains the fossils of 800 billion vertebrate animals, while the Miocene shales fossil bed of California indicates that one billion fish died within a 4-square-mile zone.

Although according to uniformitarianism, sediments of several feet thick should reflect thousands of years of slow development, it is common to find entire mountains of fossils, from Alaska to Africa, indicating spontaneous deaths. Commenting on one as seen in Belgium, paleontologist Dr. Edwin Colbert, possibly the foremost dinosaur expert in the world, has observed: "Thus it could be seen that the fossil boneyard was evidently one of gigantic proportions, especially notable because of its vertical extension through more than a hundred feet of rock."

Sudden death is a common sight over the whole globe. Imprints in fossiliferous rock, all that remains after some buried creatures decayed, have revealed the image of a fish half devouring its meal—another small fish—whose tail is still sticking out of its gaping mouth. Fossils have been unearthed of animals caught while giving birth or, as in the case of a herd of Triceratops, discovered by their broken legs and bones to have been overwhelmed by a wall of water while stampeding, no doubt while trying to escape. When Trachodon, a dinosaur discovered in sediment formation in Kansas in 1908 (now in the American Museum of Natural History in New York), was unearthed, its impression was largely intact. Its skin shows remarkable detail, including the absence of any significant signs of decomposition or predation by other carnivores and carrion-eaters. In August 1971 an expedition unearthed two fossilized skeletons in the Gobi Desert. The dinosaurs, Velociraptor and Protoceratops, were still locked in mortal combat, their backs arched, indicating a sudden load of sediment overwhelmed them and froze them in death. One of the largest dinosaurs in the world, Seismosaurus ("ground-shaking lizard"), was found sufficiently intact in fossilized form that proteins were still preserved within its bone.

Mountains of fossilized animals, as noted above, are so common they have led to some interesting theories on what type and scale of flood hit the Earth. It is speculated that as the flood waters rose, scores of animals managed to reach the highest hills. As the water levels rose still farther, they were slowly swept away by the swift flood currents and deposited in quickly building sedimentation, individually or, where tidal action swept away an entire hill, in great heaps.

This theory would far better explain the general order of animals noted in the sediments: sea invertebrates toward the bottom and land animals and dinosaurs closer to the top, the latter representing the more agile or fierce animals that could make it to the top of the hills and thus be swept away last and deposited higher up in the rapidly building sedimentation.

Discoveries of man-made objects buried even deeper in the sediments reveal the catastrophic nature and recent date of such a flood and the extent of civilization that was wiped out. A clay doll was found 300 feet down at Nampa, Idaho, while an intricately incised iron square was found in deeply buried coal deposits in Europe, and ancient jewelry (necklaces) has been unearthed in coal deposits in Africa and America, all dated to millions of years ago if assuming uniformitarian sedimentation.

However, the fallacy of such an assumption, together with an idea of the volume of the flood and its recentness, can be gleaned from the depth at which human fossilized remains continue to be found and retrieved. The most surprising is a perfectly fossilized human forefinger discovered by Dr. Carl Baugh at the Paluxy River in Texas. The cuticle and nail could clearly be made out and, when sectioned, the ring delineating the bone and tendon was quite evident. This was found so deep it could only be dated by uniformitarian theory to 70 million years ago (Cretaceous Period), long before that theory of slow sedimentation allows for any form of man on the Earth, much less a perfect human specimen as of today.

Another example of how recent was such a flood are the detailed descriptions of just such an event contained in the biblical histories of the Judeo-Christian-Islamic traditions, as well as in some five hundred worldwide legends, many of them remarkably similar. The universality of such stories would seem to rule out local incidents, since many of the mountain tribes have little to fear from floods, and those that have lived near great rivers have been used to the frequent and disastrous overflows of the Nile, Euphrates, and Indus, to exaggerate a seasonal inundation into the legends so dominate of one great flood. Also, since so many peoples have a collective memory of such an event, it would seem that it happened in fairly recent geologic times and truly had global repercussions.

In addition, some of the most ancient cultures in the world preserve surprisingly clear and detailed recollections of a far greater amount of water in the atmosphere. In the Sumerian and Babylonian creation accounts, the firmament is personified by the god Mummu, who is the rising mist between the great first god Apsu, the sweet waters, and Tiamat, the salt waters, and is eventually divided by Marduk, while in Genesis this same concept is reflected in God dividing the waters above and below with the firmament. It is a fact, however, that only 0.015 percent of the atmosphere today is made up of water, and if it all came down it would be sufficient to cover the whole Earth with less than two inches of rain. But ancient worldwide flood stories show a remarkable consistency in the number of days that it rained—an average from forty to sixty days—and the fact that such phenomenal rain had never been seen before.

It was only in the 20th century that some surprising evidence was unearthed (literally) that produced startling corroboration of these ancient accounts and therefore links to an antediluvian civilization. Worldwide sedimentary corings have confirmed a vastly different atmosphere existed in the past. Fossilized plants and animals known to thrive only in tropical climates are found globally, from Antarctica to Alaska, indicating that the Earth at one time had a largely stable and warm temperature. However, there is currently enough water on the Earth, embodied in the polar ice fields, to flood it completely in such a temperate environment. But the undisputed presence of past continents and thriving terrestrial ecosystems can only mean that much of this water was not on the Earth until recently.

Many catastrophist geologists and geophysicists point to the fact that a vastly greater amount of water in the atmosphere (specifically, the troposphere), sufficient to form a water vapor canopy much like the one Venus, our twin planet, still possesses (though carbon trioxide), is the only thing that can explain this. The only other elements that can create a globally warmer Earth would be more ozone or carbon dioxide. But in this case we are back in the same boat—literally—because this planet would be one vast ocean. Not only would a greater abundance of water in the atmosphere create a greenhouse effect, but the loss of this vapor canopy, for reasons still unknown, would have brought huge amounts of water onto the Earth and caused a great flood.

Dr. John Morris, well-known flood geologist, proposes that the Bible alludes to this scenario from his study of passages dealing with the antediluvian environment. In Genesis 2:5–6 it reads that "the Lord God had not caused it to rain upon the Earth, but there went up a mist from the Earth, and watered the whole face of the ground." This is precisely what would have been the case on an Earth with a water-vapor canopy. With a steady temperature there would have been no air-mass circulation and therefore there would have been no rain. The temperature drop at night would have brought down some of the water as dew, then with the heat of day it would have risen, watering the vegetation in the process. In the passage dealing with abatement of the flood, further corroborating information was found. It is recorded that a great wind came—something noted perhaps because it was the first time mankind had ever experienced a strong wind. This would indicate that the atmosphere of the Earth had undergone a great change and now air-mass circulation was possible. With far cooler temperatures, the formation of polar ice and an "ice age" was possible and the waters would recede.

Study of the atmosphere adds an unexpected dimension to all this—as well as confirming a date for it within the span of intelligent mankind. The isotope carbon 14 should have achieved equilibrium in the atmosphere within 30,000 years (that is, the amount entering the atmosphere from the Earth is equal to the amount exiting into space, thus causing a steady level in the atmosphere), but repeated and reliable tests have proven that carbon 14 is still building, something that can only be explained by a massive shake-up of the atmosphere within this time frame.

Dr. Melvin Cook of the University of Utah undertook a further study of the nonequilibrium factor. He discovered that this nonequilibrium was so significant in carbon 14 dating that it "reduces the computed age by an amount dependent upon the age of the sample by amounts increasing in time from about 20 percent in 1,000 years, 30 percent in 4,000 years, and finally telescoping all the very long ages to 12,500 years or less."

Though this method brings a plausible global event sufficient to upset the atmosphere closer to the known era of intelligent man, the Earth's magnetic field may help in narrowing this event down to a more precise period. For the last 150 years the magnetic field has steadily declined by about 6 percent. Dr. Thomas Barnes, of the University of Texas, El Paso, who has devoted much of his life to studying it, explains, from the aspect of its decline, its significance:

The consequences of the stronger magnetic field in the past was better shielding of the Earth and its atmosphere from primary cosmic rays. This also reduced the rate of production of carbon 14 in the atmosphere. . . .

Primary cosmic rays interact with the atmosphere to produce neutrons which in turn transmute nitrogen atoms into carbon 14. Hence, with the lesser number of cosmic rays striking the atmosphere per second, a smaller rate of production of carbon 14 existed in the past. A smaller production rate of carbon 14 in the atmosphere than has previously been assumed would reduce the age of carbon 14 dates.

In commenting on Dr. Cook's time period of 12,500 years ago, Dr. Barnes adds: "When the effect of the larger magnetic field in the past and the consequent lesser rate of production of carbon 14 is included, these ages will be telescoped still further."

This lesser date would be within the last 7,000 years. This time frame now becomes oddly coincidental with those applied by our earliest legends to a cataclysmic flood wiping out a previous civilization. This time period, furthermore, has been considerably strengthened by quite fascinating discoveries made only recently—again in sedimentary deposits.

Among these the case of "radio haloes" in coalified logs deeply buried in the Colorado Plateau is cause for comment for a number of interesting reasons. First, they have been found in logs across a wide part of the plateau; second, the sediments here are rich in uranium. One of the isotopes in the radioactive decay chain of uranium-to-lead was found to have leached quickly into the logs. This isotope, polonium 210, has a radioactive decay life of only around four years. This decay, as with other isotopes, shoots an identifiable halo, or concentric shadow or ring, rippling out from its core into whatever substance it is lodged in. In the case of polonium 210, only one concentric ring is emitted during decay. The polonium 210 halos in the logs show that the core is surrounded by both an elliptic and a concentric halo, indicating that the logs were quickly buried under enough weight to compress them and thus also the initial halo emitted by the decay. Furthermore, after this compression there was still enough time in polonium 210's radioactive decay life to form another halo, this time one that remained concentric. This discovery indicates that the huge Colorado Plateau was created quickly by flood; in doing so the flood buried part of an antediluvian forest with a load of sediment sufficient to compress the logs before the radioactive decay life of polonium 210, and its ability to create another halo, was finished—that is, under four years' time. The ratio of uranium-to-lead, roughly 64,000

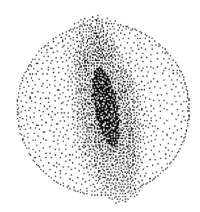

A radio halo of polonium 210. Examination of the cores of uranium halos in the same wood discovered a large amount of uranium 238 but almost no lead 206, in a ratio of up to 64,000, indicating all deposits were only 5,000 to 7,000 years old. Uniformitariams attempted to date these deposits at 35 million to 245 million years old, unaware of the precise work on radio halos done by Dr. Robert Gentry.

times, in the same samples indicates this happened only 5,000 to 7,000 years ago.

Perhaps some of the most conclusive evidence for a recent massive flood is the existence of fossil fuels—in other words, the by-products of the flesh of marine invertebrates, animals, dinosaurs, and, presumably, in this view, people, billions and billions of each. Laboratory conversion of organic material (garbage) into hydrocarbons and then into petroleum has aided in the destruction of the old uniformitarian paradigm of oil formation. A hands-on demonstration showed that it was more a matter of temperature and pressure than time—in 20 minutes oil was produced. It is tempting to think that oil proves the existence of a flood, since oil is not formed naturally otherwise—huge "seas" of vertebrates are not deposited daily into many square miles, packed over with enough water-laid rock so that the pressure of such a mass and the heat of the decomposing flesh can produce the vast beds of oil we have beneath us today. As a matter of interest, most oil is in the Middle East, where biblical and legendary sources say civilization was concentrated before a flood.

Not only is the hypothetical chronology of uniformitarianism lacking in geologic studies, radiometric dating of rocks in an attempt to justify this chronology has come under serious criticism by modern neocatastrophist geologists. No matter what results are obtained, if they do not match the hypothetical age applied to the strata by the geologic column concept of slow Lyellian development, they are thrown out in favor of uniformitarian assumptions. This has proven embarrassing when this method was used unknowingly on rock formations known to be recent. Dates like 22 million years were announced for the 200-year-old subsurface Kilauea flow in Hawaii. Potassium-argon tests yielded ages from 160 million to 3 billion years for the 1801 Hualalei flow, also in Hawaii, while 23-year-old Mount Saint Helens flow in Washington state in 1980 has already been accorded ages in excess of millions of years.

Despite these and other discoveries, there are still adherents of uniformitarianism who seek to deny or explain away, often feebly, their existence. Often there is a certain amount of success in this since some institutions or some textbook orthodoxy still adheres to this philosophy. They also invoke the Progress Theory, another Victorian-uniformitarian concept dominant in the West, which states that progress is also a steady and natural climb to the present and that therefore ancient man had no choice but to be primitive. Taken to its logical conclusion, one cannot believe anything written down or passed on by ancient man because it is not history but primitive exaggeration. Only *our* written records are history, and only *our* experiences are facts.

Yet according to the tenets of this theory, mankind has existed with a similar degree of intelligence as today for tens of thousands of years. We are so used to the millions of years of uniformitarian ideology, we forget how long a thousand years really is and yet, paradoxically, how short a period the last 5,000 years of human history is, compared with the potential it could (should) have had.

Any assertion that there could have been an advanced global civilization in prehistory is usually greeted with derision because no cause for its utter destruction could be conceived by uniformitarian methods. Nevertheless, the proof of the disasters ancient records repeatedly describe continues to be discovered in spite of uniformitarianism's philosophical denials.

Many of these discoveries support the proposition that the splitting asunder of the "megacontinent" happened in the 4th millennium B.C. This proposition, found again in the massive buckling of flood sediments, is corroborated by the chronology of ancient legends, for they speak of a great flood first and then they speak of a great destruction of civilization thousands of years later by division and splitting of the Earth just before the dawn of our own histories.

We know that the 4th millennium B.C. is the most puzzling point in the history of mankind. In the late part of this millennium, around 3100 B.C., a mere 5,000 years ago, our history suddenly begins with the complex written language of Sumerian, recording business and legal transactions, religious incantations, and legends of the many city-states of southern Mesopotamia. Around this same time the culture of Egypt begins, as well as the unknown culture of the Indus Valley at the gateway to the Asian subcontinent. The Mayan calendar of Mexico and Central America is so precise, its beginning date can be calculated as coequal with our date of 3114 B.C.

Besides the legends about the destruction of a great civilization that had existed before them, each year all these cultures also celebrated festivals of renewal or of the dead, recalling some past horrific event that the Egyptians even located as being centered in the Western Ocean (the Atlantic).

Traces of a prehistoric single language have been suggested by the finding of a form of early Sanskrit in South America. Vincente Lopez, a 19th century French scholar, discovered that the earliest peoples of South America included Indo-Aryans and that their leaders used *Ayar* prefixed before their names, identical to Sanskrit *Ajar*—"chieftain." The four original "leaders" of this people may symbolically reflect an entire culture set on the move after a calamity. Lopez notes their names were Ayar-Mancotopa, Ayar-Chaki, Ayar-Aussi, and Ayar-Uyssu, meaning in Sanskrit "believers, wanderers, soldiers, husbandmen"—a caste system not unlike the Old World's earliest societies, but in this case trying to rebuild in South America.

Aside from alluding to a single-language civilization preceding ours, biblical texts place a significant event as occurring during the same epoch. In the genealogical recital in Genesis 10.25 it is written: "And to Eber were born two sons, the name of the one, Peleg, because in his days the Earth was divided."

The biblical reference has traditionally been interpreted by the clergy as referring to nations, despite the fact that the Hebrew word *eretz* and the Greek word (in the Septuagint) *gaien* mean the ground or earth and not *goyim* or *ethnos* or *phyla* which respectively refer to nations and tribes in Hebrew and Greek. But the word *peleg* means earthquake, a name that would not be relevant to a mere scattering of tribes. According to the chronology of some biblical scholars, such as Dr. Merrill F. Unger, Eber's life span would coincide with about 3500 to 3100 B.C.

The candidacy of the 4th millennium B.C. for the age of the splitting of "megacontinent" is gaining ground from some other unusual developments. The most remarkable are from uniformitarian methods, no less. This evidence once again involves the rate of sedimentation. Over the last 100 years a careful study of the rate of sedimentation at river mouths reveals all river deltas in the world to be only 4,000 to 5,000 years old, suggesting the creation of all rivers about that long ago. This can be explained if the continents split and underwent titanic movement, with cliff and shoreline transformations. Either old rivers were rerouted and formed new deltas in their present locations or new rivers, created from the upset of juvenal sources, flowed to the sea for the first time.

Another clue is found in uniformitarianism's neat time periods for dating the Earth's geological strata. Even if we were to take these as accurate, it is worthy to note that the fracture zone between the continents (that is, where the continents can be placed back together like pieces of a puzzle), most apparent between western Africa and eastern North and South America, goes up directly between all "time periods" of the uniformitarian geologic column, from the most ancient to the most recent, indicating a split for the continents within the Holocene Epoch in the last 10,000 years.

It has been suggested by a number of catastrophists that the ending of the Ice Age may have started with this event. As the continents suddenly moved over the seabed, they pushed land into new temperature zones and possibly caused the Earth to lose its balance and go off kilter, perhaps by as much as 26 degrees until it regained some of its balance and evened out at its present 23.5-degree inclination.

Major shifts of land and sea are evident on the continental shelves, which show signs of cliff erosion from the surf, though now hundreds of feet below the present surface. The deep underwater beaches at the Azores could have been created only by the prolonged pounding action of the surf on the shoreline. Corings on the continental shelves have bored into fossil graveyards of land animals, and the retrieval of ancient man-made tools in the same area indicates habitation when the shelves, now deep below the surface, were once above.

Vast and deep subsurface ocean changes in relatively recent times are also indicated by the rippling of bottom sands on seamounts and even on the deep ocean bottom, something unexpected in the uniformitarian model of perpetually calm ocean depths for 200,000,000 years. Concerning this discovery, Dr. Edwin L. Hamilton, who studied the phenomena closely, describes the unexpected find, as seen in the Pacific. "A feature of immediate interest was the fact that ripple marks, long considered evidence of shallow water deposition by land geologists, were found in the deep sea. Two remarkable photographs taken on the top of Sylvania Seamount in the Marshall Islands area establish the fact that the soft Globigerina ooze between the manganese-coated boulders was definitely rippled." Further deep-sea expeditions by the Navy Electronics Laboratory have extended the surprising discoveries even farther down. Hamilton comments that "well-defined ripple marks down to a depth of about 6,000 feet" have been found.

Corings and retrievals of igneous rocks (granites, basalts) in the Atlantic's soft (therefore presumably young) seabed have found counterparts to the great beds of lava on land, like the Deccan Traps in India and the Columbian Plateau. The only explanation seems to be the same event: massive continental movement.

Then the 4th millennium B.C. again arises in computations of the Earth's magnetic field. We again find that its disturbing decline indicates the Earth was jolted relatively recently. If this decline (6 percent in the last 150 years) were extrapolated backward linearly, as is the standard in uniformitarian reasoning, only 7,000 years ago the Earth would have had a magnetic field the strength of a magnetic star, which this Earth could never have supported. This would suggest that the Earth had a rather steady conductor generating its magnetic field until recent history, when something upset the globe, such as a tilt of the Earth on its axis sufficient to disturb its rotational core and hence to disturb the generation of the magnetic field.

Former exemplars of uniformitarianism are now seen to point directly to the 4th millennium. Strongholds such as the Grand Canyon were dashed by the discovery in our generation that the headwaters of the Colorado River (which uniformitarianism proposed slowly etched out the canyon over eons of time) are actually at a lower altitude than the plateau through which the Grand Canyon is cut. Since water does not run uphill, the old theory was junked in favor of a breach that would have cut the canyon quickly, as an inland sea (apparently the one that covered large parts of the American southwest) emptied through it. From the recent estimates of how fast Niagara Falls recedes, a date no earlier than perhaps only the 4th millennium B.C. can be offered. But so far nothing can be offered, in uniformitarian ideology, to explain what jolted the American continent enough to split open a canyon in the southwest and drop or uplift parts of the strata near Canada.

"Apparent age" is often a deceptive excuse to claim that identical geologic features can look different in age. Following the titanic eruption of Mount Saint Helens in 1980, almost every geologic feature of "extreme old uniformitarian age" on Earth had been created, only on a much smaller scale. Heat winds laid down a 60-foot ridge of sediment, a "gravity collapse" of land created a valley with extreme weathering around its lip, and a mud breach created a ¹/₅ scale "Grand Canyon" and then diverted a creek to flow down its center, much as the Colorado does in the Grand Canyon today. Spirit Lake sloshed back and forth so violently against the sides of the mountain that huge tidal waves created cliffs looking "thousands of years old" overnight. At the same time the blast of the volcano ripped more than 1 million trees out of the forest and threw them into the lake. Over time these floating logs rubbed all their bark off against each other and, becoming waterlogged, sank to the bottom root end (heaviest end) first to become embedded in the rising sediment, there to sit as a dead forest—precisely what is seen in vast ridges of sediment like Petrified Ridge in the Dakotas, where fossilized trees, denuded of their bark and with only 3-foot-long roots (as in Spirit Lake), are buried as great dead forests. But by the size of these dead forests they indicate floods and upheaval on a global or continent-wide level.

The downsizing of carbon 14 dates has turned the tables on our view of the slow ascent of mankind's civilization from Mesolithic foragers to Neolithic stoneworkers to Bronze Age artificers. Probably as the dates continue to be compressed these time periods will be eradicated altogether. In their place carbon 14 has indicated a cataclysm, for which dating beyond seems barred by the extent it so changed the isotope ratios upon which our current dating methods rely. Catastrophist ideologies are causing the abandonment of dating an object merely by its depth in sediment. Petrification of relatively modern implements, such as bags of flour in Arkansas, a derby hat from a mine in New Zealand, and an entire water wheel in Australia, has erased the whole concept of "apparent age." Without this philosophical dating chronology, the foundation of our timetables disappears into a world of contradictory artifacts and ambiguous interpretations—of whether one is older, coequal, or even later than another.

The ability to spread agriculturally and organizationally over one megacontinent would require a high level of science and technology to remain linked and cohesive. Therefore it is unavoidable to consider the existence over the whole world of unknown ruins as further evidence that a great civilization preceded our own time. They contain within them more than just the arguable paradoxes of small artifacts, but the undeniable fact that they all seem designed by the same collective science. Their stones are enormous in size, intricate in their cutting, mysterious in their method of hauling and arrangement, and resemble each other from as far as Peru to Malta, Britain, and even Africa. Today we classify them as "cyclopean" because of the colossal size of the blocks used—the greatest paradox, for they surpass anything our engineering can achieve today, yet they are so old not even our most ancient cultures knew who built them (aside from the "gods," that is).

Many of these megaliths, from the Mediterranean to Canada, had been arranged into crude henges or "wheels," almost all of which seem to incorporate into their key angles astronomical alignments to specific stars. The principal alignments are with the passages of the equinox, solstices, and other seasonal indicators. The plurality of such sites would seem to indicate the widespread need for a new calendar, one perhaps necessitated by the cataclysm mentioned above. After a devastating continental upheaval the entire heavens would be altered (from our perspective), and the beginning and ending of new seasons would need marking. However, it is true that primitive though accurate enough astronomical calculations and computations of heavenly bodies and their movements and risings could have been derived from placing tree trunks in appropriate places to mark stars on the horizon (as the Egyptians did). The use of such huge monoliths, of a size that even our own modern cranes cannot lift, suggests a science and engineering beyond even our own. But the crudeness in the cutting of the blocks indicates expedience and a culture on the wane, one that soon disappeared, to leave what was left of their science and engineering a mystery to later peoples. As far as anybody can tell, the oldest appear to date to about the late 4th millennium (circa 3100) B.C.— another echo of the time of "peleg" and prehistory.

It stands to reason that if these represent early rebuildings after a cataclysm, most of those found underwater, having been covered by rising ocean levels over the centuries following, might be even older and might be some of the most fantastic and intact ruins anywhere, since they would have been spared the ravages and quarrying by successive cultures on land. It is in the Bermuda Triangle, on the Bahama Banks, where just such an idea is being proved with each successful dive. Discoveries here even include some elaborate tiled floors deep beneath the bottom sands— details of prehistoric civilization not found anywhere on land. If all the observed geometric patterns prove to be man-made, then the shallow Great Bahama Bank actually becomes the most extensive prehistoric site left on Earth, on the scale of a vast city.

Already the downsizing of carbon 14 has revealed a clue to this lost civilization and the Triangle. The Bimini Stones had been previously dated to 12,000 years ago by testing the mangrove roots that had overgrown some. Overgrowth would obviously imply abandonment. This time period was coequal to the date for the ending of the last so-called glaciation of the Earth. However, the downsizing of dates now places both events in the 3rd to 2nd millennium B.C.—providing the intriguing prospect that the Bahamas are indeed the last part of the former remnant of one great continent, broken in the 4th millennium B.C. to succumb slowly to the sea.

Other underwater discoveries of even greater gargantuan stones have been turning up on both sides of the Atlantic, to very much impress upon the observer a culture torn in half. These underwater stones seem older in nature because they are more finely and accurately cut (as opposed to crude henges), perfectly square or rectangular and precisely positioned one against the other. For example, for 9 miles a cyclopean stone wall runs along the continental shelf off Morocco, made up of square stones two stories high set upon smaller stones, while some similar walls or roads have been traced by aerial survey off South America. Other cyclopean stone constructions exist off Spain, Portugal, and Yucatán.

The only other place on land where similar stones have been found is at Baalbek, in Lebanon. Archaeologists, in their investigation of the ancient site, have established a veritable timetable of human architectural evolution, from the present to the past. Tumbled or cast about from wars and quarrying are the square stones of Turkish mosques of the Renaissance period; then even older are the massive amounts of the small mud kiln-baked bricks of medieval and Saracen Arab dwellings; even older still are the Byzantine rectangles of Justinian's time, the 6th century A.D.; even grander and older are the monumental blocks and columns of the Roman Imperial period; still older are the great stones of Antiochian Syria of the Hellenistic Age. Still older are the Phoenician stonework and sarcophagi of the age of Hiram (950 B.C.), then older still are primitive Canaanite constructions and sun-dried bricks (2000 B.C.). And then there are the oldest of them all—colossal stones of 1,200 tons, the largest and heaviest worked stones on Earth, arranged neatly to form a foundation so huge the purpose of which no one can conceive, and upon the length of only three of its blocks a huge classical Roman temple was later built and is still partially standing. Nearby lies the largest stone worked by man—a gigantic rectangle measuring 68 by 15 by 15 feet, weighing 1,400 tons. It lies strangely prostrate near the remains of others, toppled by some unknown prehistoric event.

Tales of lands sinking and disappearing to the west (as recorded by those indigenous peoples nearer Europe and Africa) and memories of a homeland to the east across the sea (as remembered and passed on by Amerindian peoples) were still in existence by the time the Spanish sailed across the Atlantic but never associated, of course, with recalling perhaps the same prehistoric event: a vague remembrance of the opposite continents as they split and moved over the horizon, and a vague remembrance of a homeland fractured.

These native Atlantic legends have often been used as proof of a vague recollection of an Atlantean continent sinking, as in Plato's tale or Edgar Cayce's trances. It has been pointed out by critics of Atlantis, however, that when all the continents are moved back into their theoretical places in a megacontinent, there is no leftover landmass large enough to be accorded to the Atlantean continent or island first spoken of by Plato. This is also true of the legends of Lemuria or Mu, a vanished paradise land in the Pacific. But the questions could be asked, "Was the megacontinent Atlantis?" "Was it Lemuria?" Are the legends, borrowed and tailored though they may be, refering to this lost civilization on a single continent? Was its type of destruction confused with its "name"? It is interesting to note that in Sanskrit, one of the earliest languages on Earth, traces of which are found even in South America, the word meaning great cataclysm is *Atyantica!* Did the Atlantic receive its name from the earliest languages of mankind?—not from the Greek legend of Atlas, son of Zeus, but from great disasters that were at the heart of the Earth and destroyed that one culture?

A consideration of this over the next chapters may explain how the ruins beneath the Triangle's jade waters could hold the last clue to a fantastic civilization of the past and the most fantastic clue to the current riddle of the Bermuda Triangle.

8

Atyantica!

SEVERAL OF THE most dedicated searchers for Atlantis have agreed that Plato's tale is derived only from bits and pieces from what might be termed one vantage point of a much broader upheaval. It is also apparent to any observer of history that there exist far older tales of cataclysmic upheaval, destroying a vast prehistoric civilization at its zenith, that possess this same quality, though they are without any direct reference to the Atlantic.

But when the Atlantic-centric theme of Atlantis or, rather, Atyantica, is taken into account, a remarkable ingredient is added that all too ably explains otherwise mysterious elements credited for their various destructions. For example, in our Judeo-Christian-Islamic traditions we know that Babilu (Babel) preceded the dawn of our own histories and was destroyed by scattering and division, so that its towers and buildings came crashing down. In India this civilization is known as Rutas, destroyed by earthquake "before the Himalayas existed"—another echo of a time before great continental movement, since the catalyst of orogeny, or mountain building, is buckling land in response to the whole continent moving. The Chinese recall the world destruction of Mu by being overwhelmed by tidal waves and inundation. In Peru the inhabitants of this civilization who survived were called Viracochas—"sea foam" and by extension "stormy sea"—because they arrived in Peru at a time of unparalleled oceanic upheavals in order to build the first great city, Tiahuanaco.

Taking the above as caused by one event, one can view these as stages of destruction of the same civilization, yet from different vantage points on what was a single continent. The cities at the epicenter of the cataclysm—on both sides of the Atlantic—were destroyed quickly, so entire populations were forced to relocate; powerful earthquakes tumbled down cities on what are now the plains of Mesopotamia; the great uplifting mountains, where the continental strata buckled, uprooted cities in India; cities along the eastern coast of this megacontinent (present-day China) were overwhelmed by tidal waves as the Euro-Asian continent slammed forward into the Pacific, with tidal waves crashing over Peru for the same reasons.

The crucial instigating factor within these tales—destruction caused by God or the gods—might be given startling scientific body from an unusual source. Harold Wilkins, in his *Mysteries of Ancient South America,* notes many aboriginal Indian legends that were originally recorded by the first Spanish and Portuguese explorers. All these distinctly recall four successive impacts, and that the sun and moon turned various shades of yellow, red, and blue. These atmospheric changes, if taken in the context of the continents ripping apart, could easily be explained by the massive amount of methane gas entering the atmosphere from the Atlantic seabed. This incredible incident was followed by another disturbing visual observation. Toward the east—in other words, where the Atlantic is now—darkness *rose up from the earth* to the sky, a memory perhaps recalling the horrific furnace with billowing plumes of smoke that would have belched out of the Midatlantic Ridge as the Earth split open.

Somehow the idea of just such a bombardment of comets or meteors, and the destruction of a prehistoric civilization, was recalled even by the Old World's most ancient cultures. As the following excerpt from Plato indicates, it was an event so old the Greeks, relative newcomers to civilization, had preserved it in myth, but that more ancient cultures like Egypt preserved it with startling scientific regard. We again go back to his *Timaeus* dialogue and the story of Solon of Athens journeying to Egypt in search of ancient knowledge. During his conversation with the priest of the delta city of Sais, Solon tries to figure out when the Great Deluge hit the Earth, but the priest curtly interrupts him:

O Solon, Solon, you Hellenes are never anything but children, and there is not an old man among you. [Solon in return asks him what he meant.] I mean to say that in mind you are all young; there is no old opinion handed down among you by ancient tradition [bear in mind the priest was speaking 2,400 years ago], nor any science which is hoary with age. And I will tell you why. There have been, and will be again, many destructions of mankind arising out of many causes; the greatest have been brought about by the agencies of fire and water, and other lesser ones by innumerable other causes. There is a story, which even you have preserved, that once upon a time Phaethon, the son of Helios, having yoked the steeds of his father's chariot, because he was not able to drive them in the path of his father, burnt up all that was upon the Earth, and was himself destroyed by a thunderbolt. Now this has the form of a myth, but really signifies a declination of the heavenly bodies moving in the heavens around the Earth, and a great conflagration upon the Earth.

This myth seems startlingly to embody the relationship, as noted visually, between Helios (the sun) and a comet (a small version of the sun) from the moment it entered the Earth's atmosphere—the thunderbolt being its explosion in the atmosphere. This exact chain of events was witnessed over Siberia on June 30, 1908, when a bright burning pillar traveled slowly through the sky and exploded about 5 miles above the surface of barren forests near an area called Tunguska. This is almost unanimously believed today to have been a small comet, perhaps the short-lived comet Encke. It laid waste more than 700 square miles of forest, started flash fires, and felled trees in a neat domino effect as far as 12 miles from its epicenter.

Placing these events in an obvious chronological order, the cause of the great splitting apart of the megacontinent and the destruction of a vast single civilization by confusion and scattering, by the gods or from above, seems to be explained by massive impacts of meteors, comets, or asteroids. Developing this further, one could assume that such a great force might have shaken the Earth literally to its core, so that the crust cracked and the mantle poured forth to uplift and split this supercontinent.

An idea of the extent of this widespread destruction can be appreciated by the fact that no known great meteorite impacts can be located anywhere near Greece or Egypt, nor is there evidence of an impact causing a "great conflagration upon the Earth" in the histories of adjacent civilizations. But as the Egyptian priest said, according to Plato, such an event may have been so long before and possibly so far away that many peoples, like the Greeks, regarded it only as myth. Older cultures, however, may have preserved the memory factually as a holdover from a prehistoric civilization that directly experienced its results.

Abundant evidence has come to light in the last twenty-five years, however, to support the proposition that areas now encompassing the Bermuda Triangle and the Caribbean had been the epicenter of catastrophic comet or meteor impacts that ignited forests around the globe. This evidence includes Stishovites (shock-heated grains of quartz), more numerous in the Caribbean than anywhere else on Earth. They have so far only been found at meteorite impact sites and nuclear explosion test beds, where the massive explosions sent shock waves passing through the rock at such force they shock-heated and compressed mineral grains of normal quartz.

One piece of evidence may even establish titanic movement of the American continent in the wake of this impact. Tempestites, or deposits left by tsunamis (huge tidal waves), have been identified in Mexico, the southeastern United States, and the Caribbean on a colossal average. One consisted of a 150- to 300-foot band and of a mixture of both big and small rocks, indicating that a violent and tremendous tidal wave ripped through what is now the Caribbean and the Gulf of Mexico in the wake of something definitely Earth shaking.

This apparently happened even before the "dust settled." On top of the tsunami deposit a layer of iridium-rich silt had settled—and, apparently, had settled over almost the entire globe, if recent studies are to be embraced. A trace metal, iridium seeks the presence of iron and is therefore an extremely rare terrestrial metal, but one that is more common in the mantle and presumably in the core, where the greatest deposits of iron are thought to exist. It is located today in some "hot" volcanoes, such as those in Hawaii, where it comes up from the mantle in the lava flows. But it is also associated with identified iron meteorite impact sites. This worldwide layer usually measures 2 to 3 centimeters thick, but in the Caribbean and Haiti it is as much as 17 centimeters thick, with the iridium content being much higher than elsewhere, on an average of ten to fifty times more.

This iridium layer contains several "peaks"—that is, periods of greater concentration—around the globe. A possible explanation for this is that early peaks were caused by the varying impacts of iron meteorites and then later ones were caused by successive volcanic eruptions as the Earth was jolted and great eruptions sent more iridium into the atmosphere at varying intervals based on the duration and timing of the flows, such as those seen at the Columbian Plateau or the Deccan Traps. These flows, a world apart, would seem to be impossible events without the continents undergoing massive upheaval and upsetting the mantle below. Widespread forest fires at this time seemed to have sent soot around the world, since this global iridium layer is found intermixed with carbon ash. But, once again, it is thickest in the Caribbean, again indicating that this area was near the primary epicenter.

Attempts to correlate the evidence above with an impact site have centered around the so-called subsediment Chicxulub Crater in the Yucatán. Geologist Walter Alvarez was the first to propose this back in 1980. Using uniformitarian methodology, he dated the crater to 65 million years ago, even suggesting that the impact wiped out the dinosaurs. Recently, however, as that paradigm and its dating methodology have fallen apart and as further tests indicate Chicxulub is not an impact crater, the search for impact sites has centered on the ocean bottom.

Crater-hunter Rufus Johnson has been able to pinpoint a chain of possible comet impacts along the Bermuda Triangle's continental shelf, with a minimum estimated age of 6,000 years. They extend out from Virginia and then, following the coastline, down to Florida, where possibly one of the largest in this shower might have hit. Although the craters are by now so weathered by the elements and the ocean that identifying them is highly subjective, Johnson continues to discover other evidence of massive impacts in this general area, like smooth and rounded river rocks in the middle of fields far from any river, some of them weighing up to 32,000 pounds! He observes: "Yet these boulders are scattered around on the ground as if some unseen giant just casually tossed them aside."

While the lead of this theory seems, at first glance, more suited to explain only the colossal ruins on the various sunken plateaus of the Bermuda Triangle, it may have more direct bearing on explaining its infamous enigma if we more thoroughly explore aspects of its legendary destruction.

If we assume that these are the impact sites heard by the ancient peoples of the Americas, a rather interesting correlation with the enigma of the Bermuda Triangle is uncovered. In commenting on the Tunguska impact's aftereffects, Dr. I. Vasilieyev, who contributed significantly to its study, reported that there had been "absolute electromagnetic chaos at the center of the site." He continued: "There was clearly an electromagnetic hurricane of enormous proportions which has shattered, perhaps permanently, all the normal alignments with the earth's magnetic field"— a coincidence that adds another dimension to the origin of electromagnetic anomalies in the Triangle.

Unlike a meteor or an asteroid, a comet has a coma, or head, that is a vast reactor of energy. The damage done by several comets measuring hundreds of miles in diameter might have distorted the magnetic field enough so that even today, triggered by current changes, weather, or perhaps even the presence of a plane or ship, anomalies will spontaneously swirl into and out of existence. One may justifiably ask, however, if this is not going too far in trying to pin down a source for electromagnetic anomalies in the Triangle and the connection between them and unidentified underwater ruins.

Yet we may also ask: how did a "tale" of destruction of a prehistoric supercivilization evolve the idea that such an event divided all languages of mankind? And if not a tale, how could a real event like this have happened? It must be remembered that the earliest languages we know of, all dating to around 3100 B.C., even when spoken by peoples in adjacent lands, seem to pop out of nowhere—Sumerian, Babylonian, Elamite, pockets of Sanskrit in South America, and so on, many of which have absolutely no affinity with the other.

Similarly, today we have been confronted by mysterious moments wherein people have suddenly spoken languages they were never taught, or dialects so old experienced scholars had to be called in to decipher what was said. While some try and explain this as supernatural or "reincarnation," it overlooks a far more acceptable answer that fits into a more understandable framework. Pursuing this angle also uncovers one of the most intriguing proofs that such a legend of language creation was inspired by a real cataclysm capable of deranging the electromagnetic frequencies of the Earth.

In his articles and books on electromagnetic field effects, Albert Budden has drawn our attention to the wide array of poltergeist effects on physical matter, such as mirrors cracking, tables overturning, and nonflammables exploding. But examples of its effects on electrical equipment and computers indicate a certain potential on the human brain, itself a similar though vastly more complex electrical device. He describes how "Television sets switch themselves on and off, repeated telephone connections are made which engineers consider 'impossible,' and computers show programmes that have not been installed by anyone or information that is inaccessible through normal use."

In developing his electromagnetic pollution theory, Budden has become convinced that poltergeist phenomena can be explained by electromagnetic aberrations. Identical phenomena have been created around power poles that mimic those reported throughout medieval history that were then attributed to noisy ghosts—"poltergeists," according to German priests. They apparently have been occurring randomly (as far as we understand today) for hundreds of years. One can assume such a phenomenon is a mild upset of the magnetic field in a local place, though what causes the aberration remains mostly unexplained.

At the very least, anyway, it seems that electromagnetic aberrations can cause almost anything in any device subject to their effects, including the implanting of information not personally experienced and altering the reception of information. The aberrant fields might engineer this effect by warping other wavelengths with which they come into contact.

Especially of interest here are extremely low frequency (ELF) electro-magnetic waves and fields. Physicist Thomas Valone, director of the Integrity Research Institute in Washington, D.C., notes that the alpha rhythm of the human brain is the same frequency as the Schumann Frequency, the Earth's fundamental resonant frequency. (Taking the speed of light—186,000 miles per second—and dividing it by the median circumference of the Earth equals 7.8 Hz—the brain's alpha rhythm.)

On the amazing potential of all this, Valone further comments:

In fact, Dr. Robert Wecker in the *Body Electric* cites an experiment conducted by the Max Planck Institute in Germany in which Dr. Rutger Wever found that after totally desynchronizing subjects' biorhythms (metabolic and circadian), the introduction of a weak 10 Hz field (2.5 V/m) "dramatically restored normal patterns to most of the biological measurements. Wever concluded that this frequency in the micropulsations of the earth's electromagnetic field was the prime *timer* of biocycles." Another study done by an Indian biophysicist Sarada Subramanyam showed that humans' EEG not only responds to the earth's micropulsations but also depends on the direction in which they are facing in relation to the earth's field.

These dramatic examples of the intricate connection between the human bioprocesses and the Earth's electromagnetic frequencies show us the potential effect a global cataclysm, like massive impacts and a rending continent, could have on the human brain. In some cases, people can even be "allergic" or "hypersensitive" to certain forms of electromagnetism or its "pollution," while others can withstand varying degrees of it, some to the point that they seem quite immune. This may have been a key factor in how various languages could be created out of one, although it may also depend somewhat on the geographic location where the persons were in the world when the cataclysm struck.

With so much evidence pointing to the general possibility of the key points to these legends of a prehistoric destruction, it seems logical to assume that an advanced one-world civilization—a very specific and integral part of these worldwide legends of destruction—could also have existed and been destroyed by this event and by the accumulative action of its geologic aftermath during the centuries following.

While this prehistoric civilization's capabilities are only hinted at vaguely in our own legends, Edgar Cayce was the only one to get specific on details of its supposed science and, furthermore, claim the Bahamas was its last intact remnant. This is one of the most astounding assertions made in the Cayce records. While most anybody could fabricate a super civilization from the legends, no one could fabricate its last remnant on the Bahama Banks, as Cayce proposed, albeit via a highly unorthodox method, nor would anybody else have the guts to assert that obscure Bimini held archeological evidence for this civilization.

Along with this disturbing coincidence come others. In his revelation of the final exodus from the Bahama Banks, Cayce asserted that part of this exodus was accomplished using their advanced power sources one final time to "guide the ships in the sea and in the air" to Peru, Egypt, Spain, among others, and lastly Yucatán. Although all the Old World civilizations seem, surprisingly, to appear around 3100 B.C., in America the Mayan civilization, like all the others of Mexico, seems to have no architectural roots older than 1500 B.C. This disparity might be answered by the Mayan calendar, which maintains a beginning date equivalent to our 3114 B.C.— another echo of the time of peleg and Atyantica.

But there is no question that Amerindian cities, as we know them, do not go back that far in Mesoamerica. Reports made from aerial surveys may contain a clue. These repeatedly refer to evidence of sunken cities on the expansive and shallow Yucatán continental shelf much like those at the Great Bahama Bank. These may represent cities inundated just prior to the Amerindian retreat to higher ground to build the cities of which we now know.

Mayan oral histories assert that early Mayans first came from a great land across the Eastern Sea or a land "to the rising sun" that sank beneath the waves, implying a land beyond the Gulf of Mexico, toward the Great Bahama Bank. An older civilization destroyed is recalled as Aztlán or Atlán, reminiscent again of Atyantica, Atlantis, and great upheaval.

The Yucatán is, of course, the oldest civilized area of Mexico. In Honduras, at the Mayan ruins of Copán, the Athens of the Mayans, there is a famous mural showing a stylized retreat from volcanoes erupting from under the sea—men fleeing in canoes and temples crashing and falling into the ocean. Whether this recalls inundations of the alleged Yucatán cities or those of the Great Bahama Bank or the prehistoric destruction of a civilization by the splitting apart of the megacontinent (or a mixture of them all), the mural also shows in stylized form a strange flying object with landing gear. This is neither a stylized bird nor a cloud, as the mural commendably portrays realistic fish in the sea and the billowing smoke of volcanoes. Caycean assertions about the last evacuation from "Poseidia" could scarcely be justified only by these artistic inferences.

Nevertheless, Caycean overtones of a previous civilization or "mighty men" influencing the beginning of our civilization are not found or inferred only in the artwork or legends of the Maya, but in almost every early tribe or race. Exactly what degree of advancement these references imply has often been the subject, or victim, of contemporary and later interpretations, as in the mural at Copán.

The Egyptians maintained that before them there was the "reign of the gods" from whom they received their knowledge of civilization, passed down from a silver dish or saucer. This last inference may have come about to symbolically convey "gift" from a higher source. But it is also common to all these cultures to recall, perhaps fancifully, flying machines and that the last known uses of these were for evacuation, before their knowledge was eventually restricted to the rulers and then lost. The Babylonian *Hakatha* (laws), possibly derived from early Sumeria, states

Part of the glyph from Copán, Honduras. Copán flourished in the 7th century A.D. The Maya are the product of a long line of Amerindian civilizations going back to the mysterious Olmecs, around 1500 B.C. They, in turn, flourished 1,600 years after the Amerindian calendar begins. Whatever this glyph recalls, it must be older than the 2nd millennium B.C. The most fantastic elements of a prehistoric destruction may have been stylistically retained (though improperly understood). An unusual object is floating above the Mayan's head.

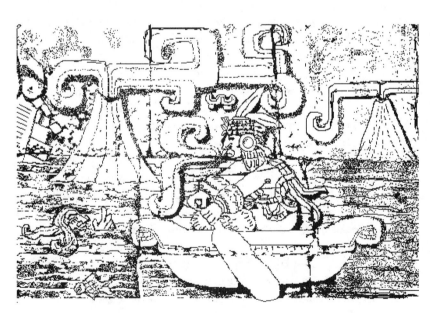

unambiguously: "The privilege of operating a flying machine is great. The knowledge of flight is among the most ancient of our inheritances. A gift from 'those from upon high.' We received it from them as a means of saving many lives." The ancient Chaldean work *Sifrala* even becomes technical, mentioning words that can be translated only as "graphite rod," "copper coils," "crystal indicator," and "vibrating spheres" and other indications of some form of novel power so suggestive of Cayce's "Atlantis."

A reevaluation of these legends is not being inspired by Caycean concepts which are, on the whole, anathema to standard scientific inquiry. It is in the study of mankind's first cities that we are finding what can only be catalogued as a leftover science, though our timetables allow for no civilization having preceded them.

This revelation is especially productive in Peru, far removed from the torrent of Middle East and Mediterranean civilizations from which much has been lost through the plunder and obliteration of countless wars and famines and superstition. Peruvian legends likewise refer to the earliest arrivals as "coming down" to build the first great city, Tiahuanaco, in circumstances suggesting evacuation in the aftermath of continental upheaval. The Inca regarded the city's original inhabitants as a "divine" people and called them the Viracochas after the creator god Viracocha, who first "descended" to create Tiahuanaco "after the receding of chaotic flood waters." Whether Viracocha was a composite of the abilities of this "divine" people or their original leader, it is interesting to note in this regard that some of his unusual appellations include "Lord Creator of the World" and, interestingly, "Old Man of the Sky."

Tiahuanaco's extent, easily seen in aerial surveys, is revealing it to be a riddle of incredible engineering. It is no longer believed to have ever been a ceremonial capitol of a relatively few priests

Despite the appearance of Mayans in later stylized artwork showing them retreating from sinking cities, the earliest inhabitants of the Yucatán, as in this slate relief from the Totonac culture, Vera Cruz, were very non-Mayan bearded men, with unusual headdresses. Evidence for this early Indo-Aryan race is found throughout the Americas.

and kings as previously thought, but a thriving culture with an estimated population of 350,000 or more. The choice of the 12,500-foot altitude to build Tiahuanaco may reflect a desire to be as far from the ocean as possible; and it had to have been built by a people with the pre-science to adjust crops in order to support such a culture at this height, far better than the modern farmers can accomplish today. How these people arrived is a further mystery, since all the earliest cultures of Peru, as we understand them by the ruins they have left behind, began in the Andes. Yet migrants do not land on the coast or migrate into plains and then forsake the convenience of rivers and fields to straightaway march up a mountain into the thin air of 12,500 feet.

While the references to flying machines, evacuation, and so forth can be variously interpreted, Tiahuanaco represents tangible mysteries of construction, especially considering that its monumental megalithic blocks are often 200 tons or more, placed in perfect polygonal joins, so that a knife blade cannot be inserted between them—a considerable feat anywhere, much less at almost 2 ½ miles' altitude.

The "divine race" of Viracochas is hardly myth. They appear in the oldest Peruvian artwork found. This human-form vessel from the Moche culture (about 100 B.C.) shows a Viracocha flute player. The Viracochas, who wore long white robes and clothes similar to those of the Sumerians, were also noted for their light skin, auburn or strawberry-blond hair, and weights placed in their earlobes to lengthen them.

A pervasive paradox exists throughout all our earliest civilizations. The excavations of the Indus cities and those of earliest Mesopotamia, both of which were founded around 3100 B.C., reveal these, the oldest cultures we accept, had the marks of a higher civilization than those that followed (until modern times). For organization and layout, cleanliness and convenience, these earliest cities were designed to accommodate up to 50,000 people. Mohenjo-Daro (along the Indus) was built on a grid, with broad avenues bisected at right angles by smaller lanes. An advanced sewer system, superior to any in Europe only two hundred years ago, ran under the streets. Manhole covers were made of brick, with holes in

The Incas insisted that the Viracochas built Tiahuanaco and Sacsahuaman at the earliest of times by burning stone until it was as light as cork and then applying a liquid to the edges to soften it so that polygonal stones fit perfectly into place. This is an example of the joins between 200-ton blocks at Tiahuanaco.

The ten-ton Gate of the Sun at Tiahuanaco, one of its many mysterious buildings.

them to allow for inspection. A drain led from each home; there were bathrooms, toilets, subterranean aqueducts with corbeled arches, and a central pool. These conveniences can be extended to Tiahuanaco, Ur of the Chaldees, and even Machu Picchu, where water was somehow pumped up 2,000 feet to supply running water.

Indications of advanced science and even the use of electricity continue to be found from periods formerly reserved for "cavemen." A skull discovered in Arabia, believed to date to 6,000 years ago, had been operated on. Examination proved that delicate brain surgery was performed after an herbal anesthetic was used; bone regrowth indicated that the patient lived another two years. Under close scrutiny the teeth of a skull found in Pakistan, near the Indus, have upset our views of prehistory. The skull, also about 6,000 years old, has revealed under microscopic examination the results of advanced dentistry. Molars contain drilled holes lined inside with connective grooves, telltale signs of drill bits, and with this the

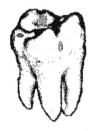 implication of the use of magnifying mirrors. It is inconceivable that any force other than electrical could have been used to create these perfect concentric holes in such a small working area as the human mouth. We are equally at a loss to explain any *known* ancient technology that could have formed such precise minute drills in the first place, plus the ball-bearing science required for their rotary function.

These discoveries, along with their implication of still more "modern" scientific knowledge behind them, are hardly freaks. Nor are they limited to Pakistan. The earliest Peruvian cultures excelled in brain surgery, and they left admirable examples of what must be electroplating—an art, it is believed, the Egyptians also mastered.

Although these are tangible evidence for inferring an ancient knowledge of some form of electrical power, none of them prove it beyond a doubt without the presence of the machine or instruments that created the power. Cayce was not alone in the 1930s, of course, in his belief that there was a prehistoric supercivilization. But he is the only one ever to have insisted that a machine capable of producing a form of electrical energy would be found near Bimini, foretelling in a strange way unknown ruins and the epicenter of unexplained electromagnetic phenomena in the Bermuda Triangle.

If only, *if only*, Cayce had never mentioned Bimini, it would be easy to deal the occult out of the world of investigating very tangible things like boats and airplanes. When approaching Cayce's other comments about this civilization one is faced with some that are so fantastic they could hardly be real. Yet, at the same time, the Bimini prediction haunts one to wonder if they, too, have any merit.

Dealing with the validity of Cayce's prophecies has proven difficult even for his followers. The most objective view of his Atlantis readings may still come from no less than his son, Hugh Lynn Cayce, who, after his father's death, headed the Association for Research and Enlightenment (ARE), which Cayce had founded. He observed: "They are the most fantastic, the most bizarre, and the most impossible information in the Edgar Cayce files. . . . If his unconscious fabricated this material or wove it together from existing legends and writings, we believe that it is the most amazing example of a telepathic clairvoyant scanning of existing legends or stories in print or of the minds of persons dealing with the Atlantis theory." In struggling with an assessment of his father's overall psychic contributions, he further added: "Life would be simpler if Edgar Cayce had never mentioned Atlantis."

There is, of course, great influence from Ignatius Donnelly's hallmark book *Atlantis: The Antediluvian World,* published in 1882, though Donnelly, writing before the air age, was *sans* the supercivilization aspect so dominant in Caycean readings. Cayce's dependence on the Platonic legend of an island or continent in the middle of the Atlantic is another case in point, one now completely disproved by studies of megacontinent via ocean bottom mapping of the continental shelves. Then again he deferred to Plato's date of 11,400 years ago, which seems to be a purely Platonic fabrication. Cayce even incorporated the "Land of Oz" into Atlantis. Other Caycean prophecies concerning Atlantis and future inundations have miserably failed, such as Japan and California falling into the ocean in 1998, to name only one. Cayce himself expressed puzzlement at his own Atlantis readings. On one occasion, after glancing at a transcription of what he had said, he remarked: "I wonder where that came from and if there is anything to it?"

Whether Cayce was really seeing the incremental destruction of a past supercivilization or was merely inspired by ancient tales of destruction and popular contemporary theories, some of his adherents hold that the truth lies somewhere between. They contend that knowledge of the ancient tales might have influenced some of Cayce's interpretations of what he was actually seeing. After all, he was not a geologist and therefore, already knowing the stories of Atlantis, as we all do, he assumed what he was seeing was the "fabled continent" breaking up and sinking into the Atlantic. In this context it is noteworthy that, in a 1938 reading covering the initial breakup, he declared that Atlantis split into five "islands," which, in essence, the megacontinent has—the five continents on the Earth today.

But, taking Cayce's failures into account, is there really any reason for the serious student of prehistory to credit his successes as more than coincidence or Procrustean interpretations after the fact? It would seem to be more than ridiculous to use Cayce's trances as a basis to postulate the theory that these ancient power complexes may still be functioning and causing ships and planes to vanish or disintegrate in the Bermuda Triangle. It is, however, in an uncanny discovery that more than coincidence is drawn between Caycean power crystals, a civilization of prehistory, and the Bermuda Triangle.

The theory that ruined "Atlantean" power complexes were once built in the Bermuda Triangle and may still be functioning today has taken an unexpected twist from the possibility that some of these have been seen *on land* and apparently still functioning. This was not in the Bermuda Triangle but deep in the jungles of Brazil, in its Mato Grosso region. Legends have persisted here since the first Spanish and Portuguese explorers arrived in South America of a prehistoric civilization tumbled down and overgrown. Detailed descriptions of these ancient cities, furthermore, have been made by native Indians unfamiliar with any Caycean readings or any advanced science, and relayed to a Westerner *before* Edgar Cayce began his trances and not published until 1950, *after* Cayce's death. Yet they share a remarkable identity with what Cayce was recording about Atlantis thousands of miles away in Virginia Beach.

The very year Cayce began to give readings on Atlantis (1924), Colonel Percy Fawcett made worldwide news when he announced that he was journeying into the Mato Grosso to search for what he believed were the only clues left of a civilization of prehistory. Fawcett was led to this belief by the knowledge he had accumulated over the previous twenty years (1905 to 1924) of surveying and exploring South America to determine boundary lines.

In his *Lost Trails, Lost Cities*, published after his death (or rather disapearance) by his son Brian Fawcett, he refers to the uniformity of South American legends describing what is by now a familiar event: the Andes mountain range violently uplifting, inland seas draining, great portions of land splitting, with portions rising and later sinking, and great buildings tumbling down and being devoured by subsequent jungle growth. Fawcett also noted that the seabed sediment between South America and the Galápagos

The actual continental shelf around the Caribbean before ocean levels rose, possibly after the continents split. A land bridge connected the shelf with South America. Some believe that a civilization rebuilding after the splitting of the megacontinent could have thrived along the Bahama Bank and into Brazil for centuries before being inundated here and choked out in Brazil by jungles.

Islands is full of tree trunks—consistent with a great deforestation by tidal waves sweeping over land as the South American continent catastrophically smashed into the Pacific, ripping trees back into the Pacific, forming great log mats that eventually sank to the bottom into the sedimentation (as we have seen in Spirit Lake, Washington, and in North Dakota).

Fawcett's evidence for an advanced civilization in Brazil goes impressively beyond native legends when what they describe is reconciled with the Cayce Records. These lost cities are described as having pyramids, rectilinear street plans, and in one case a great temple with a huge rock crystal cut into a disc. Although Hollywood-esque re-creations of Cayce's Atlantis show pyramids with great crystals atop them, Cayce in fact associated these with temples, as did the Brazilian Indians. An unexpected correlation with Caycean power columns for centralizing energy between the crystal's generating source is found when a near-savage Indian, captured and shown the splendors of a Spanish church in Peru, remarked that it was nothing compared to a ruined city deep in the jungle where great halls were lit by a single column of brilliant crystal (or glass). Fawcett's belief that these Indians tales were indeed referencing some unique forms of energy was reinforced by his firsthand examination of some of the most ancient dwellings in Colombia. He wrote: "They were windowless houses with narrow entrances, their interiors free from the grime of every cooking or illuminating agency known to us except electricity!"

Fawcett was not a dreamer. Nor was he a fool. He had been a colonel in the British army and is responsible for fixing many of the national boundary lines in western South America that are still recognized today. He was so sure the "lost cities" existed that he sacrificed his life to locate them. Before he left on his final expedition—from which he, his son Jack, and his friend Raleigh Rimmel, never returned—he wrote this (published posthumously) for those who might one day follow: "Whether we get through, and emerge again, or leave our bones to rot in there, one thing's certain. The answer to the enigma of Ancient South America—and perhaps of the prehistoric world—may be found when those cities are located and opened up to scientific research. . . . The existence of the old cities I do not for a moment doubt. How could I? I myself have seen a portion of one of them—and that is why I observe that it was imperative for me to go again. . . . I have traveled much in places not familiar to other explorers, and the wild Indians have again and again told me of the buildings, the character of the people, and the strange things beyond."

If Edgar Cayce "saw" remnants of this civilization in reality or whether he was inspired by knowledge of these stories and our earliest legends, the upshot seems approximately the same. In other words, if the growing evidence suggesting that mankind reached a technically high degree of science in prehistory is correct, then the possibility that advanced power sources were built is even more real, since they are the product of deduction from evidence and not from trances. Considering that we are now developing power sources of limitless duration, it is easier to imagine that a highly technical civilization could have existed in prehistory that perfected power sources capable of harnessing the energy in elements all around us: within rocks, water, even "air"—that is, protons and electrons, by means of what is now being viewed as vortex compression.

By expurgating the Caycean view of this prehistoric civilization, the only difference is an elimination of the Bahamas and Bimini from its discourses. But it is in the eerie fulfillment of his prophecies here that interest in the Caycean view is sustained. This once again reintroduces one of the most fantastic theories for explaining the mystery of the Bermuda Triangle. In this case, however, though not entirely made up of what might be termed devoted Cayce followers, or at least those who wholeheartedly feel his readings are without error, they do believe that his psychic wanderings locked on to these power devices because these were, naturally, the most interesting elements he saw.

It is true, of course, that the greatest electromagnetic and undersea phenomena do recur where Cayce predicted that Atlantean ruins would exist. However, the argument can also be made that this is purely coincidental—although it seems to be yet another coincidence among so many. The "white waters" of the Bahamas have also been used as evidence that Atlantean power sources are still working below. These white flumes are proposed to be "exhaust" of some sort. Although they have proven to be perfectly natural (though still mysterious in origin), a rare photo of them taken in 1999 by Lynn Gernon, while flying near Andros with her husband, Bruce, revealed something inexplicable. They were at 6,500 feet altitude almost precisely where Bruce had experienced the unusual lenticular cloud in 1970. Their attention was drawn to the ocean surface because big blotches of the glowing white waters were venting up and floating on the surface. In the midst of one blotch, which Gernon estimated covered about 10 acres, there was an almost perfectly circular area of clear water into which the glowing phosphorescence was incapable of intruding. So far, there is no natural explanation that can explain it.

More than anything, this phenomenon could be used to argue that there is something below capable of saturating the water in a neat column extending from the seafloor to the surface and perhaps beyond, revealed briefly by a natural venting of phosphorescent gas nearby. There seems to be no other source but electromagnetic or radioactive energy capable of repelling the phosphorescence in the white waters, and thus when drifting with the gentle current they traced the geometric outline of what would otherwise be an invisible . . vortex?

This adds disturbing ramifications to a discovery by diver and explorer Dr. William Bell in 1957. When investigating the seafloor south of Bimini he found in 40 feet of water a metal column of sorts, greater in width at its base. Although it was covered with sea growth, after he chipped this away, he saw that beneath was a gray substance. Farther down in the seabed he uncovered adjoining gearlike constructions, about 2 feet in diameter. When he developed his pictures, he noted that the column had an odd glowing aura to it, akin to ionization, that made the energy in the water photographically visible. During this time, and for several months afterward, he experienced bloody noses and other signs of radiation.

The building or tower that had housed this column seemed to have collapsed with time or in a catastrophe. Scattered about were thin slabs of some kind of stone, cut to precise though now weathered squares. Since Bell believed the column extended downward another 40 feet, these thin slabs, with little imagination, could conceivably have come from the uppermost part of the edifice or have been used to line the interior walls—another echo of the nonconductive tiles surrounding the power chamber or domes of Caycean readings and now our own reactors.

But like the existence of the Bimini stones, is all this proof? Supposing the most fantastic theory—that these are sunken power complexes—doesn't explain disappearances of boats and planes. Cayce may have predicted unusual power columns, but he didn't predict that they were working or that they could cause ships and planes to vanish. So-called followers of his put that together, along with a wide array of claims of finding glowing pyramids below and statues holding crystals.

If all these claims were fact, one would also expect the jungles of Brazil to have a reputation for mystery similar to that of the Bermuda Triangle. One reason the "green sea" of the Amazon does not is that aircraft usually avoid flying over the area, since crashing there means certain death. Percy Fawcett's notes, once again, become a damn nuisance, preventing one from finally slaying the Medusa. He recorded the existence deep within the jungle of ancient stone towers, glowing within. One lone stone sentinel, which lay on the route to the legendary city Fawcett sought, "is the terror of the surrounding Indians, as at night it is lighted from door and windows."

The possibilities of a sunken civilization like Atlantis or a lost one in Brazil have enlivened our imaginations for generations, possibly because they imply an intact link with our past: the depths of the Atlantic or the jungles of Brazil are both inaccessible to the ravages of quarrying by later cultures, so one is inspired to believe that the keys to what may have been our prehistoric past lie fallen but preserved here.

Edgar Cayce's readings continue to keep the question very much alive. In addition, the growing scientific study of what may cause "psychic" abilities in some people has given interest in Cayce's readings a boost in forward momentum. For sometime now instances of "remote viewing" have been accepted. This psychic ability is thought to be related to the possible existence of superluminal particles called tachyons, which are particles that move so rapidly they constantly exceed the speed of light and therefore are almost impossible for us to detect. No one imagined these might exist in biological life and cause a link between similar species until scientists in the Soviet Union went to great lengths to study extrasensory perception (ESP) in plant life. The tests were conducted under the following conditions: they separated the plants by hundreds of miles, placed them in specially designed, sealed-off tanks that shield all frequencies by which the plants might communicate, and then they were connected to polygraphs. Despite these measures, the plants still were able to respond and communicate. When one plant was singed by a cigarette, or even when the technician merely thought of burning it, the plant hundreds of miles away responded.

By the very postulated nature of tachyons—that they exceed the speed of light—it was theoretically possible that tachyons could penetrate any shielding and therefore might be responsible. Dr. Hal Puthoff, of Stanford University, an expert in lasers and in theoretical zero-point energy fluctuations, came to this theory and proposed that beds of algae could be linked with others by lasers to see if one bed's electromagnetic pulse reactions were transmitted along the laser beam to the other bed, which, sensing these wavelength changes, would react identically. This would tend to substantiate the idea that even faster particles could form a connecting link between humans, far more complex than lasers, and explain some psychic phenomena.

In one incident he recalled, Dr. Puthoff invited, through mutual acquaintances, the famous medium Ingo Swann to participate by being placed in a chamber such as the ones the Soviets had surrounded their plants with in their ESP tests. When Swann merely approached the chamber, all the gadgets, indicators, and lights went on and reacted violently. Swann then immediately drew an accurate picture of what the interior of the complex chamber looked like, though he had never seen it and the chamber had never been photographed or the classified descriptions of it circulated in any published form.

After being shown disturbing information that the CIA had obtained on Soviet psychic spies' "remote viewing" of the United States, Dr. Puthoff agreed to head the U.S. counter "remote viewing" program, selecting sensitive people to counterspy with no other means than their minds. According to some published accounts, the U.S. psychic spies were able to roam the Soviet Union in every dimension of the three planes of space we occupy, as well as the fourth . . . of Time. The results of this data, obtained over Puthoff's fifteen-year tenure, are still highly classified.

Within the supporters of this method it is noted that to yield the best, or at least statistically acceptable, data several psychics have to be employed on the same subject at once and that a distilling of their results composes a far more accurate mosaic. To them, since Cayce engaged in his trances alone, the margin of error through infiltration from his personal beliefs is much higher. Therefore elements of Cayce's readings may be reliable, but those that tend to repeat themselves, like the continued references to power sources, may be the most reliable.

Naturally, interest in Cayce's readings of Atlantis is now concentrated on his descriptions of these fabulous power devices, receiving even greater impetus from the discovery recently by our generation of the possible source of their limitless power, which was so difficult for him to convey—zero-point energy. If Cayce's power sources are a complete mental myth, they are no longer impossibilities. They are, as found in a reading from 1939 predating any use of nuclear or atomic power, as potentially real for the near future as Cayce's prescient warning for that future: "Influences of atomic energies or electrical force of any nature become a channel for good or bad today."

A similar warning is shared in common by our earliest legends: that this great civilization went too far to begin with and the great meteors, asteroids, or comets that may have destroyed it by instigating great Atyantica were its final judgment. In our own tradition we find Babilu or "gate of the gods" destroyed because of its hauteur, encapsulated in its attempt to reach or command the heavens. In the biblical narrative, God does not dismiss what the unity of Babel can do, but rather says: "And now this they begin to do. And now nothing shall be restrained from them, which they imagine to do"—not exactly the comment the Almighty would make for primitive men putting mud bricks together, nor is that a sin worthy of its destruction by division, scattering, and confusion, and that their speech should be made strange.

It reminds us rather of what Viktor Schauberger entered into his diary after gazing into the vacuum of zero-point energy: "I stand face to face with the apparent 'void,' the compression of dematerialization that we are wont to call a 'vacuum.' I can now see that we are able to create anything we wish for ourselves out of this 'nothing.' "

Just how far a prehistoric civilization could have been capable of going before its destruction may be obscured by a cataclysm on Earth—but its evidence might strangely still be held in the heavens. A civilization consumed with the heavens may have directed itself there, as we are today. All our great discoveries of the "enlightened age" have been upstaged. We now know we were not the first to the Americas; we were not the first with the gear system or with astronavigation; we were not the first with the battery and perhaps with aerodynamics. Because of the Bermuda Triangle we may discover we were not the first into space—a proposition that may launch us into the most chilling theory to explain the entire mystery of the Bermuda Triangle.

9

The Warnings of Lunar and Martian Anomalies

MORE THAN ONE investigator of prehistoric ruins has noted the pattern of their astronomical alignment with other planets and stars and that there is a remarkable similarity between these patterns and geometric shapes seen on other heavenly bodies. This raises the question of exactly how far back civilization on this planet goes, and what stage it actually reached before, perhaps, being destroyed. If it had attained a significant degree of scientific and technological knowledge, it doesn't seem unlikely that it should have been preoccupied, as we are today, with space exploration and other planets.

Richard C. Hoagland, Mike Bara, Lan Fleming, Dr. Stanley McDaniel, and other lunar observers are of the opinion that the unusual shapes and patterns on the moon formerly called lunar anomalies or geologic eccentricities are man-made or, at least, intelligence-made artifacts built at some ancient time. Over the last fifty years reports of these objects have proliferated. In 1954 reports of a 20-mile-long bridge over parts of the surrounding mountain range of the Mare Crisium elicited wide attention after being reported by distinguished English astronomer Dr. H. P. Wilkins, who described it vividly during a live BBC radio broadcast.

In 1966 the greatest stir was caused by photographs taken of the Mare Tranquilitatis by *Lunar Orbiter II* when searching for landing spots for the upcoming Apollo manned mission in 1969. These photos revealed a rectangular "pool" flanked by what appeared to be tall pyramids or obelisks, noted for the long shadows they cast and their regular spacing. William Blair of the Boeing Institute of Biotechnology innocently reported that they appeared man-made, which then set off a sensation, followed by several caustic denouncements of the whole idea as absurd.

The proliferation of such reports in the last decade may in part be because superior yet affordable telescopes capable of delineating far greater detail than in the past have been developed and marketed, enabling large numbers of amateur astronomers to gaze at the moon. In addition, NASA's Jet Propulsion Lab and Malin Space Sciences System upload the latest official photos on their websites. There is also an increasing reexamination of the photos taken by many earlier lunar expeditions and overflights, like *Apollo 15* and, most recently, *Clementine* (1994).

Among the anomalous objects on the moon are geometric shapes—a triangle, a cross, and possibly a pentagon. Their placement implies they were designed for viewing from the Earth (all of which can be seen with a modest telescope). Other oddities include enigmatic flashing lights, especially in the crater Aristarchus, and reflections off what appear to be broken glass fragments.

Ridicule is naturally hurled at the idea by people who cannot conceive that man—or anybody else—would build huge complexes on a body that cannot support life. But this is often only justified of the extreme "lunar buffs" who see just about any shape or formation on the moon, like "Roman cities," missile complexes, Los Angeles, and 600-square-mile glass boxes covering parts of seas and whole craters—just as there are people who can make out any forms they fancy in clouds, ink blots, and large trees if they study them long enough and are diligent enough to find exotic topography. Lunacy—no pun intended—is attached in a sort of "guilt by association" to the far more conservative discussions of long-documented facts and observations that remain unexplained.

The Mare Crisium (Latin for Sea of Crisis) has been a hotbed of anomalous sightings of reflected glares and sparkling flashes for the last fifty years. Most recently, lunar anomalists Mike Bara and Steve Troy have noted what appear to be huge glass domes in the old sea basin. Examination of NASA photos from *Apollo 10* yielded the unexpected detail. One photo, indexed as AS10-30-4421, was an angled shot of the small crater Picard on the mare "seabed." In the distance, however, Bara noted an unusually high point of albedo (derived from Latin, meaning whiteness) bright enough to appear as reflective glare. Blowing up the area of the photo revealed two perfect domes, one much closer to the crater than the other, with the texture of crystalline glass. This was suggested by the background mountain range clearly appearing through the transparent dome. Concentrating their examination on the nearest dome revealed there to be some sort of chimney on top, standing perfectly erect. On the hillside, in the distance behind it, there were what appeared to be a face and, less subjective, a "phoenix"—some sort of flail or bird symbol etched vaguely in the hillside. This stood out because of its albedo—the natural character of moon rock beneath the old and undisturbed gray surface.

Brief flashing or reflective lights on the moon have been recorded in astronomical observer records for the last two centuries. More recently, they have been seen by such distinguished astronomers as Winifred Sawtell Cameron of the Goddard Space Flight Center and Audoiun Dollfus of the Observatoire de Paris. Dollfus proposed that phosphorescent gases were escaping from the bottom of the crater Langrenus in 1992, when he made his observations. He noted the glowing lights actually changed shape over several days.

Steve Troy, on the other hand, believes the flashing lights could be sunlight hitting glass constructions or fragments of them at the right angle during the lunar sunrise. Why they are not seen at other times, he offers, can be explained by the theory that the sun has to hit them at just the right angle to produce a reflective glare. At all other times they are invisible because of the transparency of the glass and the fact that the moon has no atmosphere. Some of the observations, he notes, have been of brilliant and brief flashes, which are suggestive of sunlight or other light briefly striking glass.

From the *Apollo 16* Preliminary Science Report, subheading "crew observations" page 5-4, comes the following detailed sighting of a typical TLP or Transient Lunar Phenomena:

One of the most intriguing orbital observations was made at approximately 123:07 GET (3:01 CST) April 21, 1972. The CMP [Command Module Pilot] was watching the stars rise over the approaching sunrise horizon while he was waiting to execute one of the zodiacal light photographic sequences. While in a totally darkened cockpit, he noticed a bright flash that appeared to the south of the ground track and several degrees above the horizon. This flash was of very short duration and did not remain long enough to permit recording of a geographical position.

If these are the remnants of ruined glass artifacts or abandoned glass artifacts *in corpus toto*, the question naturally crops up: Why build on the moon? To this Troy has a suggestion: There may have been ancient mining operations seeking the moon's very valuable minerals, although operations now plainly seem to have ceased. Some craters, in which mining for minerals might have been more advantageous, do have various dwellings or bunkers of odd circular and horned shapes presenting the appearance of large bases and companion tubes, like the wide variety of objects together making the so-called village in the vast impact crater Tycho.

From the point of view of an alien race, there seems little reason to build on the moon when a very habitable and rich planet is nearby. But from the perspective of an Earth culture reaching out into space—and one whose religious ideas may have centered on signs and geometric shapes and planetary grids—it does make sense that they would mark their first step into the solar system—mark significant astral alignments and perhaps place religious markers to commemorate the event. The use of glass, however, remains unexplained, as it offers no protection from the scorching heat of the lunar day (250°F) or the freezing cold of the lunar night . . . unless, of course, atmosphere was pumped into these glass domes.

Martian anomalies are, however, a different matter altogether. They have been seen since Giovanni Schiaparelli first sighted the "canals" of Mars in 1877. More credence is attached to the idea of life on Mars since it does have water and an atmosphere, though the water is believed to be frozen carbon dioxide and the atmosphere very thin compared to Earth's. This allows for more excitement when new discoveries are made, something with which Schiaparelli was familiar. His Italian *canali* for "channels" was misinterpreted by the English press to mean *canals* and taken to imply man-made irrigation ditches. The excitement caused dozens of telescopes to be trained on Mars to see if our most intriguing neighbor was indeed inhabited. Percival Lowell was perhaps the most famous astronomer to do so. He even went to the expense of building his own Lowell Observatory in Arizona in 1894 and devoted his life to studying Mars to determine if there were civilizations there; he eventually concluded that there were.

Although Viking and Mariner overflights and landings have indicated there is no civilization on Mars, the question "Was there ever?" is being asked by an increasing number of observers. This is being prompted by some strange formations and images clearly captured in Mariner and Viking photography, some of which, under closer scrutiny, still cannot be explained as natural formations.

One of the most interesting of these formations is the "tunnels" or "glass sandworms" of Mars, long cylindrical tunnels that appear to have been made of a form of crystalline glass and reinforced at even intervals with supportive ribs. These extend for miles under the Martian desert, as determined by ground depressions, but for about a mile, one is exposed in an open fissure in the desert floor to reveal the startling appearance of a metro tube or a subterranean aqueduct.

Measurements in photographs indicate that this tube is about 600 feet wide for most of its distance, but a curious area of distortion shows that it has "ballooned." The effect is strikingly similar to that seen in hot glass when the craftsman blows through a glass tube to shape the hollow piece he is working on. This part of the tunnel also reflects the most light—something that is clearly visible even high up—and this seems to confirm that its appearance as glass is not illusionary. The ribbing around the glass "tunnel" seems evenly spaced, and where it has "ballooned" the ribs appear stretched proportionately. However, some of the ribs seem to be creases in the "glass" as if to indicate it is not necessarily hard glass but a softer, transparent material, like plastic designed for some give—though it has apparently undergone far more undulation than intended, with some of the frosted creases appearing as ribs where the long tube creased back and forth beyond its limitations.

Among the most studied Martian anomalies is the so-called "Face on Mars," a curious plateau in which some see the heavily eroded features of a feline, sphinx, or human face. Since man has gazed at clouds and trees and seen any number of novel forms therein, with no two witnesses agreeing, the "Face on Mars" may reflect this same surrealism, or simply show the ability of individuals to see what they wish to see. The plateau on which the "face" is chiseled, however, is perhaps itself the most extraordinary testimony to the fact that a natural formation was worked on to create some representation. Its shape is almost that of a perfect shield, with severe erosion having occurred on one side. Some straight lines, never found in nature, can still be made out around its rim. Using the plateau as a scale, the length of the remaining straight lines would still be remarkable.

The "Face" is not an isolated anomaly in this region of Mars. Anomaly researchers, primarily Richard Hoagland, have named this area Cydonia—the city on Mars—after the section of Mars on which it appears. There are many more neat geometric patterns here, including some odd shapes and possibly a pyramid.

Other unusual sights include neat lines in the smooth bottom of the Valles Marineris, a vast canyon stretching around nearly one third of the circumference of Mars. The lines extend for miles, crisscrossing both diagonally and tangentially, in a way similar to those on the Nasca Pampa in Peru. They bisect natural lines, indicating that they are not a natural formation or typical buckling from geologic action in the valley or wind or water erosion. Some are even curved or oblique. It is hard to imagine what natural process could so neatly make one line straight and then make another curve around it or over it without disturbing or obliterating the previous line.

Nearby there are a number of enigmatic "igloos" on the valley floor. Although craters can appear as domes from a distance due to the shadowing of sunlight, the shadows cast by these circular formations are on the *outside* of the circle, on the opposite side from where the full force of the sun is hitting, rather than on the inside, where they would be if these were craters in the valley floor. A number of these "domes" show "ejecta," that is, material ejected out of craters by the force of an impacting object. However, the "ejecta" sprays in only one direction, not all around the perimeter, as one would expect from an impact. Rather, it appears to vent only one way, as if debris coming out of a chimney was blown with the wind and discolored the valley floor.

A prominent feature of all the nearby "lines" is that they do not appear to be etched into the soil but appear to be mounds, possibly covering something below. One is tempted to imagine more "tunnels" like the one exposed. If so, perhaps Schiaparelli and Lowell will be vindicated, at least in thinking that canals or channels for irrigation existed on Mars, though they may represent subterranean irrigation. But unlike Lowell's later certain belief, there is no indication that they prove there is any present life on Mars.

It is often speculated that any water on Mars must be channeled from its polar caps, where the greatest abundance lies frozen. Lowell believed the "channels" that he saw were designed to direct the melting water during the Martian spring and irrigate the vegetation that he believed was the darker strands he saw on the Martian surface. However, it is tempting to consider in this context that daily need for water would require subterranean channeling to underground or domed "hothouses" to maintain year-long vegetation in the less than desirable and cold atmosphere of Mars.

If there were native vegetation on Mars's surface, it is thought that it would most likely grow near the polar caps where it could access some of the frozen water and thrive when it melted in spring. It is precisely in this area where coloration startlingly suggestive of vegetation has recently captured the attention of our world.

What appear to be trees have been photographed by Mars Global Surveyor. They measure about 300 feet across and are about 50 feet high, and they appear to shed and change foliage with the seasons. Oases, forests, and sandy arroyos with bushes also seem indicated in recent photographs, although officially these are explained as marks left by the defrosting of the polar caps during the Martian spring. It must be said, nonetheless, that this defrosting happens in very familiar patterns that we associate with greenbelts on Earth.

The appearance of botanical "life" on Mars has prompted a number of lively debates and comments. Sir Arthur C. Clarke, the inventor of the communications satellite and father of the *2001: A Space Odyssey* concept, has publicly (at the Werner von Braun Memorial Lecture) declared: "I'm quite serious when I say 'have a really good look at these new Mars images.' Something is actually moving and changing with the seasons that suggests, at least, vegetation." He noted their likeness to banyan trees and added: "I'm 95 percent sure that there are extensive areas of vegetation—or its equivalent—on Mars." In addition, he has recalled the scientific community's attention to the unexplained tunnels or worms on Mars, commenting, "I'm still waiting for a good explanation of that colossal 'sandworm.' "

The Mars Orbital Camera has also detected the possibility that ice was near the equator of Mars in the recent geological past, increasing the possibility that life could have existed in some form over most of the planet.

Mars's future seems to be one of life, but in this case Earth life. NASA has already tentatively scheduled placing man on Mars by 2020 and by 2041 possibly our first permanent colony. It is then, and only then, that we may determine what was on Mars in the past and if there was life and civilization there, what happened to them.

Until then we are left with some sobering and disturbing suggestions. Some of the most surprising Martian geologic anomalies involve a number of large craters that taper from the wide circumference of the lip down to a narrow bottom, like a giant funnel in the ground. These are quite unlike the common impact craters with their large flat bottoms and splatterlike rays (ejecta) streaking out from their circumference. But they do have distressing counterparts on Earth. In the Nevada desert 65 miles northwest of Las Vegas, the area of the Mojave and Great Basin Deserts is pockmarked by hundreds of huge craters. One of the largest, Sedan Crater, is 1,000 feet across. This crater was created by a 100-kiloton underground atomic blast. The 900 craters there were all created by atomic bomb tests conducted during the Cold War from 1951 to 1992, their respective sizes directly reflecting the strengths of the bombs tested.

Tourist guides who now conduct their curious charges through this formerly top-secret area (a source of revenue for the federal government) liken the area to the surface of the moon, and it is advertised as "getting a taste of another world." The craters here, however, are nothing like anything seen elsewhere in the solar system—on our moon, the moons of Jupiter or Saturn, or any planet save the odd craters on Mars.

Ancient texts of India describe several forms of warfare of a prehistoric civilization that are so unusual and fantastic they were naturally declared to be pure myth or heroic epics written by an ancient Indian Homer. Yet there is such a diaspora to the references of this type of warfare, they cannot be considered as from one imaginary source. They describe aerial warfare, give detailed descriptions of weapons remarkably similar to modern missiles and atomic bombs, give dimensions of flying machines called *vimanas,* and even go into great detail about various different kinds of *vimanas,* including those that traveled through space to other worlds, fired missiles, and were used in battles between heroes and demigods in space.

It is possible, of course, that much of this recollection reflects Indian philosophical thought—were it not for the fact many of them were already obscure in ancient times, discarded by Indian priests and prophets as impossible to understand. An indication of their neglect can be gleaned from Dr. V. R. Ramachandra Dikshitar, who, holding the chair of Indian Studies at Oxford, lauded in his *War in Ancient India:* "We owe much to the energetic scientists and researchers who plod persistently and carry their torches deep down into the caves and excavations of old and dig out valid testimonials pointing to the misty antiquity of the wonderful creations of humanity."

Why these texts have been lost in deep caves or buried and ignored can be explained by their content, for there is much in these Indian Vedas (scriptures) that seems to have no religious or moral instructional purpose whatsoever, such as details about great "chariots" accelerating beyond the atmosphere. Elements of these extraordinary records, however, may have been extracted in very ancient times to inspire the background for some of the famous Indian epics. In the *Mahavira Charita,* Sita, a passenger in a chariot accelerating into orbit, gets a very accurate answer to her question: "How can it be that in daytime we see this circle of stars?" To which her husband, Rama, replies naturally enough: "Owing to the great distance we cannot perceive it in the daytime as our own eyes are dimmed by the rays of the sun, but now that is removed by the ascent of this chariot, and thus we see the circle of stars."

Where the writer of the *Mahavira Charita* got his information nobody knows, only that it was very ancient, perhaps 3,500 years ago. And these compilations (roughly at the time of Moses) are said to come from ear-lier sources, as are other Indian epics that tell of great wars and the deeds of the gods and demigods. They may go back so far as to recall the same prehistoric civilization that Genesis mentions only in passing. After a flood, it must be remembered, mankind moved "eastward" to build their great civilization, and India is certainly east from Mesopotamia. Here Babilu, "gate of the gods," flourished and spread. As a matter of interest, all early cities around the Indus Valley in Pakistan were built of fired brick (the same material that the builders of Babel insisted on using).

The cities of the Indus Valley were for some reason abandoned and lost for millennia. This so-called Harrapan culture is hard to date, though it is thought to have flourished around the same time as Sumer and early Egypt. When excavation started on one of its cities, Mohenjo-Daro (Mound of the Dead), intaglio seals were discovered engraved with remarkably fine detail, bearing a script so old it remains undecipherable. This script became more mysterious when it was discovered to match closely the script of Easter Island, which some archaeologists believe

Top: Finely incised steatite seals from Mohenjo-Daro. These same types of seals and writing have been found in Mesopotamian cities, dated to the 3rd millennium B.C. Do they represent contact or the leftover trinkets of a previous single language and civilization? *Bottom:* Rongo-Rongo from Easter Island.

came from the nautical expeditions of the Viracochas of Peru. Parenthetically, we once again are reminded of that prehistoric civilization of one language, to that early Sanskrit used even in South America, to "peleg," and to legends of that one great civilization that went too far and was destroyed in what Sanskrit would call Atyantica.

The Jewish attitude of religious devotion and the Egyptian attitude of glorification of the state never made it conducive for either to recall past secular or foreign events with astounding detail. But the Indian attitude embraced recording great and sweeping events, travels, wars, man's interaction with gods and demigods, and man's enlightenment through these epic events. We may wonder today if this was because they were closer to some of these incredible events.

Proximity to these alleged prehistoric events may not be the only reason Vedic literature is so detailed in its account of this fabulous civilization. Another suggestion may be justified in light of the theory that language division was caused by a cataclysmic disturbance of the electromagnetic frequencies of the Earth (see chapter 8). Since the studies of electromagnetic effects show that there is varying degree of influence on the human brain, dependent on the individual's location on the Earth and their specific biochemistry, one is tempted to believe that a sudden division of languages, as contained in such stories of the Tower of Babel and dozens of others around the world, would not have wiped out the "mother language" but that it may have continued to be spoken by those unaffected. Pockets of Sanskrit having been identified even in ancient South America are hard to explain otherwise. Is it possible that Vedic Sanskrit (only dating to the 2nd millennium B.C.) is actually the direct descendent of the "mother language" and therefore the storehouse of a previous civilization's knowledge was still accessible to its scribes?

Considering the quantity of Vedic writings, they must represent the heritage of what must have been the most prolific language in the prehistoric world. Although their content later came to be represented in stylized form, the older texts being uncovered today are disturbingly precise and scientific in their body.

In the Sanskrit *Samarangana Sutradhara* an entire chapter of about 230 stanzas laboriously details the principles of construction underlying many types of *vimanas*. They are said to move so fast as to make a noise that can be heard only faintly from the ground. In describing a *vimana*, the *Sutradhara* says:

Strong and durable must the body of the Vimana be made, like a great flying bird of light material. Inside one must put the mercury engine with its iron heating apparatus underneath. By means of the power latent in the mercury which sets the driving whirlwind in motion, a man sitting inside may travel a great distance in the sky. The movements of the Vimana are such that it can vertically ascend, vertically descend, move slanting forwards and backwards. With the help of the machines, human beings can fly in the air and heavenly beings can come down to Earth.

This could almost be read as an advertisement for Piper, Cessna, or Beechcraft, except none can enter the solar system (yet). . . . None of the above has any religious or philosophical aspect to it, but seems rather like a truncated understanding of what had once long before been a basic science. More detailed scripts have been found to contain descriptions of various types of jet *vimanas*. In the *Samar, vimanas* are said to be "iron machines, well-knit and smooth, with a charge of mercury that shot out of the back in the form of a roaring flame."

As an example of how detailed and, in many cases, monotonous are the references to such machines, Indian journalist Mukul Sharma wrote in "Flight Path," which appeared in the *Times of India* (April 8, 1999), that the *Yantra Sarvasva* (traditionally ascribed to Maharshi Bhardwaj the Wise) "consists of as many as forty sections of which one, the *Vaimanika Prakarana* dealing with aeronautics, has eight chapters, a hundred topics, and five hundred sutras." In it he comments that Bhardwaj describes there were three types of *vimana:* "Those that travel from place to place; those that travel from one country to another; those that travel between planets."

The *Vaimanika Shastra* was discovered in a temple in 1875. This 4th-century B.C. text, extensively copied and recopied over the preceding millennia, touches on several aspects of air travel, including steering, precautions for long flights, avoiding lightning and storms, switching to solar drive, and, to draw an interesting connection with zero-point energy, switching to some free-energy source that remains elusive in translation but seems associated with gravity. The author of this Veda (sacred writing) even cites as many as seventy authorities and ten experts in aviation in antiquity, almost in bibliographical terms, but these sources are now lost or await discovery in the future.

Myth and fancy cannot explain the details in the ancient epics and Vedas of India. To the ordinary listener in those days there is much of the technical that would seem boring if repeated word for word by a contemporary raconteur. Because they differentiate between types of *vimanas* for various lengths of journeys and comment that space travel involves a different element "past the atmosphere," there seems to be some advanced knowledge of an earlier science which is contained, perhaps imperfectly, in the transcriptions of these texts during the last 3,500 years. In the myth of Persian flying carpets, the reader will remember, they could fly anywhere and did so magically, without pages and pages being devoted to how they could. The Indian texts, however, are little concerned with magic, only with instruction about an actual object. Considering the style of the writings and how laboriously detailed they are, Andrew Tomas *(We Are Not the First)* thinks it is better to view these as flight manuals on the care and control of *vimanas*. The *Samara Sutradhara* might even be called a scientific treatise, since it deals with construction, takeoff, cruising for thousands of miles, normal and forced landings, storage in a hangar (a *Vimana Griha*), and even possible collisions with birds! He has expressed: "If this is the science fiction of antiquity, then it is the best that has ever been written."

Examination of some recently found Vedas has proven they had never been translated in the past when the vernacular changed. As a result, many of the words in the narrative are not translatable even by Sanskrit scholars, since the original word has no equivalent in succeeding dialects or modern tongues. For example, in the ancient *Vymanka-Shastra,* which is believed to be the embodiment of the ancient science of aeronautics, the description of a *vimana* as an "an apparatus which can go by its own force, from place to place or globe to globe" is followed by a detailed description on how to build one. Dr. V. Raghaven, the retired head of the Sanskrit department of India's prestigious University of Madras, observes: "The text's revelations become even more astounding. Thirty-one parts of which the machine consists are described, including a photographing mirror underneath. The text also enumerates sixteen kinds of metal that are needed to construct the flying vehicle: 'Metals suitable, light, are sixteen kinds' but only three of them are known to us today. The rest remain untranslatable."

When remembering that they can go from "globe to globe," one wonders if these missing metals are terrestrial metals at all, and one equally can wonder if an answer has not been found for the oddities on the moon which have suggested ancient mining operations. Dr. Ruth Reyna, of the University of Chandrigarh, was recently called upon to translate old Vedas found in Tibet. She reported that they spoke of how to build interstellar spaceships and antigravity drives, in stylized form, and that a voyage to the moon was discussed.

Space-age weapons such as lasers and rays are also mentioned in Vedas, as well as nerve gas and numerous types of projectiles that spit forth fire. From the perspective of a land observer, they are described as zooming upward into the heavens, belching out fire from behind. One is the *Mohanastra*—the "arrow of unconsciousness," which was hurled at the enemy and caused entire armies to fall asleep. In the great war epic the *Mahabharata*, a compilation of 200,000 verses considered to be the Indian *Odyssey*, there is a description of the powerful weapon called the *brahmaastra*, cruelly used against other peoples. It is described not in the detached manner of a legend, but with the clarity of an ancient journalist:

Gurkha flying in his swift and powerful Vimana hurled against the three cities of the Vrishis and Andhakas a single projectile charged with all the power of the Universe. An incandescent column of smoke and fire, as brilliant as ten thousand suns, rose in all its splendor. It was the unknown weapon, the Iron Thunderbolt, a gigantic messenger of death which reduced to ashes the entire race of the Vrishnis and Andhakas.

The corpses were so burnt they were no longer recognizable. Hair and nails fell out. Pottery broke without cause. Foodstuffs were poisoned. To escape, the warriors threw themselves in streams to wash themselves and their equipment.

But the most destructive weapons were launched from land. The impact of the *Agneya*, a dreaded projectile, after it was fired against an enemy, is described with commendable detail:

Dense arrows of flame, like a great shower, issued forth upon creation, encompassing the enemy. . . . A thick gloom swiftly settled upon the Pandava hosts. All points of the compass were lost in darkness. Fierce winds began to blow. Clouds roared upward, showering dust and gravel. Birds coaked madly . . . the very elements seemed disturbed. The sun seemed to waver in the heavens. The Earth shook, scorched by the terrible violent heat of this weapon. Elephants burst into flame and ran to and fro in a frenzy . . . over a vast area, other animals crumpled to the ground and died. From all points of the compass the arrows of flame rained continuously and fiercely.

In other sutras the "cloud roaring upward" is described as "parasols opening up one over the other"—a disturbing parallel, as linguist Charles Berlitz notes, "with a modern mushroom cloud" after an atomic blast. It was so dreadful that it was banned by the "gods."

In this context it is worth considering that the "tower" in Babel to reach "heaven" was an impoverished recollection of a launching platform to send "towers"—an epic term to describe projectiles—*into* the heavens, and for this reason God destroyed and scattered the civilization "for this they begin to do, and now nothing will be restrained from them which they imagine to do." Incidentally, no archaeologist has ever discovered any great actual tower that could possibly fit "Babel."

It is interesting to note that the great stones at Baalbek in Lebanon are actually not the *first* course of blocks, but the *top* course. They sit on blocks of monumental though comprehensible size, indicating that the large 70-foot stones on top were necessary to withstand some terrific repelling force from *above*.

All of this could, of course, represent pure imagination and reflect the ability of man to spin tall tales and equally to believe them. But the dogma that it could not have happened is just as, if not more, unwarranted and without any supporting evidence. It hinges of the basic precept that change and progress are one and the same. In the words of Indian philosopher Shri Aurobindo Ghosh, in observing occidental thought: "European scholarship regards human civilization as a recent progression starting yesterday with the Fiji Islander and ending today with Rockefeller, conceiving ancient culture as necessarily half savage culture. It is a superstition of modern thought that the march of knowledge has always been linear." He goes on to lament: "Our vision of 'prehistory' is terribly inadequate."

In this context it might be wise to inject the population problem today—not too many but too few. This has confounded mathematicians, biologists, anthropologists, and sociologists. If mankind is as old on Earth for as long as believed, the present world population is only a fraction of what it should be. Presuming an estimate of 100 million inhabitants for the Roman Empire (a generous estimate) at its zenith and taking into account other peoples of the world, a rough estimate of 300 million souls on Earth 2,000 years ago can be made. Even with civil collapse in the Roman

Baalbek. What the actual huge edifice must have looked like before the Romans built their temple on it. They resemble the great stones underwater off Morocco.

Empire, the ravages of China by the mighty Kahn, wars, plagues, famines, and the like all over the Earth, mankind has reached over 6 billion souls today in fewer than 2,000 years. But if rational man goes back as far as 40,000 or 50,000 years or even 10,000 years before that, there should be billions and billions more of the human species everywhere . . . unless, of course, billions were killed or died in some unexplained event long ago.

Could the great upheavals that might have overwhelmed the Earth in the last 10,000 years have been unleashed by human beings themselves? A great flood could have been initiated by pollutants, forming nuclei that could have brought down a water vapor canopy; a splitting of the continents might have been precipitated by a society's own destructive weapons. Indian Vedas give tragic body to the succession of impacts recalled by Amerindians in South America and of the craterlike configuration in parts of the Bermuda Triangle's coastlines. It is interesting to comment while on this topic that some of the enemies these ancient texts mention are not even historically known to ancient India but may represent cultures far away on the Earth. We must remember that certain *vimanas* were capable of long flights.

Furthermore, in northern India and the Gobi Desert fossils are found to be highly radioactive, as are certain ruined "city" sites in the northern part of India that are still not completely excavated or identified, though they are linked with the mythical seven cities of Rish (which may end up not to be mythical at all but simply to have existed so far back in time that concrete knowledge of them was lost). There is also the fact that some of the ancient cultures of the Americas and India mysteriously vanished—all of which is suggestive of sudden destruction. There would appear to be no enemy locally, but if the Vedas are true, an ancient world war might be implied. We must remember the great abundance of ancient tektites and shtishovites in areas of the Bermuda Triangle can only be found elsewhere at nuclear test beds or meteorite impact sites. In this context, one might view the great disheveled stones in the Americas and the sunken ones of the Bahamas to be what is left of the enemies at which such things as *Angeyas* and *brahmaastras* were hurled.

According to D. Hatcher Childress, author of *The Anti-Gravity Handbook*, one type of early *vimana* is described as "a double-deck, circular aircraft with portholes and a dome, much as we would imagine a flying saucer"— thereby making it impossible to avoid the topics of UFOs and ancient astronauts and that this technology did not come from Earth to begin with. He further observes some startling parallels between these ancient aircraft and modern reports of UFOs. "It flew with the 'speed of the wind' and gave forth a 'melodious sound.' There were at least four different types of vimanas; some saucer shaped, others like long cylinders ('cigar shaped airships')."

Childress believes that the unidentified ruined cities of Pakistan and northern India (called the Rama Empire by modern scholars) were a vast civilization that flourished many thousands of years ago and back into prehistory. (The hypothetical time period is the 5th to 4th millennia B.C.— again, the era just before and during the time of Babel and then "peleg.") He identifies these with the legendary "seven cities of Rish" mentioned above. The earliest writers of the Hindu texts refer to this empire as having these wondrous flying machines. But, to draw a disquieting parallel, the cities are now, like the Bimini stones, mere ruins of unidentified cultures.

After his long study of the ancient texts, Dr. Raghaven came to perhaps the most controversial conclusion: that this fantastic Earth culture of prehistory *was* influenced by extraterrestrials. He has stated categorically: "Fifty years of researching these ancient works convinces me that there are living beings on other planets, and that they visited Earth as far back as 4000 B.C." He adds: "There is just a mass of fascinating information about flying machines, even fantastic science fiction weapons, that can be found in translations of the Vedas, Indian epics, and other ancient Sanskrit texts . . . in the Ramayana there is a description of Vimanas that navigated at great heights with the aid of quicksilver and a great propulsive wind. These were space vehicles similar to the so-called flying saucers reported throughout the world today."

Raghaven's conclusions have not been maverick. Dr. A. V. Krishna Murty, professor of aeronautics at the Indian Institute of Science in Bangalore, has expressed a concurring opinion in which he observes: "It is true that the ancient Indian Vedas and other texts refer to aeronautics, spaceships, flying machines, and ancient astronauts. A study of the Sanskrit texts has convinced me that ancient India did know the secret of building flying machines—and that those machines were patterned after spaceships coming from other planets."

Extrasolar planets, or exoplanets, are believed definitely to exist. Some have even been "charted" by "wobbles" or eccentricities in other suns indicative of the gravitational pull of another heavenly body nearby. It was by this method that Urbain Laverrier discovered Neptune from an eccentricity in Uranus's orbit. This led him to calculate precisely where the other planet must be.

Modern high-precision radial-velocity measurements are, as described by the European Southern Observatory in Geneva, a "fundamental observational method based on the detection of changes in the velocity of the central star, due to the changing direction of the gravitational pull from an (unseen) exoplanet as it orbits the star. The evaluation of the measured velocity variations allows us to deduce the planet's orbit, in particular the period and the distance from the star, as well as a minimum mass."

This method has led to a number of significant discoveries, including 130 known candidates for exoplanets, eleven of which were recently "discovered" through international efforts organized by the CORALIE and ELODIE and ELODIE-HIRES programs carried out primarily at Geneva, Grenoble, and Haute-Provence observatories and the Center of Astrophysics in Cambridge, Massachusetts.

Famed planet hunters Geoffrey Marcy and Robert Butler made a dual exoplanet discovery in 1996 in the 70 Virginis and 47 Ursae Majoris systems. Both had confirmed the 1995 discovery of a planet around 51 Pegasi. A triple exoplanet system orbiting Upsilon Andromedae was discovered in 1997 and confirmed by leading authorities, such as Dr. R. Noyes and Dr. S. Korzennik. Strong interest remains centered around other stars such as Gliese 876 and Epsilon Eridani, where frequent eccentricities are noted.

In searching for other planets, the primary interest is, naturally, to find life or where life may be possible. Although many of the exoplanets discovered are gas giants many times larger than Jupiter, on which life would be impossible, they offer some intriguing prospects. According to a press release from the international program based in Geneva:

With the exception of the planet Iota Hor b . . . circular orbits among exoplanets have only been found for short-period systems, contrary to what is the case for the giant planets in our own Solar System. However, the orbit of the newly found planet near the sun-like star HD 28185 is very nearly circular and with a period of 385 days (close to 1 Earth year), its distance from the star, 150.6 million km, is almost equal to the distance between the Sun and the Earth (149.6 million km).

This new planet is therefore located in the "habitable zone" where temperatures like those on the Earth are possible. Still, it is a giant, gaseous planet (with a minimum mass of 3.5 times that of Jupiter, or about 1000 times that of the Earth) and thus an unlikely place for the development of life. Nevertheless, it may be orbited by one or more moons on which a more bio-friendly environment has evolved. The presence of natural satellites ("moons") around giant extra-solar planets is not a far-fetched idea, just look at our own Solar System.

It stands to reason that moons of such huge planets could be the size of Earth and support a thriving culture. Though not having a moon like ours, they would have as a night-light the light of their sun reflecting off the breathtaking view of a multicolored planet like Jupiter, with gaseous festoons, great spots, "eyes," and swirling bands.

Of course, what we are doing could be true on other planets and may have been ongoing for a considerably longer period of time. We must bear in mind that intelligences from other worlds may long ago have reached out toward the Earth. They may even have influenced the development of a previous civilization on Earth, as suggested above. The lunar and Martian anomalies noted, if indeed they were made by intelligences, may be footprints or celestial maps and markers of their pioneering toward Earth and, as such, are leftovers of a civilization with no connection to the Earth other than having interfered with it ages ago.

Indian epics are not alone in describing men coming down to Earth. The progenitors of the great antediluvian civilization in Genesis are called the Beni Elohim (Bney HaElohim) or "sons of God" or "gods." Although today we interpret Bney HaElohim variously as angels or Seth's (as opposed to Cain's) descendants , when it was translated by ancient Jewry (when they translated into the Greek of the Septuagint in the 3rd century B.C.), this one passage retains a direct translation as *uioi tou theou*—sons of God—perhaps because they felt "angels" was out of context when referring to inbreeding with women. Their progeny became the great men of the Earth. Their origin is described in Genesis 6.1–4:

And it came to pass when men began to multiply on the face of the Earth, and daughters were born to them, that the sons of God saw the daughters of men that they were beautiful; and they took them wives of all whom they chose. Then said the Lord God, by no means will my spirit remain in these men forever, for they are also flesh, for yet shall be their days 120 years. There were giants [Nephilim] upon the Earth in those days; and after that, whenever the sons of God came into the daughters of men, they bore children to them: those were mighty men [ghibbor] which were of old, the men of renown.

—Or, as the Greek translation of the Hebrew Testament reads, "men of great name." Whoever the "sons of God" were, it is only their progeny who did things worthy enough to make them stand out and be called great men. The tone of clarification in these verses also indicates that the people of the time were very familiar with the stories of great men and that here they were being told exactly who these "great men" were and from where they had come, plus a rough estimate of when it was. In any case, they and their civilization were long gone by the Flood.

In the Hebrew book of Enoch, a dominant book during the time of Christ, the Hebrew tradition that these were angels is clearly reflected, the belief being that they were two hundred who came down to Mount Carmel under the leader Azazel. However, the language in Genesis clearly indicates that these were men, for God in his contempt says of the sons of God, "they are also flesh," which could be interpreted "they are also *only* flesh." Genesis evidently implies that this went on for a considerable time, for their descendants were already upon the Earth when other sons of God continued to sire children by the daughters of men.

Identification of this progeny as both *nephilim* and *ghibbor* remains obscure. It may be because *nephilim* only connotes heritage, whereas *ghibbor* connotes abilities. *Nephilim* can have a duel meaning implying a caste or group from one origin: "sons of the fallen ones" or "fellers," that is, those who can destroy mightily, as seen in the Indian Vedas. While the words are translated as "giants," neither implies physical stature, merely greatness. Later, in the books of Numbers and Deuteronomy, *nephilim* and *ghibbor* are used for the *anakim,* physical giants, the sons of Anak, who are not credited with any special divine heritage. Og, king of Bashan, is regarded as the last of the *anakim;* the victorious Israelites were so impressed by his bed made of iron that they measured it—13$\frac{1}{2}$ feet long, 6 feet wide. Possibly this association with "giants" inspired early Jewry to translate such a rare word as *nephilim* as "giants." (Greek obtained a number of words from Semitic languages. The base of *nephilim*, "nephal," is a part of *nephalos* = clouds, an interesting aside to the connotation "fallen ones.")

By the time of the Genesis compilation (15th to 14th centuries B.C.), their origin had long been only dim oral traditions that had been handed down and then tersely recorded on clay tablets in cuneiform. They exist in a paragraph in Genesis and that is all. We must also remember the purpose of Genesis was not to write down in detail what other scrolls in circulation or other oral traditions said, but merely to give an overview of a very distant time leading up to Abraham and the Jewish people. The "sons of God" remain enigmatic, as do their offspring. But to insist they were spacemen is to overlook the possibility they could have merely been men from a more advanced earthly society who toyed with less-developed cultures before a great flood.

It is intriguing to contemplate this angle—also to wonder whether elements of a previous Earth civilization may have gone to other planets before a terrible flood, continental upheaval, or unrestrained warfare. Descriptions of saucer-shaped craft in ancient India, or the heavenly dish in which the gods gave information in Egyptian legend, could reflect the last vague memories of an advanced Earth civilization capable of having colonized the heavens.

If UFOs today are definitely from another planet, one may wonder whether the civilization that sent them may indeed have originated on Earth long before it was reduced by cataclysms. If Earthmen have mounted to the stars at some ancient time, or if Earth has been visited by humans from other worlds, it is possible they came back to this planet, perhaps rediscovering it by accident or revering it as a sacred place of their own origin. They might at first have been extremely surprised by the present appearance of the planet, which their records and maps may indicate looked remarkably different when their ancestors emigrated to colonize other planets.

Nevertheless, it remains to be explained why so many UFOs are seen in the area of the Bermuda Triangle. Instead of considering modern UFO and possible USO reports as representing little green men visiting Earth, they might just as well represent human beings, as frail and as imperfect as we are, returning to what is to them their mother world. They may view the ruins beneath the Triangle as being the most valuable remnants remaining of a civilization they left behind long ago on a planet very different from ours today.

But there is another possibility—indeed a striking one, unavoidable when ancient legends and recent developments in medicine are put together. This may tell us why men from other worlds or from a previous Earth would have to be based by the sea, and the geography of this part of the Atlantic may tell us why they would choose the Bermuda Triangle.

The seabed of the Mare Crisium on the moon, showing crater Picard center front. In the far distance the highest point of albedo on the far right attracted lunar anomalists when studying the print. Blowing it up further revealed 2 domes, possibly crystalline glass. (NASA Goddard Space Flight Center, 70mm film frame, AS10-30-4421)

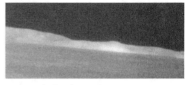

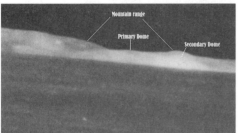

Enlarged, the domes become apparent, their right sides reflecting the most light. (NASA)

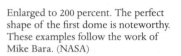

Enlarged to 200 percent. The perfect shape of the first dome is noteworthy. These examples follow the work of Mike Bara. (NASA)

The Mars Orbital Camera picked up a high point of albedo on Mars's surface. Enlarging the photo reveals long "worms" with the appearance of crystalline glass, exposed at areas where the Martian surface has cracked to create gorges. (Malin Space Science Systems/NASA "Fine Channels" MO 400291)

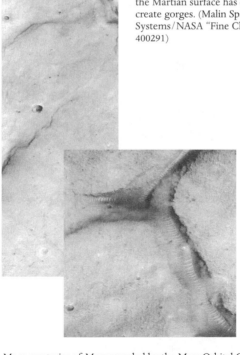

Enlarging further shows the "worms" of Mars in more detail. The high point of albedo originates at the area where the formerly subterranean "worm" has ballooned or been expanded by distortion. It is believed to measure 600 feet across here. It also appears that "exhaust" is coming out of its end where the gorge forks. (Malin Space Science Systems/NASA)

More mysteries of Mars revealed by the Mars Orbital Camera. A Martian oasis? Notice the growth is heavier and thicker where it appears "water" once ran. Farther away the growth "bushes" are smaller, more malnourished. (Malin Space Science Systems/NASA "Gullied Rise" M 804668)

Martian trees? They reminded Sir Arthur C. Clarke of banyan trees. (NASA)

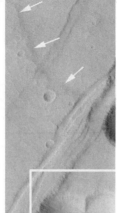

Left: A weathered Martian mound in the shape of a heart. (Malin Space Science Systems/NASA "Martian Heart" MOC 2-135a)

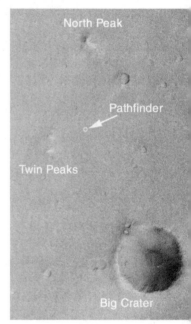

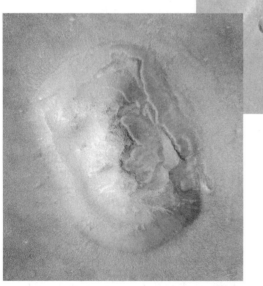

Another unusually shaped mound, the Face of Mars. Many believe this near perfect "shield-shaped" mound was worked on in the past, but its features have long been eroded. (Malin Space Science Systems/NASA "Cydonia Massif" EO 3-00824)

An unusual crater on Mars, the Big Crater, which funnels to a narrow bottom. Compare this with the Sedan crater. (Malin Space Science Systems/NASA "Pathfinder Location" MO 400291)

The Sedan crater, created in the Nevada desert, by one of the 900 underground atomic test explosions.

10

Interest from a Past World?

MORE THAN ONE investigator of the Bermuda Triangle has offered that the pattern of UFO sightings, increasing dramatically since the atomic age, indicates an expressed concern by the UFO entities for our welfare or, possibly, for their own. This last point of view presupposes there has been a long-standing interest in the Earth that must imply a connection to it or requires extensive bases on the planet along with a dependence on its ecology.

There is no question that over the last 4,000 years people have looked up and at one point or another expressed astonishment at, as the Romans put it, *naves in aerae uisse sunt*—"ships in the sky are seen." Although many times the "ships" took the form of a speeding light, torch, spear, or hovering orb of light, for 216 B.C. the annalist Julius Obsequens recorded, "at Arpinium [Rimini, in Italy] a thing like a round shield was seen in the sky"—not a bad simile with our own "flying saucers." In 98 A.D., "at sunset a burning shield passed over the sky at Rome." Encounters like these were rare compared to today. But the theory that there must be bases somewhere on the Earth combine some undeniable and intriguing facts about the pattern of UFO reports over history. The rarity of ancient reports may represent periodic checkups on what could be viewed as harmless and distant civilizations. But the flurry of sightings since 1947, in a period of stupefying technological progress, may indicate that we can no longer be viewed as harmless, and so UFOs are busily assessing our civilization's exponential progress.

Ivan Sanderson points out that we are no longer distant, either. Civilization until the last five hundred years was clustered in the Mediterranean, Mesopotamia, and a few other places, giving UFO occupants a greater range of free, relatively uninhabited space to operate in, unobserved on Earth. Instead of viewing the increased number of sightings as new visits to the Earth, he observes that historically the sightings have increased as mankind has moved westward. With the consequence: "they are not coming to us, but that we have been coming to them."

Over his long study, J. Manson Valentine has uncovered evidence suggesting that "coming westward" means to bases in the Triangle. He has noted that UFOs commonly come and go from the sky to the sea and vice versa with little effort. They zoom under the sea with as much speed as they do in the sky. He speculates that this might explain the phenomenon of "furrows" etched in the shallow bank bottoms, like something literally plowed over the banks at such a speed its wake cleaved a ditch. He has observed many of these, including a straight furrow extending for 18 miles, even *over* small islets. They can only be seen shortly after whatever it was has passed, before the currents obliterate them. Following them once led to clear circular patches of bottom sand devoid of any customary sea bottom growth, precisely where the lines terminated, as if something had slipped below or had emerged.

An apparent long-standing interest in the Earth, coupled with what appears to be little interest in open contact with us, poses the question: just what is the nature of the UFO occupants' interest and what predicates their choice of the Triangle?

A wide array of ideas has been put forward that hinge on observing our space center at Cape Canaveral or that the area is itself ideal for trajectory into outer space (the reason we selected Cape Canaveral for our space center) or as John Spencer, himself a ten-year veteran of the U.S. Air Force, proposed, "aliens" used the area of the Bermuda Triangle as a "catching ground" for "specimens" from Earth; he noted that both the area's seclusion and its isolated traffic made it easier for the UFOs to get in, interdict travelers, take what specimens they first chanced to find, and then get out without being detected. But none of these theories can explain the incidents earlier than a mere fifty-five years ago.

A far more sanguine theory for the presence of UFOs could be suggested by the legends of a past Earth, by ancient writings describing a prehistoric civilization as having had such aircraft, and by a sunken civilization from an unknown date in the midst of the Bermuda Triangle.

Another one of the most universal traditions in ancient legends is that of long life spans for past mankind. This is not only contained in Babylonian accounts but it is also an ancient obsession in Chinese thought, and also matter-of-factly applied to all peoples in Genesis both before and after the Flood. The only difference is that after the Flood they slowly began to lose this natural longevity.

Accidental discoveries in the last forty years are shedding remarkable light on how we can understand this and also why we should have expected it if these accounts detail facts. And these accidental discoveries occurred within the Bermuda Triangle because it is ideal for one thing: pressure and isolation tests on the many accessible undersea banks it so ubiquitously offers.

The Aquanaut Program of the 1960s was cannibalized to prepare astronauts for the isolation they would undergo on the moon shot and even, according to the hopes of the time, during prolonged living in small bases on the moon and other planets. Prospective astronauts were placed in watertight domiciles, usually some form of submersible affixed to the bank's bottom, to simulate a completely closed-off mode of living. Shallow banks were ideal for submerging these base stations at depths endurable by man and still making them accessible to terrestrial contact should an emergency occur. The emergency came in the form of a severe and deep cut to one aquanaut's hand. After it was bandaged, his fellow aquanauts sharing that particular domicile determined that he should be brought up the next day. However, the next morning before preparing him for transfer, his hand was unbound in order to replace the old bandage with a clean one. It was then noted that his hand had healed miraculously, far beyond any exception.

Studies eventually yielded the answer: the pressure at those depths had increased helium within the domicile and body chemistry. The profound affect helium has on the healing process was later confirmed and employed in hospitals in the form of hyperbaric (Greek *hyper baramos*— increased pressure) chambers to treat severely burned patients in critical need of healing in order to survive.

What the Aquanaut Program had done by accident was to possibly duplicate an environment that might have existed on the Earth several thousand years ago, before a flood. It has been noted by a number of catastrophist geophysicists that if there were sufficient mass to the antediluvian water-vapor canopy, it could have increased gravity at sea level to perhaps as much as twice what it is today. This in turn would have increased helium by perhaps as much as three to four times. Mankind, in essence, would have been living continually in an environment that today we struggle to obtain in specially designed chambers to speed healing.

Also, a water-vapor canopy would have acted as a second ozone layer, giving greater protection to the Earth from harmful ultraviolet light and other solar contaminants that tax our immune systems today and no doubt allow nasty diseases to get a foothold by simply making the human body divert too much energy to fend off the constant geophysical attacks. The end result is that we degenerate—"age"—faster.

Another factor (touched on in chapter 8) might be the timing of bio-rhythms based on the Schumann Frequency (fundamental frequency of the Earth = 7.8 Hz) and the possibility that such catastrophic changes in the atmosphere could alter that frequency to its present rate and with it alter the human bioprocesses or "tune" them to operate and burn out more quickly.

Along with this are genetic alterations. Geneticists and biologists have long known that the human genome and biochemistry can be affected by cataclysm—new species emerge after atomic tests and foliage grows more quickly, for example. They also know the body is essentially designed to eat, drink, reproduce, sleep, and live forever if only the aging process could be blocked and cell division maintained without degeneration. Footprints of biological potentiality, both positive and negative, have proven that manipulation or, rather, *adjustment* of life spans is possible. For example, the average life span of the Pygmy is only thirty-five years, while the Protozoa Globergina never dies; it divides and becomes two separate entities *ad infinitum*.

Perhaps the most astounding success so far in the field of "quantum longevity" involves the study conducted in 1985 by Daniel Rudman of the University of Wisconsin. He is the first physician in history to literally retrogress the age of a human being. By injecting synthetic human growth hormone (HGH) in twelve men, ages sixty-one to eighty, three times a week for six months, he was able to turn them back in time twenty years. Gray hair returned to its previous color, wrinkles on hands and face disappeared, skin thickness increased by 7 percent, fat was reduced by 14 percent, and lean muscle mass increased by 8 percent—sixty-year-old men literally looked forty again. Liver, spleen, and bone density were returning to their youthful states.

It was not surprising that the human body handled the high doses of injected hormone, since they were doses it once produced itself. Studies have proven that at age twenty the human biochemistry is signaling 500 micrograms of HGH to be released per day. This, however, decreases by age eighty to a mere 25 micrograms. The reasons have never been determined, for further tests have proven that the pituitary, the master gland, is capable of releasing as much HGH when old as when young, but seems to lack the stimulation—in other words, it lacks the correct bio-friendly environment to maintain its stimulation.

Induced blood poisoning like the bends (nitrogen poisoning of the blood) demonstrates the myriad chemical changes that occur in the body just by changing pressure too quickly. But the effects of increased pressure, as experienced in undersea domiciles, on the stimulation and reception of HGH have not been studied (yet), principally because the effects of HGH were not fully appreciated until the Rudman study was published in 1990 and also because uniformitarianism cannot accept that the geoenvironment has ever been any different than today.

In the biblical account of the post-Flood ages, one thing is immediately apparent—Noah's son, Shem, lives remarkably shorter than his father, dying at 600 years instead of his father's 950 years. Generationally after him the ages noticeably decrease. This, however, is exponentially along the lines of a truly physical equation. But myth does not abide by the rules of physics. The decrease in longevity is recorded as follows: Shem lived 600 years; Arphaxad, 535; Cainan, 460; Shelah, 460; Eber, 404; Peleg, 339; Regau, 339; Seruch, 330; Nachor, 304; Tarra, 205; Abraham, 175. The exponentiality is seen in that the greatest decrease is right away, then continues at a slower pace. This might be explained by the initial change in the atmosphere from a water-vapor-canopy loss—in other words, the human body was deprived of its accustomed pressure, perhaps subjected to different wavelengths, and was adjusting to the new environment, at the cost of its longevity.

One can well imagine that even a moron living to the ripe old age of 900 would be a genius by our standards today. An entire civilization of very healthy people living for a thousand years might indeed have been capable of astounding feats, not least of which would be space exploration and amazing city-building, the latter of which man seems to have excelled in the Genesis records. Loss of knowledge over several generations would not pose a problem, since literally dozens of generations could be alive at once.

While the life spans of postdiluvian men, those of the time period to which the great megacivilization of Indian Vedas, biblical Babel, even perhaps Bimini, belong would have been much less, they are still recorded as living long ages as compared to us, such as three hundred or four hundred years. With our ages continuing to dwindle until the present eighty-year average, it is not surprising that man lost knowledge and that succeeding cultures remembered the era of a remote past of long ages and great accomplishments as the time of the "gods."

What if UFOs represent a sampling of a prehistoric Earth culture returning to this planet? Considering the lower atmospheric pressure and the greater infiltration of solar forces and ultraviolet light on mankind

This tablet shows pictographs, an even earlier form of writing than Sumerian cuneiform. Pictographs are hardly primitive; they are the basis behind most languages. But over time they change to a cursive, easier to write, form, an evolution readily apparent in Chinese even today. However, the mysterious scripts of the Indus Valley and Easter Island seem to have advanced beyond pictographs. Everything in Genesis and Mesopotamian accounts of cataclysm indicates they are truncated from earlier more detailed versions, thus explaining why some scribes mistranslated a number system and instead of coming up with 930 years for an antediluvian life span came up with 28,000 years (in Babylonian).

after the loss of a water-vapor canopy, the present atmosphere would not be conducive to their, presumably, longer and healthier life spans. Out of necessity they would have to seek bases that more closely match Earth's earlier atmosphere, again, presumably the natural atmosphere of a healthy planet with an intact vapor canopy, to which they might also have migrated. This would require existence under the oceans, but only at depths that could replicate the delicate balance of oxygen, helium, and other vital homeostatic elements belonging to an earlier Earth. In the entire world, the ideal areas for this purpose are the continental and island shelves of the Bermuda Triangle, which occupy advantageous depths. They might also seek the ruins of a vanished civilization, hoping to determine just what went wrong.

Spencer has also offered an alterative for the disappearances of planes and ships that may be more worth considering in the above light. He felt that the UFO occupants might be assessing our technological development to see how far we are progressing and therefore how much in danger we might be of effecting our own destruction, as mankind may have done before—tragically altering the Earth's natural ecology and atmosphere in the process. If UFOs carry a sampling of former Earthmen who took to the stars long ago, this might be regarded as a conservationist and preventive measure. This would, of course, presuppose an ultimately altruistic purpose to their actions, one that seems belied by the destruction of so many ships and planes—if UFOs are to blame.

If the repeated sightings of UFOs are genuine, no one can explain their continued presence as mere disinterested interlopers. They make no attempt at contact; leave no trace or residue (despite claims); and do not openly wage war—all this is tantamount to indifference yet they continue to be seen in the Earth's atmosphere though they have developed an avoidance of crowded areas. Essentially what it approximates to is an interest in the Earth but no desire to expose themselves to our atmosphere or culture.

No one interested in faithfully discussing missing planes and ships can avoid references to UFOs or "flying saucers." Many do not like to do so because of the erratic behavior the subject often excites today. Discussion of UFOs may elicit giggles from some, scorn from others, derision, dismissal, awe, or even dangerous devotion. One can be accused of religious or cult associations or, contrariwise, be labeled apostate. But no one can deny that since 1947 some phenomenon has developed in the skies above us that deserves study or, at least, serious comment.

Thousands of reports from both civilian and military pilots have detailed a host of unexplained aerial phenomena. They are often described as a "disc," "flying saucer," "cigar," or just a very brilliant light or glow. They have often paced, harried, and dogged aircraft or they simply streak past at phenomenal speeds. Some show signs of intelligent control, while others do impossible things; they make 90-degree turns at high speed, they hover, ascend, descend, and disappear, all indications of unknown propulsion and mind-boggling power.

Radar observations have been particularly useful. The UFOs have been clocked at tremendous speeds by several stations monitoring the same object. They can appear in a single turn of the radar antenna and disappear just as quickly. They clock in as doing 3,000, 4,000, and 10,000 miles per hour. The figures are tabulated by many stations, making it conclusive that they are "good returns"—that is, solid objects and not temperature inversions, a meteorological phenomenon of cooler, heavier layers of air trapped in higher altitudes between warmer layers.

At first (1947–50) they showed special interest in our large cities, then our vegetation belts and military installations. From New York came reports, over Rome, Paris, and London, off Sicily and circling Buenos Aires; they descended on Washington, D.C., and streaked past other world capitals: Sidney, Tokyo, Lisbon, and Madrid. One hundred and twenty-two sightings in 1947 increased by increments of thirty each succeeding year until they reached a crescendo in 1952, with 1,501 reports of lights, saucers, discs, and cigar-shaped objects flitting about the Earth.

UFOs also come in "flaps" (or waves) and then leave, as in 1952, then again in 1966, then in 1973, and again in 1990, over Europe and Russia.

This might be explained by copycat reporting, that is, one actual sighting inspiring a whole host of bogus reports from spontaneous stargazers and erratic minds. But such well-placed people as Russian generals; The Lord Hill-Norton, former Chief of Defense Staff for Great Britain; U.S. governors; former Vice President Al Gore; former USSR president Mikhail Gorbachev; and former President Jimmy Carter have either seen them or actively pursue an interest in them. Disappearances of aircraft have directly resulted when our interceptors got too close to unknown "blips" or "targets" on the scope, as in the case of a missing F-89 jet on November 23, 1953, when its "blip" was observed to "merge" with an "unknown" violating U.S. airspace over the Great Lakes. This does not imply any form of predation but could merely represent accidental destruction or self-defense. However, a disappearance off Australia is poignant for the pilot's inability to identify the craft that was harassing his plane—a disquieting similarity to the disappearance of José Maldonado Torres and José Pagan in the Bermuda Triangle in 1980.

On October 21, 1978, Fred Valentich was en route from Australia to nearby King Island. What passed before his eyes was recorded by Melbourne Flight Service Unit and included in the Summary Report issued by the Department of Transport of Australia. It is so extraordinary it must follow verbatim:

The pilot obtained a Class Four instrument rating on 11 May 1978 and he was therefore authorised to operate at night in visual meteorological conditions (VMC). On the afternoon of 21 October 1978 he attended the Moorabbin Briefing Office, obtained a meteorological briefing and, at 1723 hours [5:23 p.m.], submitted a flight plan for a night VMC flight from Moorabbin to King Island and return. The cruising altitude nominated in the flight plan was below 5000 feet, with estimated time intervals of 41 minutes to Cape Otway and 28 minutes from Cape Otway to King Island. The total fuel endurance was shown as 300 minutes. The pilot made no arrangements for aerodrome lighting to be illuminated for his arrival at King Island. He advised the briefing officer and the operator's representative that he was uplifting friends at King Island and took four life jackets in the aircraft with him.

The aircraft was refuelled to capacity at 1810 hours [6:10] and departed Moorabbin at 1819 hours [6:19]. After departure the pilot established two-way radio communications with Melbourne Flight Service Unit (FSU).

The pilot reported Cape Otway at 1900 hours [7:00 p.m.] and the next transmission received from the aircraft was at 1906:14 hours [7:06:14]. The following communications between the aircraft and Melbourne FSU were recorded from this time: (Note: The word/words in parentheses are open to other interpretations.)

TIME	FROM	TEXT
1906:14	VH-DSJ	MELBOURNE this is DELTA SIERRA JULIET is there any known traffic below five thousand
:23	FSU	DELTA SIERRA JULIET no known traffic
:26	VH-DSJ	DELTA SIERRA JULIET I am seems (to) be a large aircraft below five thousand
:46	FSU	DELTA SIERRA JULIET what type of aircraft is it
:50	VH-DSJ	DELTA SIERRA JULIET I cannot affirm it is four bright it seems to me like landing lights
1907:04	FSU	DELTA SIERRA JULIET
:32	VH-DSJ	MELBOURNE this (is) DELTA SIERRA JULIET the aircraft has just passed over me at least a thousand feet above
:43	FSU	DELTA SIERRA JULIET roger and it is a large aircraft confirm
:47	VH-DSJ	er unknown due to the speed it's travelling. is there any airforce aircraft in the vicinity
:57	FSU	DELTA SIERRA JULIET no known aircraft in the vicinity
1908:18	VH-DSJ	MELBOURNE it's approaching now from due east towards me
:28	FSU	DELTA SIERRA JULIET
:42		// open microphone for two seconds//
:49	VH-DSJ	DELTA SIERRA JULIET it seems to me that he's playing some sort of game he's flying over me two[,] three times at a time at speeds I could not identify
1909:02	FSU	DELTA SIERRA JULIET roger what is your actual level
:06	VH-DSJ	my level is four and a half thousand four five zero zero
:11	FSU	DELTA SIERRA JULIET and confirm you cannot identify the aircraft

:14	VH-DSJ	affirmative
:18	FSU	DELTA SIERRA JULIET roger standby
:28	VH-DSJ	MELBOURNE DELTA SIERRA JULIET it's not an aircraft it is // open microphone for two seconds//
:46	FSU	DELTA SIERRA JULIET MELBOURNE can you describe the er aircraft
1909:07	FSU	DELTA SIERRA JULIET as it's flying past it's a long shape // open microphone for three seconds // (cannot) identify more than (that it has such speed)// open microphone for 3 seconds // before me right now Melbourne
1910:07	FSU	DELTA SIERRA JULIET roger and how large would the er object be
:20	VH-DSJ	DELTA SIERRA JULIET MELBOURNE it seems like it's stationary what I'm doing right now is orbiting and the thing is just orbiting on top of me also it's got a green light and sort of metallic (like) it's all shiny (on) the outside
:43	FSU	DELTA SIERRA JULIET
:48	VH-DSJ	DELTA SIERRA JULIET // open microphone for 5 seconds // it's just vanished
:57	FSU	DELTA SIERRA JULIET
1911:03	VH-DSJ	MELBOURNE would you know what kind of aircraft I've got[,] is it (a type) military aircraft
:08	FSU	DELTA SIERRA JULIET confirm the er aircraft just vanished
:14	VII-DSJ	SAY AGAIN
:17	FSU	DELTA SIERRA JULIET is the aircraft still with you
:23	VH-DSJ	DELTA SIERRA JULIET (it's ah nor) // open microphone 2 seconds // (now) approaching from the southwest
:37	FSU	DELTA SIERRA JULIET

:52	VH-DSJ	DELTA SIERRA JULIET the engine is rough idling I've got it set at twenty three twenty four and the thing is (coughing)
1912:04	FSU	DELTA SIERRA JULIET roger what are your intentions
:09	VH-DSJ	my intentions are ah to go to King Island ah Melbourne that strange aircraft is hovering on top of me again // two seconds open microphone // it is hovering and it's not an aircraft
:22	FSU	DELTA SIERRA JULIET
:28	VH-DSJ	DELTA SIERRA JULIET MELBOURNE // 17 seconds open microphone //
:49	FSU	DELTA SIERRA JULIET MELBOURNE

There is no record of any further transmissions from the aircraft.

The weather in the Cape Otway area was clear with a trace of stratocumulus cloud at 5000 to 7000 feet, scattered cirrus cloud at 30000 feet, excellent visibility and light winds. The end of daylight at Cape Otway was at 1918 [7:18] hours.

The Alert Phase of SAR [Search and Rescue] procedures was declared at 1912 hours [7:12] and, at 1933 hours [7:33] when the aircraft did not arrive at King Island, the Distress Phase was declared and search action was commenced. An intensive air, sea and land search was continued until 25 October 1978, but no trace of the aircraft was found.

OPINION AS TO CAUSE

The reason for the disappearance of the aircraft has not been determined.

If we compare the array of inexplicably missing planes and ships in the Bermuda Triangle with such a case as this, or Torres and Pagan's, it is liable to give form to a nightmare of possibilities. The worst, naturally, again comes back to the idea of intentional kidnapping of human and technological specimens for reasons which we cannot, or would not like to, fathom.

Long before any of these incidents, Spencer and several other UFOlogists proposed that the rarely seen "cigar-shaped" UFO could actually be a base ship in which several saucers could fit, as well as several specimens of aircraft and boats from Earth. Valentich's disappearance is noteworthy for his description of one of these long spaceships.

The relentlessness with which the "unknown" bore down on Torres and Pagan also makes the encounter seem more unnerving in light of these long-held opinions. Moreover, after the Phantom II jet's disappearance in 1971 an unexplained oblong shape was seen in the water that quickly disappeared. This shape was estimated to measure 100 by 200 feet, similar to Valentich's UFO and Spencer's "mother ships."

A July 1985 mass sighting over Zimbabwe reported a similar large luminous object hovering at 17,000 feet. When two jet interceptors arrived from Bulawayo, the object ascended vertically with incredible speed and disappeared. Air Marshal Azim Daudpota confirmed: "Scores of people saw it. It was no illusion, no deception, no imagination."

On March 21, 1990, several pilots and radar stations in Russia tracked an enormous disc or flying saucer near Pereslavl-Zalesskiy, near Moscow. This case was confirmed by General Igor Maltsev, Chief of the General Staff of the Soviet Air Defense Forces. A description of its behavior, as given by General Maltsev in an April 1990 official statement, is advisable: "According to the evidence of the eye-witnesses, the UFO was a disc with a diameter from 100 to 200 meters. Two pulsating lights were positioned on its sides. When the object flew in a horizontal plane, the line of the lights was parallel to the horizon. During vertical movement it rotated and was perpendicular to the ground. Moreover, the object rotated on its axis and performed an 'S' turn in flight, both in the horizontal and the vertical planes. . . . Next, the UFO hovered above the ground and then flew with a speed exceeding that of a modern-day jet fighter by two or three times. All of the observers noticed that the flight speed was directly related to the flashing of the side lights. The more often they flashed, the higher the speed." General Maltsev's impression was that: "The movement of the UFO was not accompanied by sound of any kind and was distinguished by its startling maneuverability. It seemed that the UFO was completely devoid of inertia. In other words," he added, "they had somehow come to terms with gravity. At the present time, terrestrial machines hardly have any such capabilities."

Echoing somewhat this impression, Admiral the Lord Hill-Norton has stated: "The enormous and very consistent weight of evidence from sightings, and even optical and radar measurements, make it clear enough to me that the technology of construction and propulsion of these devices is far in advance even that of our space probes, never mind our manned space flights." He comments that "were such technology in actual use anywhere on Earth it would have surfaced, either in war or, perhaps more likely, in industry." Noting that a disc is the most common shape, he has offered the opinion that "U stands more for unexplained than unidentified."

In a flap over Belgium in the same year (1990) Colonel Wilfried de Brouwer said with refreshing though dispassionate candor, "There was a logic to the movements of the UFOs."

When faced with the unusual reports from around the world by persons who have had no interface with each other and yet remarkably describe the same phenomena, such a fact may elicit from the reader a similar opinion as expressed by Mikhail Gorbachev: "The phenomenon of UFOs does exist, and it must be treated seriously."

The disc shape often reported seems more than coincidental with the observed abilities of UFOs. Physicist Alan Holt suggests that a disc would be ideal to generate an electromagnetic pattern that would nullify or disconnect the Earth's own gravitational field around it, allowing it to travel in "hyperspace" in which huge distances can be attained at slow speed. Noting in his NASA published article "Field Resonance Propulsion Concept" (1980) some attributes of UFO sightings, he poses an interesting solution: "If the speed of light is the true limit of velocity in space-time, then the potential extraterrestrial visitors must utilize a form of transportation which transcends space and time to keep the trip times short. UFOs are often observed to disappear instantaneously. In a subset of these cases, the UFO later reappears at a nearby location, implying a disappearance from and a reappearance into space-time."

For some time now the theoretical difficulties of travel in space-time have been the greatest objection to the idea that spaceships could be visiting the Earth from other planets. Recently, however, we have been urged to reconsider the limitations of space travel by some surprises involving the velocity of light and objects in deep space. When three of our space probes (*Pioneer 10* in 1972, *Pioneer 11* in 1973, and *Ulysses* in 1989) left our solar system, the last NASA detected of them was "an incomprehensible acceleration." An analogy may help to explain this phenomenon. If space can be viewed as an ocean of electromagnetic wavelengths, the heliosphere—the electromagnetic-gravitational force of our sun—that creates our solar system can be viewed as a choppy harbor, distorting, bending, and causing a tug of war of forces. When the probes entered deep space, just as when a boat enters calm water, they zoomed along on the smooth electromagnetic ocean of billions of wavelengths speeding uninterrupted between solar systems and galaxies.

Part of Einstein's predictions about space and light (an electromagnetic wavelength) seems proved by this discovery. He postulated that space itself curves around a massive object like a planet, and with this so will light bend. Yet the more light bends, the more it slows. The speed of light around here, within both the gravitational field of the Earth and then that of the sun, travels at a constant of 186,284 miles per second. But outside our solar system, free of its gravitational pull, it is only logical to assume that light travels at speeds far greater than what it does within this heliosphere, no longer having to contend with our own sun's massive pull.

With such increased acceleration comes a shortening in the amount of time it takes to traverse space. With a speeding object, however, there comes an increase in its mass and along with this, theoretically, a curving of space around the object and a resulting slowing of time. We must remember that our own planet travels at just over 66,000 miles per hour, and with its gravity and curving of space we have detected a definite slowing of time at its surface, as compared to its orbital heights.

The principle of the increase of mass with speed was also predicted by Einstein and proven in the cyclotron at UCLA when the atom was increased to speeds near that of light, and its mass was detected to increase.

A spaceship traveling at the speed of light or greater speeds would have an increase in mass, thus causing a bending of space around it and with this a slowing of time within the spaceship's field. It would be theoretically possible to travel long distances in relatively short time spans (from the perspective of those inside the spaceships), but time would still progress at its normal speed (or at least our acceptable progression) outside the craft. A round trip from here to Sirius (nine light years away) at light speed would only require a box lunch for those inside the spaceship, but Earth's time would have progressed eighteen years. But if a speed greater than 186,284 miles per second could be attained in intergalactic space, as now seems probable, the time disparity would be shorter unless with a greater bending of space time would slow even more.

Observed in-flight behavior of UFOs has, interestingly, inspired our own theories on how to eliminate all these worrisome conjectures. The goal is to achieve total "counterbary" or antigravity around a craft—it is within its own gravitational field and capable of barycentric control (control of the gravitational field from within) while also being able to repel the gravitational fields and wavelengths of other bodies. Like a bubble with an ant floating inside, it would be the field of antigravity that is accelerating while the craft inside merely moves with the field, thus traveling at fantastic speeds but without the increase of mass or curving of space and perturbation of time, making it possible for craft to travel frequently in space without encountering dreadful time lapses between their home worlds and ours. Such craft would also be capable of any maneuver, including 90-degree turns at high speed, since the occupants, in their own gravitational field inside, would be unaware of the g-forces of such movements, just as our Earth's gravitational field makes us unaware of our own planet's incredible acceleration through space.

Despite the instant official denials that UFOs exist and pose any danger, it is cautioned that if any of our conventional craft were too near to an intense electromagnetic-gravitational field—as such a hypothetical craft would generate—the field would cause all electronic gear to go haywire—coincidental, one might add, with the effects reported in the Triangle and in UFO encounters throughout the world.

Paul LaViolette, systems scientist and physicist, as well as having served on NASA's Space Exploration Outreach Project, has proposed that a less intense form of such a field is generated by the B-2 Stealth bomber, created, in this case, by the engines sending positive electrical charges toward the leading edge of the batwing and negative charges to the trailing part of the batwing. Physicist Thomas Townsend Brown was the first to discover this method of propulsion and used it on discs, once again, finding these the best suited. This created a pull in the direction of the positive charge and a push from the negative charge causing lift without the need for air to flow over the wing.

Although highly classified, elements of the B-2 are known, and these tend to indicate that some form of electrogravitic force is in use. For instance, the U.S. Air Force admits the B-2 leaves no vapor trail at high altitudes; the cockpit sits in a Faraday Cage, which is used to shield electronics from massive amounts of static electricity; the batwing shape is ideal to drain off the buildup of static electricity because its jagged design is equivalent to seven wing tips (from which on a regular aircraft the static lines leach off the accumulated electrical charges); and the skin of the bomber is made of depleted uranium crystals. One can well imagine what a conventional aircraft would encounter if it got too close to the field of a B-2.

When Brown's model discs first flew in 1952, he believed that a full-sized disc with engines capable of generating appropriate electrical charges would be capable of Mach 3 speeds. In order to belie the criticisms that he had merely created a form of electrostatic propulsion, he carried out the tests in a vacuum chamber, detecting, once again, the unusual nonconventional electrogravitic phenomenon.

In describing Brown's discs, his colleague Mason Rose asserted that they "had no moving parts at all. They create a modification of the gravitational field around themselves. . . . They act like a surfboard on a wave . . . the electrogravitic saucer creates its own 'hill' which is a local distortion of the gravitational field, then it takes this hill with it in any chosen direction." He further commented: "The occupants of one of Brown's saucers would feel no stress at all, no matter how sharp the turn or how great the acceleration. This is because the ship, the occupants, and the load are all responding equally to the wavelike distortion of the local gravitational field."

While T. T. Brown postulated no theory for how this was done, aside from saying it was neither predicted by Relativity nor by theories of electromagnetism, LaViolette's analysis is worthy of some comment:

However, recent advances in theoretical physics provide a rather straightforward explanation of the principle. According to the novel physics of subquantum kinetics, gravity potential can adopt two polarities instead of one. Not only can a gravity field exist in the form of a matter attracting gravity potential well, as standard physics teaches, but it can also exist in the form of a matter-repelling gravity potential hill. Moreover, it predicts that these gravity polarities should be directly matched with electrical polarity: positively charged particles such as protons generating gravity wells and negatively charged particles such as electrons generating gravity hills.

The wave-like line depicts how the gravitational field would be distorted around one of T. T. Brown's "antigravity discs" into a pulling trough and a propelling hill, as predicted by Dr. Paul LaViolette's subquantum kinetics theory. It also portrays the concept that Dr. Mason Rose was conveying. (Based on an illustration in Dr. LaViolette's paper, "The U.S. Antigravity Squadron," and in his book, *Subquantum Kinetics*. Reproduced by permission of Dr. Paul LaViolette.)

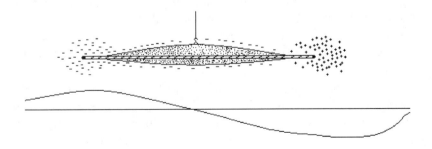

With this we are reminded that the very structure of matter—the atom—is mostly space, a minisolar system comprised of a nucleus with protons inside and an equal number of electrons orbiting it. The electrons are never pulled into the nucleus, but they are also never repelled out of orbit. The harmony—the gravity and antigravity that maintain their perfect orbits—are the result of basic electromagnetic forces between them.

In his study of the Triangle, Valentine came to other opinions on how to connect the electromagnetic anomalies with UFO travel. He was of the opinion that these were the result of a combination of natural forces and induction by UFO activity. This could explain, he proposed, very localized and severe magnetic storms causing the aberrations in electronic equipment. He said: " 'Space engineers' may be utilizing the electrical potential of a very special area of the Earth." Before completely materializing, "these interdimensional craft may be quite invisible to us while their presence in our atmosphere is being felt magnetically."

This idea about UFOs and special areas for magnetism sounds less fanciful now that elements of Project Magnet have been declassified. This Canadian project, carried out under electrical engineer Wilbert B. Smith in the early 1950s, contains some surprisingly pertinent information. Its goal, as outlined by Smith in a memorandum recently discovered by Nick Balaskas at the University of Ottawa Library, was specifically to determine a means "whereby the potential energy of the earth's magnetic field may be abstracted and used." On this basis, he continued, Project Magnet built a small unit to test the hypothesis, with this result that: "The tests were essentially successful in that sufficient energy was abstracted from the earth's field to operate a voltmeter, approximately 50 millivolts."

However, it is in the purpose of the ensuing field tests that a most intriguing coincidence with these theories regarding the Bermuda Triangle is uncovered. Smith officially wrote: "This project is for the purpose of studying magnetic phenomena, particularly those phenomena resulting from unusual boundary conditions in the basic electromagnetic field. There is reason to believe their discovery will open up a new and useful technology."

While it has often been reported before that Project Magnet located unusual areas of magnetism over the Earth, the purpose of the Project to specifically *find unusual areas* to see if energy was more accessible here, or if these anomalous places could point the way to creating these conditions and accessing the field's potential at any given location, are only now being discovered.

The purpose again is to find a source of limitless power, the current obsession of our own society in its healthy attempt to finally end our dependence on our dwindling supply of fossil fuels. He further elaborated:

The design is now completed for a unit which should be self-sustaining and in addition provide a small surplus of power. Such a unit, in addition to functioning as a "pilot power plant," should be large enough to permit the study of the various reaction forces which are expected to develop.

We believe that we are on the track of something which may well prove to be the introduction of a new technology. The existence of a different technology is borne out by the investigations which are being carried on at the present time in relation to flying saucers.

This coincidence is extraordinary. In trying to determine how flying saucers can fly and even be here, Project Magnet was led to magnetism as a power source and its unusual areas as a better tap for this energy. In trying to account for disappearances, Triangle theorists uncovered unusual magnetic properties, sudden and unexplained electromagnetic power drains, the many UFO and USO reports in the area, and evidence of unusual energy pulses from the seabed. (Except in the above scenario they would not be prehistoric Atlantean complexes but modern ones—or for those who believe there is a connection, these are revitalized ones or engineered on the same principle.) Both groups involved appear very much to have walked up a foggy avenue from opposite directions and suddenly met head on.

Disappearances also increased in frequency at approximately the same time "flying saucer" reports began. Trying to avoid UFOs as the connecting link between them all is like trying to avoid a scorpion in your underwear.

An example of how confidential were aspects of Project Magnet can be seen in how open Smith was in his 1952 memorandum about his own investigation into UFOs. Concerning his "discreet inquiries" through the Canadian Embassy in Washington, D.C., he discovered: "a. The matter is the most highly classified subject in the United States Government, rating higher even than the H-bomb; b. Flying saucers exist; c. Their modus operandi is unknown but concentrated effort is being made by a small group headed by Dr. Vannevar Bush; d. The entire matter is considered by the United States authorities to be of tremendous significance."

A UFO, as seen near Brazil. From a photograph taken from an Argentine pursuit plane, late 1954.

The tremendous significance is, of course, that the mere presence of flying saucers, their shape, speed, and the fact that they seem to be here, led us to considering electromagnetism and gravity as means of propulsion. Every bit of our research has led us to believe that such propulsion is possible, that discs are the best shape for this propulsion, and that phenomenal speeds and perhaps some very novel conduits of travel are easily attained—a most remarkable achievement if UFOs end up being only hallucinations, as they are frequently officially condemned.

The whole trend of this becomes even more provocative when considering the theories of magnetic opposition and how the shape of this sphere is a determining factor for where magnetic phenomena will take place along its field lines. This transmitting of force along invisible magnetic field lines to its magnetic opposite, as determined by shape and mass, shows the frustrating relationship of shape, mass, and energy fields. But it also shows that "portals" for this energy do exist.

It is possible that Bruce Gernon actually flew along a field line briefly while in a magnetic vortex caused by charged particles swirling around the line of force, proving perhaps that one day we can project matter along lines of magnetic force. This method may be the most foolproof for ensuring that no bending of space will be encountered with hyperacceleration, and that we can achieve the speed of light, which, yet again, we must recall is an electromagnetic wavelength.

This movement of energy over the Earth along its lines of force is only the tip of the iceberg. There are magnetic and gravitational waves in the vacuum of space, though to us they seem to be out of place, for there is nothing from which they could have evolved. But if there is such a thing as galactic magnetic opposition, these waves could represent the field lines of the Milky Way. If we learn to project matter along our own magnetic field lines, it seems logical we could travel in space in the same way. One presumably could travel along these magnetic field lines to their opposite in the Milky Way—if such a magnetic opposite also exists in the galaxy, and it seems logical that it could.

Our magnetic opposite in the Milky Way could be a lively and inhabited solar system that, though on the opposite side of the galaxy, could be our easiest first step to other planets instead of conventional jet engines to laboriously get us to Mars or elsewhere. A number of UFO researchers have suggested that UFOs may indeed travel along magnetic wavelengths, and that likewise we too could be an easy first step for men on the opposite side of the galaxy, if they use these magnetic and gravitational waves as highways.

In this theory, the Bermuda Triangle might itself be the portal for this galactic magnetic opposition, and the high number of UFO reports in the area might merely represent UFOs coming, not out of space, but out of hyperspace, from the exact magnetic opposite in the galaxy.

Known magnetic faults in the Triangle have been the busiest places for UFO activity, especially around the Tongue of the Ocean in the Bahamas, the Puerto Rico Trench, and other areas of Puerto Rico. The famous 1972 Adjuntas Flap in Puerto Rico lasted for months, beginning near the mountain village of Adjuntas (near the center for natural gamma aeroradioactivity, according to the U.S. Geological Survey map) and radiating down toward the island's western coastline. During these night flaps of unexplained lights, a number of derelict sailboats were found near Aguadilla and Cabo Rojo and towed to port, with no evidence suggesting why they were abandoned.

Continuing UFO activity is especially prevalent around these areas today, the precise area where Torres and Pagan disappeared after reporting the "weird object." During one encounter on April 11, 1992, several witnesses, including Frederico Cruz, director of Civil Air Defense at Lajas, Puerto Rico, saw a huge disc being pursued by a military jet. According to Cruz: "The saucer was metallic, silvery, and highly polished, and it seemed to be playing with the jet. It would continually stop in the air suddenly, then just as the jet was about to catch up, it would move away quickly." Concerning the concentrations of coastal sightings at Laguna Cartagena, he firmly stated: "We have seen brightly colored ovoid and round objects as they overfly the area, making right-angled turns, and sometimes they enter the lagoon and disappear underwater"—thereby recalling to mind yet again the idea that they prefer bases beneath the sea's pressure. "The UFOs are there, they really are. So that's why I can't remain silent while others ridicule those who have seen these things."

Others have braved ridicule by placing in an affidavit a clear statement about things that official investigators are perhaps hesitant to include in their narrative reports. After his son's disappearance in 1980, José Pagan Jiménez did not defer to the nebulous wording of the official report and dub the "object" merely "weird," but he specifically called it a "glowing object"—a discovery he made during his own investigation as a police lieutenant. For fifteen years he tried to find his son, even traveling to the Dominican Republic in hopes he and Torres had returned but were being detained. He finally gave up in 1995 and refuses to talk about it to this day. The only link left to an explanation for the family is that "weird object."

One can understand why there would be an amalgam of theories about the Bermuda Triangle, but it is amazing how so many intertwine. All these attributes of UFOs seem strangely to recall Edgar Cayce's readings, given long before modern UFOs realization, of craft that flew in the air and underwater using gravitational and magnetic wavelengths in a previous Earth civilization before a cataclysm. Modern propulsion theories suggest that such craft are possible. Past cataclysms may explain why beings from other worlds would prefer to be based beneath the sea, and the ideal geography of the Bermuda Triangle—its magnetic faults, its past dead civilization, and its convenient banks—may tell us why and how they are there.

In this context, it may not be appreciated but advisable to reemphasize that aircraft disappearances involving UFOs only seem to happen over water. And the Triangle, because of its heavy volume of traffic, is the one place where it is easiest to interdict travel, since a disappearance is naturally dismissed as an accident, whereas over land, if no trace is found an acceptable excuse can never be offered. Incidents like Valentich's and Torres's disappearances may become known only because they happened close enough to land for the pilots to contact a base and warn others about what was happening. The others may have been silently taken.

But there may be another reason altogether for such sightings and disappearances—a final piece in the puzzle, befittingly final as the ocean is itself the final frontier on this planet, an integral part of its function and the element that makes this planet hospitable. It is best that we gaze not to the stars for this answer, but to a world that is just as old and even more perplexing.

11

Let the Oceans Speak

THE RATIO OF this planet that is water is nearly three quarters of its surface, or about 170,000,000 square miles versus 60,000,000 square miles of land. Any consideration of an answer for the many disappearances in the Bermuda Triangle, as well as what appear to be escapes from unusual phenomena within it, cannot omit the ocean, itself the one tangible thread that runs throughout the litany of all these incidents. It is certain that nowhere else in the world *over land* does anything comparable to the events in the Bermuda Triangle take place.

To consider why so many phenomena reported in the Bermuda Triangle are all seemingly tied into electromagnetism (EM) field effects, we cannot overlook its most important element: water. Water is an essential conductor of electrical charges. We may note mentally that this planet operates on electromagnetism, but we often forget the crucial role of water in electricity and thus on electromagnetism. Water is, scientifically speaking, merely the compound H_2O, or two parts hydrogen and one part oxygen. Sharing the oceans' chemical base are minerals of varying concentration, primarily sodium (salt), calcium, magnesium, and conductors of electrical currents like the metals copper and mercury. Erosion from the land and sea sediments account for some of these.

The atmosphere is not as dense molecularly as this "hydrosphere," but it is just as complex, and its balance is far more crucial to maintain the orderly recycling that takes place between the sea and sky. Besides H_2O, other elements exist in the atmosphere, by ratio: molecular nitrogen (N_2), molecular oxygen (O_2), carbon dioxide (CO_2), argon (Ar); and in smaller amounts methane (CH_4), nitrous oxide (N_2O), carbon monoxide (CO), hydrogen (H_2), ozone (O_3), and helium (He), neon (Ne), krypton (Kr), xenon (Xe).

To illustrate how these gases are not just "air," it is estimated that 1 part per million of atmospheric CO_2 equals 2.13 gigatons of carbon, that is, 2.13 billion tons.

As can be imagined, an excess of any particular one of these elements could be potentially harmful, as an element absorbed into the ocean or perhaps in the atmosphere itself, by altering the chemical makeup of the atmosphere and therefore creating an upset in the delicate processes that occur between ocean and atmosphere. These are, however, kept in a fairly steady ratio because of a complex recycling of them by the Earth, primarily over the ocean.

But the burning of fossil fuels is a comparatively recent process, one that has existed in major degrees, first with coal and then with oil, only within the last two centuries—a brief span compared to the age of the Earth and mankind. Every five years about 6.2 gigatons of carbon are added to the atmosphere through fossil-fuel burning (for example, burning 1 gallon of gasoline yields 19.6 pounds of carbon). Roughly 92 gigatons are absorbed into the oceans during this same five years from the atmosphere. Of this, 90 or so gigatons reenter the atmosphere. Much of this is natural recycled carbon: from erosion, deterioration, and even human breathing. But there is a difference between recycling carbon and adding it. The burning of fossil fuels is not a natural event, and it adds billions of tons of carbon to the equation every decade—and this has now been ongoing for two hundred years. We may suppose that if any undesirable change is going to be triggered by a chemical imbalance, it would first appear over the oceans, where the greatest amount of carbon is absorbed, stored, and prepared for recycling back into the atmosphere.

This theory is intriguing because it proposes that we ourselves are slowly orchestrating these events and phenomena. This may explain why they have not been reported before, or at least as frequently until now inasmuch as they may not have been possible until the present chemical makeup of the atmosphere and oceans. An airplane or ship at the right moment may even be the deciding factor in setting off these electromagnetic phenomena. One recalls how fogs have attached themselves to an airplane or ship. One reason for this may be that airplanes and modern vessels are metal and perhaps attract any unusual electrical phenomena to them or create the friction necessary to generate them.

Developing this theory more may also provide a very good explanation for why many UFOs appear over the oceans and behave with apparent indifference: it could be that they are nothing more than strange atmospheric or electromagnetic phenomena materialized over the ocean at the right temperatures, winds, and humidity, a combination for which the tropical Bermuda Triangle may be ideal.

We must remember that UFOs are mostly identified as blue-green or white-orange lights. These colors are so often seen in the Bahamas and Gulf Stream waters that they are frequently pointed out to tourists. These greenish "pools" of phosphorescence are caused by a number of things, not least of which are algae growth, marl, and often plain unidentified luminescence. Some dance and flit about underneath and then disappear or zoom away. In many ways this is starkly suggestive of atmospheric ball lightning, though implying an underwater version of it.

It seems clear that the humid and often volatile atmosphere of the Triangle is equally capable of creating numerous lights and glows, or possibly even reflecting some of those from the water in the heavy haze—areas of visible humidity—to which the area is particularly prone. At night they could clearly be identified as speeding lights.

Vivid descriptions of UFOs as saucers might rule out the supposition that all UFOs are some sort of electrical phenomena (except where the phenomenon is said to be an ovoid or saucer-shaped *glow*). On the other hand, UFOs might still be atmospheric even where the clear shape of a saucer or disc is reported. One remembers that in the Hutchison Effect odd multicolored lights and "objects with a cling of gray fog" materialized during high-voltage tests. The potential electrical power in the atmosphere, especially powerful in humid weather, could be astounding. One should not be surprised that places like the Triangle could produce extraordinary lights and even, under unusual circumstances . . . the appearance of "objects"?

Laboratory discoveries of this last manifestation have some interesting applications when interpreting unusual aerial phenomena. We must remember that water (as well as many other materials) is capable of assuming three major states: liquid, solid, gaseous. Is it logical to postulate that under the right conditions other gases of the atmosphere are capable of solidifying and appearing as objects? If so, they would of course be aerodynamic in shape—as they form in the currents or begin to fall when first solidifying, before assuming their gaseous state again. In this context we should note that many UFOs are, curiously, described as small. Precise measurements have indicated 2 feet or smaller.

Powerful forces disturbing the magnetic field might be the trigger. Unexplained objects like those noted above were seen during some of the heaviest aerial bombing over Germany during World War II and often labeled as "foo fighters." A clear description of them, however, as contained the records of the Eighth Air Force, Mission 115 (the Schweinfurt bombing 14 October 1943), confirms their size as minuscule. This report details that clusters of silver discs were reported in the path of the 384th Formation and seen by bombardiers, turret gunners, and pilots alike. They were no bigger than 1 inch thick and 3 inches in diameter. In the words of one pilot attempting to evade them: "My right wing went directly through a cluster with absolutely no effect on engines or plane surface." Further questioning of several aircrews after they returned to base in England led to no explanations whatsoever for what these discs were. From another pilot: "Also observed two other aircraft flying through silver discs with no apparent damage. Observed discs and debris two other times but could not determine where it came from."

This "debris" is remarkable for its proximity to the cluster of discs— it clung near them much like the gray fog seen in the Hutchison Effect during high-voltage electricity tests. The records of many groups, both before and after the devastating Schweinfurt mission, confirm these same type of silver discs were seen during the heaviest bombing and antiaircraft fire. These were never explained, but remain, as noted in a memorandum in the files of U.S. Air Force history, "one of the most baffling incidents of World War II, and an enigma which to this day defies all explanation."

But suppose, and always suppose, a concentration of atmospheric gases could briefly solidify harmlessly under the incredible electromagnetic stress of antiaircraft bombardment? This seems astounding, but no less astounding than H_2O in the atmosphere changing into ice merely by a change in temperature.

In attempting to minimize the Bermuda Triangle enigma, some have caustically pointed out that unexplained disappearances have happened in the Atlantic hundreds or thousands of miles from the Triangle, and naturally with such an attitude they rhetorically add: "Why not consider the entire sea as the mystery zone?"

This is something to which Dr. Ivan Lima might agree, though without the sarcasm. He experienced something "Triangle-esque," though far from the Bermuda Triangle. It was October 8, 1995, when he and seven other members of a research team were on a scientific cruise in the Pacific, off California. A trained and qualified electrical engineer and a specialist in the magnetic field, he was partaking in the cruise in that capacity, with the others aboard being of the medical sciences.

According to Dr. Lima, they were about 50 miles off San Francisco Bay. After they had just thrown their anchor, they noted a radiation manifestation 50 feet from the vessel. Aware that solar radiation cannot produce such an effect in water (especially before 10 A.M., at such a short distance), they all began to take a keen interest. What happened next is so startling it should be reported in Dr. Lima's own words.

The following moment the formation of a fog began, exactly from the point of the radiation. The fog was low and thick, not more than a meter above the water and it . . . formed as a rectangular platform. . . . Next to the extremity of that platform, which was almost in the direction of the ship, it began to grow upward, and its size arose. It started to expand laterally, until it reached an approached height of one hundred feet long and it stabilized its oval general structure.

Then at the last moment, that gigantic and well-structured formation of clouds (at least that is what it seemed) began to rotate clockwise. And at the same time it showed signs of forming a spiral, from the extremity to the center of the formation. . . In no moment the weather changed. The sky was completely blue, cloudless, windless and without any sound.

Dr. Lima recalled that the formation had an enormously hypnotic effect on them. But like other members of the team he felt an urgent need to leave when seeing the "cloud" take on its spiral formation. When they reached the dock in San Francisco, they still noticed disturbing side effects of radiation, like nausea and dizziness, even though it was hours later. Lima has dubbed this manifestation the Gate Phenomenon because "at the last moment we all had the same impression that the center of that moving formation would open up as a gate and literally it would gobble our ship."

While the others have sought to forget the experience, Dr. Lima has continued to study it from the point of view of electrical engineering and physics. He notes that the Earth acts as an enormous electric circuit and that the atmosphere is a weak driver. The greatest potential for effects he believes is in the cavity between the sea surface and the ionosphere about 35 miles up. His studies have convinced him that: "The electromagnetic waves identified as existent Resonance in this cavity are not caused by any internal activity in the globe or surface. They are related to electric activity in the atmosphere and chemical properties of the ocean and its platform, not yet identified, particularly during times of intense ray activity in any part and moment of the terrestrial globe."

He has come to the conclusion that the Gate Phenomenon is directly related to this cavity and is created by the introduction of radiation into the atmosphere and by the chemical transformations that develop as a result among the millions of chemical processes generated by the ocean at its surface. Noting the relationship of time to gravity and electromagnetism, he speculates that this phenomenon "may explain many ship and aircraft disappearances over the oceans in the last century" as it may act as "a 'Teleportation to nowhere' or 'Time Travel' event."

Dr. Lima's theory provides a fascinating, though certainly not conventional, natural explanation for the fogs and vapors in the Triangle, as well as why electromagnetic anomalies might be noted before or when near the epicenter of such an event; the theory may also be considered an adjunct to the theories touched on in chapter 6. The Bermuda Triangle might one day prove his theory, plus the potential of electromagnetism in time-travel theories. As this book goes to press, he is currently aboard the research vessel *Emily*, conducting the first part of his project to map these electromagnetic areas worldwide, with special emphasis to the "ill famed Bermuda Triangle."

Dr. Lima is not the only observer who has likened the unusual spiral or "electronic" clouds to a doorway—implying for now a figure of speech, although in the case of the many planes and ships missing in the Bermuda Triangle, one is tempted to imagine this doorway to be a literal one in which planes and ships are destroyed or sent into another dimension. One cannot help but to recall the strange case of Peter Jensen's disappearance in which he reported he was disoriented in clouds at an altitude of only 150 feet off Miami, although the weather was perfect. In his case, eleven hours after his disappearance, long after fuel starvation, he calmly reported himself about 600 miles away, and yet no trace was ultimately found of him anywhere.

Bruce Gernon's experience may be worth reexamination in light of this evidence. His lenticular cloud first formed low over the ocean at about 500 feet altitude and then suddenly expanded into the peculiar shape of a huge doughnut, and then from this a spiraling tunnel opened up. All of this indicates, yet again, peculiar electromagnetic properties arising from the ocean.

A search of scientific literature has turned up an eyewitness account of another doughnut-shaped cloud, the only other time one has been recorded. This was on March 1, 1965, over South Sea, England. It too was undergoing surprising vortex kinesis. The Royal Meteorological

Society publication *Weather* contains the witness's description: "Flat-base cumulus clouds formed an almost perfect circle of some miles in diameter, the whole formation resembling a ring doughnut, as the centre was devoid of clouds. In this central area, air appeared to be circulating in a clockwise direction, indicated by small wisps which had detached themselves from the inside of the circle."

Walter Nemanishen, a Canadian engineer, prospector, and geophysicist whose work also includes confidential government consulting on atmospherics, suggests that upper-atmosphere electrodynamics may be the best explanation. He speculates that this could also explain why electronic aberrations seem to go hand in hand with the swirling clouds and fogs in the Bermuda Triangle.

What may make these phenomena more frequent in the Triangle, intensify their effect, or allow them to occur at much lower altitudes where they have been more consistently observed can be implied by some very interesting theorizing. He offers that one could be highly radioactive radon gas emanating from the seabed because of the disintegration of extremely high-grade uranium deposits in underlying geological formations. This could ionize a column of air and therefore make it more electrically conductive. He observes: "The greatly increased electrical conductivity of the air would explain certain other mysterious effects, like electrical equipment failing and engines sputtering and even dying. Coronal arcing would occur in piston-driven engines without electrically shielded high-tension wiring." He recalls that one isolated farm in the uranium-rich areas of northern Saskatchewan, in Canada, is situated over only a low-grade uranium deposit but nevertheless still has had "an inordinate number of lightning strikes."

In examining Paul Vance's sighting, he noted the very coincidental fact that the unusual swirling vapor was in a vertical column and that Vance's engine began to sputter at the same time, an indication of coronal arcing. The behavior of the light, however, remains obscure.

An indication this could have a bearing on Bruce Gernon's experience comes from the extraordinary photograph his wife, Lynn, took April 26, 1999, in almost the precise area where his meteorological formation began off Andros in 1970. Their attention was drawn to the area because the "glowing" or "white waters" of the Bahamas were venting up in an exotic pattern. This blotch revealed a circular clear area of undisturbed water in the center into which the phosphorescence could not intrude, thus outlining what would otherwise be a completely invisible circle of water. Again, such a phenomenon seems to suggest something either radioactive or electromagnetic below.

Regarding another possible explanation for the electromagnetic peculiarities of the Triangle, Nemanishen further comments:

I would not rule out high-energy particles (from the solar wind) as a possible cause of some of the phenomena. In addition to massive magnetic disturbances, they could also ionize the upper atmosphere. Little is still known about the effects these particles create in the stratosphere because of the paucity of electrical data. But if the interplanetary magnetic field is south during a massive coronal ejection, the extreme energy particles would not be deflected by the magnetosphere and consequently broadside the Bermuda Triangle region.

It is intriguing to consider a combination of the above as an explanation for the Triangle's phenomenon of sudden engine failure and its possible role in having caused some of the disappearances. Sudden, unexplained

Diamonds mark the areas where electronic fogs, electromagnetic aberrations, and unexplained turbulence most frequently strike. The most spectacular and frequent disappearances also happen around here. Are high-grade uranium deposits below the seabed, or areas of magnetic vortices attracting charged particles?

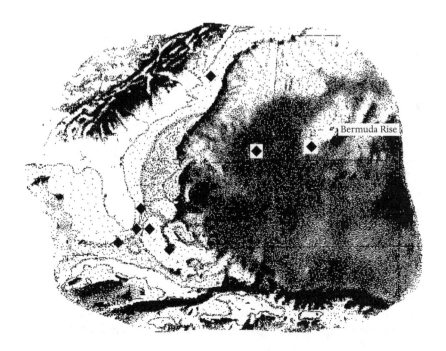

power loss *does* happen to many aircraft along the same routes over the Bahamas where so many have disappeared, except in these cases there is evidence that it happened, or someone survived.

Most recently this befell a Cherokee Lance on July 20, 2002, when it suddenly plunged from radar 15 miles from Freeport, Grand Bahama, killing all five aboard. One year before, in exactly the same spot, a Cessna 172's engine suddenly faltered and died, and the pilot was forced to ditch. Numerous incidents have occurred around Bimini. On April 26, 2001, an Aerospatiale en route from Great Exuma, Bahamas, to Miami flew into a cloud "that was not depicted on the weather avoidance radar" and encountered severe turbulence within, the jamming of its autopilot, and caused a severe injury to one person—an extraordinary coincidence with the "electronic fogs" and electrodynamics mentioned above.

In this same area the cruise ship *Sovereign of the Seas* lost all electrical power in December 2000 while en route back from the Bahamas to Cape Canaveral. She was eventually able to limp to Fort Lauderdale. The *Dolphin,* another cruise ship, lost power in this same area back in 1982, between Bimini and Florida, and ended up beached at Fort Lauderdale. The passengers were not amused, nor were the beachfront homeowners who opened their drapes that morning to find their ocean view blocked by a large liner.

Considering all this, one should wonder why the windless calm of the Sargasso Sea may also be so subject to electrical power loss—the explanation may be because it has no strong winds to deflect any of these particles, and they descend in an ionizing blanket. The sudden loss of power to steamships continues to happen more often within this area than anywhere else. Scrutiny of Lloyd's database, searching for the files containing "Bermuda," reveals that about 80 percent of vessels that pull into her port unexpectedly do so reporting engine trouble or generator failures. In some cases, this has been so severe they are able to only signal "dead in the water" in time to receive help and a tow into port. Searches under other port names like Dakar, Cape Town, Brisbane, etc., reveal that a far greater incident of diverted course is due to water ingress and fire.

Ironically, our own technological progress may be an unexpected accomplice to the mystery of the Bermuda Triangle. According to the report of the panel of leading scientists commissioned by the European Space Agency, issued January 2, 2001: "With the increasing use of microelectronics of ever diminishing feature size, systems are becoming increasingly susceptible to single event effects (SEE) arising from the highly ionizing interactions of individual cosmic rays and solar particles." It further states: "While the Earth's atmosphere shields out most of the primary cosmic rays at conventional altitudes (30,000 to 40,000 feet), there is a buildup of secondary particles (neutrons, mesons, and electrons) which reach a maximum at around 60,000 feet and are only a factor of three diminished at 30,000 feet. By sea level there is a further factor 300 diminution. As a result of this mechanism the radiation hazard at aircraft altitudes is as severe as in certain low-earth orbits. During the past ten years there has been increasing evidence of single event effects on aircraft electronics as well as in sea-level systems."

Perhaps the deadly potential of the increasing ionization of the atmosphere (a result of the weakening magnetic field?) on aircraft or ships was best illustrated when the Space Shuttle *Columbia* blew apart on reentry February 1, 2003. It is believed the missing tile (damaged on takeoff) allowed the hot ionized plasma from the friction of reentry to enter the hull and cause the explosion. It was only after this that NASA considered it time to pursue alternative propulsion systems, which will no doubt entail something electromagnetic, using a force that can repel the charged

The great currents of the world and the large seas they interlock. All energy is at a level of vortex kinesis. The planet rotates in response. But this rotation in turn causes other masses, like the oceans, to swirl, and this might interfere with the primary energy fields. If we could paint a picture of the upper atmosphere, would it look any different?

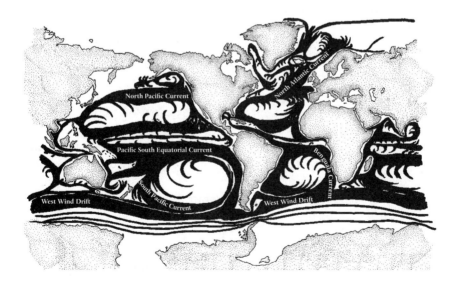

particles responsible for ionization. As early as 1992, Dr. Paul LaViolette informed NASA in detail about T. T. Brown's electrostatic engineering, and the benefits of an electrostatic charge on the leading edge of a wing in reducing the heat of drag and friction—studies that even Northrup had duplicated in its wind tunnels. The result of lack of interest was tragic on February 1, 2003.

Although the atmospheric ionization may be more deadly in the Triangle because it is more humid or over the ocean, another possibility—magnetohydrodynamics—although very speculative, may nevertheless solve some of the puzzles.

The existence of whether there are great currents in the upper atmosphere beyond even the range of the jet stream is largely a mystery, and if they are there, what drives them and the jet stream. And do they follow predetermined pathways like the currents of the sea? There are theories that either upper-atmosphere currents may be partially driven by charged solar particles, of which they are constantly in contact, or that preexisting currents from rotation may usher charged particles; either may help explain how certain parts of the Earth can become more "electrified" than others. As in the case of the currents of the oceans, there may be places where these upper-atmosphere currents collide, spin off, and possibly in the process direct charged particles lower to Earth, where they may, at certain times of the year, make the atmosphere more electrically conductive. For anyone who has lived in the Triangle or other tropical areas between 20 to 30 degrees North latitude in the winter months, there is no denying that there seems to be a greater electrical potential, providing more static electrical shocks than at other times. One can wonder if this may account for the Triangle's notorious Christmastime Hex, a term coined because many of the strangest disappearances seem to happen between November and early February.

Aside from providing an approachable explanation for many of the electromagnetic anomalies reported in the Triangle, can the possible hyperconductivity of the Triangle's atmosphere at varying times of the year also provide the genesis to give body to some of the more esoteric theories to explain the disappearances? One wonders what sort of bizarre chain reaction could be set in motion, considering that electromagnetism is the energy that is at the heart of all matter. Bizarre doughnut-shaped clouds and vortex kinesis high in the atmosphere can be explained by charged particles ionizing the air; but something is bringing them down and concentrating them. Perhaps it is radon, perhaps magnetic anomalies, perhaps magnetic vortices. The result could be electronic drains, swirling fogs, time discrepancies, and unusual and sudden winds or no wind at all. But electromagnetism seems to need the ocean in order to speak the loudest.

This is evident in the study of a science that may very well explain much about the Triangle's peculiar electromagnetic anomalies. This science, little known in the West as yet, is Hydrides and an expanding mantle. In his exhaustive book, *Hydridic Earth* (the result of thirty years of research), Russian geologist Vladimir N. Larin describes a hydride in detail. What it amounts to is an unstable hybrid metal that had scores of hydrogen nuclei driven into the electron orbits of its atoms at some ancient time. Over time these heavy metals have been brought to the surface of the seabed with saline and other processes. It oozes out along favorable areas such as where continental shelves drop off to the abyssal ocean depths—of which much of the Triangle is composed—allowing the hydrogen to "degas."

In his section Geophysical Peculiarities of Oceans, a familiar phenomenon to the reader of this book stands out as pinpointing such locations:

Other interesting geophysical data include peculiar magnetic field anomalies on Atlantic-type transitions from continents to the ocean. Some workers (Bennett & Liliey 1971) attribute these anomalies to conductive mantle material ascending from the ocean side upward in scarp-like sutures. Our scenario interprets a scarp bordering the silicate buffer in the mantle along the continent-ocean margin. Then, with jetlike streams of inflowing hydrogen, uneven silification results. This scenario should leave blocks of unoxidized or incompletely oxidized intermetallic compounds. The presence of the highly conductive admixture in the silicate buffer explains the high electrical conductivity of the newly formed mantle layer and may be the cause of the coastal geomagnetic anomalies.

One must remember that the Triangle's magnetic anomalies predominate along its continental shelf area, the deep Puerto Rico Trench, the Tongue of the Ocean, and other sharp submarine cliffs and plateaus like the Great and Little Bahama Bank, all these in the lee of the great North American continent's catastrophic slide over the unstable Atlantic seabed—perhaps another memory of ancient catastrophe unique, once again, to Atyantica.

We must not only consider the potential interplay of the oceans as a key element for creating unusual phenomena, but also for creating many sudden, volatile weather patterns that can spell disaster to boats or planes, destroying them quickly and then scattering the debris, thereby causing them to effectively disappear. We must remember that in no other place in the world are land and sea so thinly, so disharmoniously, divided. Very often hundreds of square miles of the Bahama Banks are only a few fathoms below the surface and are constantly being scoured by swift currents. The deep and fast Gulf Stream sends currents along the sides of the banks. The changes in ocean temperatures are drastic and frequent as colder currents sweep over shallow and warm water banks and as cold and warm waters collide in swift, frictional currents and eddies.

The oceans of the world are always in motion, but the unpredictability of this movement is more true in the Triangle than anywhere else. Dr. Hans Grabber of the University of Miami extension on Key Biscayne is the world's foremost authority on rogue waves. "Rogue wave" is rather self-explanatory: it doesn't travel with the pack, it is volatile, and its actions are unpredictable. Dr. Grabber's studies have led him to be able to predict where rogue waves are most likely to strike. Among the most probable areas are those near strong currents, like the Gulf Stream, and on the leeward side of islands, of which the Bermuda Triangle can boast thousands (the Bahamas alone consist of 700 islands). As an example of the volatility of rogue waves, he notes that in 1994 a huge rogue wave slammed into Daytona Beach, Florida, on what was an otherwise calm and perfect day weatherwise. Another example involved the Bahamian cruise ship *Europa,* which was slammed abeam by a rogue wave in November 1999. These rogue waves have been noted to attain heights of more than 100 feet, as seen aboard the Dutch passenger liner *Rotterdam,* which was hit by one in 1977.

Eddies of the Gulf Stream are not so noticeable, but their swirling, contrary, quartering, and crosscurrents can take any boater unawares. From aerial survey, these appear as vast whirling vortices along the edge of the fast current of the Gulf Stream. They look like larger versions of the familiar eddies in the shallows of riverbanks, where the fast currents bounce along the slower waters of the banks and take on a tumbling or swirling motion. A skipper on the ocean, unaware he is entering an eddy, especially at higher speeds, could suddenly encounter waves from unexpected directions and founder.

Among the possible causes of missing boats is the North Wall Phenomenon, a potent threat to boats in the northern waters of the Bermuda Triangle, off the Virginia capes and north of Bermuda. The U.S. Coast Guard describes it as follows:

The North Wall phenomenon is one of rapidly increasing wind and seas in the area of the northern boundary of the Gulf Stream where the sea surface temperatures can change dramatically. In such a region of large surface temperature contrast, a potential for damaging and volatile weather frequently exists. When cold air flows over this narrow zone of warm water, the air is rapidly warmed and rises. The rising air displaces the heavier, colder air aloft which descends generating strong, gusty winds at the surface.

This is not only pertinent for boat losses, as in the case of the *Miss Charlotte II* in 1998, but also for aircraft. This area is where many of the well-known aircraft disappearances have taken place (at least they were on courses that called for them to pass here). This could explain some of the reports of unexplained turbulence over the Triangle that do not qualify as regular clear air turbulence (CAT). But the explanation would apply to this northern area only, since it is the area of most appreciable contrast in the warm and cold fronts of the Atlantic. It would not apply however in other areas of the Triangle, as over the Bahamas or in the Sargasso Sea, where the variables are not so drastic.

CATs are not the completely mysterious entities they once were. They are expected in areas near the high-altitude jet stream, where its fast current bounces along the slower currents and creates eddies, as in the analogy of the riverbank. They can also precede a storm because the atmosphere is being pushed before its building and oncoming mass. These types of turbulence would have an oscillating motion, since the air is moving laterally like wave troughs of the sea.

For low-flying aircraft, however, there would be little chance of encountering any significant CATs, especially while coming in for a landing. On the other hand, von Kármán's Vortices might apply. These swirling, choppy winds were first described by Dr. Theodor von Kármán to exist at the lee side of an island or mountain; they are essentially created by the peak of a tall island diverting strong winds around it. Again, an analogy from a moving current of water might best elucidate it—imagine the swirling downstream river current in the wake of a rock. For a landing aircraft these can prove the most potentially upsetting because it is approaching at low speed as opposed to more open throttle when taking off.

Not only can the unique shallows of the Bahama Banks cause a vessel to wreck, but paradoxically they can help hide its remains more than the depths. From the vantage point of living at one of the Triangle's hot spots of Bimini, Bill Keefe believes that the treacherous currents scouring the shallow banks "would not let a boat or plane remain for long. After two or three days they are broken up or swept away to deep water." These few days constitute a narrow window of time for locating a sunken boat or plane if it was not reported missing right away and if its last position was not known with precision. Old pros consider many parts of the Bahama Banks as dangerous, and consider them especially hazardous for a neophyte sailor. Changes in water color from light green to yellow to white are crucial, as they may be the only warning that critically shallow water or rocks and reefs are approaching. The water is so shallow in certain areas that even the shadow of a passing cloud can be trouble, hazing the distinctions between good water and bad, requiring a sailor to do lots of eyeballing. A neophyte, however, does not even know exactly what to eyeball and can wreck a boat suddenly and fatally. Even where there are no rocks or reefs and where there is no land in sight, the Banks can be shallow and deadly.

"Sand bores," the colloquial expression for shifting underwater dunes, exist in the Bahamas where the water is only a fathom or a few fathoms deep, even miles from landfall. The temperamental currents etch these dunes into parallel ridges or complex mazelike patterns. The only navigable water is between them, measured here in terms of 1 or 2 fathoms and then only temporarily. From the deck of a boat the navigable channels are not always discernible, and skippers can suddenly find themselves trapped in a maze, yawing to try and follow the channels of clear water. Even the most experienced yachtsman can beach himself on these dunes as he tries to escape them. While one is often harmlessly and briefly detained until the current shifts the bore, one wonders if a boat could not be swallowed by the moving bores—especially dangerous for a sailboat with a deep keel being manipulated by the shifting sand.

Another intriguing oddity of the continental shelves off the Bahamas and Florida is the large number of underwater funnels called blue holes, They are so dubbed because of their picturesque appearance as deep blue and bottomless holes in the nearby and often very turquoise shallows. Their depths taper into narrow bottoms that apparently continue to other blue holes many miles away or even to inland lakes. Changes in tides can bring about whirlpools in the holes, which on some occasions have swallowed small outboards. Divers have found some wedged in varying levels of the funnels but have never, of course, found any of the larger yachts, ships, or planes that have vanished in the Bermuda Triangle.

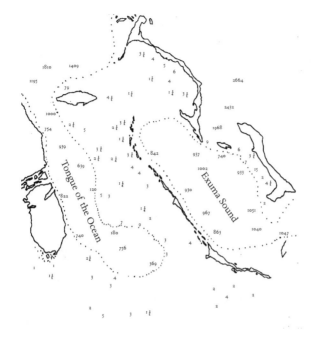

Depth readings for the Great Bahama Bank in fathoms (1 fathom = 6 feet). The numbers indicate how treacherous the area can be for a boat.

Some have offered that invisible "whirlpools" might be created by methane gas released from the sea bottom; the methane then rises to the surface in frothing funnels until it breaks the surface. Here the water is proposed to be molecularly thinner and therefore not to be able to support a vessel sailing over it. The vessel would suddenly lose buoyancy and sink to the bottom, with no crew getting off and no lifeboat launched (or even if it were, it would sink, as well). However, to truly upset any boat would require that enough gas seeps up through thousands of feet of sediment and then through thousands of feet of water. This is thought to be so rare as to happen no more than once every four hundred years. It could not affect aircraft, in any case. When an oil rig drilled into a bed of methane it did sink slowly, but news helicopters circling overhead recording the dramatic sight were unaffected.

Cyclones, atmospheric versions of the whirlpool, strike with suddenness in the Triangle and can destroy both planes and ships. At night they would naturally be completely invisible to a pilot who, not being aware he was dangerously near one, could not take evasive action until his plane began to shake violently with the swirling currents—in other words, when it would be too late for him to do anything. A boater might be able to hear a cyclone, even detect pelting spray and perhaps even illuminate it with a searchlight, but all to no avail since the boat would not be able to move quickly enough to escape it.

Highs and lows, plus updrafts and downdrafts, can be more pronounced and drastic over the ocean, especially in the Triangle because of its humidity and temperature changes. These can cause unexpected altitude changes and even vertigo for pilots taken unawares. In some cases, these updrafts and downdrafts can remove all the lift from an aircraft, essentially creating a pocket in which the plane drops so far that recovery is impossible. (A 200-foot downdraft was forecast off St. Thomas the night Irving Rivers mysteriously vanished while coming in for a landing; the downdraft could have slapped him into the sea, although this wouldn't explain the absence of an ELT signal.)

The updrafts and downdrafts of rising storm clouds can cause an aircraft to crash by creating such a tailwind that the plane loses lift and falls to the Earth or into the ocean. This is a possibility that one must keep in mind in a report of a missing plane that was diverted around storm clouds, though still on the perimeter.

Underwater earthquakes can cause ships to vanish. Spiking waves have been recorded reaching 325 feet high, like off the western coast of Mexico on September 19, 1985, after a devastating earthquake. According to the Mexican government, two merchant ships, five trawlers, and two dozen small boats were missing in the Pacific off Acapulco after the earthquake.

The ocean is not only a far greater part of this planet than the land (three-fifths as opposed to two-fifths), but its territory can be measured in cubic miles, which effectively triples its already vast domain. Moreover, unlike human beings and terrestrial animals, life in the ocean is not limited to the bottom of the hydrosphere—the sea bottom—as we are limited to the bottom of the atmosphere. In the last two centuries, the discovery of land animals previously unknown except in legends, such as the Komodo dragon and the gorilla, demonstrates what surprises may still await us in the ocean depths—which remain even more outside our view than Indonesian islands or African jungles.

Sea serpent reports made throughout the world's oceans have described huge ichthyosaurs or lizardlike fish (resembling a museum-housed skeleton of an *elasmosaurus*), whose most famous representative in the world is

Nessie, the Loch Ness monster in Scotland. Giant eels with hard scales, not unlike the fire-breathing Leviathan described in the Septuagint, have also been reported, as at Gloucester, Massachusetts, in August 1917. Even though people making these reports have been condemned as "losers," "nuts," and "cranks," the work of the late Dr. Bernard Heuvelmans reinforces the reality of some sea-serpent sightings *(In the Wake of Sea Serpents)*.

Any discussion of sea monsters cannot overlook the giant squid *(Architeuthis dux)*. This "sea monster" may be responsible for a wide range of reports of sea serpents when only its long and large tentacles were seen flapping about at the surface. Although it usually averages about 20 to 43 feet in length, the largest ever captured was 60 feet long and weighed 2,200 pounds, which opens the door to the possibility that there are even larger versions in the deep, since this squid is happiest at 13,000-foot depths. The ones we have had even fleeting glimpses of are most likely those that prefer the 700- to 3,000-foot depths. Its territorial range is well within the Triangle, the North Atlantic, and the Gulf Stream, which it might use seasonally to migrate north.

A U.S. Navy frigate (USS *Stein*, 1985), out of San Diego, suddenly had to turn back to port when her sonar went on the blink. Examination of the rubber sheath that cocoons the bow "bubble" containing the sonar showed it was ripped and shredded, and found still embedded in it were several strange claws or teeth, resembling the small teeth or claws of

A man, a boat, a Great White . . . Megalodon.

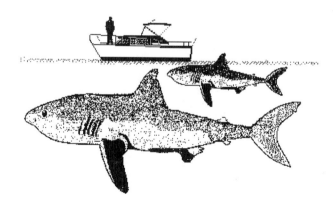

octopi but by their size indicating a significantly larger species. Recent reports of encounters with what appears to be a very large shark must be taken seriously. The length of this shark is roughly estimated by the size of its dorsal fin and by the distance from it to its tail fin trailing behind— all of which suggests a shark similar to a Great White but of an enormous size comparable to that of *Megalodon,* a species of great white known to us today only by fossilized teeth measuring more than 6 inches long.

Even the behavior of known species beneath the sea is still the subject of an imperfect science. An incident befell the Dougal Robertson family on June 15, 1972, near the islands of Galápagos while they were sailing around the world in their 43-foot sailboat *Lucette.* Suddenly three killer whales broke off from a pack of twenty and rammed their boat, sinking it in 60 seconds. Robertson was later able to write about this harrowing experience—after he and his family survived thirty-six days at sea on a small life raft. Recalling his first thoughts after the *Lucette* sank, he expressed perhaps what all those lost in the Bermuda Triangle might also have briefly felt: "I climbed wearily into the yellow inflatable, a sense of unreality flooding through me, feeling sure that soon I would waken and find the dream gone."

12

A Vast Horizon: An Answer from Without, Within, and All Around Us

IF WE ARE to label why the Bermuda Triangle holds any particular relevance, it must be found in the potential to which a search for an answer has directed us. In this case the Bermuda Triangle has forced our approach to the dawn of the final horizon, and by the slivers of sunrise breaking over its dark silhouette inspired us to contemplate what lies beyond for our own future.

There are those who prefer to remain where we began, eyes perpetually locked on the sure foundation of that dark and unchanging silhouette, rather than lift their heads to chase the beams of light streaking into the sky. They should not be blamed. It is easier and often more respectable to blame things at hand. To chase beams of light is to chase something that cannot even leave a shadow. We have followed them to the heights of improbability and down beyond the horizon to where their source is given form only by imagination. Yet the streaks of sunrise are there. If they can really take us to the infinite we do not know or if they really indicate that there exists the fanciful source we sometimes wish to imagine, we cannot yet tell.

Dominant among the hypotheses are things we thought we would never be confronted with, much less contemplate. Among these, there may exist bases under the ocean established by aliens or other humans, whether from another planet or descendants of an ancient Earth civilization, interested in observing or even assessing mankind. The reason for the disappearances is offered as being caused by the electromagnetic propulsion methods of the spacecraft or even by intentional abduction. The Bermuda Triangle's specific accompliance with UFOs may be due to the fact the ocean is forever in motion and can easily dispel the evidence of a disaster (or presumed disaster if a kidnapping took place) and therefore allay any suspicions on our part that something unusual is happening in all these disappearances—a *modus operandi* not entirely far-fetched considering the lengths some people go in order to debunk even the possibility of the unexplained. On the other hand it might equally provide the isolation for bases from which UFOs can operate or even the right conditions for them to materialize into our dimension or world.

However bizarre or repulsive such theories might be to many, they are not likely to go away. The idea that there are unexplained observers of mankind is hardly a new one. In ancient Hebraic writings, principally the Book of Enoch, there are repeated references to the "Watchers." They are classed as different from the traditional ranks of angels, and a subgroup of them are even considered to be the wicked ones who came down in Genesis—the enigmatic "sons of god" who saw the daughters of men and sired an entire advanced civilization. They are not angels—cherubim or ophanim—but are referred to as the "children of heaven." In a number of ancient writings there are equally enigmatic references. They may be pure fables or primitive superstitions or they may be, as is much in modern UFO lore today, overexaggerations of unexplained aerial phenomena, capitalized on by ancient writers and priests.

Our development of the air age, then the atomic age, and then the space age, has given rise to several theories that beings from other worlds might be greatly alarmed at what they have been observing on Earth, especially nuclear explosions, because these could represent a threat to them. This seems far-fetched unless we allow the supposition that they have some form of long-standing connection with or residence on the Earth or that they in fact travel along magnetic field lines or waves to their magnetic opposites (in this case, Earth) and that they realize that if we discovered this method of travel we could be at their doorsteps in moments, complete with deadly arsenals.

One must remember that civilizations do not have to develop along the same lines. If beings of another planet stumbled on zero-point energy created by high-voltage electricity and electromagnetic fields, they might never have thought about the atomic. Splitting the nucleus of an atom may be beyond them, and something quite fascinating and disturbing to them.

Several investigators of UFOs have speculated along these lines—that UFOs are assessing our flight and propulsion technology. They even point out that reports of frequent UFOs do not antedate World War II and the initiation of the atomic age. Among these one can even include U.S. Air Force Intelligence which in an early and confidential summation of the UFO phenomenon in 1949 expressed: "Such a civilization might observe that on Earth we now have atomic bombs and are fast developing rockets. In view of the past history of mankind they should be alarmed. We should therefore expect at this time above all to behold such visitations." It is interesting to note that the intelligence officer responsible for this assumed mankind had been observed by alien beings for a considerable period of time. This opinion may have been inspired by legends of the ancient "Watchers," the *bney h'elohim* of Genesis, or the originators of the ancient disc *vimanas* of India. What is repeatedly fascinating is that so many ancient cultures allude to such craft or visitations. Why?

The most important part in the consideration of any theory are the circumstances in which the plane or ship vanished. While in many cases this is simply unknown, in others they are so unusual as to suggest that the aircraft pilots and ship captains were faced with something completely foreign to them. Automatic alarms that should have sounded when disaster struck have consistently been silent. Vessels have vanished in calm weather without trace while others lost in storms have left debris scattered over beaches. In other disappearances, messages were picked up hours after the aircraft disappeared, ran out of gas, and subsequently was assumed to be destroyed—though this is by our norms completely impossible. In still other disappearances, entire planes with crews, passengers, and automatic electronic signals have been swept away even while on approach to an airport, while on radar, with no trace found whatsoever.

Considering such sudden and traceless losses, it seems hard not to consider theories of sudden vortices or time travel and dimensional exchange, even if they are still largely only fringe science. Along with this it is impossible not to speak about the vast underlying world within— of the atomic and subatomic world.

Mankind has long wondered about the possibilities of traveling through time and, indeed, has been consumed with trying to discern exactly what time is. In the atomic age we have been able to glimpse vaguely at the mouth of its labyrinth by noting the relationship of gravity to the performance of atomic clocks, to the curvature of space, and to the speed of light and of such things as black holes in space and thus the relationship of mass itself to the equation.

The importance of mass and shape to the invisible force fields about us is a repeating conundrum. We know by measurements of an object's fall at the poles and at the equator that acceleration and rotation affect gravity. In addition, Magnetic Opposition indicates that shape and mass can determine where energy reactions will also take place. But how is *time* affected by energy?

The clue may have been so large it was invisible to us, for now we know that by its mass and speed of revolution the Earth curves space around it, and with this comes a vectoring or curving of all the energy fields and wavelengths in space around it. Time's pathways must lie along these, and when curved, time slows. Imperceptible though it may be to all those within this field (for it is normal progression to us on Earth), to those in different curvatures of space there could be an alarming difference.

Yet the power required to slow time, even insignificantly, seems beyond any natural process except our planet speeding through space. Yet it is equally true that we believed some metals could never melt or shatter except in very high temperatures, but John Hutchison was able to accomplish this with very weak energy and no heat at all, merely by manipulating electromagnetic waves and perhaps zero-point energy. At the same time as these alarming effects stunned their observers, liquids registered only *mild* vortex action going on.

Another mystery of electromagnetic wavelengths and their potentials is Scalar Fields and their ability to interfere with magnetic fields and then even vector electrons. Within their potential some quantum physicists speculate there may even lie clues to *time reversals* and other phenomena.

The transportation and even transmutation of matter via wavelengths seems very possible if they are disrupted and then directed efficiently. So far, the Hutchison Effect indicates that strong electromagnetic waves can even cause flight (he has produced speeds of 433 feet per second, or 295 miles per hour), but we are still at a loss to control and direct these. When, and if, we do, perhaps with control will come instantaneous travel and communication through space . . . and even time.

But this is, again, just another example of the massive world within that is all around us. There are thousands of waves and frequencies flitting about the Earth, with numerous fields around them. We have seen in the Hutchison Effect that the levitation of objects is dependent on their shape. Thus some force fields and their vectors are dependent on, or activated by, the shape of the mass in question.

The instigating factor may be how the shape of something causes it to convolute, bend, or interlock the wavelengths around them under electromagnetic manipulation. This may be associated with zero-point energy, of which so many have hopes of tying into to provide unlimited power and propulsion; but the fact that an orientation seems present might suggest there is an entirely different force within matter itself, as undiscovered as "gravity" was for many centuries. If so, this force goes part and parcel with matter: the greater the mass of an object, the greater its power of orientation. This would seem a logical explanation. The Earth is the greatest mass near to us, and thus anything created on it is pulled toward it. This may explain why objects placed on their sides in Hutchison's tests did nothing, while others, when placed upright, levitated. During their forming, a force within their atoms was naturally aligned toward the greatest part of the force that is in mass—in other words toward the Earth.

It may be that there truly is more than one type of gravity: both Einstein's curvature of space around a massive object and a force within mass that orients toward the greatest part of itself. Equally, it may be wondered if this last type of "gravity" is not a force at all but a void created by several wavelengths and energy fields interacting and thereby neutralizing each other, explaining why no physicist has yet been able to find "gravity." The discovery of zero-point energy may be the greatest step toward the unraveling of both gravity and Time, for it may be the link between them both. Indeed, it may be the link between all things.

Although we have catalogued all the atoms and know how all materials are made up of what atoms, the charged particles that make up the atom are a great mystery. They are so tiny they can never be seen. What is different in the structure of the proton from that of the electron that makes it take a positive charge of electricity? And what is it about the electron that makes it take a negative charge of electricity? And for that matter, from where do they get this charge—where is this constant current of energy? How can it be that these particles never loose their charge?

It was in a vacuum chamber lowered to zero degrees Kelvin ($-273.15\,^{\circ}C$)—the true zero point of all existence since all the tremendous activity in the atom ceases—that oscillations of energy were still detected. Zero point was discovered. Some background radiation exists—constantly. It cannot be in mass. It is the energy, the current if you will, from which the particles that make up all atoms and thus all mass, get and maintain their charge of energy in order to create the multiplicity of materials we enjoy. The proton and the electron and the neutron are perfectly formed to take the appropriate charges, and the most remarkable process begins: mass, energy, time, and space-creation. That is the significance of zero point. It has to be before all things, and it must remain to support all things. If the charge should die out, we are plunged into the zero point of all existence.

Dr. Hal Puthoff may be right. Gravity may be a zero-point fluctuation.

Einstein's theory of a curvature of space may indeed enable a curvature or bending of this current or wave of background radiation, this zero point, around the Earth. In doing so, orientation and attraction—gravity—may come about. This may explain why no physicist has yet discovered "gravity" inasmuch as zero point has only recently been discovered and remains mysterious as to how it can be self-generating, be everywhere, and be independent of mass. During Hutchison's tests perhaps the fields his machines created disturbed these wavelengths and hence the "void of gravity" they create, and the objects naturally floated as if in space, free of the Earth's influence.

We must keep in mind that those who have survived unexplained encounters at sea repeatedly testify to unexplained fogs, vapors, electromagnetic aberrations, and sometimes unusual lights—phenomena that suggest immense disruption of frequencies and wavelengths. Particularly interesting reports concern fogs beginning to swirl or attach themselves to the aircraft or ship, indicating that friction or metal content is attractive and conductive.

High-voltage electricity experiments have also created strange metallic fogs, as well as multicolored coronas. As we know, both of these have been reported in Bermuda Triangle disappearances, often in some of the most perplexing cases. If repeated reports of encounters with fogs and compass aberrations in the Bermuda Triangle and in other areas of the oceans are to be accepted, it would seem that electromagnetism is the culprit and that the ocean, with its currents, chemicals, and mass, is the accomplice. How together they create these force-field disruptions, however, remains teasingly out of our reach at present, just as Hutchison's electromagnetic effects have accomplished similar phenomena in a lab. But electromagnetism's relation to gravity, time, and the like leaves "disappearance" open to interpretation.

It does not seem to be beyond nature's power to imitate Hutchison's work, provided the right circumstances are present. The estimated voltage potential of the atmosphere is enormous, about 200,000 watts. Since it seems to require the sea, the ancient enigma it always possessed, and which our generation pompously removed, is firmly replaced.

There is also the possibility put forward, and a rather interesting one that we are contributing to these effects by our pollution of the atmosphere, and therefore the oceans, through modern-day technology and the burning of fossil fuels. In this light we may be witnessing an unplanned experiment that is going awry, for unlike a lab we cannot control the greater routine of the Earth.

At the very least we should not ignore the possibility that we might be to blame in some respect. W. H. McCrea, himself a distinguished cosmologist, saliently observes the prospects for the universe from the theories of its origins: "The naive view implies that the universe suddenly came into existence and found a complex system of physical laws waiting to be obeyed. . . . Actually it seems more natural to suppose that the physical universe and the laws of physics are inter-dependent. This leads us to expect that, if the universe changes in the large, then its laws might also change in a way that could not be predicted."

Is it logical to assume that we might be witnessing a small example of this on our own planet? Our changes in the chemical makeup of the Earth may first begin to show themselves in peculiar ways, which on the face of it may seem completely harmless, like unusual fogs, electromagnetic anomalies, and so forth. But from the point of view of somebody in proximity to such phenomena, it may be disastrous, since these could be the only signs that the frequencies and electromagnetic wavelengths in the vicinity are disturbed.

In the West we tend to see things by their appearance and not as their substance. With such a mindset we tend to overlook the vast complexity of the subatomic world and the force fields all about us. We see a human being as a figure and forget the molecular, cellular, and electromagnetic machine that it is. An example of this perfect molecular orchestration can be found in the human brain, unfortunately an often overlooked commodity by humans themselves, for we have learned to take for granted its daily functions. And for its relationship to "time," an apt analogy was made a long time ago. This was in an 1895 novel by H. G. Wells, *The Time Machine,* foretelling the popular notion of time travel. Trying to convince his colleagues, the Time-Traveler says:

That is the germ of my great discovery. But you are wrong to say that we cannot move about in Time. For instance, if I am recalling an incident very vividly I go back to the instant of its occurrence: I become absent minded, as you say. I jump back for a moment. Of course we have no means of staying back for any length of Time, any more than a savage or an animal has of staying six feet above the ground. But a civilized man is better off than a savage in this respect. He can go up against gravitation in a balloon, and why should he not hope ultimately he will be able to stop or accelerate his drift along the Time-Dimension?

Or, as the Traveler concludes, "go the other way."

The ability of the human memory illustrated so clearly above by H. G. Wells is in fact the marvelous working of electricity along predetermined pathways in the human brain, based on minerals, vitamins, acids, proteins, hormones, and various electrical impulses created by them, mixed together at the right time under the right and proper functioning of the body's chemistry—an analogy to our own Earth's complexity.

Our brains can produce a blurry or bright image of a past event, in color or black and white, moving or still. Through the chemical process, the human eyes, ears, and brain are like a camera and recorder: a medium for electric signals that project the image into the brain for storage and retrieval, complete with sound, yet it does not need to cast it upon a screen or to use a projector.

With the advent of the computer age perhaps we are in a better position than ever to understand the vast machine of the human body and especially the nervous system. It has often been said that we use only 10 percent of our brains. This, however, may prove false in light of computer engineering. The greatest bulk of computer hardware is the "hard disk," designed for storage so that the tiny processor, the actual computing device, can access information and commands in order to operate efficiently at correct speeds—not unlike the ratio in size and function of the cerebrum to the small area protected by the corpus callosum where the tiny pituitary gland sets the pace for all functions. A great part of our brain may in fact be a massive hard disk capable of unlimited storage, retaining everything ever seen and experienced—perhaps explaining why later in life we suddenly recall events we had not thought about for fifty years. If they had not been saved somewhere, the mental images could not be brought back up into, what shall we call it now—RAM? A computer's random access memory can be likened to our own mind during daily activities: essentially what people view on their computer monitor during their work.

Considering that the brain is also responsible for psychomotor functions (of which a desktop computer need not worry), the actual area devoted to memory must be remarkably smaller than our own computer hard disks, yet capable of infinitely more storage, billions and billions of terabytes.

In conjunction with the brain, the nervous system also has functions reminiscent of computers, or vice versa, as the case may be. During sleep at night several automated processes occur that suggest a mechanism closely aligned to "scandisk" is checking the body. The autonomic nervous system checks to see if everything is functioning and attached. The heart may beat faster temporarily, the breathing may alter or shut off for 10 seconds, along with a whole host of other "system checks." Delays between one check and another may even in future be used to indicate where a problem is in the body between these points, as "scandisk" has stopped its system check and is trying to identify a problem and repair it by sending forth a host of immune-system chemicals and nutrients, including human growth hormone, which is released in greatest quantity during deep sleep to literally begin bodily rejuvenation.

We must remember the maxim "for dust thou art"; that essentially all that we are made of, or the bases of chemicals our own body can create, exist in the Earth, in our atmosphere and oceans. Considering the power of the brain, the potential chemical interactions in the entire Earth for creating phenomena are incomprehensible.

Several researchers into electromagnetic effects have come to the conclusion that many of the phenomenal events we have recorded throughout history, and which were then subsequently attributed to the supernatural, have an understandable origin elsewhere. Concerning his personal experience, Dr. Ivan Lima has written: "My research made me believe that this phenomenon is related to an event that is disturbing, inexplicable and yet undiscovered . . . [But it is] a realistic, physical and transitory event created by nature that humanity thinks to be just a psychic phenomenon."

Commenting on the wide range of effects related to "poltergeist" activity, Alfred Budden has observed that fires start behind locked doors and in enclosed places impossible to reach easily, furniture moves about, objects levitate and sometimes fly around the room, water mysteriously vanishes and reappears, "objects do appear to arrive from nowhere and seem to vanish just as strangely," iron bars are found twisted and broken, and mirrors are shattered—everything noted in the Hutchison Effect . . . and perhaps in the Triangle.

In his investigation of one house "haunted" by these same effects, Budden took a magnetic field meter. "It soon became clear to me as I went from room to room that the place was subject to sudden and powerful power surges. I could have foreseen this, even if I had not developed the electromagnetic pollution approach (for which I am known) for the understanding of anomalies, as there was a 40-foot-tall radio mast for transmitting line-of-sight microwave signals erected just five feet away from the outside wall. Apparently, as the planning and safety authorities do not regard siting power lines over residential properties as hazardous to health, a microwave tower is thought of as nothing to be concerned about."

We are familiar with other sources of interference with our natural wavelengths, such as sunspots, but we remain ignorant of what our own tampering can do to these vital force fields and wavelengths. Do we now confuse the natural signals with our own cellular, satellite, telephone, microwave, and other radio signals, causing us to "stir up the pot" and create aberrations?

From this last point of view it is clear that the potential exists for man to create changes accidentally and to not even be aware he is doing it. Such destruction may have come to past civilizations without their knowing it, if they walked in paths similar to the ones we now are walking. Some of the great upheavals of early legends may indeed have been in the Atlantic, perhaps in areas that are now the Caribbean and the Bermuda Triangle. While these may have caused latent tensions that may make the area still prone today to electromagnetic anomalies, one still must wonder if these electromagnetic anomalies are not reminders of a past cataclysm but harbingers of a future one which we ourselves may be bringing. Then the sorry cycle of history repeats itself: retrogression, barbarism, slow climb back to city building, with future man denying that any cataclysm or super-civilization ever could have existed before and brought its destruction.

This is a repeating warning in the Edgar Cayce records. While it may seem easy to ignore such warnings, due to the method by which they have been presented to us through the channel of trances, there still lie on the bottom of parts of the Bermuda Triangle, and in other areas of continental shelves around the Atlantic, the buried remains of an unidentified civilization. Cayce's readings have appeared prescient in many ways, foretelling in a strange way UFO and USO movements in the Triangle, buried ruins near Bimini, and universal forces and machines by which they were manipulated to give the cumulative effect of what zero-point energy now seems capable.

Although his warnings about future upheavals have heresofar failed miserably, the overall story of his Atlantis and its end may impart to us a much-needed parable when we reach the point of his fabled Atlantis—and it seems we will. As an object lesson, it may prevent us in the future from going too far, as other civilizations may have done in the past.

A view of Caycean Atlantis in this light seems more acceptable, and whether fact or fiction if it prevents us from fulfilling its destiny it has accomplished something valuable. Likewise so has the Bermuda Triangle of missing planes and ships since it has drawn our attention to the patterns below the sea as a proverb of foolish abuse.

The Bermuda Triangle calls to mind so much we can learn from: of powers all around us, of past misfortunes that could avert future and tragic reenactments, our own inadequacies as a species, and a respect for the greater design in nature that we often overlook. Armed with this knowledge, in future we may be more hesitant than we would otherwise have been to tamper with nature unwisely, seeing its perfect and delicate design.

Mystery should not cause us to recoil, nor make us cower, deny, or even worship. It is an invitation to look and to learn. When aircraft flew straight into the ground while flying around mountains, we did not attribute the crash to "mountain gods" and prostrate ourselves; nor did we dismiss it as of no significance. Investigation led to the discovery of wind shear. The sky, the sea, this entire planet have been conquered because of tragedies. Other worlds within and without will undoubtedly be conquered with their share of the same.

The Bermuda Triangle's presumed tragedies (since there is little evidence of death) may lead us on the road to conquering time and space, for their abode lies over that vast horizon whose crest the Triangle has made us approach. There is no such thing as an empty or vain act unless we choose to make them that through ridicule and dismissal, and the pursuit of even "unconventional theories" has enriched the study.

In his humorous article "Zen and the Art of Debunkery," San Francisco journalist Daniel Drasin plays the satirical adviser to debunkers on how to perfect their art publicly. He begins under General Debunkery: "Before commencing to debunk, prepare your equipment. Equipment needed: one armchair." In the long body of his advice, one point strikes a familiar chord: "Equate nature's laws with our current understanding of nature's laws. Then label all concepts such as antigravity or interdimensional mobility as mere flights of fancy 'because what present-day science cannot explain cannot possibly exist.' Then if an anomalous craft is reported to have hovered silently, made right-angle turns at supersonic speeds or appeared and disappeared instantly, you may summarily dismiss the report."

But the reality of one such point of debunking, seen and promoted far too often, justifiably elicits our feelings of contempt. As Drasin's article states, "Label any poorly understood phenomenon as 'occult,' 'fringe,' 'paranormal,' 'metaphysical,' 'mystical,' 'supernatural,' or 'new-age.' This will get most mainstream scientists off the case immediately on purely emotional grounds. If you're lucky, this may delay any responsible investigation of such phenomena by decades or even centuries!"

It is time we grew beyond this. If the debunkers of old had not insisted that such phenomena as poltergeists were supernatural, priests would not have been called in to exorcise what were really electromagnetic anomalies, and today we might be hundreds of years wiser about electromagnetism. We might in fact have gone to the stars in ways we can only dream of today. Instead we sit in the midst of a battery of ridicule from naysayers.

Mankind now prepares to fulfill what earlier generations thought impossible. We plan to travel to Mars, to colonize other worlds. Our science fiction has, eerily, gained the status of "prophecy"; things dreamed about decades ago, even hundreds of years, first by Jules Verne and then by others, have and are coming to pass. We prepare for greater travels than Jonathan Swift could imagine. We stand ready to embark upon the Principles of Immortality and Eternal Life beyond the imagination of Mary Shelley. Whether we like it or not, we are guided by the hopes of the future expressed in science fiction, in esoteric debates, and in fringe or "mad" science—of hyperspace, dimensions, space colonization, and travel in the space-time continuum. We must be ready to meet what we will, and dismissing their eventual advent may prove a tragic blunder, however pert some of the debunkers' comments may seem.

If the Bermuda Triangle reminds us of this potential and inspires us to look more deeply into the blueprint of nature, then those who died or at least disappeared in the Triangle did not do so in vain. They were shipmasters and pilots, adventurers and explorers, who braved an already dangerous and tumultuous world of the sea and sky. In doing so their loss may unexpectedly guide us to future energies from which we may all profit and to future forms of travel by which we may explore space and other worlds; and their loss may have sobered us enough that now, for the first time, we may be able to use these forces to edify mankind instead of obliterating him.

We stand on the threshold of worlds without and worlds within. We can now look into a gene and see a greater complexity than anything man can create. Our generation is the first to discover planets outside our solar system. Our horizons are constantly being extended, whether through our greatest telescopes or through our smallest microscopes. The immense, dizzying complexity of our galaxy is merely a macrocosm of the microcosm out of which it is built—the atomic world of which we ourselves are composed.

A brilliant microbiologist, Dr. Michael Denton, has observed: "To grasp the reality of life as it has been revealed by molecular biology, we must magnify a cell a thousand million times until it is twenty kilometers in diameter and resembles a giant airship large enough to cover a great city like London or New York. What we would then see would be an object of unparalleled complexity and adaptive design. On the surface of the cell we would see millions of openings, like the portholes of a vast spaceship, opening and closing to allow a continual stream of materials to flow in and out. If we were to enter one of these openings we would find ourselves in a world of supreme technology and bewildering complexity."

Of the opposite—the infinity of the universe—astronomer J. C. Maxwell has said: "In the heavens we discover by their light . . . stars so distant that no material thing can ever have passed from one to another; and yet this light . . . tells us also that each of them is built up of molecules of the same kinds that we find on Earth . . . !"

. . . Everywhere the proton is still the proton, the electron is still the electron. Now perhaps we can add zero point in everywhere.

Right here is the gateway to the universe. The ocean starts at our dock and leads us across the sea to new lands. The subatomic ocean connects us with even more and can lead us across the Universe to new worlds, within and without. They collide everywhere; they work intertwined: mass, shape, energy, time, and space.

Can this energy be churned into vortices? Can proton and electron spins be redirected? Can this energy bend space? Bend time? Is there really enough energy to do this on Earth? Is there really enough zero-point energy in a shoe box of the quantum vacuum to disintegrate the Earth? We shouldn't wonder after what splitting only the uranium atom culminated in at Alamogordo, New Mexico, on July 16, 1945.

We have too long denied that a blueprint exists. The unexplained are the keynotes of its greater orchestration throughout nature, critical parts of the whole that are drawing our attention to the future and to the future of exploration.

Well, in the long run it's true. We go back to our habit again. And with immovable assurance in our dominion over that small twirling globe, we handle it, size it up, or at the very least just dust it. We interpret events, improvise, and extrapolate them to fit into our current frame of mind. Life goes on as before and mystery seems far from our daily lives. We forget; more immediate things crowd our minds. There is an answer somewhere, of course—in time, in time. We go on our way. That globe will continue to spin until the end. What will an answer bring? Things we ridicule today?

Time will tell . . .

Notes

2. The Riddle of Missing Planes

16. **meet you anyhow.** Board of Investigation into the Five Missing TBM Airplanes and One PBM Airplane Convened by Naval Air Advanced Training Command, NAS Jacksonville, Florida, 7 December 1945, and Related Correspondence. Naval Historical Center. (All quotes hereafter are from the same source unless otherwise stated.)

21. **or fifteen knots."** *Kansas City Star.*

22. **finally ended up."** Captain Don Poole, interview by author.

22. **an entire flight?"** David White and Joe O'Brien, interviews by author.

23. **visibility which prevailed."** Report of the Court Investigation of the Accident to the Tudor IV Aircraft *Star Tiger* GAHNP on 30 January 1948, Held under the Air Navigation Regulations, 1922. His Majesty's Stationery Office, Air Accidents Investigation Branch.

24. **an unsolved mystery.** Report, *Star Tiger.*

24. **you accept control?"** Report on the Loss of Tudor IVB *Star Ariel* G-AGRE which Disappeared on a Flight between Bermuda and Kingston (Jamaica) on 17 January 1949. Ministry of Civil Aviation, Department of Transport, London.

24. **question of icing."** Report, *Star Ariel.*

25. **inability to do so."** Report, *Star Ariel.*

26. **is unknown."** Report of Independent Investigation of Major Aircraft Accident Involving R7V-1 Buno 128411 at Sea on the Great Circle Route Between Shad Intersection (Lat 37-40N; Long 73-00) and Lajes Airport, The Azores, on 31 October 1954. U.S. Navy, Navy Safety Center, Norfolk, Virginia.

27. **Oceanic Air Control."** Air Force Aircraft Mishap Report, KB-50K, 8 January 1962. Kirtland AFB, New Mexico.

28. **their investigation."** Air Force Report, KB-50K.

28. **magnetic particle,"** Air Force Aircraft Mishap Report, C-133A, 27 May 1962. Kirtland AFB, New Mexico.

29. **one-four-thousand."** Air Force Aircraft Mishap Report, C-133A, 22 September 1963. Kirtland AFB, New Mexico.

30. **no apparent hazards."** Air Force Mishap Report, MATs C-119G, 5 June 1965. Air Force Safety Center, Norton AFB, California.

35. **turn at this time."** Air Force Accident Report, Disappearance of Phantom II F-4E About 82 Miles Southeast of Miami, September 10, 1971. Kirtland AFB, New Mexico.

36. **appeared to be above."** Air Force Report, Phantom II F-4E.

37. **lost at sea."** Investigation into the Circumstances Surrounding the Loss of AB 524 (Buno 149945) and the Subsequent Death of Lt. Paul T. Smyth, USN, [SSN] and Lt. Richard W. Leonard, USNR, [SSN] at about 1437R, 22 February 1978. Navy Mishap Report, Office of the Judge Advocate General.

38. **clear through there."** Factual Aircraft Accident Report: Missing Aircraft on Flight from Fort Pierce, FL, to Nassau, Bahama Islands, Piper PA-28R-201, N47910, May 19, 1978. National Transportation Safety Board.

39. **I could, please."** Factual Investigation Report: Missing Aircraft Between Fort Lauderdale, FL, and Havana, Cuba, September 21, 1978, Douglas DC-3, N407D. National Transportation Safety Board Report via National Technical Information Service, Department of Commerce, Washington.

39. **Coast Guard Miami, FL."** Factual Report, Douglas DC-3, N407D.

43. **of Aguadilla VOR.** Factual Aircraft Accident Report: Near Puerto Rico, Ercoupe 415-D, N3808H, June 28, 1980.

44. **same stuff, sir."** Factual Report, Ercoupe 415-D, N3808H.

44. **will be undertaken."** Factual Report, Ercoupe 415-D, N3808H.

45. **vanished from radar."** Factual Aircraft Accident Report: Missing Between Fort Lauderdale and Bimini, Bahamas, Cessna 402B, N44NC, March 31, 1984, MIA-84-F-A126.

3. The Riddle of Vanished Ships

53. **[Wednesday, October 3].** Extracts from Fray Bartolomé de Las Casas's *Diario* appear in many publications. The most complete and accurate is Carlos Sanz's facsimile edition published in 1962. *The "Diario" of Christopher Columbus's First Voyage to America 1492–1493* edited by Dunn and Kelley Jr. contains both the original Spanish and Dunn and Kelley's translation. The translation here is mine.

56. **has been received.** *London Times*, November 6, 1840.

57. **mysteriously deserted.** The incident of the *Ellen Austin* was first mentioned by British Commander Rupert T. Gould in his *Stargazer Talks*, 1944. Lloyd's and the New York Historical Society have records of the vessel.

59. **felt towards Master."** *Cyclops* Papers, Boxes 1068–1070, Modern Military Branch, National Archives, Washington.

66. **is still afloat."** *New York Times*.
67. **capsizing or foundering."** SS *Poet*: Disappearance in the Atlantic Ocean After Departure from Cape Henlopen, Delaware, on 24 October 1980, with Loss of Life. Marine Casualty Report, U.S. Coast Guard G-MMI-1.
69. **lifeboat can do so."** Sanderson, *Invisible Residents*.
69. **persons on board."** Lloyd's Casualty Reports.
70. **on the right side.** "Report on the Investigation of the Disappearance of William and Patricia Kamerer: Foul Play is Suspected," in *Nassau Guardian*. Department of Archives, Ministry of Education, Nassau.
73. **only speculation."** Waters, *Rescue at Sea*.

4. Can It Be That Simple?

84. **55° to 85° West."** Sanderson, *Invisible Residents*.
84. **triangle or trapezium."** Winer, *Devil's Triangle*.
84. **once more to Bermuda."** Spencer, *Limbo of the Lost*.
91. **in real trouble."** George Smith, recorded interview by author.
93. **Board of Inquiry assessed.** Report of Independent Investigation of Major Aircraft Accident Involving R7V-1 BuNo 128441 at Sea on the Great Circle Route Between Shad Intersection (Lat 37-40N; Long 73-00) and Lajes Airport, The Azores, 31 October, 1954. U.S. Navy, Navy Safety Center, Norfolk, Virginia.
94. **to sink the ship."** Kusche, *Bermuda Triangle Mystery Solved*.
94. **have been discovered."** Ibid.
94. **an added bonus."** Kusche, interview by Wanda Sue Parrott in Ebon, ed., *Riddle of the Bermuda Triangle*.
95. **the salvage business."** Lloyd's Casualty Reports.

5. Those Who Lived to Tell

97. **shoulders sore."** Factual Aircraft Accident Report: Incident over the Atlantic: Boeing 737, N12221, Continental Airlines Flight, 180 miles south of Bermuda, July 8, 1999.
97. **aircraft was hit."** Factual Report, Boeing 737, N12221.
99. **helplessness it created."** Factual Aircraft Accident Report: Incident MIA94LA074, Crash at Culebra, PR, Cessna 172K, N79401, February 15, 1994. National Transportation Safety Board.
99. **slow heeling over."** Capsizing and Sinking of the U.S. Sailing Vessel *Pride of Baltimore* in The Atlantic Ocean, May 14, 1986. Marine Accident Report, National Technical Information Service.
100. **this same time."** Chuck Willis, interview by author.
102. **I'm next!"** Don Henry, interview by author, Port St. Lucie, Florida, 1992.

102. **closer to it.**" Landsburg, *Secrets of the Bermuda Triangle*.
103. **might have been.**" Ibid.
103. **making up a story.** Don Welch and Don Reyes, interviews by author.
104. **navigational equipment.**" William "Al" Kittinger, interview by author, December 3, 2000.
105. **worked perfectly.**" Ibid.
106. **scramble on us.' "** Alan Oneida, communication to author.
106. **(about 700 miles).**" Ibid.
107. **on board with us.**" Marsha Pilgeram, communication to author.
107. **in the Bahamas.**" Zink, *Stones of Atlantis*.
108. **Bermuda Triangle.' "** Bill Keefe, interview by author, October 2000.
108. **number on us!**" *Miami Herald*.
108. **state by then.**" David Angstrom, communication to author.
112. **regular submarines.**" Berlitz, *Bermuda Triangle*.
113. **away very fast.** Berlitz, *Without a Trace*.
116. **Star exactly.** Translated from the Spanish by the author. The author recommends again the scholarly work of Dunn and Kelley, *"Diario" of Christopher Columbus's First Voyage to America 1492–1493* and Carlos Sanz's facsimile edition, 1962.

6. Space-Time Vortices, Zero-Point, and Sunken Worlds

120. **mystical about it.**" Valentine, quoted in Berlitz, *Without a Trace*.
122. **high-powered microscope.**" Moon, *Facts of Faith*.
123. **mutually interactive.**" Ibid.
124. **caught up in it.**" Valentine, quoted in Berlitz.
127. **them is important.**" Budden, "Poltergeist Machine."
129. **bowl of water.**" Solis, "Hutchison Effect."
129. **or movement effect.**" Hutchison, quoted in Solis, "Hutchison Effect."
130. **matter of moments.**" Solis, "Hutchison Effect."
130. **dimension or domain.**" John Hutchison, interview by author.
130. **So it exists.**" Hutchison, interview.
131. **because of this.**" John Hutchison, Report, Alternative Energy Institute, Inc.
133. **Earth's atmosphere.**" Cayce, *Edgar Cayce on Atlantis*.
134. **motivating forces.**" Ibid (440-5; Dec. 20, 1933).
134. **other elements also.**" Ibid.
134. **brought destruction.**" Ibid (519-1; Feb. 20, 1934).
134. **people in the land.**" Ibid.
137. **of this 'nothing.' "** Viktor Schauberger, quoted in Cook, *Hunt for Zero Point*.
138. **country being left.**" Plato quoted in *Great Books of the West*.
139. **coast of Florida.** Cayce, *Atlantis* (440-5; Dec. 20, 1933).
139. **then rise again.**" Ibid (5750-1; Nov. 12, 1933).

139. **not so far away."** Ibid (958-3; June 28, 1940).
140. **covering broader sections."** Valentine, quoted in Berlitz, *Bermuda Triangle*.
140. **go under the sand."** Valentine, quoted in Berlitz, *Atlantis*.
141. **ancient peoples."** Valentine, quoted in Berlitz, *Atlantis*.
142. **a natural formation."** Valentine, quoted in Berlitz, *Atlantis*.

7. Clues from a Shifting Paradigm

149. **mountains arose anew."** Creation ex nihilo, 2002.
154. **feet of rock."** Colbert, *Men and Dinosaurs*.
157. **years or less."** Cook, *Prehistory and Earth Models*. See also Barnes, *Origins and Destiny of the Earth's Magnetic Field*.
157. **carbon 14 dates.** Barnes, *Origins and Destiny of the Earth's Magnetic Field*.
157. **telescoped still further."** Ibid.
159. **oil was produced.** "Oil Made from Garbage," *Science Digest*.
161. **in South America.** Lopez, *Les races aryennes de Pérou*.
162. **have been found.** Edwin L. Hamilton, quoted in Whitcomb and Morris, *Genesis Flood*.

8. Atyantica

172. **tossed them aside."** Johnson, *Comet of Doom*.
172. **earth's magnetic field"** I. Vasilieyev, quoted in Welfare and Fairly, *Arthur C. Clarke's Mysterious World*.
173. **through normal use."** Budden, "Poltergeist Machine."
174. **the earth's field.** Valone, *Electromagnetic Fields and Life Processes*.
181. **mentioned Atlantis."** Cayce, *Edgar Cayce on Atlantis*.
183. **except electricity!"** Fawcett, *Lost Trails, Lost Cities*.
183. **strange things beyond."** Ibid.
186. **door and windows."** Ibid.
187. **good or bad today."** Cayce, *Atlantis*.
188. **this 'nothing.' "** Viktor Schauberger, quoted in Cook, *Hunt for Zero Point*.

9. The Warnings of Lunar and Martian Anomalies

191. **geographical position.** Apollo 16 Preliminary Science Report, "crew observations," 5-4 (1972).
195. **colossal 'sandworm.' "** Sir Arthur C. Clarke, Wernher von Braun Memorial Lecture.
196. **creations of humanity."** Dikshitar, *War in Ancient India*.
199. **travel between planets."** Sharma, "Flight Path."

200. **ever been written.**" Tomas, *We Are Not the First.*
200. **remain untranslatable.**" V. Raghaven, quoted at A Tribute to Hinduism, Sushama Londhe's website (2001).
200. **moon was discussed.** Ruth Reyna, quoted at A Tribute to Hinduism, Sushama Londhe's website (2001).
204. **shaped airships').**" Childress, *The Anti-Gravity Handbook.*
204. **the world today.**" Raghaven, quoted at A Tribute to Hinduism, Sushama Londhe's website (2001).
204. **from other planets.**" A. V. Krishna Murty, quoted at A Tribute to Hinduism, Sushama Londhe's website (2001).
205. **own Solar System.** "Swiss Telescope at La Silla Very Successful," press release, European Southern Observatory, Geneva, April 4, 2001.

10. Interest from a Past World?

210. **coming to them.**" Sanderson, *Uninvited Visitors.*
212. **their youthful states.** Rudman, "Effects of Human Growth Hormone in Men Over Age 60."
220. **no imagination.**" Good, *Above Top Secret.*
220. **such capabilities.**" Good, *Alien Contact.*
221. **than unidentified.**" Ibid.
221. **movements of the UFOs.**" Ibid.
221. **treated seriously.**" Ibid.
224. **gravitational field.**" LaViolette, "The U.S. Antigravity Squadron," 82–101.
224. **generating gravity hills.** Ibid.
225. **being felt magnetically.**" J. Manson Valentine, quoted in Berlitz, *Without Trace.*
226. **to flying saucers.** Wilbert B. Smith, Top Secret Memorandum, November 24, 1952, at University of Ottawa Library (found by Nick Balaskas).
226. **tremendous significance.**" Ibid.
228. **move away quickly.**" Frederico Cruz, quoted in Good, *Alien Contact.*
228. **seen these things.**" Ibid.

11. Let the Oceans Speak

233. **where it came from.**" Eighth Air Force report, Mission 115 (bombing of Schweinfurt ball-bearing factories), 14 October 1943.
234. **without any sound.** Lima, *Gate Phenomenon Project.*
234. **gobble our ship.**" Ibid.
235. **the terrestrial globe.** Ibid.
235. **'Time Travel' event.**" Ibid.

236. **inside of the circle."** *Weather.*
236. **high-tension wiring."** Walter Nemanishen, communication to author, 2002–3.
237. **Bermuda Triangle region.** Ibid.
241. **geomagnetic anomalies.** Larin, *Hydridic Earth.*
243. **winds at the surface.** SS *Poet,* U.S. Coast Guard G-MMI-1.
248. **find the dream gone."** Robertson, *Survive the Savage Sea.*

12. A Vast Horizon

255. **not be predicted.** Maxwell, "Cosmology After Half a Century."
255. **the Time-Dimension?** Wells, *Time Machine.*
257. **a psychic phenomenon."** Lima, *Gate Phenomenon Project.*
257. **be concerned about."** Budden, "Poltergeist Machine."
259. **dismiss the report."** Drasin, "Zen and the Art of Debunkery."
261. **bewildering complexity."** Denton, *Evolution.*
261. **find on Earth . . . !"** Maxwell, "Cosmology After Half a Century."

Bibliography

In order to maintain the continuity of the narrative, the author has eliminated the use of endnote references within the body of the work or at every quotation. The reader, however, will find the sources for these listed below *inter alia*. The official reports, acquired through the Freedom of Information Act, are listed alphabetically under appropriate headings.

Books and Articles

Antigravity Report: A Collection of Seminal Papers for Futurists. Washington DC: Integrity Research Institute.

Arnold, Kenneth, and Ray Palmer. *The Coming of the Saucers: A Documentary Report on Sky Objects That Have Mystified the World.* Boise ID. Privately published, 1952.

Barker, Ralph. *Great Mysteries of the Air.* New York: Macmillan, 1967.

Barnes, Thomas G. *Origins and Destiny of the Earth's Magnetic Field.* San Diego: Institute for Creation Research, 1973.

Berlitz, Charles. *Atlantis: The Eighth Continent.* New York: Putnam, 1984.

———. *The Bermuda Triangle.* Garden City NY: Doubleday, 1974.

———. *The Dragon's Triangle.* New York: Wynwood Press, 1989.

———. *Mysteries from Forgotten Worlds.* Garden City NY: Doubleday, 1972.

———. *Without a Trace.* Garden City NY: Doubleday, 1977.

Budden, Albert. "The Poltergeist Machine." *NEXUS Magazine,* 4:1 (Dec. 1996–Jan. 1997).

Budge, Sir E. A. Wallis. *An Egyptian Hieroglyphic Dictionary: With an Index of English Words, King List, and Geographical List with Indexes, List of Hieroglyphic Characters, Coptic and Semitic Alphabets, Etc.* 2 v. New York: Dover, 1978.

Burgess, Robert F. *Sinkings, Salvages, and Shipwrecks.* New York: American Heritage Press, 1970.

Burland, C. A. *The Gods of Mexico.* New York: Putnam, 1967.

Caidin, Martin. *Ghosts of the Air: True Stories of Aerial Hauntings.* St Paul MN: Galde Press, 1995.

Cayce, Edgar Evans. *Edgar Cayce on Atlantis*. Edited by Hugh Lynn Cayce. New York: Paperback Library, 1968.

Charles, R. H., trans. *The Book of Enoch the Prophet*. Boston: Weiser Books, 2003.

Childress, David Hatcher, ed. *The Anti-Gravity Handbook*. Rev. 3rd ed. Kempton IL: Adventures Unlimited Press, 2003.

Clarke, C. Simeon, Letter to author August 22, 1992, re: Merchant ship *Rosalie*.

Colbert, Edwin H. *Men and Dinosaurs: The Search in Field and Laboratory*. New York: Dutton, 1968.

Cook, Melvin A. *Prehistory and Earth Models*. London: Parrish, 1966.

Cook, Nick. *The Hunt for Zero Point: Inside the Classified World of Antigravity Technology*. New York: Broadway Books, 2002.

Costello, Peter. *In Search of Lake Monsters*. New York: Berkeley, 1975.

Custance, Arthur C. *Genesis and Early Man*. Grand Rapids: Zondervan, 1975.

Delaney, Frank. *Legends of the Celts*. New York: Sterling, 1991.

Denton, Michael. *Evolution: A Theory in Crisis*. Bethesda MD: Adler & Adler, 1986, 1985.

Dikshitar, V. R. Ramachandra. *War in Ancient India*. Delhi: Motilal Banarsidass, 1987.

Dobler, Paul E. Ph.D. *Biophysical Experiments on the Radiation of Matter, Divining Rods, Electric Waves*. Washington DC: Integrity Research Institute.

Donnelly, Ignatius. *Atlantis: The Antediluvian World*. Alexandria VA: Time-Life Books, 1991.

Drasin, Daniel. "Zen and the Art of Debunkery," 1997.

Dunn, Oliver, and James E. Kelley Jr., trans. *The "Diario" of Christopher Columbus's First Voyage to America, 1492–1493*. Norman: University of Oklahoma Press, 1989.

Ebon, Martin, ed. *The Riddle of the Bermuda Triangle*. New York: New American Library, 1975.

Edwards, Frank. *Flying Saucers, Here and Now!* New York: Stuart, 1967.

———. *Flying Saucers, Serious Business*. New York: Stuart, 1966.

The Electro-Gravity Device of Townsend Brown, File 24-185; Subject: Special Inquiry— A comprehensive evaluation by the office of Naval Research, with accompanying documents, 15 September 1952. Washington DC: Integrity Research Institute.

Fawcett, P. H. *Lost Trails, Lost Cities*. New York: Funk & Wagnalls, 1953.

Fell, Barry. *America B.C.: Ancient Settlers in the New World*. Newly rev. and updated ed. New York: Pocket, 1989.

Gaddis, Vincent. *Invisible Horizons: True Mysteries of the Sea*. Philadelphia: Chilton, 1965.

Gish, Duane T. *Evolution: The Challenge of the Fossil Record*. El Cajon CA: Master Books, 1985.

Godwin, John. *This Baffling World*. New York: Hart, 1968.

Good, Timothy. *Above Top Secret: The Worldwide U.F.O. Cover-Up*. New York: Quill, 1989.

————. *Alien Contact: Top Secret UFO Files Revealed.* Rev. ed. New York: Morrow, 1993.

Gould, Rupert Thomas. *Enigmas.* 2nd ed. New Hyde Park NY: University Books, 1965.

————. *Oddities: A Book of Unexplained Facts.* 3rd ed. New Hyde Park NY: University Books, 1965.

————. *Stargazer Talks, by Lieutenant-Commander Rupert T. Gould.* London: G. Bles, 1946.

Gourley, Jay. *The Great Lakes Triangle.* Greenwich CT: Fawcett, 1977.

Growse, F. S. trans. *The Ramayana of Tulasidasa.* 2nd rev. ed. Edited and rev. by R. C. Prasad. Delhi: Motilal Barnarsidass, 1987.

Hart, Jerrems C., and William T. Stone. *A Cruising Guide to the Caribbean and the Bahamas: Including the North Coast of South America, Central America, and Yucatan.* Rev. ed. New York: Dodd, Mead, 1982.

Heuvelmans, Bernard. *In the Wake of Sea Serpents.* Trans. Richard Garnett. London: Hart-Davis, 1968.

Heyerdahl, Thor. *Aku-Aku: The Secret of Easter Island.* Chicago: Rand McNally, 1958.

————. *The RA Expeditions.* Trans. by Patricia Crampton. Norwalk CT: Easton Press, 1988.

Hoehling, A. A. *They Sailed into Oblivion.* New York: Yoseloff, 1959.

Hynek, J. Allen. *The UFO Experience: A Scientific Inquiry.* New York: Marlowe, 1998.

International Registry of Sunken Ships: Worldwide Database and Information Centre; Hugh Brown, President.

Jeffery, Adi-Kent Thomas. *The Bermuda Triangle.* New York: Warner Paperback Library, 1975, 1973.

Jessup, Morris K. *The Case for the UFO: Unidentified Flying Objects.* New York: Citadel Press, 1955.

Johnson, Rufus. *The Comet of Doom.* Kerr Books, 2001.

Jones, E. V. W. In Associated Press, 1950.

Keyhoe, Donald E. *Aliens from Space: The Real Story of Unidentified Flying Objects.* Garden City NY: Doubleday, 1973.

————. *The Flying Saucer Conspiracy.* New York: Holt, 1955.

————. *Flying Saucers from Outer Space.* New York: Holt, 1953.

————. *Flying Saucers: Top Secret.* New York: Putnam, 1960.

Klass, Philip J. *UFO Abductions: A Dangerous Game.* Updated ed. Buffalo NY: Prometheus Books, 1989.

————. *UFOs Explained.* New York: Vintage Books, 1976, 1974.

————. *UFOs—Identified.* New York: Random House, 1968.

————. *UFOs: The Public Deceived.* Buffalo NY: Prometheus Books, 1983.

Kolbe, R. W. "Turbidity Currents and Displaced Freshwater Diatoms," *Science.*

Kusche, Larry. *The Bermuda Triangle Mystery Solved.* Amherst NY: Prometheus Books, 1995.

———. *The Disappearance of Flight 19.* New York: Harper & Row, 1980.

Landsburg, Alan. *Secrets of the Bermuda Triangle.* 1977.

Larin, Vladimir N. *Hydridic Earth: The New Geology of Our Primordially Hydrogen-Rich Planet.* Edited by C. Warren Hunt. Calgary: Polar, 1993.

LaViolette, Paul A. *Subquantum Kinetics: A Systems Approach to Physics and Cosmology.* Alexandria VA: Starlane, 2003.

———. "The U.S. Antigravity Squadron." In *Proceedings,* 1993 International Symposium on New Energy, Denver CO. Reprinted in *Electrogravitics Systems: Reports on a New Propulsion Methodology.* Edited by Thomas Valone. Washington DC: Integrity Research Institute, 1994, 82–101.

Lima, Ivan. *The Gate Phenomenon Project: The Phenomenon of Time Travel by Nature.* Project overview (private website), 2001.

Lindbergh, Charles A. *Autobiography of Values.* New York: Harcourt Brace Jovanovich, 1978.

Lopez, Vincente. *Les races aryennes de Pérou.* Paris, 1872.

Lord, Walter. *A Night to Remember.* New York: Bantam, 1997.

Lyell, Charles. *The Principles of Geology, Being an Attempt to Explain the Former Changes of the Earth's Surface by Reference to Causes Now in Operation.* New York: Johnson Reprint Corp., 1969.

Marx, Robert F., with Jenifer G. Marx. *In Quest of the Great White Gods: Contact between the Old and New World from the Dawn of History.* New York: Crown, 1992.

Maxwell, J. C. "Cosmology After Half a Century," *Science,* 1968.

McKee, Alexander. *Great Mysteries of Aviation.* New York: Stein & Day, 1982.

Meredith, Dennis L. *Search at Loch Ness: The Expedition of the New York Times and the Academy of Applied Science.* New York: Quadrangle / New York Times Book Co., 1977.

Miami Herald: June 6, 1997; November 12, 24, and 27, 1984; February 25, 1985; March 9 and 15, 1983; July 5, 1990; November 14, 1985.

Moore, William L. *The Philadelphia Experiment: Project Invisibility: An Account of a Search for a Secret Navy Wartime Project That May Have Succeeded—Too Well.* New York: Grosset & Dunlap, 1979.

Moon, Irwin A. *Facts of Faith.* In *Sermons from Science* film series (Chicago: Moody Institute of Science, 1955).

Morris, Henry M., ed. *Scientific Creationism.* 2nd ed. El Cajon CA: Master Books, 1985.

Morris, Henry M., and Gary E. Parker. *What Is Creation Science?* Rev. and exp. El Cajon CA: Master Books, 1987.

National Geographic Society. *Mysteries of the Ancient World.* Washington DC: The Society, 1979.

Nervig, Conrad A. In *Proceedings,* Naval Institute.

New York Times: August 28, 1982 *(Dolphin);* January 13, 1980 *(Sea Quest);*

December 5, 1977 *(L'Avenir)*; November 11–26, 1980 *(Poet)*; September 21, 1985; February 27, 1978 *(Fighting Tiger 524)*; August 5, 1986; December 26, 1976; May 4, 1985; August 13, 1979; October 17, 1982; October 18 and 19, 1976 *(Sylvia L. Ossa)*.

Nicholson, Irene. *Mexican and Central American Mythology.* New rev. ed. New York: Bedrick Books, 1967.

Nickell, Joe, with John F. Fischer. *Secrets of the Supernatural: Investigating the World's Occult Mysteries.* Buffalo NY: Prometheus Books, 1991.

Pauwels, Louis, and Jacques Bergier. *The Morning of the Magicians.* Translated by Rollo Myers. Chelsea MI: Scarborough House, 1991.

Phillips, Edward H. *Beechcraft: Pursuit of Perfection.* Eagan MI: Flying Books, 1992.

Robertson, Dougal. *Survive the Savage Sea.* Dobbs Ferry NY: Sheridan House, 1994.

Robinson, Bill. *A Sailor's Tales.* New York: Norton, 1978.

Rudman, Daniel. "Effects of Human Growth Hormone in Men Over Age 60." *New England Journal of Medicine* 323 (July 5, 1990): 1–6.

Ruppelt, Edward J. *The Report on Unidentified Flying Objects.* Garden City NY: Doubleday, 1956.

Sand, George X. "Sea Mystery at Our Back Door." *Fate* (October 1952).

Sanderson, Ivan T. *Invisible Residents: A Disquisition upon Certain Matters Maritime, and the Possibility of Intelligent Life Under the Waters of This Earth.* New York: World Pub., 1970.

———. *Uninvited Visitors: A Biologist Looks at UFO's.* New York: Cowles Education Corp., 1967.

Septuagint (Vaticanus and Alexandrinus), translated by Sir Lancelot Charles Lee Brenton, Hendrickson, 1992.

Sharma, Mukul. "Flight Path." *Times of India* (April 8, 1999).

Slocum, Victor. *Capt. Joshua Slocum: The Life and Voyages of America's Best Known Sailor.* New York: Sheridan House, 1950.

Solis, Mark A. "The Hutchison Effect—An Explanation" (February 16, 1999). John Hutchison's website, www.geocities.com/ResearchTriangle/Think-tank/8863/HEffect1.html.

Spencer, John Wallace. *Limbo of the Lost: Actual Stories of Sea Mysteries.* Westfield MA: Phillips, 1969.

———. *Limbo of the Lost—Today: Actual Stories of the Sea.* Rev. and exp. New York: Bantam Books, 1975.

Steiger, Brad, ed. *Project Blue Book: The Top Secret UFO Findings Revealed.* New York: Ballantine Books, 1976.

Stone, May. Letter to author from New York Historical Society, New York, March 9, 1993, re: schooner *Ellen Austin.*

Swanborough, Gordon. *Civil Aircraft of the World.* Completely rev. ed. New York: Scribner's, 1980.

Tedlock, Dennis, trans. *Popol Vuh: The Mayan Book of the Dawn of Life.* Rev. ed. New York: Simon & Schuster, 1996.

Titler, Dale. *Wings of Mystery: True Stories of Aviation History.* Rev. ed. New York: Dodd, Mead, 1981.

Tomalin, Nicholas, and Ron Hall. *The Strange Last Voyage of Donald Crowhurst.* Camden ME: International Marine, 2003.

Tomas, Andrew. *We Are Not the First: Riddles of Ancient Science.* New York: Putnam, 1971.

Tredree, H. L. *The Strange Ordeal of the Normandier.* Boston: Little, Brown, 1958.

Tute, Warren. *Atlantic Conquest: The Men and Ships of the Glorious Age of Steam.* Boston: Little, Brown, 1962.

U.S. Navy and Marine Bureau Numbers, Third Series, 00001–10316, 80259–90019, 111479–120341, as compiled by Joe Baugher.

Vallé, Jacques, Ph.D. *Revelations.* Parapsychology, 1991.

Valone, Thomas, ed. *Electrogravitics Systems: Reports on a New Propulsion Methodology.* 2nd ed. Washington DC: Integrity Research Institute, 1995.

———. *Electromagnetic Fields and Life Processes.* Washington DC: Integrity Research Institute.

———. *T. T. Brown's Electrogravitics Research.* Washington DC: Integrity Research Institute.

Villiers, Alan. *Posted Missing: The Story of Ships Lost without Trace in Recent Years.* New York: Scribner's, 1974.

Waters, John M. Jr. *Rescue at Sea.* 2nd ed. Annapolis MD: Naval Institute Press, 1989.

Weather. Royal Meteorological Society publication.

Welfare, Simon, and John Fairley. *Arthur C. Clarke's Mysterious World.* New York: A & W Publishers, 1980.

Wells, H. G. *The Time Machine.*

Whitcomb, John C. *The World That Perished.* 2nd ed. Grand Rapids MI: Baker Book House, 1988.

Whitcomb, John C., Jr., and Henry M. Morris. *The Genesis Flood: The Biblical Record and Its Scientific Implications.* Philadelphia: Presbyterian & Reformed Pub., 1961.

Wilkins, Harold T. *Flying Saucers on the Attack.* New York: Ace Books, 1967.

———. *Mysteries of Ancient South America.* New York: Citadel Press, 1956.

———. *Strange Mysteries of Time and Space.* New York: Citadel Press, 1959, 1958.

Wilson, Clifford, and John Weldon. *Close Encounters: A Better Explanation, Involving Trauma, Terror, and Tragedy.* San Diego: Master Books, 1978.

Winer, Richard. *The Devil's Triangle.* New York: Bantam, 1974.

———. *The Devil's Triangle II.* New York: Bantam, 1975.

Wood, Derek. *Jane's World Aircraft Recognition Handbook.* 5th ed. Coulsdon UK: Jane's Information Group, 1992.

Wraight, J. M. (Miss). Letter to author, September 5, 1991, Lloyd's Marine Collection, re: *Marlborough, Timandra, Rubicon, Ellen Austin.*
Zink, David. *The Stones of Atlantis.* Rev. ed. New York: Prentice Hall Press, 1990.

Official Accident Reports

Aircraft Accident Investigation Summary Report V116/7831047 Cessna 182L VH-DSJ, October 21, 1978. Bureau of Air Safety Investigation, Canberra, Australia.
———. Eastern Airlines, Incorporated L-1011, N310EA Miami, Florida, December 29, 1972. NTSB Report, National Technical Information Service.
———. Florida Commuter Airlines, Inc., Douglas DC-3, N75KW, Grand Bahama Island, Bahamas, September 12, 1980. National Transportation Safety Board.
———. Northeast Jet Company Gates Lear Jet 25D, N125NE, Gulf Of Mexico, May 19, 1980. National Transportation Safety Board.
Air Force Mishap Report, F-89C, 23 November 1953; Kirtland Air Force Base, New Mexico. Cleared Feb 1995.
———. SAC B-52G, 15 October, 1961; Kirtland Air Force Base, New Mexico.
———. MATs C-119G, 5 June 1965. Air Force Safety Center, Norton Air Force Base, California.
Air Force Aircraft Mishap Report, C-133A, 27 May 1962; Kirtland Air Force Base, New Mexico.
———. C-133A, 22 September 1963; Kirtland Air Force Base, New Mexico.
———. KB-50K, 8 January 1962; Kirtland Air Force Base, New Mexico.
———. MATS C-118A-20-70, BuNo 53-3250A, in Washington State, near McChord AFB, 1 April 1959.
———. F-89C-1-Lo, BuNo 51-13559A, 2 July 1954, near Griffiss AFB, New York. Maxwell AFB.
———. P51D, BuNo 44-63869, 7 January 1948, near Franklin, Kentucky, 3.5 miles SW. Maxwell AFB.
———. MATs C54G BuNo 45-539, Atlantic Ocean, Kindley Field, Bermuda to Morrison AFB, Florida, 3 July 1947. Maxwell AFB.
Air Force Accident Report Summary, KC-135A BuNo 61-0319, 600 NM NE of Homestead AFB (29.00N, 69.57W); KC-135A BuNo 61-0322, ditto, 8-28-1963. Kirtland AFB.
Air Force Accident Report, Disappearance of Phantom II F-4E #67–0310 about 82 miles southeast of Miami, September 10, 1971, Kirtland Air Force Base.
Board of Investigation into the five missing TBM airplanes and one PBM airplane convened by Naval Air Advanced Training Command, NAS Jacksonville, Florida, 7 December 1945, and related correspondence. Naval Historical Center.
Capsizing and Sinking of the U.S. Sailing Vessel Pride of Baltimore in The Atlantic Ocean, May 14, 1986, Marine Accident Report, National Technical Information Service.

Computer Search of the Records of the National Transportation Safety Board for all aircraft posted missing from 1983 through 1992 as requested by the author on May 12, 1993.

Database Search of Vessels on Record for Fiscal Years 2000 & 2001, US Coast Guard, 7th District, Miami.

Disappearance of the SS Marine Sulphur Queen on or about 4 February, 1963. Marine Casualty Report; U.S. Coast Guard G-TPS.

Factual Investigation Report: Missing aircraft between Fort Lauderdale, Florida and Havana, Cuba, September 21, 1978 Douglas DC-3 N407D. National Transportation Safety Board Report via National Technical Information Service, Department of Commerce, Washington, D.C.

Factual Investigation Report: New England Airlines, November 28, 1989. Pilatus Britten Norman Islander BN 2A N127JL, National Transportation Safety Board.

Factual Aircraft Accident Reports by the NTSB (NTIS, Department of Commerce). Near St. Thomas, U.S. Virgin Islands November 3, 1978 Piper PA-31-350, N59912.

————. Missing between Fort Lauderdale and Bimini, Bahamas, Cessna 402B, N44NC, March 31, 1984, MIA-84-F-A126.

————. Unknown 1-24-90, Cessna 152, N4802B, MIA-90-L-A061.

————. Missing aircraft between Andros Island Bahamas and West Palm Beach, Florida, October 4, 1979, Aero Commander 500, N3815C.

————. Missing between Bimini and Nassau, Bahamas, January 6, 1981, Beech c-35, N5805C.

————. Missing A/C between Marsh Harbour, Bahamas and Fort Pierce, FL., Beech H-35, N5999, September 28, 1982, MIA-83-L-A009.

————. Factual NTSB Accident/Incident Report 6120.4A for N777AA; MIA-83-F-A017. [Highly uninformative].

————. Missing between Bimini and Eleuthera Island, Bahamas, Beech 65-B80, N1HQ, November 5, 1982, MIA-83-L-A025.

————. Long Boat Key, Florida, Piper PA-24-250; N6376P, 5-3-91, MIA-91-F-A155.

————. Missing Aircraft on Flight From Fort Pierce, FL., to Nassau, Bahama Islands, Piper PA-28R-201, N47910, May 19, 1978.

————. Key West, Florida, Piper PA-28-160, N5488W, September 8, 1985, MIA-85-L-A249.

————. Missing Aircraft, 12-21-87; Cessna 152, N757EQ, MIA-88-L-A073.

————. Near Fort Lauderdale, Florida, April 24, 1979, Piper PA-28R, N7480J.

————. Missing Aircraft (Between Fort Lauderdale, FL., and Cat Island, Bahamas), 4-2-79, Beech E18s, N444Z.

————. Missing Between Santa Marta, Columbia and Port-au-Price, Haiti, July 18, 1978, Piper PA-31, N689WW.

————. Missing Aircraft Between Dillon, S.C. and Daytona Beach, Florida, Cessna 172, N1GH, April 30, 1978.

————. Missing Aircraft Between Opa Locka and Great Inagua, Bahamas, January 11, 1979, Beech A23A, N925RZ.

————. Missing Aircraft, April 27, 1978, Smith Aerostar 601, N555BU.

————. Missing Aircraft From St. Croix, V.I. to St. Thomas V.I., June 30, 1979, Cessna 150J, N60936.

————. Missing Aircraft Between Delray Beach & Key West, Florida, November 19, 1979, Beechcraft D50B, N1706.

————. Gulf of Mexico, 10-31-1991, Grumman F9F-8T, N24WJ, FTW-92-F-AMS-1.

————. Atlantic Ocean, 3-26-1986, Piper PA-31-350, N3527E.

————. Missing After Departure From Freeport, Bahamas, 6-3-1987, Cessna 401, N7896F.

————. Missing Between Andros Town, Bahamas, and Fort Pierce, Florida, Cessna T-210-J, N2284R, October 4, 1983.

————. Unknown PA-28-150; N6946D 8-10-1990, MIA-90-L-A170.

————. Caribbean Sea; Piper PA-28-140; N7202F 6-5-90, MIA-90-L-A139.

————. Missing Between Nassau, Bahamas & Miami, FL., Piper PA-32R-301, N8341L, July 12, 1985.

————. Missing Between Aruba and Santo Domingo, 2-7-88, Beechcraft 65-88, N884G, MIA-88-L-A104.

————. Missing Between Miami, FL & Port-au-Prince, Haiti, Cessna 210, N9465M, May 8, 1985.

————. Missing Aircraft Between Aguadilla, Puerto Rico & South Caicos Island; December 21, 1979; Piper PA-23, N1435P.

————. Unknown—Missing Aircraft, February 11, 1980, Beech BE-58, N9027Q.

————. Missing Aircraft Presumed to be Between DeFuniak Springs & Gainsville, Florida, November 20, 1978; Piper PA-23-250 N54615.

————. Missing Between Immokalee, Florida and Freeport, Bahamas; Aero Commander 680, N128C; Approx. March 25, 1978.

————. Missing Between Haiti and Bahamas, May 26, 1978; Beech BE-65, N809Q.

————. Missing Aircraft Between Jamaica, W.I. & Nassau, Bahamas (International Waters) October 27, 1979; Piper PA-23-250, N13986.

————. Near Puerto Rico, June 28, 1980; Ercoupe 415-D, N3808H. From General Microfilm, Wheaton, Maryland.

————. Cessna 152, N93261, Missing, near Marco Island, Fla., 9-30-93.

————. MIA95FAMS1, N5916V, MISSING; 12-25-1994.

————. MIA95FAMS2, N6844Y, MISSING; 09-19-1994.

————. MIA94FAMS1, N69118, MISSING; 08-28-1994.

————. MIA93FAMS2, N93261, UNKNOWN; 09-30-1994.

————. Cessna 172, crash of at Indian Shores, Fl., 7-15-94, MIA94FA179.

————. Missing N50GV Aero Commander 500, 5-2-96, ATL96FAMS1.

————. Atlantic Ocean, near Nassau, Bahamas, N6138X, Aero Commander 500, 5-12-99.

————. Missing N11214, Near Winter Haven, Florida, 10-27-2000 MIA01FAMS1.

————. Incident MIA94LA074, Crash at Culebra, PR., Cessna 172K, N79401, 2-15-94.

————. Incident over the Atlantic Ocean: Airbus N13983 Continental Flight 267 near Slapp Intersection, airway Green 431, 6-25-95.

————. Incident over the Atlantic: Airbus N70054, American Airlines Flight 918, near Miami, 10-27-99.

————. Incident over the Atlantic: Airbus N50051, American Airlines Flight 2009, 30 miles south of Champs Intersection, 1-7-97.

————. Incident over the Atlantic: Boeing 767 N649UA, United Air Lines Flight 990, 450 nautical miles southeast of Miami, 10-22-93.

————. Incident over the Atlantic: Boeing 757 N653A American Airlines Flight 935, 300 miles west southwest of Bermuda, 4-7-96.

————. Incident over the Atlantic: Boeing 737 N12221, Continental Airlines Flight, 180 miles south of Bermuda, 7-8-99.

F/V Navigator—Investigation into the disappearance of with loss of life on or about 1 December 1977. U.S. Coast Guard, G-MMI-1.

Halvorson, S. Report of Assistance on Gloria Colita, 1940. National Archives and Records Administration.

Holt, Alan. "Field Resonance Propulsion Concept," NASA Report, 1980.

"In The News"—Bulletins of the U.S. Coast Guard. 5th District: May 1, 1998 (Miss Charlotte II); August 5, 1999; November 15, 1999; March 23 and 24, 2000 (Leader L.); November 14, 1998 (Carolina); August 10, 1998 (Erica Lynn); January 1 and 2, 1998 (Formosa).

Investigation into the circumstances surrounding the loss of AB 524 (BUNO 149945) and the subsequent death of Lt. Paul T. Smyth, USN, [SSN] and Lt. Richard W. Leonard, USNR, [SSN] at about 1437R, 22 Feb 1978. Navy Mishap Report, Office of the Judge Advocate General.

Lloyd's Casualty Reports. March 25, 1995 (Jamanic K.); November 25, 1992 (Coyote); May 14, 1999 (Genesis); December 21, 1995 (Fou de Bassan III); November 4, 1992 (Mae Doris); December 22–31, 1993 (Captain Sarantis); October 16, 1996 (Intrepid); September 2, 1991 (American Airbus); April 24, 1999 (Miss Fernandina); February 22; March 12 and 19, 1992 (Dairyu Maru No. 3); February 20 and 24; April 20; March 3 and 5; June 22; August 6, 1993 (Vast Ocean); December 1 and 21, 1995; August 16, 1996; (Alkashem); January 31, 1992 (Yuko Maru No.8); April 16 and 19, 2001 (Also Times of India 12 April 2001) (Honghae Sanyo); December 11, 1993 (St. George); November 24, 1999 (Europa); May 9, 1991; (Kurika); March 27, 29, and 31, 2000 (Leader L.); August 31; September 1, 2, and 6, 1999 (Andra).

Loss of the U.S. Fishing Vessel Amazing Grace about 80 Nautical Miles East of Cape Henlopen, Delaware About November 14, 1984. National Transportation Safety Board.

M/V *Southern Cities:* Sinking with loss of life, Gulf of Mexico, 1 November 1966. U.S. Coast Guard Marine Board of Investigation Report and Commandant's Action. U.S. Coast Guard, GTPS.

Marine Casualty Report: SS V.A. Fogg, Gulf Of Mexico, 1 February, 1972. U.S. Coast Guard, National Technical Information Service.

Mary Celeste, Brigantine, RG59: State Department Records. RG36: Custom Service Records. RG41: Bureau of Navigation Records. RG84 Foreign Service Posts Records, 187 pages. National Archives and Records Administration, Washington, D.C.

National Archives and Records Administration: Carroll A. Deering, RG59 General Records of the Department of State; RG41 Records of the Department of Navigation; RG45 Coast Guard Correspondence; RG65 Records of the Federal Bureau of Investigation.

RG45 Naval Records Collection of the Office of Naval Records and Library. Subject File: USS Cyclops, 1,356 pages, boxes 1068–1070. The Modern Military Branch: RG59 Department of State, 49 pages; National Archives and Records Administration, Washington, D.C.

Navy Mishap Report: PBM-3S #6545, 10 July 1945, between Nassau and Banana River, Fl. Navy Historical Center.

Navy Mishap Report: PB4Y-1 #32046, 24 June 1943, Missing North Atlantic. NHC.

Navy Mishap Report: PV-1 7 August 1943, Missing North Atlantic. NHC.

Navy Mishap Report: PBM-3S # 6717, Lost at Sea, North of Bermuda, 20 August 1944. NHC.

Navy Mishap Report: PV-1 #33097, Lost at Sea, near Nevassa Island, Caribbean, 12 July 1943. NHC.

Navy Mishap Report: PV-1 #33229, Missing Caribbean, 21 June 1943. NHC.

Navy Mishap Investigation Report, P5M-1 BUNO 127705, 9 November 1956; Navy Safety Center, Norfolk, Virginia.

Preliminary Report Aviation MIA97WA181, N570VR, Piper PA-23-250, Missing, 5-4-97. NTSB.

Preliminary Report Aviation MIA99WA123, N33YR, near Crooked Island, Bahamas, F33A, 12-30-98. NTSB.

Preliminary Report Aviation ATL98FAMS1, Piper PA-28-181, N25626, Missing 8-19-98. NTSB Report of Court (No. 7952) SS "Samkey" O.N. 169788. Department of Transport, London.

Report of Independent Investigation Of Major Aircraft Accident Involving R7V-1 BUNO. 128441 At Sea On The Great Circle Route Between Shad Intersection (Lat 37-40N; Long 73-00) And Lajes Airport, The Azores On 31 October, 1954. U.S. Navy, Navy Safety Center, Norfolk, Virginia.

Report of the Court investigation of the accident to the Tudor IV. Aircraft "Star Tiger" GAHNP on 30th January, 1948, held under the Air Navigation Regulations, 1922. His Majesty's Stationary Office. Air Accidents Investigation Branch.

"Report on the Investigation of the disappearance of William and Patricia Kamerer—foul play is suspected," via *Nassau Guardian*. Department of Archives, Ministry of Education, Nassau.

Report on the loss of TUDOR IVB "STAR ARIEL" G-AGRE which disappeared on a flight between Bermuda and Kingston (Jamaica) on 17th January 1949. Ministry of Civil Aviation. Department of Transport, London.

Search and Rescue Case File, F/V Heidi Marie. 1st Coast Guard District, Boston, Mass.

SS Poet: Disappearance in the Atlantic Ocean After Departure From Cape Henlopen, Delaware on 24 October 1980 With Loss Of Life. Marine Casualty Report. U.S. Coast Guard G-MMI-1.

Tug KING CO-BRA—INVESTIGATION INTO THE DISAPPEARANCE OF WITH SUBSEQUENT LOSS OF LIFE ON OR ABOUT 2 JANUARY, 1979. U.S. Coast Guard, G-MMI-1.

National Transportation Safety Board Incident/Accident Briefs of (received individually)

N7210B, Beech j35 File # 2-1164.
N8040L, Cessna 172, File # 3-3058.
N5126K, Navion A, File # 3-1156.
N564E, Lockheed 1049H, File # 6-0038.
N7956K, Beech s35, File # 3-3723.
N39385, Lake LA-200, File # 6-0066.
N83CA, Piper PA-32, File # 3-2732.
N9074W, Piper PA-28, File # 3-1003.

Briefs by Computer Searches of NTSB Database File

Computer Search No. 1 (1983–1993)

N2284R, Cessna T-210-J, File # 2534.
N4437T, Piper PA-34-200, File # 3117
N85JK, Cessna 340A. File # 2727.
N39677, Piper PA-28-235, File # 0633.
N44NC, Cessna 402B, File # 0673
N81947, Aeronca 7AC, File # 2839.
N505CX, Cessna 337, File # 0279.
N9465M, Cessna 210K, File # 1118.
N8341L, Piper PA-32R-301,
    File # 1423.

5488W, Piper PA-28-160, File # 2030.
N24MS, Piper PA-34-200T, File # 2314.
N3527E, Piper PA-31-350, File # 0294.
N2652B, Cessna 402C, File # 0803.
N757EQ, Cessna 152, File # 2149.
N6834J, Piper PA-28-151, File # 0201.
N4802B, Cessna 152, File # 0147.
N7202F, Piper PA-28-140, File # 1510.
N6946D, Piper PA-22-150,
    File # 1016.
N6567Z, Cessna TU-206G,
    File # 1137.
N6376P, Piper PA-24-25-, File # 1089.
N24WJ, Grumman F9F-8T,
    File # 0477.
N5913A, Cessna 172, File # 1567.

Computer Search 2 (1975–1982)

N414DG, Piper PA-30, File # 3-2185.
N86011, Cessna 337D, File # 3-2186.
N8936V, Cessna 172, File # 3-3641.
N5182R, Cessna 172, File # 3-4046.
N1157, Beechcraft D50, File # 3-2420.
N6377J, Piper PA-28, File # 6-0025.
N5665D, Beechcraft E-50,
    File # 3-4014.
N4573P, Piper PA-23, File # 3-4039.
N128C, Aero Comdr 680,
    File # 3-1553.
N555BU, Ted Smith 601, File # 3-2475
N44196, Piper PA-32, File # 3-3386.
N47910, Piper PA-28, File # 3-1445.
N809Q, Beechcraft 65, File # 3-2771.
N689WW, Piper PA-31, File # 3-3385.
N407D, Douglas DC-3, File # 3-4127.
559912, Piper PA-31, File # 3-4304.
N54615, Piper PA-23, File # 3-4173.
N925RZ, Beechcraft A23A, File # 3-
    1848.
N4442, Beechcraft E18s, File # 3-1155.
N7480J, Piper PA-28R, File # 3-1080.
N60936, Cessna 150J, File # 3-2838.

N3815C, Aero Comdr 500,
    File # 3-3140.
N13986, Piper PA-23, File # 3-3242.
N1706, Beechcraft D50B,
    File # 3-3112.
N1435P, Piper PA-23, File # 3-3309.
N9027Q, Beechcraft 58, File # 3-0979
N3808H, Erco 415D, File # 3-1585.
N5805C, Beechcraft C35,
    File # 3-0329.
N505HP, Piper PA-28R-201T,
    File # 1763.
N5999, Beechcraft H35, File # 2279.
N777AA, Piper PA-31, File # 2177.
N1HQ, Beechcraft 65-B80, File # 2874.

Computer Search 3 (1964–1974)

N2157P, Piper Apache, File # 2-0926.
N81089, Cessna 140, File # 2-0984.
N8063H, Beech C18s, File # 2-1053.
N4010D, Cessna 182, File # 2-1106.
N99660, Ercoupe F01, File # 2-1056.
N6077P, Piper PA-24, File, # 2-1099.
N92877, N. American B-25, # 2-1087.
N7090P, Piper PA-24, File # 2-1096.
N122E, Chase YC-122, File # 2-1161.
N7210B, Beech J35, File # 2-1164.
N4129P, Piper Apache, File # 2-1166.
N5100W, Piper Cherokee,
    File # 2-1172.
N8165W, Piper Cherokee,
    File # 2-1173.
N3775K, Piper Cherokee,
    File # 2-1175.
N7121E, Cessna 182, File # 2-1178.
N9443J, Piper Cherokee, File # 6-0130.
N1483F, Cessna 172, File # 3-3881.
N944MH, Cessna 180, File # 3-4217.
N8653P, Piper PA-24, File # 3-0019.
N9490S, Beech 95-C55, File # 3-1596.
N3821, Douglas DC-4, File # 3-1675.
N609R, Beech 50, File # 3-1613.

N8040L, Cessna 172, File # 3-3058.

N590T, Beech B-95, File # 3-3521.

N8971C, Piper PA-22, File # 3-3003.

N852JA, Britt-Norman BA-2A, File # 3-3565.

N9078P, Piper PA-24, File # 3-0010.

N1166T, Cessna 310G, File # 3-1177.

N9364P, Piper PA-24, File # 3-2496.

N30844, Cessna 177B, File # 3-0304.

N61155, Cessna 150J, File # 3-4418.

N7050T, Cessna 172, File # 3-0663.

N5126K, Navion A16, File # 3-1156.

N7956K, Beech s35, File # 3-3723.

N50143, Cessna 150, File # 3-2845.

N8103Q, Cessna 414, File # 3-0382.

N864JA, Britt-Norman BN-2A6, File # 3-0545.

N83CA, Piper PA-32, File # 3-2732.

N632Q, Beech K35, File # 3-3340.

Acknowledgments

THE AUTHOR WOULD like to thank the following persons, organizations, and institutions who, over the twelve years of researching this work, have lent expertise and contributed information, advice, contacts, personal experiences, photographs, and documents. Mention of them below does not imply any endorsement of or advocacy for any conclusions expressed in the work.

Air Combat Command, Langley Air Force Base, Virginia; Aircraft Accident Investigation Bureau, London; Air Mobility Command, Scott Air Force Base, Illinois; Louis F. Alley, FOIA manager, Kirtland AFB; Lori-Ellen Amason; David Angstrom, pilot; Australian Embassy; Joe Baugher, aviation historian; Joan Beckett; Hugh Brown, researcher; Bruce Burgess, producer; CAA, London; Doug Church/National Air Traffic Controller's Association; C. Simeon Clarke, researcher, London; June Clark; Tristram Coburn; Robert Corner; Chris Corner; Debbie Corwin; Patrick R. Davis/Carroll A. Deering Family; Department of the Navy, Judge Advocate General's Office; Department of Transport, London; Department of Transport, Canberra, Australia; Carrie Durand; Jason Fox, researcher; General Microfilm, documents contractor; Don Garner; Doug Gerdon; Bruce Gernon, pilot; Goddard Space Center; Mary Gordon; Jack Green, archivist/U.S. Navy Historical Center, Washington Navy Yard; Jonathan Grupper, producer; George Hathaway, P.Eng.; John Heffernen, shipbuilder; Don Henry, salvor, diver, shipmaster; Her Majesty's Stationery Office, London; Walt Houghton, pilot, Assistant to the Director of Aviation, Broward County; John Hutchison, inventor, electromagnetic pioneer; Bill Keefe, Bimini diver, Bimini Undersea; NASA/Jet Propulsion Lab; The Keeper, Lloyd's Marine Collection, Guildhall Library; William A. Kittinger, pilot, air traffic controller, fisherman; Paul A. LaViolette, Ph.D., systems scientist; Daniel Lieb, researcher; Ivan Lima, Ph.D., geophysicist, engineer; Lloyd's of London, Register of Shipping; Jessica Louchheim, associate producer; Ian McIntyre, Director of Civil Aviation for Bermuda; Malin Space Sciences System; Harry Marx, pilot; Kathryn Marx; Suzanne K. Marx; Judith Marx; Alan F. McElhiney, naval historian, President of Naval Air Station Fort Lauderdale Historical Association, U.S. Navy, Ret.; Robert MacGregor, author, pilot; Gerry Meyer, boat dealership manager and salesman; Ministry of Education and Department of Archives, Nassau, Bahamas; Ministry of Works and Communication, Saint Vincent; NASA; National Air and Space Museum, Smithsonian Institution; National Archives and Records Administration; National Archives Still Pictures Branch; National Military Personnel Records Center; National Technical Information Service, Washington, D.C.; Alida Nattress; Navy Safety Center, Norfolk, Virginia; Walter Nemanishen, P.Eng.; The New York Historical Society/May Stone; Salvatore A. Nicoscia; Joe O'Brien, Ret., U.S. Navy TBM pilot; Jim Olchefske; Alan Oneida, pilot; Gary E. Parker, Ed.D., biologist, geologist, lecturer; Peggy Pflager; Marsha Pilgeram; Captain Don Poole, U.S. Navy, Ret.; Carmen Rivera; Evelyn Rivera; John H. Romero III; Richard Romley, pilot; Saint Vincent and Grenadines Embassy; Bill Smith, TBM pilot, and wife, Rita Smith; George Smith, Ret., U.S. Navy PBM pilot; Robert Strange, producer; U.S. Coast Guard; U.S. Navy; Dr. J. Manson Valentine; Tom Valone; Paul Vance, pilot; Angie S. Vandereedt/National Archives, Washington, D.C.; Larry Vardiman, Ph.D., geophysicist; Pedro Velez; David White, Ret., U.S. Navy TBM pilot; Ronald Welch, shipmaster, fisherman; and Chuck Willis, shipmaster, fisherman.

Index